6 May 01

To Keith

Warm regards

Leon Spears

Also by
Leon Speroff:

A Slow-Pitch Summer:
My Rookie Senior Softball Season;
Arnica Publishing, Inc. (2007)

The Deschutes River Railroad War;
Arnica Publishing, Inc. (2007)

Carlos Montezuma, M.D.:
A Yavapai American Hero
The Life and Times of an American Indian, 1866-1923;
Arnica Publishing, Inc. (2003)

A GOOD MAN

GREGORY GOODWIN PINCUS

A GOOD MAN
GREGORY GOODWIN PINCUS

The Man, His Story, The Birth Control Pill

LEON SPEROFF, M.D.

Professor Emeritus of Obstetrics and Gynecology
Oregon Health & Science University
Portland, Oregon

Arnica Publishing, Inc.
Portland, Oregon

Library of Congress Cataloging-in-Publication Data

Speroff, Leon, 1935-
A good man : Gregory Goodwin Pincus : the man, his story, the birth control pill / Leon Speroff.
   p. ; cm.
Includes bibliographical references and index.
ISBN 978-0-9801942-9-6 (hardcover)
1. Pincus, Gregory, 1903-1967. 2. Biologists--United States--Biography. 3. Oral contraceptives--History. I. Title.
[DNLM: 1. Pincus, Gregory, 1903-1967. 2. Biology--Biography. 3. Contraceptives, Oral--history. 4. History, 20th Century. WZ 100 P647s 2009]

QH31.P536S64 2009
570.92--dc22
[B]

2008045872

Cover design by Aimee Genter
Text design by Josef Garibaldi

Arnica Publishing, Inc.
3880 SE 8th Ave. #110
Portland, Oregon 97202
P: 503.225.9900 F: 503.225.9901
http://www.arnicacreative.com

Arnica books are available at special discounts when purchased in bulk for premiums and sales promotions, as well as for fund-raising or educational use. Special editions or book excerpts can also be created for specification. For details, contact the Sales Director at the address above.

DEDICATION

PERSONAL ACKNOWLEDGMENTS

My secretary, Judy Lunki, deserves this public recognition of my deep appreciation for her twenty years of dedication to my needs, assistance in my projects and books, and her warm, unwavering friendship.

My thanks to Ellen More, Head, and Kristine Reinhard, Archives Assistant, Office of Medical History and Archives, The Lamar Soutter Library, University of Massachusetts Medical School, for their interest, time, and assistance.

A special, heart-felt thank you to Thoru Pederson, Director of the Worcester Foundation for Biomedical Research and Professor of Biochemistry and Molecular Pharmacology at the University of Massachusetts Medical School, John McCracken, a scientist at the Worcester Foundation for thirty-four years, and Michael Pincus and Geoffry Dutton, Gregory Pincus's nephews, for their enthusiastic and friendly editorial input and overall support.

I especially want to express my gratitude to Laura Pincus Bernard, daughter of Gregory Pincus, who trusted me to interpret her father's history, cooperated without reservations in providing answers to my questions, suggested (with addresses and phone numbers) relatives to contact, and never ran out of patience and encouragement.

TABLE OF CONTENTS

xv	**Maps and Diagrams**	
xvii	**Prologue**	
xxi	**Gregory Pincus Timeline**	
1	**Chapter 1**	Beyond the Pale
9	**Chapter 2**	Three Russian Families
21	**Chapter 3**	Down on the Farm — The Woodbine Colony
53	**Chapter 4**	Goody and Lizzie
81	**Chapter 5**	Harvard and "Pincogenesis"
97	**Chapter 6**	It's Not Even in Worcester — The Worcester Foundation for Experimental Biology
131	**Chapter 7**	The Laurentian Hormone Conference
141	**Chapter 8**	Russell Marker Solves a Problem
165	**Chapter 9**	The Samurai and the Dowager

191   **Chapter 10**   John Rock: A Catholic Proponent of Contraception

201   **Chapter 11**   Clinical Trials in the Caribbean

225   **Chapter 12**   June 23, 1960: The FDA Approves the Pill

233   **Chapter 13**   The World Reacts to the Pill

251   **Chapter 14**   Fame and Illness

275   **Epilogue**

279   **Appendix:** The Endocrinology of Female Reproduction

287   **Chapter References**

327   **Illustration Acknowledgments**

337   **Bibliography**
      Collections, 337
      Books, 337
      Book Chapters, 344
      Journal Articles, 345
      Magazine Articles, 356
      Newspaper Articles, 356
      Internet, 358
      Unpublished Manuscripts, 359
      Dissertations, 359
      Miscellaneous, 360
      Personal Interviews or communications, 361

351   **Index**

MAPS AND DIAGRAMS

2   The Pale of Settlement

13   Western Russia

17   Family Tree

26   New Jersey

61   The Bronx

108   Massachusetts

185   Progestin Structures

194   World Population

280   Steroid Structures

281   Steroid Structures

282   The Cycle

283   Embryo Transport

285   Timing

PROLOGUE

ON A FRIDAY AFTERNOON IN TOKYO, October 28, 1955, fifty-two-year-old Gregory Pincus walked to the podium facing 150 delegates attending the fifth annual Conference of the International Planned Parenthood Federation.[1] He wasn't hurried; as always, he seemed calm and confident. Pincus's daughter said, "He was not a person who became nervous."[2] His bushy hair and mustache had not yet turned all white, but almost. The pigmented, baggy skin under his eyes was more pronounced than when he was younger, but his dark-brown, serious eyes were as penetrating as ever. He was of average height, a trim 160 pounds, and always well-dressed. A newspaper reporter observed, "Dr. Pincus is one of those rare people who looks as if he should be doing the work he does."[3] Pincus spoke steadily and clearly in a baritone with a pleasant timbre, without unnecessary pauses or sounds, and never in a monotone. The resonance and depth of his voice would increase and his eyes would widen to emphasize a point, but not enough to detract from his message. He had become one of science's most experienced speakers, making innumerable presentations to audiences that varied from the lay public to distinguished scientists and clinicians.

As Pincus made his way to the podium, did he for a brief moment wonder how far he had come, from the son born in a farming colony of Russian immigrants to a scientist making presentations on oral contraception that would eventually reverberate around the world? Did he expect this first presentation on the possibility of an oral contraceptive to have a major impact? If so, he would be disappointed in the short-term, but he knew it would take more work, and he must have believed that his work would eventually change the lives of millions of women.

Gregory Pincus, 1955

Pincus had already acquired fame as a scientist, and his role in the development of the birth control pill would push him to new heights. Just not yet. There was even disagreement among his colleagues. The major clinician involved in the studies, John Rock, thought it was premature to present their findings in Tokyo and refused to attend the meeting. Rock said, "He was a little scary. He was not a physician and knew very little about the endometrium (the lining of the uterus) though he knew a great deal about ovulation."[4]

Katharine McCormick, the wealthy dowager who funded the early research and made it possible, paid for Pincus and his laboratory colleague, Min-Chueh Chang, to fly to Tokyo. Chang presented first, in the morning, reviewing his work on the mechanisms of fertilization. He concluded, "Unless and until we know more about the basic mechanism of fertilization or reproductive physiology, and external as well as internal factors that control it, to devise an effective measure for its control is only a hit or miss affair."[5] Thus the mood was already a discouraging one when Pincus stood to make his presentation. He told the audience of the effective inhibition of ovulation and thus the prevention of pregnancy achieved with the administration of synthesized progestational hormones to animals. And he gave a preview of the results in women in the studies currently being conducted by John Rock and Celso-Ramón Garcia.

One would think that his news would have electrified the audience, but it did not. Perhaps it was obvious that this was an early report of ongoing work, but Pincus nonetheless concluded that the drugs he was testing, the synthetic progestational agents, norethindrone and norethynodrel, offered great promise, saying, "We cannot on the basis of our observations thus far, designate the ideal anti-fertility agent, nor the ideal mode of administration. But a foundation has been laid for the useful exploitation of the problem on an objective basis. ... That objective will undoubtedly be attained by careful scientific investigation."[6,7]

Typically cautious scientific talk, and it is not surprising that the respected scientist, Sir Solly Zuckerman, Professor of Anatomy at the University of Birmingham, summarized the presentation by saying, "It is fair to conclude that the observations reported by Dr. Pincus do not bring us as close as we should like to the goal of our researches." Indeed, a contraceptive pill is "so remote from realization that ... no one could say how, when, or even whether success would ever be achieved." [8,9]

Sir Alan S. Parkes, the famed reproductive physiologist from the University of Cambridge later reflected, "Few of us who heard Pincus speak at the 1955 Conference of the International Planned Parenthood Federation in Tokyo on the inhibition of ovulation by progestational and other steroids foresaw the future. I, for one, was more impressed by the fact that there was nothing new in the principle involved than by the enormous potentialities of new developments. It remained for Pincus to recognize the potentialities of the newly developed, orally active progesterone-like compounds as anti-ovulatory and, therefore, contraceptive agents." [10]

Many scientists would have been discouraged by a reception such as that received by Pincus in Tokyo. But Pincus had a personal characteristic that time and time again drove him and his colleagues to success. He made deliberate, logical decisions, and he had confidence in his reasoning; that confidence sustained not only himself, but his entire research group, to see through disappointments, wrong turns, a pace that seemed excruciatingly slow, and lack of acceptance by others. One of his many strengths was the ability to communicate his confidence to his colleagues, his technicians, and even his funding sponsors. Sheldon Segal, distinguished scientist at The Population Council, observed that "He was never fazed by whatever reaction. He was very self-assured. He knew what he knew; he knew what he believed, and he wasn't shaken easily by comments or criticism."[11] His experience in Tokyo proved that he was the right man at the right time for a scientific-clinical development that would have an enormous impact on human society.

Sir Parkes wrote years later, "… I have no doubt that the perspicacity and driving power required to bring the pill to widespread practical use came from Pincus. His enthusiasm was backed by an extraordinary knowledge of all aspects of the biological control of human fertility … ."[12] According to Howard J. Ringold, from Syntex's Institute of Hormone Biology, "Pincus had the vision to see that the idea would work. And he had the drive to see it was carried out. … saying the accomplishment is possible is not the same as having the foresight and the imagination to actually do it."[13]

Sometime after Pincus's death, his widow, Elizabeth, recalled:

> When he finally told me, he said, "Lizuska, I've got it."
>
> I said, "What have you got?"

He said, "I think we have a contraceptive pill."

I said, "My God, why didn't you tell me? … when these women asked you to produce a contraceptive pill, this was a fantasy. These were bright, intelligent women but they wanted something in never-never land. Did you think you could ever get the pill?"

He said, "Lizuska, everything is possible in science."[14]

GREGORY PINCUS TIMELINE

1903	Born in Woodbine, New Jersey
1908	Moved to New York City
1916–1920	Morris High School in the Bronx
1920–1924	Cornell University
1924	Graduate student at Harvard University
1925	Marriage to Elizabeth Notkin
1927	Sc.D. degree from Harvard
1927–1930	National Research Council Fellow
1930	University of Cambridge, Kaiser Wilhem Institute
1931	Instructor, Department of General Physiology, Harvard University
1936–1939	Assistant Professor, Harvard University; *In vitro fertilization and parthenogenesis in rabbits*
1937	University of Cambridge
1938	Visiting Professor of Experimental Biology, Clark University, Worcester, Massachusetts
1944	Founding of the Worcester Foundation for Experimental Biology and the Laurentian Hormone Conference
1949	Adrenal perfusion system
1951	Pincus meets Sanger and McCormick
1951–1952	President of the Endocrine Society
1951–1953	First contraceptive studies in rabbits by Chang
1954	First attempt at a clinical trial in Puerto Rico
1956	First major clinical trial in Puerto Rico
1960	FDA approves oral contraception
1965	National Academy of Sciences
1967	Death from myeloid metaplasia

CHAPTER ONE:

BEYOND THE PALE

GREGORY PINCUS was the eldest child of Joseph William Pincus and Elizabeth Florence Lipman, who were both born in Russia, "that most unfortunate of all birthplaces for the Jew."[1] Their families emigrated to the U.S., fleeing Russian anti-Semitism and eventually meeting in a Jewish farming colony in Woodbine, New Jersey.

Over several hundred years, many Jews migrated to Poland and Lithuania to escape persecution in Western Europe. By the late nineteenth century, the largest Jewish community in the world was in the Russian Empire, numbering about five million people, about one-half of the entire world Jewish population.[2] This was a consequence of the successive annexations under Catherine the Great of eastern Poland between 1772 and 1795.

The foundations of Russian anti-Semitism were established after the Polish annexations, and incorporated into government policy by the Tsars, beginning in 1825. This policy underwent cycles of repression and relaxation with each change in Tsars. Anti-Jewish teachings and patterns of discrimination by the Catholic Church (including expulsions of entire Jewish communities) were common in medieval Europe, establishing stereotypic myths and beliefs regarding the Jews. Russian dislike of Jews was a widespread cultural response to the Christian conversion of the Slavic tribes. The Russian Orthodox church institutionalized anti-Jewish doctrines. The Russian church was included in Tsarist governments, and, ultimately, anti-Semitism became government policy as the Russian Tsars were expected to "protect the faith."

By law, Jews were not allowed to move from the area called "The Pale of Settlement." Within the Pale of Settlement, Jews constituted 30 percent to 50 percent of the population in major cities, where they pursued industrial and commercial occupations. "Pale" was a medieval word for a pointed stake forming part of a fence, and came to refer to a barrier or a limit, beyond which it

was not permissible to go. In the 1897 Russian census, only 300,000 Jews were living beyond the Pale in the rest of Russia.[3]

A "Narodnik" (go to the people) movement began in Russia in the late nineteenth century, promoting assassinations of prominent officials. This was a period of great expectations for Russian Jews and many moved beyond the Pale. The Jewish communities in Moscow, St. Petersburg, and Odessa grew rapidly. Russian

Jews of the late nineteenth century were confronted with three major choices. Most retained their traditional Jewish identity. Some tried to modernize, attending Russian private schools where attempts at assimilation often created revolutionaries. And some converted to Christianity, the pathway to assimilation into Russian society.

Government policy changed with each new Russian ruler in the nineteenth century, relative liberalism alternating with reaction. The reactionary Nicholas I was followed by the reforms of Alexander II, but his assassination dashed Jewish hopes and aspirations. On a Sunday afternoon, March 1, 1881, Tsar Alexander II left the palace in St. Petersburg to review a battalion of troops. His carriage was bombed by members of the Narodnaia Volia (The People's Will) organization, and an hour later, Alexander II bled to death. Despite Alexander II's reputation as a liberator and reformer, he was still viewed by revolutionaries as an autocratic despot, an enemy of the people. A quarter century of relative quiet was followed by a wave of pogroms.

Pogrom is derived from a Russian word meaning "to smash" or "to conquer."[4] Pogrom at first was used to refer to destruction as a consequence of a hostile invasion, but beginning in 1871, it came to stand for anti-Jewish riots. In the Western world, the use of the word implied the knowledge and support of government officials.

Modern scholarship has attributed Russian pogroms to a complex interplay of forces, not just a simple anti-Jewish motivation.[5,6] Although the violence was directed at Jews, it was a consequence of poverty, a lack of food, unemployment, and changing urban-rural demographics (movement of peasants to the cities) that led mobs of uneducated, jobless, often homeless Christian men to spontaneously express their desperation by unleashing anger against employed and better-off Jews. The notion that pogroms were government-supported stemmed from the fact that local police usually offered no opposition. However, the local police in almost every case were incapable of exerting control; they were poorly trained, poorly paid, woefully undermanned, and often, incapable of discipline. Given this atmosphere, it didn't take much to spark a riot: a tavern brawl or a perceived sleight during a rite such as an Easter parade. The violence was largely directed toward Jews, but students, intellectuals, and other minorities frequently bore the brunt of pogrom anger.

Gregory Pincus's mother, Elizabeth, recalled that one of her first memories was the coronation in 1881 of Alexander III.[7] Living in Moscow with her wealthy family, her nurse, Praskovia, took her to the plaza in front of the Kremlin to watch the royal procession. When the open carriage approached with the new Tsar and his wife, Princess Sophie Frederica Dagmar of Denmark, known in Russia as Maria Fyodorovna, Praskovia lifted the three-year-old Liza to her shoulders. Liza remembered the cheers of the crowd, the decorated white horses, the Tsar's white uniform trimmed in gold, the numerous medals on his chest, and his tall military hat with a long plume. Prince Nicholas followed, riding by on his white horse. But the new royal family would prove to be no friend of the Jews. Even the wealth of Elizabeth's family could not protect them against discrimination and oppression, although the impact was far more intense on the Jewish poor.

The new Tsar, Alexander III (1881–1894), three-year-old Elizabeth Lipman's hero in a white uniform, wanted nothing to do with reform and returned to autocratic rule and isolation of the Russian state from Western Europe. He regarded democracy, freedom of speech, and constitutions as Russia's enemies, and he despised Jews. Pogroms spread throughout Western Russia, and in 1882, anti-Semitism was officially codified in new laws that prohibited Jews from living in the countryside outside large and small towns. Jews already living in the countryside were forced to leave. A strict quota system was imposed for Jewish students in Russian schools, and decrees were declared that restricted vocations and property ownership. In 1891, all Jews (about

20,000) were expelled from Moscow, except for a few privileged and wealthy families.[8]

It is not surprising that many Jews sought their liberation through the socialist movement, but the most popular Jewish response to these difficult times was emigration. Around 7,500 Russian and Polish Jews emigrated to the United States between 1820 and 1870.[9] In the decade after 1870, the number rose to 40,000, and in the decade after the pogroms that followed 1881, 135,000 left for the U.S. The numbers steadily increased, and between 1891 and 1910, nearly one million Jews left Russia for the U.S. Thousands of others went to other countries around the world, but eventually nearly one-third of the Jews in Eastern Europe emigrated to the U.S.

Nicholas II (1894-1917) succeeded his father, Alexander III. He was dedicated to his motto: "Orthodoxy, Autocracy, Nationality."[10] The land was his personal property, and the people were his subjects. Most of the Russian people accepted this absolute monarchy, viewing the Tsar as their "Little Father" who demanded their loyalty and obedience. Nobles and clergymen, their positions and titles earned by their service to the government, enjoyed extensive privileges, but workers in the cities and peasants in the countryside, who made up 80 percent of the population, were still eking out only a subsistence living, the details of which were largely unknown by the upper classes.[11-14]

Peasants lived in small, dark one-room log cabins with earth floors and without chimneys and conducted their lives with religious piety. In order to stay warm in the winter, they shared the space in crowded turmoil with their animals. Bathing and soap were unaccustomed experiences. A privy was rarely found. Daily meals consisted of bread, kvass (a fermented beverage made from rye or barley), cabbage, and onions—rarely meat or oils. The toll on health was enormous, especially on infants and children. Recurrent infectious diseases were rampant. In the midst of the vast wealth of the autocracy, the average family in Russia in 1900 was spending seven cents a year on schools, newspapers, and books; 80 percent were illiterate.[15] With rare exceptions, Jews did not escape this poverty.

THE FAMILIES of Gregory Pincus's parents left Russia for the U.S. near the end of the nineteenth century. They were not poor, but they could easily see that life for a Russian Jew was not safe and that their economic futures were questionable. As was typical, the heads of the families, Gregory's grandfathers, went first. Once established in New York City, they sent for the rest. Gregory would be the first in the Pincus family to be born in America.

RUSSIAN HISTORY

The major ancestors of the Russian people were the Slavic tribes who moved from Asia into the lands vacated by the Germanic tribes. By the seventh century, the population of western Russia was predominantly Slavic. The Slavs adopted Christianity in 988 with their own variation of the Eastern Orthodox religion. The ruling autocracy linked church and state, using the church as an instrument of power and keeping the church dependent on the state for financial support.

For hundreds of years, most of the Russian people lived under one ruling force or another. The Mongols invaded Russia in the thirteenth century, leading to Tatar domination for about 150 years, a major reason for the contrast between rural Russia and urbanized Western Europe until the seventeenth century. Ivan III, the Great, (1462–1505) defeated the Tatars, increased the size and dominance of Moscow, subjugated the nobility, and laid the foundations for a national state of Russia. The rulers of Moscow came to be the rulers of Russia, and the principal ruler came to be known as a Tsar. "In Russia, the ruler was everything."[1]

Ivan IV, the Terrible, proclaimed himself Tsar in the mid-sixteenth century. His regime survived the death of Ivan's childless son Feodor and in 1612 elected Michael Romanov to the throne; the paternalistic Romanovs ruled until overthrown by the Revolution in 1917. The new Romanov state officially sanctioned serfdom, granting total power to the landlords over their peasants. Peasants and middle-class tradesmen and craftsmen in the cities were not allowed to move from one site to another. This strict control fostered many riots, including a major peasant uprising led by the Cossacks of South Russia in 1667. Ultimately, the Tsar's army prevailed over every challenge.

Peter I, the Great, (1672–1725) despotically ruling the largest state in the world (although made up mostly of farmers), introduced Western European technology and culture to Russia, but maintained absolute control with his army. Conscription into his army meant a lifetime enrollment; the military was the Tsar's right arm. Peter's successful campaign against Sweden brought into the fold the provinces bordering the Baltic Sea, Russia officially became the Russian Empire in 1721.

The Duma, initially a council of nobles, later came to designate a Russian legislative body. Under Peter, the Duma had the responsibility of collecting taxes. The Orthodox Church was administered by the state, and local governments were abolished. Peter was succeeded by Catherine II, the Great, a German princess who married the heir to the Russian throne. Peter's dissolute son, Catherine's husband, ruled only six months before losing his life and his position to his wife who became the Tsar in 1762. Catherine ruled the Russian nobles, and the nobles ruled the countryside. This total control of the peasants continued to breed uprisings and the threat of revolution. During Catherine's rule, eastern Poland was annexed, Ottoman rule was expelled from the south, and Ukraine and Belarusia were incorporated into the empire.

In the early nineteenth century, Tsar Alexander I (1801–1825) was instrumental in the famous defeat of Napoleon, securing a prominent political position for Russia in Europe. Nevertheless, the retention of the serf system prevented any impact of the Industrial Revolution similar to that taking place in Western Europe. Nicholas I (1825–1855), the younger brother of Alexander I, confronted an effort on the part of nobles and army officers, influenced by their exposure to Western Europe during the defeat of France, to establish an elected government. Nicholas crushed the rebellion, and further entrenched the backward autocracy. The educational system was now under total governmental control, and dissidents were shipped to Siberia.

Nicholas was followed by Alexander II in 1855. A growing reform movement motivated the new ruler to emancipate the serfs in 1861, an event that marked the beginning of the end for the landowning nobility. Movement of the serfs to the cities, although difficult because it required a government passport, stimulated the growth of industry and the emergence of a middle class. However, the new freedom of the serfs was severely limited. The released serfs were required to pay their landlords in labor or cash to compensate for the lost land. The peasants remained landless individually; the land turned over to the peasants was administered collectively by each village community just as it had been previously.

The Tsar's greatest ally in the maintenance of his monarchy was the isolation provided by great distances and primitive communications. However, the inexorable progress of the Industrial Revolution finally led to the end of Tsardom. After petitioners to the Tsar were massacred in St. Petersburg in January 1905, a general national strike forced Nicholas to allow the creation of an elected Duma, which he then proceeded to dissolve repeatedly. These events ushered in a wave of pogroms in over 300 cities, as once again, Jewish scapegoats bore the brunt of populist anger. Competing opposition forces rooted in unemployment, the effects of World War I, lack of opportunity, and exploitation would eventually lead to the fall of the Russian empire, followed by the era of the Communist Party.

CHAPTER TWO:
THREE RUSSIAN FAMILIES

ENTIRE JEWISH FAMILIES left Russia, seeking an escape from the oppression of anti-Semitism. Gregory Pincus benefited from the family strength and individual courage derived from this experience. His mother's family, the Lipmans, emigrated to the U.S. in 1888, and the Pincus family arrived three years later. H. L. Sabsovich is another Russian Jew important in our story, a man whom the Pincus and Lipman families would meet in Woodbine, New Jersey. Sabsovich, with similar roots as the Lipman and Pincus families, emigrated with his family in 1887, and later in life he would have a major impact on the lives of Lipman and Pincus family members. Working with the Baron de Hirsch Fund, he is acknowledged as the builder of the Woodbine Colony for Jewish farmers in New Jersey, and admired for his accomplishments as director of the Woodbine Agricultural School.

H. L. Sabsovich

A tall, slim man, Sabsovich was born February 25, 1861 in Berdyans'k, Russia, a small town on the Sea of Azov. Hirsch Loeb Sabsovich later in life preferred to be known by his initials, H.L., but as a boy, for unknown reasons, he was called Grisha (Gregory).[1] Sabsovich's father died when Sabsovich was four years old, leaving the older boys to support the family of seven children. Recognizing his intellectual brightness, his brothers encouraged him to remain in school, and by the age of ten, Sabsovich, fluent in Latin, Greek, French, and German, was contributing to the family income by tutoring wealthy students.

A number of boys were expelled from the Odessa Gymnasium for liberal agitation. Two,

Kostia Puritz and Lyova Albert, left the city in 1879 to live with the Sabsovich family and to attend the Berdyans'k Gymnasium, undoubtedly influencing the political ideas of young Sabsovich. After graduation, Sabsovich and his friends went to Odessa to study law. Sabsovich supported himself by continuing to tutor other pupils.

Jewish girls were not allowed to attend the free Russian schools. Sabsovich met his future wife, Katherine, in 1880 when she and a few friends opened a free school for poor Jewish girls in Odessa, a school that in the early twentieth century was still operating as the Anna Siegal School.[2]

Sabsovich belonged to the *Intelligentizia* in Odessa, mostly Christian and Jewish students active in underground activities that stirred government opposition. Assassinations were commonplace throughout Russia, culminating in the bombing of Alexander II. In 1881, the government fomented a wave of anti-Semitism, most likely part of a strategy to divert anger and violence away from the autocracy. The populist movements accepted this, pleased to see agitation among peasants and workers, and if some Jews had to pay the price, so be it.

Animosity against the Jews became prevalent in the schools, prompting the organization of self-defense groups led by Jewish students, and Sabsovich became one of the leaders. The Pogrom of 1881 began in Odessa on the fifth day of Passover, while Sabsovich was visiting Katherine.[3] He rushed out, not to be seen by Katherine until three days later when she visited him in the Odessa prison. The police had arrested the Jewish students who were trying to defend Jewish homes. Some of the students belonged to wealthy and influential families, and so the students were released after two weeks. Many of these young men became well-known scientists, social workers, physicians, and lawyers, both in Russia and as emigrants.

"The greatest hurt may have been psychic, leading many to abandon hope for a gradual but certain improvement of their condition."[4] The events of 1881 stimulated a wave of emigration among the Jews of Odessa. Sabsovich became active in an organization, *Am-olam* (The Eternal People), formed to aid emigration to America with the principal aim of establishing farm colonies as a means of achieving economic independence. Sabsovich raised funds from Jewish organizations and prominent Jewish people throughout the world to support emigrating families.

The organization's success rapidly attracted the attention of the government. In March 1882, the Chief of Police in Odessa was assassinated. The meetings of *Am-olam* in the home of Nuchem

Rubin had come to the attention of the police. During a meeting on March sixteenth, the house was surrounded by the police.[5] It was immediately apparent to the members of *Am-olam* that the captain of the police had targeted Sabsovich, a "tall, slim man with big gray eyes, eyeglasses, and a short beard," who fortunately was not present.[6] Sabsovich left the next morning for a few weeks in the country. The government made it impossible to obtain passports, and only a small number of *Am-olam* recruits succeeded in reaching the U.S.

Returning from his brief exile, twenty-one-year-old Sabsovich finished his third year of law school, and married Katherine on April 25, 1882. Letters from Jewish men successfully conveyed to America by *Am-olam* convinced him to give up law and the prospect of a comfortable career supported by his father-in-law's financial backing, and to pursue something he had been teaching in his liberal circles: "Back to the Land." Specifically, he determined to learn agriculture so he could teach and lead those Jews who left Russia, mostly from commercial or professional vocations, to return to the land as farmers.

In the face of strong opposition from his in-laws, but with his wife's support, Sabsovich and Katherine went to Paris in July 1882 to attend agricultural college. Rebuffed by a school that only accepted single men, the couple went to Zurich, where they found a large colony of Russian students. Sabsovich completed his course work in three years, achieving some prominence with articles on agriculture printed in Russian newspapers. The couple returned to Odessa in the summer of 1885 to unhappily learn that efforts to form farming colonies in America proved unsuccessful, and that most of the Odessa immigrants were in New York City working in factories.

On their return to Odessa, Sabsovich and Katherine agreed to smuggle revolutionary literature from Zurich into Russia. The documents were printed on fine tissue paper and bound within the covers of the couple's German and French scientific books.[7] The customs officials in Odessa held their trunks for further investigation, for five days, but upon claiming their books, Sabsovich and Katherine were relieved to find that the books had never been opened—a close call that saved their lives.

Sabsovich accepted a position as assistant editor of *Agriculture,* a new agricultural newspaper in St. Petersburg. But then he was informed that the new job would not be possible, because his Swiss diploma did not entitle him to live beyond the Pale. For the next three years, Sabsovich turned again to tutoring.

In 1886, Sabsovich received a letter from Professor Kusnetzoff, director of a teachers' seminary in the Caucasus, who, impressed with Sabsovich's articles in *Agriculture*, offered him the position as manager of his estate, for 600 rubles per year plus a house for his family. Sabsovich carefully informed Kusnetzoff that he was Jewish, but Kusnetzoff declared that this was of no matter to him. Sabsovich, Katherine, and daughter, Marie, settled in Yiesk, a town east of Rostov, in a newly built house on a 2,000-acre estate in the heart of Cossack country.

Sabsovich's charge was to improve the output of the fruit orchards and the fields of rye, wheat, and corn. His knowledge was immediately apparent, and peasants began traveling great distances to seek his advice. During the winter, peasant families filled a large barn on Saturday evenings to listen to Sabsovich lecture on farming, with discussions often not ending until after midnight.[8] For two years, the young couple experienced no anti-Semitism as their personal values and contributions established good friendships. In the absence of schools, Katherine taught reading and arithmetic.

The two years came to an end when Professor Kusnetzoff's father learned of their presence. He was an orthodox priest, believing all of the stereotypic government and Christian proclamations against Jews. Unfortunately, Sabsovich's grandmother came to visit, stopped at the priest's house for directions, and thus the old priest discovered the manager of the estate was a Jew. Incessant letters from father to son led to Sabsovich's dismissal.

In February 1887, the family now with two daughters, left for America with funds provided by Katherine's mother, convinced that a Jewish agriculturalist had no place in Russia.

The Lipman Family

Elizabeth Lipman, Gregory Pincus's mother, came from a union of the Birkhahn and Lipman families in Kurland (also known as Courland), the western part of Latvia (at that time, it was Friedrichstadt, Russia).[9] According to the family story, the Birkhahns could be traced to an educator from Holland who came to Kurland in the seventeenth century.[10] Kurland was annexed into the Russian Empire in 1795. In the early 1800s, many Jewish workers migrated to Kurland from Germany and from the Pale of Settlement. The German language and way of life predominated in the Kurland Jewish community.

In the late 1800s, a *Birkhahn*, a wealthy trader in furs, fathered Ida. Ida married Michael Gregory Lipman, born November 18, 1874. Ida's marriage to Michael Lipman was arranged in the Jewish custom for wealthy fathers to marry their daughters to scholars. Michael, the oldest son in a family of six boys and three girls,

was a melamed, a Hebrew teacher and scholar. Although he worked in the fur business after the marriage, he "had no business sense."[11]

The family lived on a large estate in Freidrichstaat, with many servants. Ida and Michael were to have eight children who reached adulthood: Amata, Jacob, William, Raymond, Elizabeth, Charles, Isaac, and Ethel. All had remarkable strengths and achievements.[12]

Many members of the Birkhahn and Lipman families emigrated to the U.S. Alex, Gregory's youngest brother, recalled the Pincus family visiting and being visited by an Aunt (Tante) Birkhahn from Harlem, the Passaic Birkhahns, and the Newark Birkhahns.[13] One Lipman, a young physician, set out for America as the ship's doctor on the *Exeter*, but never made it when the ship was sunk by a German submarine. Another first cousin, Wolf Lipman, disappeared in the American West, prompting Gregory's mother to periodically express a desire to search for him in Yellowstone Park, where he was rumored to be a park ranger.

Michael and Ida Lipman, Gregory Pincus's maternal grandparents, moved from Riga, where Elizabeth was born in 1877, to Moscow when Elizabeth was six months old. Her older brother, Jacob, who would become a prominent and important American, was educated by private tutors initially, then attended a classical gymnasium in Moscow.

Shortly after the coronation of Alexander III, when Elizabeth was four years old, the family moved to the shores of Chiste Prood, a large lake. Elizabeth warmly remembered the winter scenes when everyone, men, women, and children, wore furs head to feet.[14] Her parents, Michael and Ida, were strictly Orthodox and would not allow their children to eat in other people's homes. Michael was a fur buyer for a large importing company, and when Elizabeth was five years old, he was transferred to Orenburg on the Ural River in Southern Russia, near the border with Kazakhstan. Elizabeth's brother Jacob was able to attend high school in Orenburg until he came with his family to New York City at age thirteen.

For three years in Orenburg, the family endured extreme cold through long winters and blistering heat in the summers. Elizabeth remembered that "We used to cook eggs in the sand."[15] Nevertheless, this was a pleasant time, a wealthy life with nurses, servants, family picnics, boating, and playing in the woods and the nearby desert. The Lipman family was unusual; most of the Jews in Russia were impoverished. Their neighbors as well as the landlord in Orenburg were Tatars. The market hosted camel caravans from Turkestan and the Far East. Elizabeth remembered well the

Tatar feasts, especially at weddings, with roast lambs and koumiss, fermented mare's milk.[4]

Despite this good life beyond the Pale for three years, Michael Lipman could see hardship in the future.[17] Knowing his business was threatened with extinction because of anti-Semitism, he went alone to the U.S. in 1887. Years later, Elizabeth's brother Jacob, now twenty-two years old and writing in the Rutgers undergraduate newspaper, described life in Russia: "Alexander the Third with, perhaps, the best of intentions, by what he believed to be serving his God, has brought suffering and distress to countless families, and by a single stroke of the pen has driven a peaceable people from their cherished homes, to brave the perils of a long and unknown journey; has compelled them to seek religious liberty across the broad Atlantic, in a new and strange world."[18]

Michael sent for his family a year later in 1888. Ida and her seven Russian-born children boated upstream the quiet, still waters of the Volga River for several days, and connected with a train for Moscow. They were warmly received by Elizabeth's uncle's family with its six boy cousins. After a week in Moscow, they departed for Grandfather Birkhahn's home in Kurland, a town where everyone spoke only German or Yiddish, making it difficult for the Russian-speaking Lipman family.

Joined by two cousins, a party of ten Lipmans embarked by ship from Hamburg. With multiple hampers and bundles, Elizabeth, now known as Liza, thought the family looked like a regiment of soldiers.[19] They had traveled fourth class by train through Germany, sitting on their luggage in large freight cars. Although Liza's father had paid for first-class tickets on the ship, they were placed in steerage on a slow steamer named *Marsalla* that took seventeen days to reach New York, a time period lengthened to the limit of endurance by constant seasickness. After a year's separation they were warmly greeted by Michael on the pier, fittingly with something they had never before experienced—bananas.[20]

The first family home in America was a flat in a lower east side tenement in New York City. The initial challenge was to learn English, and before long Liza skipped three grades to the fourth grade. By age nine, Liza was in the sixth grade, first in her class. At home she was taking care of her new baby sister, Ethel.

Over a period of about three years, Michael lost his money in several unsuccessful business ventures and decided to join the first settlers at the new farming colony in Woodbine, New Jersey. Michael opened a small store, patronized mainly by the workers clearing the land and building houses for the colony. The once-wealthy Lipmans were starting over, with an agricultural lifestyle that was completely alien to them. In Woodbine, they would meet the Sabsovich and Pincus families.

THE LIPMAN AND PINCUS FAMILIES became one close family, providing warmth and support for each other, and Liza Lipman's siblings would always be an important part of Gregory Pincus's life. Following the old country Jewish custom that the daughters must marry in chronological sequence, Amata, now known as Annie, was quickly married off. This allowed Liza (who as she became Americanized, came to be known as Lizzie) to marry Joseph Pincus.[21] Annie soon separated from her husband, but not before giving birth to Evelyn Seltzer, who was to play an important role in the Pincus family. Evelyn went to Morris High School in the Bronx with Gregory, then to Trenton Normal School, becoming an elementary school teacher in New Jersey and New York City. She married Joseph Isaacson, a high school sweetheart, in 1924, the same year Gregory married. The Isaacson family was successful in the garment industry, and Joseph and Gregory became close friends. Annie went to work as the matron of the Baron de Hirsch Agricultural School at Woodbine, and later worked at the Bronx Hospital and as manager of several hotels and a boy's summer camp. After Michael Lipman died in 1914,

Grandmother Ida lived with her daughter Annie in New York City.

Lizzie's brothers were an accomplished lot, especially her brother Jacob (his story is told in Chapter 3). Jacob attended the Baron de Hirsch School at Woodbine in the same 1894 class as Joseph Pincus, Gregory's father.

William (Willie) Lipman was five years old when the family spent a winter in Siberia. Despite his young age, he was assigned to be an apprentice to a machinist. At Woodbine, Lizzie's brother Willie supervised the garage, selling and repairing automobiles; he also owned and occasionally drove the buses that went between Woodbine and Sea Isle City on the Atlantic coast. Add to that his duties as fire chief, running the electricity-generating plant, president of the board of education, and playing the tuba in the band. In the 1920s, he left Woodbine, opening a Dodge dealership in Egg Harbor City, New Jersey. His last days were in Vineland, New Jersey, with his wife Sophie and three sons. He invented and marketed nationally an air pump and a chicken waterer.

Raymond Lipman became an instructor at the Baron de Hirsch Agricultural School, and then managed a demonstration farm in Norma, New Jersey. He later purchased the farm and remained there the rest of his life, active in many civic organizations. He married Olga Volovick and had a son, Aaron, who continued to run the farm.

Gregory Pincus's uncles, Charles and Jacob Lipman, were instrumental in creating in young Gregory an early desire to be a scientist. Charles went to Rutgers and graduated from the famed agriculture school. After acquiring a Ph.D from the University of Wisconsin with a specialty in plant physiology and an interest in bacteria, he began a long career with the University of California, Berkeley, becoming overall dean of the graduate schools.[22] He spent many summers with a U.S. federal mission in Samoa, and for years served on the selection committee for the Guggenheim fellowships. His obituary in *Science* cited several strong characteristics. "Professor Lipman believed implicitly in the power of education to liberate the human intellect from the shackles of ignorance, provincialism and fanaticism. He insisted that higher education and graduate study should confer upon the student not only special skills, but a broad, tolerant attitude and appreciation of human cultures. He observed keenly, worked intensively, conquered obstacles and advanced science in a way which exemplified his own high ideals."[23]

Isaac Lipman graduated in agriculture from Cornell University, and then operated a fruit farm that later became a poultry business in

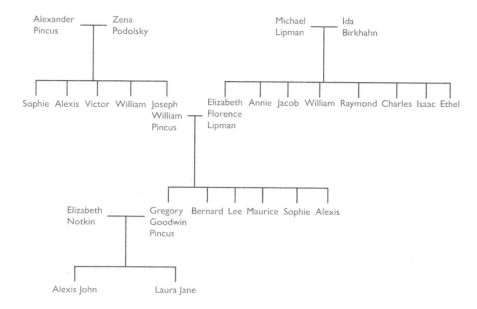

Washington Crossing, New Jersey. Ethel became a social worker, and worked all over the world. At age fifty she married Ludwig Bernstein, a distinguished social worker, and they retired to the Los Angeles area. After his death she married an oceanographer with the Coast and Geodetic Survey, Harry Marmer, who died within a year. Ethel traveled worldwide the rest of her life.

The Pincus Family

According to family legend, the Pincus men operated taverns in the Crimea, the part of Ukraine that extends as a large peninsula into the Black Sea, having been expelled from Spain in 1491 and traveling through North Africa.[24] Joseph's grandfather, also named Gregory Pincus, moved from the country to Berdyans'k; Alexander, Joseph's father, settled in Odessa, an extremely cosmopolitan city in the late nineteenth century, with many ethnic groups and many Jewish inhabitants (about 30 percent of the total population).[25] Attracted by a burgeoning economy, migrants poured into Odessa. In the 1860s and 1870s, Odessa's Jews enjoyed a period of prosperity and respect. But around 1880, their lives became progressively harder, a consequence of poor economic times and the anti-Semitic policies of Alexander III.

Warnings of a change in the involvement of Jews in the vibrant economy and the rich cultural life of Odessa were to be seen in major pogroms. On May 27, 1871, an outbreak of violence initiated by a rumor that Jews had desecrated the Greek Orthodox church and cemetery affected every inch of the Jewish neighborhoods, with damages that were twice as great as the more notorious pogrom of 1881 when Sabsovich was arrested.[26]

Alexander Pincus married Zena Podolsky. Joseph, Gregory's father, born in 1877, was the eldest of six children. Joseph's early education was in Berdyans'k, then in Odessa. Russian was the family language, but Joseph learned Latin, Greek, French, German, and English. Odessa was a multinational seaport city of 400,000 inhabitants with commercial contacts in Europe, Asia, and the United States. Learning several languages was regarded as essential for economic success.[27] Joseph did not learn Yiddish until he was twenty-one when he realized it was needed at Woodbine in New Jersey.

Alexander Gregorovich, Gregory's grandfather, went alone to America, sending for his family in 1891. They first lived on the lower east side of New York City among many Jewish families. An attempt at a restaurant business failed, and they moved to a farm in Colchester, Connecticut. H. L. Sabsovich visited the farm and talked Joseph into enrolling in the first class at the Baron de Hirsch Agricultural School in Woodbine. Joseph's decision was not difficult because he already had a high regard for Sabsovich. During the months the family was separated, Joseph's father, Alexander, had talked of Sabsovich in his letters to Russia: "a landsman of ours from Berdiansk" [sic] and described their inspection trips taken together to farms throughout New Jersey.[28]

There were only twelve graduates in the class of 1895 at the Woodbine Baron de Hirsch Agricultural School, among them Lizzie's brother, Jacob Lipman, and Joseph Pincus.[29]

Joseph, the first Woodbine student from outside the Colony, proceeded to graduate with eighteen classmates from the Storrs Agricultural College, which is now the University of Connecticut.[30] During these years, he belonged to a fraternity, the Shakespearian Society, and managed the football team. Joseph returned to Woodbine, becoming an instructor and then the head of dairy farming. He was a most eligible and pursued bachelor.

Joseph's siblings all did well. William graduated from the Columbia University College of

Zena, Victor, William, Joseph, Alex, Sophie, Alexander Pincus

Physicians and Surgeons, served as a doctor in a silver mine in Mexico, then started a family practice on Vyse Avenue near Bronx Park in New York City. Victor worked for General Electric, and then became the chief executive of Villa-Siegmund, a high fashion dress company. Alex worked on the building of the Panama Canal, sold American shoes in Japan and China, lived in Argentina during World War I, and settled first in Paris, then in Spain. Sophie married David Maimin who became president of the company that manufactured his father's invention, a cloth-cutting machine.

THE TURN OF THE CENTURY found Joseph Pincus together with the Lipman family in the colony of Jewish farmers at Woodbine, New Jersey, under the guidance of Professor H. L. Sabsovich.

CHAPTER THREE:

DOWN ON THE FARM: THE WOODBINE COLONY

THE STORY of the Jewish immigrant farm colony at Woodbine, New Jersey, is one of philanthropy, dedication, and accomplishment, stirred with hard work, economic struggles, and political conflicts. Gregory's parents, Joseph Pincus and Lizzie Lipman, fell in love, married, and started their family at Woodbine. The story features H. L. Sabsovich, a beloved and admirable man who deserves more recognition in American history.

The Woodbine Jewish Farmers Colony

In June 1887, the Sabsovich family arrived in the U.S. They stayed with various relatives in New York City, sleeping on rooftops, a common tenement practice to escape the summer heat. After a week, Sabsovich moved to Pittsfield, Massachusetts, to work in an older brother's picture-framing store. The brother was one of the men sent to the U.S. by *Am-olam*, as described in Chapter 2. Sabsovich, not satisfied, was soon peddling perfume concoctions cooked at home on the stove.[1]

After five months, the family returned to New York City. With the help of old friends from Odessa, Sabsovich, now twenty-seven years old, applied for a position with the agricultural experiment stations being opened around the country. He accepted a post as assistant to the director of the Fort Collins Agricultural Experiment Station in Colorado for $1,000 per year, a position that also included teaching obligations. Upon arriving in Fort Collins in 1888, Sabsovich discovered the reason for the director's eagerness to hire him; the director left immediately for a three-week honeymoon.[2] Upon his return, the director found the station running expertly and smoothly.

In January 1889, Sabsovich learned of the formation of the American Committee of the Baron de Hirsch Fund, composed of prominent Jewish men who were successful capitalists in New York City, such as Julius Goldman, Jacob H. Schiff, Emanuel Lehman, and Henry Rice (later the Committee became the controlling trustees of the Fund). The Committee appointed three men to organize an agricultural colony: Paul Kaplan, Herman Rosenthal, and Selig Rosenbluth.[3]

By any standard, Baron Maurice de Hirsch was enormously wealthy. He inherited money; he married money; he made money building the Oriental Railway linking Constantinople to

Baron Maurice de Hirsch

Europe, and he gave away money—a lot of it. Born in Munich in 1831, Baron de Hirsch died in 1896 on his estate in Hungary. The men in his family were the exclusive bankers to the royal courts of Europe, and his noble title was inherited from his grandfather through his father. The richest Jew of his time, de Hirsch lived lavishly in Paris and London, and raced horses in England; his winnings went to various hospitals. He wasn't religious, but he was devoted to helping the Jewish poor. His daughter died in infancy, and when his only son died of pneumonia at age thirty-one, the Baron said, "My son I have lost, but not my heir; humanity is my heir."[4]

Baron de Hirsch spelled out his philosophy in an 1891 article in the North American Review:

> In relieving human suffering I never ask whether the cry of necessity comes from a being who belongs to my own faith or not; but what is more natural than that I should find my highest purpose in bringing to the followers of Judaism, who have been oppressed for a thousand years, who are starving in misery, the possibility of a physical and moral regeneration—than that I should try to free them, to build them up into capable citizens, and thus furnish humanity with much new and valuable material? ...
>
> What I desire to accomplish, what, after many failures, has come to be the object of my life, and that for which I am ready to stake my wealth and my intellectual powers, is to give to a portion of my companions in faith the possibility of finding a new existence, primarily as farmers, and also as handicraftsmen, in those lands where the laws and religious tolerance permit them to carry on the struggle for existence as noble and responsible subjects of a humane government.
>
> ... If I devote myself, however, to this one work, I can perhaps bring it to eventual accomplishment. And all through this matter I have the certainty that he who frees thousands of his fellow men from suffering and an oppressed existence, and helps them to become useful citizens, does a good work for all humanity.[5]

The direction of de Hirsch's philanthropy was strongly influenced by his wife Clara, the daughter of Raphael Bischoffsheim of Brussels.[6] Her uncle, Solomon H. Goldschmidt, was for many years president of the Alliance Israélite Universelle in France. Clara, long involved in philanthropic activities, married de Hirsch in 1855, and in 1873, de Hirsch began to fund the Alliance Israélite Universelle to provide schools for Jews in the Orient. Today, the Alliance continues to be a principal international organization, promoting Jewish education and defending human rights.

Clara was very involved in all of de Hirsch's projects, and after his death she continued to oversee the de Hirsch philanthropy until she died in 1899. During her widowhood she gave away more than $15 million, and another $10 million was dispersed according to the instructions in her will, including $1.2 million for the Baron de Hirsch Fund in New York.

In 1885, Baron de Hirsch offered the Russian government the enormous sum of $10 million to help educate Jewish people in the Pale. Officials rejected his proposal when de Hirsch, with good insight, refused to relinquish control of the money to the Russian government. He then concluded that emigration was the best solution for Russian Jews.

In 1891, de Hirsch established the Jewish Colonization Association in England "to assist and promote the emigration of Jews from any part of Europe or Asia—and principally from countries in which they may for the time being be subjected to any special taxes or political or other disabilities—to any parts of the world, and to form and establish colonies in various parts of North and South America and other countries, for agricultural, commercial, and other purposes."[7] Large tracts of land were purchased in Argentina, Canada, and

Asia for farm colonies. In addition, the Association developed and maintained farm colonies in Cyprus and Palestine, and assisted in supporting the Woodbine Colony. The Jewish Colonization Association, through its negotiations with the Russian government, was able to secure legal emigration for Russian Jews for the first time.[8]

In the same year, 1891, de Hirsch created the Baron de Hirsch Fund in New York City, capitalized with $2.4 million and dedicated to making Jewish immigrants in the U.S. self-supporting. He established a similar fund in Montreal, Canada. Right from the beginning and consistently in their later activities, these funds were not charitable organizations. The trustees used the interest income to support the socioeconomic development of immigrants through typical financial contracts like mortgages.

By the time he died, de Hirsch had given over $100 million to his philanthropic activities. Returning Jewish immigrants to the land was not just a simple matter of emigration. Funds were required to transport the immigrants inland from the seaports. Tools, seed, and farming equipment had to be provided. Families needed support until good harvests were available. And, of course, land had to be purchased and occupied until farmers could afford repayment. Today, the de Hirsch Fund has about $6 million in assets and spends about $500,000 per year still assisting Russian immigrants.[9]

The Jewish Agricultural Society was organized in New York City in 1900 with the support of the Baron de Hirsch Fund and the Jewish Colonization Association. Over the years, using trial and error methods, the Society established about 4,900 families on American farms, distributed nearly 22,000 Jewish immigrants to farms in thirty-one states, and provided almost $15 million in loans to Jewish farmers in forty-one states.[10,11] It became the major educational resource for Jewish farmers on a wide range of topics that included social, technical, and scientific subjects. The Baron de Hirsch Trade School in New York City, founded in 1895 in a building built with a gift from Clara de Hirsch, graduated in a forty-year period, more than 9,000 students educated in the trades of carpentry, painting, plumbing, electrical work, and machine operation and maintenance. The school was turned over to New York City in 1935.

IN THE SPRING OF 1889, the three members of the Baron de Hirsch Fund responsible for developing an agricultural colony wrote Sabsovich requesting that he formulate his thoughts regarding farming for Russian Jewish immigrants in letters to the Committee. Sabsovich proceeded to do so, and in May 1890,

he was invited by telegram to New York to make a presentation at a Sunday afternoon meeting of the Committee.[12] The next day, his wife received a telegram: "Get ready. Am coming to take you and children to New York."[13] He had been offered the position to manage a new Jewish farming colony. He promptly accepted, even with no increase in salary, thrilled to have the opportunity to follow his dream of bringing Jewish people "Back to the Land." The day the family left Colorado, Sabsovich received a telegram offering him the position as chair of Agricultural Chemistry at Wyoming College, which he declined.

H. L. Sabsovich

It fell to the thirty-year-old Sabsovich to select the site for the new colony. The Fund purchased an estate of 5,300 acres, fifty-six miles from Philadelphia and 110 miles from New York City, on August 11, 1891, and named it after a vine, Woodbine. The new owner was a corporation established by the de Hirsch Fund, the Woodbine Land and Improvement Company. Sabsovich recognized that other sites had better soil, but the challenge of enriching the land with modern scientific methods proved to be too attractive to resist, and he believed that the process offered an important method to educate future farmers.

The land did have advantages: low land costs, a sparse surrounding population, proximity to eastern markets, good rainfall, and passing through it, the tracks of the West Jersey and Seashore Railroad.

Another factor that probably influenced the choice of Woodbine was the scattered presence of small Jewish farming settlements in southern New Jersey already established by the *Am-olam* movement during the 1880s in the area surrounding the town of Vineland.[14] The experience of these settlements made it clear

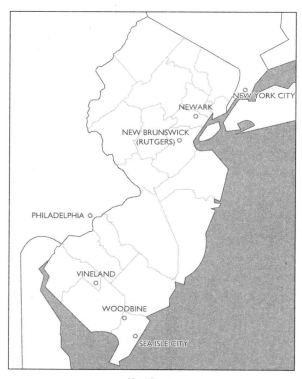

New Jersey

that this was not to be a grain belt, but that the soil and conditions required a concentration on vegetables, berries, and fruits, including grapes. T. B. Welch, a dentist and teetotaler in Vineland had developed a local grape juice industry that provided a market for the grapes grown by the Jewish farmers. In the 1890s, plant disease forced the Welch Grape Juice Company to move to upper New York state, leaving the Jewish farmers with a small effort in wine production.[15]

Sabsovich, the superintendent of the colony, and twelve new immigrants became the "pioneer farmers."[16] In fact there were no farms. The land consisted of a small railroad station and one house, surrounded by a flat and lonely landscape of pine and oak woods. The colonists constructed two six-room houses, one for the Sabsovich family, the other house, run by a widow, for boarders. Both houses were obliged to furnish food for their residents; the remaining men lived in a new barn. By winter, sixty Jewish men, including Michael Lipman, had been chosen by Sabsovich for the colony. They were not farmers. These Jewish immigrants were mostly traders involved in various commercial activities. They would have to learn agriculture, and Sabsovich would be the teacher.

Each settler was requested to invest $200, but only about half of the men could afford to do so.[17] The new home sites were leased according to five-year contracts at 5 percent interest, calling for $50 per year rent until the Fund administrators decided it was time for a purchase mortgage. The new immigrants, unfamiliar with American financial arrangements, were immediately saddled with a major debt of around $1,100.[18]

Once surveyed, the land was divided into thirty-acre farms. First, the land had to be cleared, a shock to these inexperienced tradesmen, unaccustomed to physical labor. Professional woodcutters were hired to teach by example, and soon the trees were being removed. Besides providing wood for heating the new houses, the farmers piled cords of wood on the streets, awaiting shipment for sale in Philadelphia.

Goldberg, one of the older immigrants at Woodbine, expressed his reactions to one of the younger farmers:

> Yeh, young man, ambitious, tireless. Hm, as a matter of fact, you are tired already, tired after chopping at the first tree, but you will not admit it. Of course not. Yeh, you young fellows know everything—and we older people nothing. To me the whole thing is funny. I mean my sitting here. And why I am here is the funniest thing. Can you, a learned young man, explain to me why I am here? There in my Bessarabia, I drank wine instead of water. There I ate fresh mamaliga—puffy and hot, right from the oven. I was a

respected member of the synagogue. My son Shruel—long may he live!—was simply Shruel, but here is Jack. There I was 'Tata' ('papa'), simply 'Tata' to him. In this country, I am 'Hey, old man!' Can you explain all this to me? Listen: to drink just water instead of wine; to eat wooden shavings—they call it 'corn flakes'—with cold milk instead of hot mamaliga. ... Thirty acres of land. Land! Look at the corn here. A chicken can jump over it without using its wings. There, in our Bessarabia, corn is corn. You have to use a stepladder to reach the upper ears. The corn there is juicy without the use of that, excuse me—they call it by a fancy name 'manure.' Yeh, their manure will certainly make the corn juicy. ... I don't want thirty acres of land. What for? Half an acre is enough for me—and enough for everyone![19]

And there were the mosquitoes! Not the repetitive annoying whine of a single mosquito buzzing one's face, but huge numbers that swarmed to greet the new inhabitants of this land. "In the Ukraine, with hundreds of miles of steppe, there were no mosquitoes. Here they were everywhere; in my ears, nose, mouth, and even in my eyes ... unable to drive them away."[20]

In these early months, Sabsovich would leave for the woods at 7 AM, return for an hour's lunch at noon, and after completing the day, hold office hours in his house beginning at 7 PM, often lasting to midnight.[21] No detail was too small for his attention and consideration. Plans for the farmers' houses were provided by a New York architect. The builders consisted of any of the future farmers with previous experience as carpenters and painters. The streets were named after American presidents and statesmen (except for de Hirsch Avenue, the main thoroughfare), with sidewalks lined by rows of newly-planted poplar and maple trees.

The town eventually contained a school, a firehouse, stores, a bowling alley, a theater, a synagogue, and a cemetery. The railroad tracks ran next to the town, and across the tracks were Willie Lipman's powerhouse for generating electricity and four buildings projected to be factories for winter work. On the eastern edge of town, there was the Baron de Hirsch School, and the surrounding acres contained the numbered farming plots. Sabsovich was directly in charge of paying for all expenses, including the sixty houses; the cost of each ranged from $600 to $1,300.[22]

Sabsovich was scrupulously honest and painfully frugal with money from the Fund. He had to be pressured to purchase a horse and carriage to make his rounds of the colony. In spring 1893, Sabsovich was shocked to receive a telegram ordering him to New York City, "Your integrity

The Sabsovich House

Woodbine, New Jersey

is at stake."[23] Someone with the Fund was suggesting that the Woodbine bookkeeping was poorly managed; by this time $300,000 had passed through Sabsovich's hands. Sabsovich requested an audit, and an intensive five-day examination exonerated him of any wrong doing.

From 1896 to 1902, Elizabeth (Lizzie) Lipman, soon to be Gregory's mother, worked for Sabsovich as his secretary and bookkeeper. She said, "He was not an easy man to work for. He was extremely nervous and irritable, hard to please, for he was a sick man and fought against heavy odds. Sometimes he would dictate to me for hours and then would find some flaw in his writing and tell me to destroy it, or if a cent were missing in my cash I had to work over my books for days to find the mistake."[24]

Simultaneously with the development of farming, the trustees of the Fund persuaded small factories to move to the colony. Willie Lipman's electricity-generating plant was built in 1892 to attract industrialists with offers of free power and light. The first factory opened in autumn 1892, that of the cloak maker Myer Jonasson & Co., providing work for many of the young people. A machine plant, a basket factory, a hat factory, and clothing factories rapidly followed.

Within a few years, the colony was bustling. The factories employed 180 people. The Fund had constructed twenty-two houses. Sixty-seven farms, totaling 700 acres, were under cultivation, and 200 acres were cleared for the town. Two schools served 100 students. Neighbors from nearby towns were puzzled by

Woodbine Railroad Station

some of the Jewish customs. A notable example was the crowds gathered at the railroad station to either greet or say goodbye to friends and relatives with affectionate embraces. A neighbor asked whether these were people never to return. Katherine Sabsovich informed her that most were coming back on the same train that evening.[25]

A public bath house opened in February 1893, a typical Russian structure built of brick and containing steam baths. The Woodbine Brotherhood Synagogue opened in 1896 in a building built by the farmers who made their own bricks. In 2003, the synagogue building became the Sam Azeez Museum of Woodbine Heritage, listed in the National Registry of Historic Places. The Woodbine stores, bakeries, butcher shops, barbershop, shoe stores, and clothing stores were closed on Saturday, the Sabbath, but Sunday was the day to shop for all the neighboring communities.

The Fund intended to sustain the farmers until it was time to be self-supporting. When the Fund administrators, after only one year, decided that that the time had come to be self-supporting

Woodbine Synagogue

in 1893, the farms were not ready. All but two of the sixty farmers refused to sign new mortgage agreements.[26] The Fund administrators believed that the children could work in the cloak factory to support the families until the farms were productive. They announced that they would proceed with eviction notices for farmers refusing to sign new contracts. And they did. "An old widow whose only support was a daughter working in the factory could not or was not willing to pay the rent for a little cottage which belonged to the Committee. She lost the case in court by default. The marshal, a resident of Dennisville, came to dispossess her. All her furniture, except her bed, was carried out into the street. The widow stretched herself out on the bed and refused to budge. When the marshal carried the bed—with her on it—to the street, she slapped his face."[27]

This year-long controversy with the farmers led to Sabsovich's "breakdown" in December 1893.[28] Coming home from a visit with friends, he collapsed in the street. He was carried by his wife and Ida Lipman to the nearest house. Moved to his own bed the next morning, he remained in bed for two months. Following his illness, he convalesced with the company of his eldest daughter in Florida. But the conflicts and disputes continued, spreading to the factory workers. And upon returning to work, Sabsovich suffered a "life-threatening" relapse.[29] The extent

of his unknown illness is dramatized by his need to gain thirty-five pounds to restore him to a normal appearance. Meanwhile, while convalescing, a fourth daughter, Julia, was born in summer 1893.

Finally the farmers, after refusing to till their land for over a year, filed a lawsuit against the Baron de Hirsch Fund. Years later, one of the farmers in the courtroom on the day of the trial remembered the judge as "an old man with a loose lower lip and a protruding chin; he inspired little respect."[30] The Fund was represented by four, big-city lawyers; the farmers could not afford a lawyer and spoke for themselves. The farmers appealed to logic and common sense, arguing that they should not be required to pay anything before the farms had yielded some income, but the judge decided against the farmers, upholding the legality of the financial agreements. The impasse was resolved by the legal eviction of eight men, considered to be the most irreconcilable of the farmers, and concessions from the Fund administrators such as easier payment schedules.[31,32]

This was an important learning experience for the Fund administrators.[33] The trustees of the Fund were urban financial people who believed in written contracts and agreements, in strictly following the rules. The farmers came from a background filled with dislike and distrust of bankers and big city authorities. Indeed, many were socialists forged in the unrest of

Russia, creating a wide gulf between them and their capitalist benefactors who refused to share control over the colony. The troubles generated bitterness among the farmers, a loss of faith in the project by key Fund administrators, and negative publicity in the press. And Sabsovich, an agrarian ideologue, was caught between the two sides, irritated but empathetic with his farmers, sensitive and dependent in his relationship with those who controlled his funds.

There was also a dispute between the Fund administrators and the factory workers, centering on whether Saturday or Sunday should be a day of rest. The factory owners and the nearby trade centers preferred Sunday. Of course many of the Jewish workers wished to honor their Saturday Sabbath. Devoutly secular, but highly respectful of the Jewish religion, Sabsovich prevailed in maintaining Saturday as the workers' day of rest.

SABSOVICH DREAMED of teaching the scientific approach to farming. He also knew the importance of fostering an interest in farming in the children. He started with a series of weekly conferences on Saturday afternoons. Although there was free time for this conference on the Jewish Sabbath, some of the more conservative members in the colony must have objected to the timing. The teaching sessions were held in a large barn on Farm No. 60 that became the first home of the Baron de Hirsch Agricultural School.[34] The first fifteen pupils in the school in 1894 were given practical instructions in the planting, grafting, and care of fruit trees, the growing of crops, English, U.S. history, mathematics, and surveying.[35]

Sabsovich taught botany, chemistry, and physiology at the Agricultural School. The day was divided in half, five hours at school and five hours on farm work. Three years after the school began, dormitories, a teachers' cottage, and a school building had been erected. A girls' department was teaching English, arithmetic, cooking, mending and sewing. With expansion funded by the Jewish Colonization Association, the school was serving 100 pupils, cared for by a matron, a cook, and other workers. The students received free lodging, food, clothes, and tuition. The Baron de Hirsch Agricultural School became a pioneer in the field of vocational training in agriculture.[36] Many of the students and young faculty went on to become prominent scientists and teachers in agriculture.

Sabsovich's exhibits featuring Woodbine education, methods, and products won awards at county fairs, state fairs, and at the Exposition

The Baron de Hirsch Agricultural School

Universelle of 1900 in Paris, as well as at the Pan-American Exposition in 1901. The exhibit at the World's Fair in St. Louis in 1904 won a gold medal, and, at Harvard University's request, received a permanent display in the Harvard Department of Social Science. Joseph Pincus said of Sabsovich, "There was not a happier man in the state when a Jewish farmer for the School was awarded a prize or blue ribbon for a great pumpkin, a fine hen, or a plate of superb peaches."[37]

On February 25, 1899, the colony celebrated Sabsovich's thirty-eighth birthday. The students of the agricultural school formally addressed Sabsovich with profuse thanks and respect: "… It was with tears of sorrow that we have forsaken the unwholesome temptations of our ghettos, but it is with tears of joy and pride that we come before you to announce that you have triumphed and we are converted. … With your keen insight into life, your love for your brethren and phenomenal foresight, you have conceived an idea that but few could have done—the instilling into the young generation love for what is noble and good, for farming life in its most attractive aspect. … With clear perception you have resolved to lay the foundation of agricultural life among the Jews."[38]

But the agricultural school was not without its problems. Students rebelled over maltreatment, long hours, and poor food.[39] Sabsovich promoted a professional and scientific agricultural school, whereas others wished the school to simply teach farming. And the students were not happy with the requirement for farm work that interfered with their academic studies. A major student strike in spring 1904 led to the dismissal of five boys, with another twenty-five placed on probation.[40] These conflicts were instrumental in a major review in 1905 by the Baron de Hirsch Fund that criticized the school for poor management, excessive costs, a teaching staff insufficient in numbers and poor in quality, and lack of student discipline—all attributed to unchecked expansion and Sabsovich's inexperience.

These problems led the Sabsovich family to move to New York City in 1905 when Sabsovich

was "promoted" to the position of General Agent of the Fund, an entirely new epoch in his life devoted to the growth of Jewish social service programs in a time when social work was a relatively new phenomenon. Soon he was president of the Jewish Social Workers of Greater New York. His work with farmers was taken over by the Jewish Agricultural Society. Sabsovich became ill once again in February 1914. He recovered over two months, but died a year later, only fifty-four years old, on March 23, 1915. He was buried at his request, in Woodbine. Virtually the entire community gathered at his gravesite to hear the eulogy by his former student, Jacob Lipman.[41]

THERE WERE REPEATED reorganizations of the Agricultural School instituted by the Fund, often in response to student agitation against its autocratic governance; nevertheless it continued to be moderately successful. In 1912, for example, there were 664 applicants for seventy positions.[42] The school closed in 1917 when financial support from the European-based Baron de Hirsch funds diminished during World War I. In addition, prominent Jewish agriculturalists such as Jacob Lipman believed that the school was no longer needed; Jewish youth were now able to follow multiple opportunities in American institutions.[43]

In 1921, the Fund donated the buildings and grounds to the state of New Jersey, which opened the Woodbine Colony for Feeble-minded Males. In 1983, the buildings became the Woodbine Developmental Center, an intermediate care facility for handicapped and developmentally disabled men and boys, employing more than 1,300 people. Wandering the grounds today, one cannot escape thinking that the greenhouses and vegetable gardens interspersed among the scattered brick buildings are an appropriate link to the past.

Always known as Professor Sabsovich, many Americans believed that he was sustained by a spirit of idealism learned in the pioneering revolutionary movements in Russia. Sabsovich became the soul of the colony, a man devoted to his cause, persistently getting things done, consistently demonstrating an unwavering honesty, totally lacking in racism or chauvinism, experimenting with new ideas and methods, and congenially working among his people. In Woodbine, he didn't just build a farm. He developed a community: physically, educationally, socially, and politically. He was the professor, the manager, the arbitrator, the peacemaker, and a brother and a friend to each colonist.

Joseph Pincus, Gregory's father, recalled that

the more he came to know Sabsovich the greater his affection for him grew.[44] Joseph acknowledged that it was entirely due to Sabsovich's influence and advice that he would return to Woodbine and devote twenty years to work for and among Jewish farmers. He wrote, "There has not been an agricultural movement of any kind among Jews in which Professor Sabsovich did not participate, or regarding which his valued advice was not sought; therefore it is no wonder that all the old farmers in New Jersey and other eastern states remember and revere him."[45] In 1899, Pincus succeeded Sabsovich as secretary of the County Agricultural Society, and both men traveled throughout New Jersey and neighboring states lecturing on scientific farming and dairying.[46]

JEWISH FARMERS were a new phenomenon in the late nineteenth and early twentieth centuries. Supported by Baron de Hirsch's philanthropy, multiple Jewish farming colonies and individual farms were established throughout America, in New Jersey, Louisiana, Arkansas, the Dakota Territory, Kansas, Colorado, and Oregon. Most were short-lived, succumbing to bad weather, droughts, inadequate planning and education, and even philosophical conflicts and intellectual bickering among individuals.

The Woodbine Colony survived for about forty years. By 1901, there were fifty-two farms and seven factories in Woodbine, home to 2,500 people, with each family earning about $675 per year.[47] The Baron de Hirsch Agricultural School occupied 300 acres, including 121 acres under cultivation. In 1903, the community was established as an all-Jewish independent New Jersey borough; Sabsovich was elected its first mayor without a single dissenting vote.[48] This was "a Jewish immigrant community giving life to the progressive philosophy of middle class America, focusing on such virtues as clean government, private enterprise, the absorption of newcomers into the prevailing culture, and public education as more essential for our form of government than any other."[49]

One reason for the success of this Jewish colony was the foresighted decision of the trustees of the de Hirsch Fund to develop both farming and factories simultaneously. The factories, making pocketbooks, clothing, hats, paper boxes, machine tools, and cigars, and lured by free rent, housing, and power, were able to provide work for young people who otherwise would have left the colony. As the years went on, despite the development of a vigorous poultry and egg industry, the farms began to yield to the factories, and from World War I to World War II the farms disappeared as more and more of the locally educated children left the community in pursuit

Woodbine Factory

of better opportunities. By the end of World War II, the Jewish population of Woodbine was a minority. Even the factories were gone by the mid-1960s. Today, there are no Jewish farmers in southern New Jersey, and the factories have given way to open fields.

The colony was hit hard by World War I. Funds previously derived from the de Hirsch-supported European organizations were tied up, and young men were scarce, either entering industry or the military. Finally in 1929, the de Hirsch Fund cut all its ties to Woodbine, although the final dispersion of the land did not occur until 1941. But this short lifetime was noteworthy. The colony rescued hundreds from an impoverished life. It stimulated, educated, and Americanized many individuals who would go on to make important contributions to American and even international life. Many became prominent academicians and government officials in the fields of horticulture and agriculture. Jacob Lipman, Gregory's Uncle Jake, is, perhaps, the best example.

Jacob Lipman, Gregory's Uncle

In 1892, the Lipman family moved from New York City to Woodbine into a house across the railroad track from the Sabsovich house that also contained the administrative office for the colony. Katherine Sabsovich described Ida Lipman as the "sweetest, kindest of women."[50] Michael Lipman established a small store in the colony. He died in 1914, at age sixty-three. His wife Ida died in 1937 at age eighty-nine, living her last years with her oldest daughter Annie in New York City.

Jacob Goodale Lipman, called Jake by his friends, was educated in Russia by private tutors initially, but when his family moved to Moscow, he attended a classical gymnasium. From Moscow, the family moved to Orenburg in the Ural Mountains, where Jacob attended school until he came to New York City at age thirteen. Four years later, he was living in Woodbine.

Jacob Lipman was one of fifteen pupils in the Woodbine agricultural school when it was established in 1894. Sabsovich selected Lipman and Jacob Kotinsky, later to become a teacher at Woodbine and then a prominent entomologist with the U.S. Department of Agriculture, to receive special training aimed at making them teachers and farming experts. Working on the school's model farm and studying most of each day, within eight months they sat for the Rutgers College examinations. Their performances earned them state scholarships. Jacob Lipman was destined to become the only Jewish dean of an American agricultural college.

Thanks to the free tuition his state scholarship provided, Lipman attended Rutgers College in New Brunswick, supported by $25 per month from the Woodbine school and hard work. His day began early to milk the cows in the dairy herd at 3 to 4 AM. At 7 or 7:30, he traveled a mile to the main campus, on foot or by trolley car, returning to be back with the cows for the evening milking. Determined to pursue analytical agricultural chemistry, he signed up for extra classes and laboratory work. Lipman was an excellent writer; his articles appeared in the school newspaper, including translations of Russian articles and stories, and he won prizes for his essays in English literature and composition.

Lipman graduated from Rutgers with honors in 1898, and in the fall began a graduate program in soil chemistry and bacteriology at Cornell University. Lipman enjoyed Cornell: "The

Jacob Lipman, Rutgers Student

beautiful scenery, the splendid libraries, and the fine laboratories make this an ideal place for working and for dreaming."[51]

The farmer became a scientist. Lipman received a master's degree in 1900 and a Ph.D. from Cornell in 1903, the year Gregory Pincus was born. He returned to Rutgers to establish a department of soil chemistry and bacteriology, advancing to full professor of agriculture in 1913. In 1915 he was appointed dean of agriculture. By the time Lipman died in 1939, 334 undergraduates and seventy-seven graduate students attended courses in the agriculture curriculum; and in addition nearly 500 participated in community courses and so-called short courses for young men who could not afford college, but intended to farm.[52]

In 1911, Lipman became director of the New Jersey Agricultural Experiment Station located on the Rutgers campus, a position he held until his death twenty-eight years later. His early work focused on fixation of nitrogen by soil bacteria; he described a new nitrogen-fixing organism of the *Azobacter* species. He established that manure improved soil not solely due to its fertilizing value, but by introducing bacteria that would hasten decomposition of organic matter and make nitrogen available. His many works were directed to the understanding and improvement of the productive capacity of soil. His 1908 book, *Bacteria in Relation to Country Life*, was written

for farmers and discussed topics like bacteria in wells, the understanding and use of manure, the processing of milk and diseases in milk, how to can food properly, bacteria in bread-making, the sugar industry, the preparation of hay, and finally, how to make good vinegar and wine.

In Lipman's later years, his time was devoted to administration and interactions with political bodies in order to secure adequate funding for agricultural teaching and research. His work was continued by his students, a wave of microbiology that counts the isolation of streptomycin by Waksman and Shatz as just one of many important contributions. His lectures on soil improvement were popular with farmers; he was known as the "farmers' doctor."[53] His laboratory bred the famous Rutgers tomato. In 1915, Lipman founded the scientific journal, *Soil Science*, and served as its editor-in-chief.

Lipman was a short man, with poor eyesight and a full mustache and thick, dark hair that in later years gave way to a balding large forehead with a few gray hairs on top and a fringe on the sides. He easily delegated assignments, but held individuals accountable. He had an impressive breadth of knowledge, viewed by some as an "encyclopedic mind."[54] He was a shrewd and able administrator who never stirred rancor, but with warmth and friendship he steered others toward their objectives, and never wavered from scientific principles. Waksman said, "I often thought that it was really not he who selected his associates, but they who selected him, for he could never refuse, unless it was really impossible to accept them, or funds were lacking, and he could find no way of raising the money."[55]

Another associate said of Lipman, "He was patient and understanding with the students. Discipline was a word he didn't know. I have never known him to want to punish anybody. He felt that everybody should have another chance if he wanted it. I never knew him to become angry with any of his subordinates. He disagreed with those he was working with at times, and fought strongly for his ideas, but within the family he was considerate and patient and could always see the other fellow's viewpoint. Many of the members of the faculty and staff were his 'boys' because they had been his students, and the newcomers were all young so he enjoyed respect and loyalty which present-day administrators cannot receive."[56]

Under Lipman's direction, the Agricultural College and Experiment Station expanded to 800 acres of land with multiple buildings and substations in other locations. Specialty departments arose, such as poultry husbandry, seed analysis, agronomy, and plant pathology. An inspection service of New Jersey farms provided for adherence to fertilizer, feed, and

Jacob Lipman, Dean of Agriculture, Rutgers University

insecticide control laws. Extension educational services, began in 1912, brought advances to local communities.

Jacob Lipman's name was known to scientists and farmers not only throughout the U.S., but also internationally. He was an honorary member of the French Academy of Agriculture and the Swedish Royal Academy of Agriculture.[57] He served as president of the American Society of Agronomy, the Association of Land-Grant Colleges and Universities, and the International Society of Soil Science. In a speech in 1936, he said, "Between those who teach and those who are taught there has been friendly understanding. Hence the story of accomplishment. May it grow no less."[58]

Clarence Darrow invited Lipman to testify in the famous 1925 Scopes trial in Dayton, Tennessee. Darrow, the lawyer for John Thomas Scopes, the science teacher accused of teaching evolution, invited many scientists to testify, but the judge ruled that expert testimony was not needed. The jury found Scopes guilty, but the decision was reversed by the Tennessee Supreme Court because of an error by the judge in establishing the fine. Lipman's prepared testimony was entitled "Organic Evolution from the Point of View of the Soil Investigator."[59] He said that "A direct relation may be traced between soils, plants and animals in the evolution of organic

life."[60] And he concluded: "We are indebted to science for a clearer version of the great laws of nature and of the methods of the Divine Creator. The men of science, in carrying on their labors in a spirit of reverence and humility, try to interpret the great book of knowledge, in order that the paths of man may fall in more pleasant places and the ways of human society may be in better keeping with the Divine purpose."[61] Selman Waksman, one of Lipman's students, later a colleague, and winner of the Nobel Prize in 1952 for his discovery of streptomycin, said, "He had a profound respect for the other man's faith. To him religion was a sacred personal trust—a privilege and a responsibility—not a corrective to be forced upon the unwilling."[62]

In 1902 in New York City, Lipman married Cecilia Rosenthal, who also had emigrated from Russia as a child with her family. Cecilia, the daughter of Herman Rosenthal, an administrator of the Baron de Hirsch Fund and a Birkhahn descendent, graduated from Hunter College in New York in 1899. The couple had three sons: Leonard and twins, Edward and Daniel. The three sons became businessmen; notably, Edward was a manager for Ocean Spray Cranberries, and a president of the Cranberry Growers' Association. Daniel was vice-president and sales manager for Stein Hall and Company, a manufacturer of starches and paper products.[63] Cecilia Lipman went to college again, graduating with honors from Rutgers in 1922.

The Lipmans lived in an enormous twenty-one-room house above a lake on the farm at Rutgers. The house was filled with family and students who lived on the third floor. The three sons provided music for dancing, Leonard on the piano, Daniel on the banjo, and Edward on the saxophone.[64] The house was busy with parties, teas, receptions, and picnics on the lawn.

After Cecilia's death from cancer in 1928, Lipman spent his time with his stamp collection, playing bridge, and buying books. He never passed up a bookstore, acquiring books he gave to the college and friends. Active in multiple state and national committees, he served for many years on the New Brunswick Board of Education. From 1914 to 1939, he was the director of the Jewish Agricultural Society, the organization that was supported by de Hirsch funds and dedicated to benefit Jewish farmers.[65]

One colleague said, "He lived so much faster and better than we knew. ... He could get pleasure from the smallest things; a flower, a conversation with a child, the absurdity of an incident, a practical joke upon himself or a friend, fun with his boys, or an impossible situation. He had an amazing fund of stories which seemed to fit every occasion."[66] When he traveled abroad, he did not visit museums and cathedrals. He studied "methods of farming, problems of food distribution and marketing, and the organization of cooperatives. He was always anxious to help improve the common man's lot and to recommend to others what could be done."[67] Lipman believed that, "Our strength lies in the soil; our hope, in the land; our salvation, in the upward climb toward the higher peaks of economic and social justice."[68]

Lipman died on April 10, 1939, age sixty-five, of coronary heart disease. In 1952, a building was named Lipman Hall on the New Jersey Agricultural Experiment Station campus. During his last trip to Europe in 1937, Lipman presciently observed, "The traveler is forced to conclude that, in their methods and psychologies, Communism and Fascism are not so far apart. ... Certainly, the philosophies of Communism and Fascism are the same as to the dominance of the state and the subordination of the individual. ... Contrary to all its protestations, absolutism cannot, in the long run, avoid armed conflict. ... One shudders to think of the potential catastrophe which absolutism, with its splendid armaments, is preparing for Europe. One shudders to think that the conflagration in Europe may draw other countries into the conflict. The sins of the World War have not yet been atoned. What about the next war?"[69]

Lipman's obituary in Science concluded with this sentence: "A young scientist who has not had the friendship of a man of Dr. Lipman's type is spared the grief that comes with his loss, but his life is lacking one of its greatest joys and the satisfaction that comes out of such associations."[70] His obituary in the Proceedings of the American Academy of Arts and Sciences was written by his nephew, thirty-six-year-old Gregory Pincus, concluding with a description that laid out the personal characteristics of a man who along with Uncle Charles Lipman served as superb role models for the young Gregory: "… This man worked hard all his life. He shunned no responsibilities, rested not on his laurels. And throughout a life of incessant and demanding activity he remained a simple, friendly human being. He was a kindly, affectionate husband and father. To his parents, Michael Gregory and Ida Birkhahn Lipman, he was always an attentive, devoted son. In ordinary converse the professor, the executive, the hard-pressed administrator gave way to the humorous, wise, democratic man. As friend and counselor to many, Lipman was invariably thoughtful and considerate. He was a wise man, an able man, a courteous man, but above all a good man."[71]

Lizzie Lipman, Gregory's Mother

By the time Elizabeth Lipman was in the eighth grade in New York City, her father, Michael Lipman, had lost his money in unsuccessful business ventures. His wife's cousin, Herman Rosenthal, an administrator for the Baron de Hirsch Foundation, persuaded Lipman to join the newly organized farming colony in Woodbine. While waiting for his farm, Lipman opened his small grocery store at Woodbine, patronized mainly by the workers clearing the land and building houses.

Elizabeth, now known as Liza, and her brothers were the first Jewish children in a nearby village, where the family lived while they awaited the construction of the new colony. Their father would walk the four miles each weekend to join the family. Liza recalled, "As most of the inhabitants of the village had never seen a Jew, the arrival of the bearded man from the colony would frighten the children and they would run for shelter crying, 'the Jews are coming.'"[72]

Within a few months, they moved into the new box-like house on their allotted land. The land was cleared, and the ground plowed, but the family struggled with inadequate tools, poor soil, and clouds of mosquitoes. Persevering, by the end of summer, they had vegetables, potatoes, and dairy products from their cow.

The first school was near the railroad station, a mile and a half from the Lipman farm. The teacher, a young woman from a nearby village, had a hard time coping with fifty immigrant children. Liza remembered singing the national anthem each day with fervor. "American born children can never experience that thrill nor know the deep gratitude we felt."[73] "Americanization," an important and willful endeavor by the Jewish immigrant communities, included active and full participation in America's causes, traditions, and politics, with a strong emphasis on capitalistic economic values and principles.[74,75]

But life was not easy. Jacob Lipman, only seventeen years old, confided to another farmer: "Of course, nothing is simple here— or anywhere else. My mother is worried. They also plan to build a factory here in which the farmers' children will have to work until farming brings in some income. My sister Anna is the eldest in the family and she will have to be the family breadwinner. My mother cannot think of it without horror and humiliation. You know how sensitive mothers are regarding their daughters."[76]

At age twelve in 1892, Liza quit school and went to work as an errand girl in a Woodbine factory for $2 per week. Her father's grocery store had failed. Five of the ten in the family were working, none harder than Mother Ida—baking, washing, cleaning, and hauling water and wood. A little over a year later, the factory shut down, and many of the young people went to a nearby village to work in a canning factory. Liza lived in a house with fifty young people, making money by picking berries.

Woodbine School

At age fourteen, Liza, now known as Lizzie, was sent to New York by her father, who deemed it necessary to send her and sister Annie off to find work to help the family. A relative in New York arranged for the girls to be hired by the General Electric Company in Harrison, New Jersey, where his son worked. Living with a cousin in Newark (one of the two crossing the Atlantic Ocean with the Lipmans in 1888), the girls had to travel an hour to be at the factory by 7 AM when the admitting gate was closed, locking out late-comers.

Lizzie's first job was washing bulbs, making for a tedious and unpleasant ten hours of work. From her $3 per week, she sent $2 home and spent sixty cents for carfare. "When I passed a candy store I used to avert my eyes quickly and whisper 'Get behind me Satan.'"[77] For meals, she ate bread and cold tea twice a day and cold left-overs at her cousin's house in the evening. Sister Annie lasted two weeks testing bulbs in a dark room and left for New York. Lizzie lived in Newark for nine months; in her last months she earned $6 per week inspecting flares, earning eighty cents for inspecting 1,000 flares. She worked up to 3,000 flares per day.

Lizzie was no ordinary fourteen-year-old girl.

> One dark winter morning, as I went outdoors to take the car to work, I found that as it had been snowing all night the streets were covered with snow and slush which reached to my ankles. I waited for a car for an interminable time and fearing that I would be late I started to walk. I walked for some distance before I realized that no cars were running because the streets were impassable. I walked the whole distance of several miles. By that time it started to rain, and as I had neither an umbrella nor rubbers I was soon soaked through and my frozen skirt was clinging to my legs. When I reached the factory, shivering and exhausted, I was surprised to find the gate house open though it was late. When I entered the room I worked in I found that the foreman and only two others were at work. Nobody else had dared to brave the storm. The kind men scolded me gently for coming out in such weather, made me take off my wet shoes and stockings and thaw out in front of the radiator. This act of kindness compensated for the ordeal I went through and I was elated at the thought of sending the usual amount home.[78]

But the factory work took its toll. Lizzie grew quiet and bitter; her health declined, and her mother ordered her to come home. "I shall never forget how happy I was when I said goodbye to the prison I had been in for over nine months."[79] The boys were working and the farm was now productive. After a summer, the family decided to send Lizzie to Newark to study shorthand and typing. The plan was to return with her skills to work in the new agricultural school in the colony. By now, brother Jacob was working on the farm and in the factory, studying at night to prepare for college.

Fifteen-year-old Lizzie took the 100-mile train ride back to Newark and lived again with cousins for seven months, learning shorthand and spending many pleasant hours in the Newark Public Library reading classics in literature as well as books popular at the time. Then she was off to New York City to learn typing, living with ten relatives and three boarders in five rooms, and sleeping on an improvised bed made of chairs in the living room.[80]

Upon her return to the colony in 1896, Professor Sabsovich gave her part-time work at his office for $3 per week. Lizzie was entrusted with the bookkeeping, a skill she began to learn from the New York accountant who visited monthly. This training quickly ended because "my teacher thought it more opportune to make love to me."[81] Lizzie turned to the public school for her lessons.

Lizzie worked for Professor Sabsovich for six years, running his office and eventually earning $60 per month, which she dutifully turned over to her mother. Lizzie kept her salary for the two months before her marriage at age twenty-two to pay for the wedding. She remembered these six years as wonderful "… for we were truly living an ideal life, so full and wholesome, so carefree and yet so constructive. We were pioneers, helping to build an ideal community … As there were no theatres or movies at that time we had to create our own amusements and in doing so we brought out our best qualities. We also laid the foundation for strong bodies, thinking minds, and the ability to fight our own battles unaided and unafraid. The willingness to serve and to sacrifice gladly was also a great factor in our future lives. This training helped me greatly in raising my own family in spite of many obstacles."[82]

Of course life in Woodbine was not as idyllic as young Lizzie Lipman perceived. The years were turbulent, filled with conflict between the wealthy, paternalistic trustees in charge of the colony, with their capitalistic ideas and principles, and the farmers and workers who struggled with low incomes and a difficult working environment. "In truth, the troubled colonies contained in microcosm the problems existing elsewhere. Working conditions were hard, disillusioning, and often tragic in that adolescence of industrial America."[83] But it is very likely that the hardness of those years was responsible for forging remarkable strengths in families and individuals.

Later in her life, Lizzie recalled: "These six years (16–22) I consider the most important period in my life. They brought me interesting work, education, the satisfaction that comes from service and romance."[12] But she had a major regret. "I wanted an education and begged to be allowed to go to high school, to college. My parents did not consider it important for girls to be educated as there was but one goal to be reached—marriage. Alas, I realize now how much better I would have been able to tackle the tremendous task of raising a large family if I had had the proper education. How many nights I cried myself to sleep, sick with the realization that sacrifice and service were to be my lot always, that all my ambitions and aspirations were to be stifled and buried in my heart. I often wonder how my life would have changed had I been allowed to follow my inclinations and live my own life as young people do nowadays. I finally resigned myself to my fate and found happiness in service."[84]

Joseph Pincus, Gregory's Father

In the summer of her sixteenth year, Lizzie Lipman met her future husband, but only for a brief hello. When Lizzie Lipman was seventeen years old in 1894, Joseph Pincus returned to the colony from Connecticut, raising a furor among the girls. Lizzie said, "He was so handsome that he took one's breath away."[85] After graduating from the Storrs Agricultural College (now the University of Connecticut), Joseph became an instructor at the Woodbine Agricultural School and was in charge of the dairy. An article in Horard's Dairyman in 1902 described him: "Mr. Joseph W. Pincus, whose fine bearing and handsome face make him a general favorite with visitors, and seem to fit him for a fashionable drawing-room rather than for a farm, took us one day on a tour of inspection of his dairy, which he has made a model for all the country. He pointed out eighteen pedigreed cows with

Joseph Pincus–around 1894

the whimsical remark that he would be at a loss for names for any addition to the herd, as he had already exhausted the names of all his sweethearts!"[86]

One of the school teachers, a close friend of Lizzie's, fell in love with Joseph. Because of his duties with the Agricultural School, Joseph enjoyed frequent interactions with Lizzie who was working in Professor Sabsovich's office. Parents and friends discouraged the romance between Joseph and the teacher, leaving Lizzie to console her friend who left the village

heartbroken.[87] The memory of this unfulfilled love remained as an obstacle for Lizzie in her own relationship with Joseph, and she discouraged his talk of marriage despite their own growing love.

Feeling rejected, Joseph became so depressed, a harbinger of mood problems throughout his life, that Professor Sabsovich sent him to Florida to recover. During his absence, Lizzie's love for Joseph grew, increasingly expressed in letters to Florida. Upon his return, they, both twenty-five years old, were immediately

Elizabeth and Joseph Pincus — 1902

engaged, and married in Woodbine a year later in June 1902. Gregory Goodwin Pincus was born April 9, 1903, the first of six children in the next eight years. He was named Gregory for his paternal great-grandfather and Goodwin for a teacher of his father.[88]

Lizzie's first four children were born in a house owned by her brother, William (Willie) Lipman. In his early thirties, Willie fell in love with Sophie Kenin, but she was only fifteen years old. While waiting for Sophie, Willie built a house for her across the street from his garage. At the back, he built a separate house, a small one for his parents. Lizzie and Joseph lived in the big house while Willie waited for Sophie. The first four Pincus sons were delivered in the master bed by Dr. Joffe, a Woodbine physician.[89]

Gregory's youngest brother Alex described his father as generous, charming, knowledgeable, dynamic, caring, and indulgent.[21] But, "He had limitations which kept him from realizing his potential, and this disturbed him so that he considered himself a failure."[90] He had no money sense or "ability to earn money commensurate with his talents. … He had a 'tendency to depression.' Almost daily we heard from Mama 'Papa is nervous,' meaning don't upset him. He also exhibited sudden angers

which went counter to his usual affectionateness and wanting the best for his children and for his beloved wife. He was a great tease, mainly shown in physical ways like excessive tickling, and I now realize that this was one outlet for his inner rages."[91]

Joseph often spent more than he could afford for gifts or gourmet foods. Alex remembered that "Mama had to keep close controls over his extravagances by managing the family budget and keeping bank accounts in her name. Unless he came directly home with his pay and turned it all but his small allowance over to Mama, he could stop at a cheese shop on the way and spend almost all on his favorites such as Limburger."[92]

"Another source for his low self-esteem was the success of his friend, schoolmate, and brother-in-law, Jacob Lipman, as well of his five brothers." Alex concluded, "My feeling about him during my teens and still today was that he really had a successful life and managed to do what he wanted, but he did not see it that way."[93] The family legend was "that Papa was weak and Mama was the rock that kept the family going."[94]

In 1908, the five-year-old Gregory Pincus and his family left Woodbine for New York City. The reasons for the move are unknown—perhaps

Uncle Willie needed his house.[95] Joseph went to work for the Jewish Agricultural Society as editor of a new Yiddish newspaper/magazine, *The Jewish Farmer*, and he was also an educator in the Society's extension service, traveling to Jewish farms in New York, Connecticut, and New Jersey. *The Jewish Farmer* was the first Yiddish agricultural paper in the world; in later decades, the majority of the monthly magazine was in English. Within a few years, there were over 3,000 subscribers, and by 1912, its circulation reached 5,000.[96,97] It was both a household magazine for families and a textbook for individual farmers. Joseph became the secretary of the Federation of Jewish Farmers of America, founded by the Jewish Agricultural Society as the first national Jewish farmers' organization.[98]

The first Pincus home in New York was an apartment in the Bronx on Simpson Street near the new Seventh Avenue subway. Family lived nearby, including Grandma Ida Lipman.

Pincus and Lipman Families at Woodbine — around 1908
Back row: Raymond's son, Aaron; Elizabeth Pincus; Ida Lipman, Cecilia Lipman, Raymond Lipman, Joseph Pincus.
Middle Row: Michael Lipman, Annie Lipman, Jacob Lipman, Ethel Lipman, Charles Lipman.
Front Row: Bernard Pincus, Evelyn Lipman Seltzer, Maurice Pincus, Lee Pincus, Gregory Pincus, unknown boy.

Gregory's sister Sophie was born at Sydenham Hospital in 1910, after which the family moved to Arlington, a suburb of Newark, New Jersey. Alexis, called Alex by the family, was born at St. James Hospital in Newark a year and a half after Sophie. Alex remembered Mother Lizzie talking of these days as difficult, with Joseph commuting to New York City.[21] Gregory Pincus remembered the difficulties caused by being the only family of Jews in the neighborhood. Harassed on the way to and from school, he was so intimidated that he "used to faithfully recite the morning prayer to Jesus and sing 'Onward Christian Soldiers' with a fervor unequalled by any Christian students."[99] Ten months after the birth of Alex, the family moved back to an apartment in the Bronx, 741 Jennings Street, home until 1923 when they moved to Vineland, New Jersey, and then back to New York City in 1925, following Joseph in his new jobs.

THE LIPMAN AND PINCUS FAMILIES were typical of those families whose closeness and fortitude were forged by the challenges of emigration, a strength that included great courage and high ethical standards. Mothers and sons seemed to have an intellectual and emotional closeness without confrontations that was admired by outsiders.[100] This was so for Jacob Lipman and his mother, and for Gregory Pincus and his mother, a Lipman daughter. Mother Lizzie wrote years later, "My every thought, feeling, and emotion was given unconditionally to my dear ones, and their happiness was the only reward I asked for. And so I go on to the end — hoping, praying, serving, loving — realizing that only the strong are free."[101]

CHAPTER FOUR:

GOODY AND LIZZIE

SOMETIME WHEN HE WAS VERY YOUNG, probably before the family left the Woodbine colony, Gregory Goodwin Pincus came to be known by family and friends as "Goody," the contraction of his middle name. He liked being called Goody. His close colleague, Celso-Ramón Garcia, concluded that "Called Goody, he was very appreciative of the warmth that was inferred by this reference."[1] Although not known for certainty, it is likely that his nickname of endearment came from his mother.

Mother Lizzie was always a focal point in Goody's life. Brother Alex described her as "plump, cheerful, loving, supportive, warm, sociable—a self-assured angel. We did much hugging, and all wanted to be on the bed with her when she took her regular afternoon naps."[2] Laura Pincus Bernard, Goody's daughter, said, "She was a real matriarch. She was determined everybody was going to succeed and especially her oldest son."[3]

Lizzie actively nurtured her husband, her children, her sisters, her nieces and nephews, and was involved in her community. She was secretary of the League of Russian-Jewish Women, dedicated to keeping alive the Russian culture and heritage. She arranged for religious and musical education for her children. During World War I she pledged her family to food conservation. During World War II she was actively involved with the St. Joan of Arc School, located on the street where they lived. Although Mother Lizzie's formal schooling ended after the sixth grade, her self-education produced a knowledge and culture equivalent to a college graduate. She died of liver cancer in 1946, sixty-eight years old.

Brother Alexis didn't hesitate to offer criticism. "For one I believe that her strength fostered Papa's weaknesses."[4] Alex didn't like her attitude of inferiority and subservience when among wealthier people. "She was extremely possessive of her children, and kept us attached to her for too long, even to trying to postpone our marrying till we were overdue. We used to surround Mother and ask her which child she loved best. Always her answer was that she loved all of us the same, but Goody was undoubtedly her greatest pride from start to finish."[5]

Goody's siblings had different personalities and interests, but they were good friends and companions. Bernard, nicknamed Bunzy and later Bun, was born in June 1904, fourteen months after Goody. Bun was a constant, sardonic teaser. He aspired to be a writer, but ended up in business. Goody was closest to his brother Bun, and when Goody knew Bun was dying of lung cancer, he brought him to the Worcester Foundation as a business manager. Despite some resentment among the staff, after Bun, age sixty-two, died on September 24, 1966, Goody buried

Lizzie and Joseph Pincus

Bun's ashes in a container under a newly planted small tree at the administration building.[6] Later, the ashes were retrieved and sent to Bun's wife, Amelia, in New York City.

Lee, whose full name was Leopold Lincoln Pincus, was the most charming, talented (he played the banjo), and scholarly, but he was constantly in hot water throughout his life. According to brother Alex, he was professionally diagnosed later in life as a sociopath, something Alex ascribed to the genetic trait associated with their father's depressive tendencies.[7] Lee was only thirteen when the family sent him to the National Farm School even though the school's minimum age was eighteen. The School, founded in 1897 near Doylestown, Pennsylvania, by Rabbi Joseph Krauskopf, finally became Delaware Valley College in 1989. Alex described Lee's behavior as incorrigible, a total contrast to Goody, and responsible for his inability to pursue his aim of being a farmer. His brothers tried to no avail to help him reform. But despite the difficulties, including time in prison,

Alex, Sophie, Lee, Maurice, Bun, Goody

Lee made a major contribution to the finances of the family. Alex flatly stated "I owe to him my financial support throughout my undergraduate years."[8,9]

Lee and Maurice were in the middle and never made it to college. Maurice was sweet, kind, and sociable. His middle name was de Hirsch, honoring the Baron de Hirsch who made the Woodbine farm colony possible. Maurice moved up the ladder in business, eventually managing an Isaacson family-owned factory making boy's shirts. In 1938, he married Ruth Ames, a biologist working in Goody's Harvard laboratory.

Sophie had polio at age two and a half, leaving her with a weak right leg.[10] Nevertheless she was cheerful, determined, intellectual, sociable, and very active. Alex remembered that "As a child she was famous for sitting in her high chair and correcting her brother's table manners,"[11] a good beginning for her later work as a teacher of grade-school children and even later as a child psychologist after earning a master's degree from Columbia University in child development.

Alexis Pincus, the youngest in the family, received a Ph.D. in ceramic engineering from Pennsylvania State University. He specialized in developing industrial applications for ceramics, working first at the American Optical Company in Massachusetts and later at General Electric.

He taught his specialty at the Illinois Institute of Technology and at Rutgers. After he retired in 1983, Alexis published eighteen books on a wide variety of subjects ranging from glass manufacturing to sexology. He died at age eighty-two, living his last years in Caracas, Venezuela.

Lizzie with Alex, Lee, Goody, Maurice, Bun, Sophie

The Pincuses had a very large extended family. It started with all their relatives, no matter how remote. But with Joseph's gregariousness and fondness for students and colleagues and Mother Lizzie's belief in staying connected with friends, including entire families, the extended family grew and grew. Maurice Fels, of the Fels Naptha soap fortune, for example, supported Goody with loans and encouragement during his student days.

The Pincus home was a clubhouse, filled with school friends, neighborhood friends, and extended family from the neighborhoods of their previous homes.[12] Dinnertime usually saw at least ten sitting at the table. The kids were responsible for the dirty dishes, usually with Goody or Evelyn, Annie's daughter, doing the washing. Music invariably came after dinner, sometimes with Mother Lizzie on the piano, but usually with Evelyn playing popular music for everyone to sing. The family's first "Victrola" was a cause for celebratory dancing around the table in the living room.

Later in life, Goody was not religious, but brother Alex recalled, "We were Reform Jews belonging to the Bronx branch of the Stephen Wise Free Synagogue that met in a casino."[13] The Rabbi was Louis I. Newman. Goody taught at the Sunday School. The family usually spent Passover Seders at Woodbine with Zahde Lipman, later at Uncle Willie's, and then later at Uncle Raymond's farm.

Mother Lizzie believed in summers in the country.[14] The children returned to the Woodbine area in the summers living with relatives and spending weekends at the beach and the amusement park. In the summer of 1912,

the family rented a cottage at Arverne in the Rockaways, a summer marked by the onset of Sophie's infection with polio.

Thirteen-year-old Goody and Lee went to Camp Coolbaugh near Stroudsburg, Pennsylvania, in the summer of 1916. Goody won medals in tennis and swimming. Brother Alex remembered a Goody story at camp. "One day it began to thunderstorm very hard while my adored brother was at the far end of the lake on his daily swim. I feared for his safety from the lightning. After considering running to the camp buildings for help and/or oars, I paddled a rowboat with my hands trying to reach him. When Goody caught up to me, he shouted 'Al, you stupid kid, why don't you get in out of the rain?' Till his last consciousness Goody and I remained close brothers. One of the great things about him was that he not only gave of himself, but accepted help from me, the kid baby brother."[15]

In the summers of 1918 and 1919, Goody worked as waiter and busboy in Catskill Mountain resorts. Then Goody spent the next four summers working as a farmhand on his uncle's farms near Woodbine. For the summer of 1924, Maurice Fels arranged for Goody to be assistant director of the Vineland Boy Scout camp on Parvin Pond, near Uncle Raymond's farm. This was a momentous summer, when Goody changed the direction of his life, and he met Elizabeth "Lizzie" Notkin, his future wife.

JOSEPH PINCUS made a change in 1917. His oldest sons were approaching college age. His salary was only $50 per week from the Jewish Agricultural Society, with no promise of advancement. Alex later wondered how his father's "nervous" state might have led to negative reactions with superiors.

Joseph joined Alexander Hinchuck's export-import company in the Wall Street area. Hinchuck was a refugee from Russia and Bolshevism, with connections to the White Russians fighting the Communists. Joseph's enthusiasm was such that he convinced friends and family to invest in the company. Working for this company, Joseph traveled to Europe looking for products, returning to cover the family dining-room table with samples from which the relatives could choose.[16] But by 1923, the company went bankrupt. The family struggled, and in summer 1923 they moved to the Rainbow Lake Inn, leased and operated by Aunt Annie, fifty rooms, adjacent to Raymond's farm. The family lived with the hotel staff in an old farm house. Mother Lizzie supervised the kitchen and housekeeping; Evelyn, Bun, and Morris High School friends waited on tables, and the younger ones enjoyed the life. Joseph joined the family, giving up on a business selling imported seeds.

In the fall of 1923, the family moved to Vineland, New Jersey, where Joseph again tried a wholesale seed business. During this time period, the family was significantly supported by Lee's income. Lee had graduated from the National Farm School, and at first managed a dairy herd, then worked as a salesman for Purina Chow.

Joseph had yet another new job in 1924 for a recently established company. He became the only agriculturalist for The Amtorg Trading Corporation, an American importing and exporting company owned by the Soviet Union. It later became known that for many years Amtorg served as a front for Soviet intelligence operations in the U.S. Joseph contributed significantly to the transfer of agricultural knowledge and products between the U.S. and the Soviet Union. In fall 1925, the family moved back to New York City, to an apartment at Seventh Avenue and 112th Street. The job with Amtorg lasted until 1929, and Alex viewed this time as "one of the best times of Papa's and our lives."[17] Joseph was paid in gold, $75 per week. He had earned a commission of about $6,000 for selling the Baron de Hirsch Agricultural School in Peekskill, New York. This money expanded Mother Lizzie's savings account; some of it paid for new dining room and living room furniture.

Joseph's job required him to travel throughout the U.S. and Canada buying seeds and sheep, cattle and poultry breeding stock for Russia. Joseph's granddaughter, Laura Pincus Bernard, said, "He had traveled to every state in the Union as a consultant."[18] In addition, he was selling Russian seeds to American farmers. He was accompanied by a Russian scientist and agriculturalist who planned the trip and served as a combined technical expert and interpreter. This was an enjoyable time for Joseph, traveling first-class on the railroads and in hotels, being wined and dined, and receiving the official Russian newspaper *Pravda* by airmail from Moscow.[19] By this time, Gregory was at Harvard. But during Gregory's years of growing up, it was a time of scarcity, insecurity, and humiliations.

In the 1930s and 1940s, Joseph once again worked for the organization he was with in the early 1900s, the Jewish Agricultural Society. He arranged for the settlement on farms of refugees from Nazi persecution and organized agricultural supplies for war relief in Russia.

"McCarthyism" refers to the tactics employed by Wisconsin Senator Joseph McCarthy, beginning in 1950, questioning anyone's patriotism under the guise of rooting out communism during the Cold War. Gregory Pincus applied in 1950 for part-time support from the U.S. Public Health Service for his activities at the National

Joseph with seeds donated for Russian war relief — 1943

Institutes of Health, and was required to undergo an audit by the Board of Inquiry on Employee Loyalty of the Federal Security Agency. An unspecified question arose that postponed a final judgment. A further review was performed by the Loyalty Review Board of the Civil Service Commission, and finally a decision was made that the information provided "did not constitute grounds for belief that you are disloyal to the Government of the United States."[20] It is likely that Joseph Pincus's interactions with Russia and his subscription to *Pravda* played a role in these proceedings.

Joseph Pincus developed kidney failure in the last half of 1950. First in a nursing home and then in St. Elizabeth Hospital in Boston, he suffered a minor stroke and heart failure.[21] Joseph died of pneumonia in a Boston hospital on January 14, 1951, at age seventy-four.[22]

School in the Bronx

Goody's family thought he was a genius, and his performance in school did not disappoint them. Goody attended P.S. 40 in the Bronx, across the street from the Pincus apartment on Jennings Street. It was a very large school, with about 2,000 pupils in eight grades plus kindergarten. Typical of the times, the boys and girls were in separate classrooms and used separate doors for entry and exit, a system maintained in most public schools

in New York City early in the twentieth century. Having six children at the school over an eleven-year period, it's not surprising that Mother Lizzie was very involved with the school. Goody was a top student, and the pride of the teachers.[23]

Alex remembered Goody as always reading, so intently that "he was oblivious to the talk and noises the rest of us were making around him Yet when Mother asked for someone to run an errand and the rest of us whimpered that we were too busy to go always Goody would volunteer. Mother and all of us looked upon Goody as some kind of a saint. He was serene, caring, and competent at everything."[24] Goody had a photographic memory. "He could read a book at three times the speed of a normal person (he preferred crime novels, one a night)."[25] He had a search-engine mind, organizing and retaining vast amounts of information in a mental catalogue from which he could retrieve what he needed.

Brother Alex recalled two unusual episodes. "Goody told us that when he was about ten our Polish maid, Mary, took him into bed with her and did things. I asked did she actually rape you, and Goody replied that she couldn't because she had a rag around her parts."[26] "Around 1930 Mother and Aunt Annie, those sexual innocents brought up under Victorian prudery, were lamenting that our generation was so open about sex whereas in their days they were too

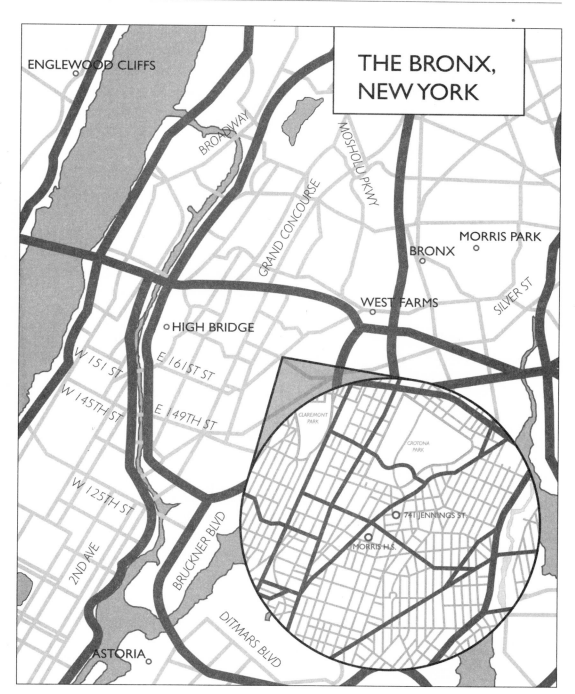

THE BRONX, NEW YORK

ENGLEWOOD CLIFFS

BROADWAY

MOSHOLU PKWY

GRAND CONCOURSE

MORRIS PARK

BRONX

WEST FARMS

SILVER ST

HIGH BRIDGE

W 151 ST

E 161ST ST

W 145TH ST

E 149TH ST

CLAREMONT PARK

CROTONA PARK

W 125TH ST

741 JENNINGS ST

MORRIS H.S.

2ND AVE

BRUCKNER BLVD

DITMARS BLVD

ASTORIA

preoccupied with literature and beauty to think about such things, much less talk about them. Goody spoke up and said that when he was a boy in their idyllic community of Woodbine, he was playing baseball in a field next to some woods when a couple came out of the woods. The ball players went to see what they had been doing in the woods and found an aborted fetus. Mother was shocked and said 'How did you know what it was?' Goody explained that he did not know then, but remembered the event years later."[27]

THE HUGE NUMBER of poor immigrants living in New York City in the late 1800s led to many social reform movements, including a new emphasis on public education. Morris High School, the third public high school to open in New York, was a short trolley ride down the Boston Post Road from the Pincus family home. The school was originally named the Mixed High School in 1897 because it was the first co-educational high school in New York City, with twenty-three teachers serving about 460 students.[28] The name was changed in 1901 to the Peter Cooper High School in honor of the inventor of the steam locomotive. However, an organized movement among the people living in the Bronx promptly changed the name a year later to Morris High School after Gouverneur Morris, known as the penman of the U.S. constitution (he wrote the final draft), whose family lived

on an estate in the area called Morrisania where the new school building was built on East 166th Street at the Boston Post Road.

The school sits on a small hill, in a remarkable and magnificent building with a capacity of 2,600 students, constructed between 1901 and 1904 for a basic cost of $469,383.[29] The final cost with furnishings and ornate trimmings came to $656,565.[30] The architect designed the building in a style prevalent in colleges and universities at the turn of the century, called English Collegiate Gothic. The five-story building featured seventy-one classrooms, twelve laboratories, a large library, separate, fully equipped gymnasiums for boys and girls, a handsome auditorium in the rear of the building with a pipe organ and seating 1,700, and a tower, housing ventilating shafts and the boiler chimney, that became the school's symbol. Beginning in 2002, the building was renovated at great cost and the high school was phased out and replaced with five smaller ones: an international high school, violin and dance, a school for excellence, an academy for collaborative studies, and a leadership academy.

In Goody's time as a high school student, 1916–1920, Morris High served a Bronx population of about 600,000 people, with a major Jewish component. Morris High was regarded by young New York Jews as the school for the "young, upwardly mobile, the first or newly immigrant Jewish boys on their way up the ladder."[31] For

Morris High School

the generation of the early 1900s, it was the entryway to college.

Goody Pincus was an honor student and won scholarships to the college of his choice. He served as president of The Morris Service League, an organization of students that provided tutors to fellow students and policed the corridors to promote good conduct and service to the high school.[32] In his senior year, Goody was vice-president of The Alacris Literary and Debating Club, whose members reviewed books and conducted short-story and recital contests. He formed his strongest friendships and was introduced to girls, "that sex which hitherto was unknown to me," at The Alacris.[33] His serviceable French and German later in life had its roots in Morris High.

Evelyn, Aunt Annie's daughter, came to live with the family so that she could attend Morris. Soon after, Goody told his mother they were in love

Goody at Morris High School

and wanted to get married.[34] But Mother Lizzie calmly pointed out that it was illegal for first cousins to marry. Evelyn later married Joseph Isaacson, and the two of them remained close to Goody the rest of his life. After Evelyn, Goody competed with his brother Bun for the favors of Goldie Shapiro, then Goody fell in love with Denah Josephson, who later married Goody's friend, Nat Harris.

Goody kept a personal diary in 1920 that began halfway through his senior year at Morris High School and ended when he went to college.[35] It was filled with idealistic, innocent thoughts on life and friends, reflecting the naivety to be expected in a bright teenager who had been "so happy all my life." "At this early date I find that I tend towards an idealistic philosophy and a happy one at that." The diary contained no pessimism or dark moods. But it did express some goals that would become consistent components of Goody's lifelong philosophy. "I shall endeavor to make the best of my opportunities to further my aspirations, keeping all the while an optimistic outlook on life, happy in what I have but constantly seeking for more happiness for myself and others, especially others. The repression of my selfish instincts and the development and conveying on of an altruism will be one of the chief aims of my life."

Goody and Evelyn

Goody, Goldie, Evelyn, Leon

The teenage Goody was an affectionate person, another trait that would persist throughout his life. "My affection easily leads me to express it in a kiss. My relations I kiss quite without constraint. My friends I cannot kiss at all. How can I express my love for them? It is bursting for expression and the kiss, the embrace, occurs not at all or is lavished on some one other than the one on whom it should have been. Thus, Evelyn receives love that is intended for others. She knows it not and calls me 'mushy.' I am such an affectionate being. I can't help it. It is better though that I do not express it to all."

Goody treasured his high school friends, especially Leon Lifschitz, with whom he had many long conversations about philosophy, politics, life, and girls. Friendship, "the holiest passion on this earth," would always be valued by Goody. His diary contained twenty-five poems, mostly about friends, nature, and the meaning of life.

> Why do we live through this eternal strife,
> Through this apparent beastly life.
> Where man fights man? Nor does he cease
> To struggle, clutch, forever making war on peace.
>
> Oh! May I ne'er be bitten with this madness,
> That yields to men but emptiness and sadness,

> And if for power or fame or such cursed things I sigh,
> Forgetting books and friends, the gentleness of life, then let me die.

At the end of Goody's senior year at Morris High School, he evoked his love of Denah in his poetry:

> Denah, you're as dear to me
> As any friend I know.
> Thoughts I'll always have of thee,
> No matter where I go.
>
> And your sweet image e'er will hover,
> So clear before mine eyes,
> As it now seems to boyish lover,
> Whose feeling too deep lies
> For language e'er to crystallize.
>
> Echoes of your voice will ring,
> Down the lanes of memory,
> And my heart will ever sing
> Of maiden young and free.
>
> And all the tenderness that in me
> Lurked, trembling to be full,
> And coming forth in caress guilty,
> That liquid flow in me
> I consecrate in memory.
>
> To Denah the clear affection
> That for you, the gods

I held in my recollection
Like tear drops of pure pearl
Will always dwell.

Thy girlish figure was by me
Waking or sleeping seen,
In dreams and actuality.
The thought of it, so green,
I'll guard, no e'er to dispel.

Denah, your blithe self doth blend
Into my life and happiness,
And to them both doth somehow lend
A certain charm and sweetness
That I hope will never fade.

In the 1960s, Denah, who had become a psychiatric social worker in New York City, sent complex, jargon-filled, philosophical letters to Goody that were hard to decipher; for example, "I can readily conceive however, that malprogramming of the cortex to moralistic definitions of human nature can control phobic avoidance of this obviously taboo territory whose exhaustive exploration is, for obvious reasons, the rational basic commitment of a biologist."[36] Goody's replies were short and formal.

Goody at Cornell

Graduating from high school, Goody wanted to follow the scientific paths of his famous uncles, Mother Lizzie's brothers, Jacob and Charles Lipman.[37] In fall 1920, he enrolled at the New York State College of Agriculture at Cornell University on a New York State Regents scholarship and a Pulitzer scholarship. The ties with Cornell were strong. Goody's uncles, Isaac and Jacob Lipman, were Cornell graduates, as were two Birkhahn cousins. His father and Uncle Jake had many friends among the faculty.

Goody planned to major in agriculture, specializing in pomology, the study of apple cultivation. Later in life, Goody repeatedly told newspaper reporters that he always knew he would be a scientist, but he originally thought it would be in agriculture.[38,39] His courses throughout his four years of college reflected his pursuit of agriculture: veterinary physiology, agricultural chemistry, plant breeding, botany, and in each of his last three years, pomology.[40] It wasn't until halfway through his senior year that Goody decided to pursue biology and science at Harvard.[21] Goody's change may have been influenced by his father. Goody's idealistic views of a farmer expressed in his diary at age seventeen were tempered by conversations with his father who emphasized the "non-paying character of a farmer's life."[41]

During his first month at Cornell, Goody continued to make entries in his high school diary. He again laid out a cornerstone of his life,

"It is my duty, therefore, and the duty of every one of us, not only to develop himself, but to help others to develop themselves, not by hammering them, but by allowing them greater freedom and by sympathetic, kindly advice, by educating and aiding."[42] After only a few days in Ithaca, Goody sat on a boulder near McGraw Hall and wrote a poem:[43]

> And the creek doth curl
> Mid all this scene,
> A silver scrawl,
> On a page of green,
> Glimpsed here, glimpsed there,
> Twixt groves of trees,
> The thread of a spider
> Dropped down by the breeze.
>
> The smoke of a pigmy train,
> And the dust of an automobile,
> One along its road of steel,
> On a curving country lane.
> The other lazily, both
> With their movement slow
> Alone stir show
> On this motionless expanse of life.
>
> Tis life in the green.
> Tis life in the bud.
> Tis a glorious paen.
> Sun in a flood
> Of beauty and peace,

> Like the quick release
> Of laughter golden
> From its fleshy dungeon human.

Surprisingly, Goody's grades at Cornell were not outstanding: eleven As, twenty Bs, five Cs, and two Ds.[44] Perhaps some of his poor grades could be attributed to a lack of interest and motivation, such as the D in Military Science and Tactics. However, in his senior year, Goody had a D in Botany and Cs in Plant Breeding and Biology, but this was the year that he was courting his future wife amidst family tension. Goody also had to devote a lot of time to earning his way; he worked most nights. Acceptance into graduate school at Harvard must have been less competitive in 1924, but Goody's grades surely must have required the assistance of personal recommendations from his famous uncles, Charles Lipman at the University of California, Berkeley, and Jacob Lipman, dean of agriculture at Rutgers and director of the New Jersey Agricultural Experiment Station.

Goody's youthful, smooth-faced picture in the 1924 Cornellian Yearbook featured his trademark, electric-shock hairdo, but his mustache, prominent eyebrows, and baggy eyes were yet to appear. Unlike most people, he wore eyeglasses when young, but not later in life. His activities were limited to the Cosmopolitan Club and *The Cornell Literary*

Review. He had no time for sports because he had no financial support from the family. He washed dishes and waited on tables for his room and board. Goody traveled back and forth between school and home by hitch-hiking.

Goody and Raymond F. Howes founded *The Literary Review of Cornell* in their sophomore year. The first issue of the eight-page, monthly magazine appeared in October 1922, available for ten cents. Goody's poem "Nocturne," appeared in the December 1922 issue:

I sense a prescience
In the moon's vague, trembling, guileless light,
Foretelling days
When the thought of moonlight shall compel
The languorous longings.
I cannot voice
The fullness of the night
As the stars do;
I cannot write in flame or starlight;
But quietly there descends

Gregory Pincus — 1924

A gleam of understanding—
Life is some dynamic strain
Loosed from the somber, all-majestic power
That guided into being all this world;
And night becomes a mystery
For haunting life,
For guiding its gauche senses
Into gropings toward their worth.
We blunder through the darkness
Thrilling to values, knowings,
Heretofore unguessed by us,
Till, when with weariness and wonder
We feel the beating of the great heart
Of this gigantic riddle,
Night flees into the dawn,
And dazzles us with day again.[45]

Goody was not involved with the magazine during his junior year when he had to drop out of school for a semester and work full time as a farmhand.[46] *The Literary Review* struggled. The editors lamented in June 1923, "We have published, for lack of better, some material which would shame a high school magazine; but certain others of our contributions deserved to be printed in a better magazine than THE REVIEW. Cornell does not abound in writers. If there are more than a score here who have a respectable command of English coupled with thoughts worthy of expression, we have missed them in our efforts to discover literary talent."[47]

Yet they resolved to expand in size to thirty pages, although the magazine would now appear quarterly, for twenty-five cents.

At the beginning of 1923, Goody became editor-in-chief of *The Literary Review,* and presided over its quiet demise in March 1924 in his senior year, only seventeen months after it first appeared. The magazine ended with a proud declaration in its final paragraph: "We are solvent." Goody contributed short stories and poems. His poem entitled "New York," appeared in December 1923 and undoubtedly reflected his years living in the big city:

I

The skies are regulated in New York,
And granted polygons through which to shine,
For they distract the men who're there to work,
And tend to make then scoffers, wasters of time.

The skies are mobile as a phantom fleet,
That men entice, with its every move,
And crowds are ever shifting in the street,
Aimless as colored clouds the wind-drifts love.

The skies flash briefly through their sharp cut space,

And seem forgotten in this stone empire;
Here songs and dreamings dying have no
place,
Nor bearers of the lotus and the lyre.

But broad flags hint of scarlet tents that
rise,
And banners tremulous against wide skies.

II

They tell of lights on Broadway, lights that
shine
To cheer the mournful city and its men;
They tell of pleasure and the dance, the
sign
Of gaiety that springs to being when

The day of toil is over, and the hum
Of business pulsings leaves the downtown
streets
Deserted, surging northward from the
slum;
The light and music come, and struggle
fleets

From nighttime, night with laughter after
day;
Men crowd into the theatres and halls,
And seek life in the concert and the play,
But on the office buildings' high built walls

Reflected night lights palely gleam with

scorn,
And in the parks men watch with forms
forlorn.

III

In New York there's a street that's never
still,
With footfalls on the flags from dawn to
dawn,
Where men with song or silence loiter till
Their fellows come to walk, or play the
faun.

And underneath the pavement subways
roar,
And disgorge wanders to join the throng
Of restless life, the spreading city's store
Of bones and protoplasm, things of song

And passing passions, creatures of unrest.
The stretching street is tireless to hold
Unfinished microcosms seeking rest,
And tireless of pageants that unfold

The mingling mockery and hope that's
flung
By New York gathering its old and young.

IV

The river under city bridges flows,
A black, foul current seeking opal seas,
And down the riverway the wind-drift

blows,
Carelessly wandering for realms of ease.

"There in the river all that defiles us dies,"
The city dwellers murmur stolidly,
"Above, the knowing carrion seeker flied,
And we must bridge it smiling scornfully."

The river soon dissolves the sweat of
those
Who work its boats, and daily trad its
docks;
The river rises, falls, but darkly flows,
Indifferent to the town that sighs or mocks,

And cuts the city like a bandit's knife
That strikes forth careless of carrion or
life.

V

And haply we find youth or mayhap fail,
The city holds us ever as its thralls;
Our cheeks flush feverish, or sadly pale,
But thoughtless of our wants the city calls,

And stifles cries that rise, Lament,
Rejoicings die, or come to birth, and love
Departs, or stays until its time is spent,
But New York stands, for cities never rove,

And New York is impassive, its deceit
Or promise are our making only; we

May meet and talk of gold upon the street,
Or see but dirt and tears there endlessly—
It matters not—all faiths and forms are
swirled
Into the gatherings of the city world.[48]

GOODY was challenged by a major crisis in his senior year that must have been an embarrassing and difficult experience. He was accused by two classmates of cheating, a charge that could lead to expulsion under the honor system in place. Brother Alex explained: "He had finished and left the room, but returned and wrote something on his exam paper. Goody said that he had forgotten to sign the honor system pledge of 'I have not received or given help on this examination,' and had merely written his pledge and signature."[49] Hearings were held. Uncle Jake, Maurice Fels, and others were called in as character witnesses. Goody was cleared, allowed to receive his bachelor's degree and to go on to Harvard.

Goody and Lizzie

"In his last year at Cornell, there came Liz, two weddings to her, and a lifelong passion and devotion. There is no doubt in my mind that Goody would never have achieved what he did without the support and pressures from his wife, Elizabeth Notkin Pincus."[50] Brother Alex went on to describe Lizzie as brilliant, witty, caring, passionate, assertive, sometimes beautiful, and sometimes hostile. Her devotion to her husband and children extended to include the entire Notkin and Pincus families. She was hazel-eyed and small, only five-feet tall, under 100 pounds until her middle years, and the whole package was completely dedicated to promoting the career and fortunes of Gregory Goodwin Pincus.

Lizzie Notkin was the fifth child in a family with five brothers. She was born in the Ukraine on April 17, 1899, the daughter of Joseph and Aneuta Spiegel Notkin.[51] After emigrating to Canada, her father eventually owned a mattress factory in Montreal. The brothers included two physicians, a lawyer, and two businessmen. After obtaining her teacher's certificate in Montreal, Lizzie taught elementary school. Alex believed that her move to the U.S. was precipitated by the end of an engagement to John Levy, who later became a prominent psychiatrist in New York City.[52]

Portrait of Lizzie in her early twenties, artist unknown

Dorothea Goodwin boarded with the Pincus family while working as a field social worker for the National Council of Jewish Women, visiting wives of Jewish farmers throughout New Jersey. Lizzie had been sent from Montreal in 1923 to associate with Goodwin for training to fill a similar position in the state of New York. She joined the Pincus household living in Vineland, New Jersey, as a boarder. Lizzie was four years older than Goody. Her daughter, Laura, recalled a family story. "She thought of him as a kid. She felt like she was a graduate and here was this student, this kid. So she said to him, 'Well, what are you going to do?' He said, 'I'm a sexologist.' At that time, you didn't use the world 'sex.' And she kind of went, 'Gulp.'"[53]

In the summer of 1924, Mother Lizzie, Joseph, Sophie, and Alex were on a trip. Alex described what happened when they came home. "When we returned we found that all hell had broken loose. All the Pincus boys fell for Lizzie, but Leon Lifschitz, Goody's high-school classmate and friend visiting at the time, won her acceptance for a canoe trip on Rainbow Lake. Paddling up a narrow channel that connected to an adjoining lake, named Parvin Pond, the canoe got stuck in a mud flat. Unable to turn around, the couple remained with the canoe until dawn. Finally successful in backtracking their route, they arrived exhausted and eaten by New Jersey mosquitoes at Uncle Raymond's and Olga's farm.

When Mother Lizzie returned home, her words were: 'Can you imagine a woman staying out all night with a man?'"[54] Alex even remembered her saying "That prostitute!"[55] This was not a good start. According to Goody's daughter Laura, "Mother and grandmother never got along, two strong-willed women competing for the love of Goody."[56] And what thoughts were stimulated by the fact that both mother and wife were called "Lizzie?"

In the fall, hitch-hiking home from Cornell in 1924 to see the family, Goody stopped outside of Albany, in Nassau, New York, to see Lizzie, now working in New York City. Lizzie and Goody would meet in the home of Nathan and Celia Naum. Nathan was Joseph's student at the Baron de Hirsch School in Woodbine. Afterwards, Joseph and Mother Lizzie would celebrate their annual wedding anniversary by taking a night boat up the Hudson to stay with the Naums.

Brother Alex told the story of their marriage: "One day in 1925 I came home to find Mother red-eyed. She took me aside to tell me that Goody had married. ... The story seems to have been that Liz had been notified by the U.S. Immigration Service that she had to return to Canada. This meant that she and Goody would have to part, maybe forever. They went before a judge in Boston and got a dispensation allowing them to marry without the usual waiting period. I recall that their pictures before the judge were published in the Boston papers because of the unusual and romantic circumstances. As the wife of an American citizen, Liz was granted a visa and moved in with Goody, Bun, and Leon. ... Later on there was a second religious wedding ceremony sponsored by the Notkins in Montreal."[57] Lizzie was granted American citizenship in 1929.[58]

In summer 1925 in New York City, the newlyweds were introduced to the extended family and friends in a series of parties. "I recall Liz rebelling at one point, and saying that she had had enough of Birkhahns. Also she explained her possessiveness by saying that the money spent on trips to New York was needed for day to day living within their cramped budget."[59] This was undoubtedly true. Brother Alex also remembered that Lizzie stayed in bed through most of the morning.

Alex described a big change in Lizzie with the move to Worcester, Massachusetts, in 1938 (Chapter 6). She began to "preach" to Goody "against the Pincus tradition of idealism rather than money-making. She would press Goody

Lizzie — 1930

to realize that there was nothing wrong in being a scientist who makes a comfortable living from his work, rather than cherishing the lifestyle of poverty and job insecurity."[60] Alex believed this was a motivation for Goody to become involved with Tom Slick, the wealthy people in Worcester, and the pharmaceutical companies (Chapter 6). "In place of her former indolence, Lizzie now was active in her home as a gourmet cook and sparkling hostess and in

Lizzie — 1937

the community through the League of Women Voters. Also she became the accompanist of Goody on most of his travels to Europe and around the world. Throughout she made her role that of the supportive wife."[61]

A Worcester newspaper reporter wrote, "Mrs. Pincus is an unusual personality in her own right, noted for her flashing wit and sense of independence."[62] Joseph Goldzieher, one of the first to study and develop oral contraceptives in the U.S., said, "She had a tongue like a razor."[63] Laura Pincus Bernard thought that her mother "was a woman born in the wrong era. She was very intelligent and she was frustrated because she was a housewife. She never pursued her own career."[64] Goody's mother and his wife shared a similar story.

Brother Alex didn't hold anything back when talking about Lizzie. "When she was good she was very, very good, but when she forgot to take her thyroid there would be demonstrations of jealousy and temper. ... More than once I was present when Goody came home to tempestuous scenes. Sweetly and lovingly he would ask Liz if she had remembered to take her thyroid pill. Then there would transpire the change in personality to the charming, caring Liz at her best. But it must also be stressed that Goody never stopped adoring Liz and that she was an essential confidante, counselor, companion, beloved lover, and generative source of his accomplishments."[65] Her emotional reactions were "mainly exhibited in an overwhelming jealousy about Goody. This jealousy extended to Mother with whom she was in conflict and

Lizzie — 1945

competition from their first meeting. But it often was exhibited when any women paid attention to Goody or vice-versa."[66]

Lizzie and Goody —1951

Alex ascribed Lizzie's moodiness to a thyroid problem, but her swings were too rapid for a dose of thyroid to have an effect. It takes several weeks for the body to adjust to dosage changes in thyroid medication. An abrupt change in behavior within minutes, even hours, of taking a daily dose of thyroid hormone cannot be a physiologic response. It is extremely likely that this was a method of communication in the Pincus marriage, a socially acceptable code, whereby Goody could signal: "That's enough. You've crossed the line. Time to back up." And she always did.

Many of Goody's old colleagues described dinners at the Pincus house with great warmth, and with great praise for Lizzie's cooking. "She was elegant when she served meals, and I don't remember her having anybody to help her, housekeeper, caterer, or anything like that. It was the first time in my life that I ever was served salad first. She was a nice woman who was very lovely to people, and she was worldly, but would talk to you down to earth about her problems and family issues."[67]

But there was another side to the story. Lizzie demanded and Goody requested that his secretary act as Lizzie's chauffer, even for shopping trips. This did not sit well with some of the secretaries, and more than one refused.[68] Those visitors who stayed overnight at the Pincus house said Lizzie never got out of bed until almost noontime.[69]

Lizzie was loud, forceful, and often opinionated. She had the low-pitched, gravelly voice of a heavy smoker.[70-73] Colleagues remembered that Lizzie was a Scotch drinker.[30] Manuel Neves e Castro, a former fellow at the Worcester Foundation and now a prominent clinician in Lisbon, Portugal, remembered her as a "short, fast-moving lady behind a cigarette, turning right or left to say hello to everybody."[74] When he first met Lizzie at a cocktail party, she told him a story:

Dr. Castro, I want to tell you a funny story. You see I'm having my second drink and I'm okay. But once I had a party at home in Northborough, with many guests, Goody's friends, that I had to see when they came in and accompany them to the bar. I had a drink with one, not having drunk more than a swallow because I had to put my glass on the table to go and welcome the next guest, and the scene was repeated. So I told the bartender, "Look here, I have to see so many people coming in, drinking a few drops from a glass, and then leaving it here, that I want to ask you not to give me more than a total of three servings, because I can hardly keep count." Later, when I could find some rest and was really needing a drink that I could enjoy for the first time, I approached the bar and asked for a drink. The bartender refused me! I insisted, and he said, "No way Mrs. Pincus. You asked me before not to serve you more than three drinks even if you used all sort of arguments to persuade me. So this it. No more drinks!" Of course, I went to the kitchen and helped myself.[75]

Joseph Goldzieher said of Lizzie: "She was a tough lady. She took no crap from anybody. She was what she was, and you accepted it or you didn't. I loved her for it, because she was a true type. I respect people who are a type unto themselves."[76]

GOODY was always concerned about Lizzie when he went off on his travels. He would use the young physicians at the Foundation to check on Lizzie. One day Goody called Edward Wallach, saying that Lizzie had a bad cold and asked him to go out to the house and see her. Wallach remembered, "I had my stethoscope and otoscope, went to the house and listened to her chest, and treated her with antibiotics."[77] Goody would tell colleagues, and the wives of colleagues, "Look after Liz, look after Liz."[78]

Lizzie had her rough spots, but her marriage of forty-three years was solid. Goody and Lizzie were totally dedicated to each other. Goody took great delight in surprising Lizzie with little gifts that she prized, such as two tins of McVittie & Price Digestive Biscuits shipped from London, England.[79] Widely available today and very popular in the United Kingdom and Ireland, the cookies originated in Edinburgh in 1799 and are believed to improve gastrointestinal functioning.

Goody rarely went anywhere without Lizzie, even if the trip was to nearby Boston or New York. On one of those rare occasions when Lizzie was left home, in 1967, only months before Goody died, she was visiting her son John in Washington and wrote to Goody in longhand on yellow, ruled legal paper, beginning with the salutation, "Darling," and signing it in a way that seemed to indicate that she recognized her two personalities:

> Do be careful with your diet and try to get some rest. Yes, I <u>am</u> taking my pills. … Goodnight darling, miss you—can't

talk to anybody as I talk to you, but it's good discipline not to talk at all—and anyway who will listen? …

> Love & kisses to you,
> your wife and Lizzie.[80]

Lizzie and Goody — 1950s

CHAPTER FIVE:
HARVARD AND "PINCOGENESIS"

GREGORY PINCUS, the first-generation American son of Russian Jewish immigrants, went to Harvard in 1924. He was admitted as a graduate student under the geneticist, William E. Castle. M-C. Chang believed that Pincus's early interest in genetics was because of his color-blindness.[1] Pincus was convinced that color-blind people had sharp, focused vision, and he was a good example. Chang recalled that Pincus said, "He could spot a four-leaf clover while walking through a field."[2] But his color-blindness was a problem when it came to his ties; his secretary could always tell when his wife hadn't made the choice.[3]

Pincus worked toward his graduate degree at the Bussey Institution in Applied Biology, a part of Harvard, a spread of greenhouses, gardens, and barns next to the Arnold Arboretum in Forest Hills, about ten miles from Cambridge, Massachusetts. The complex grew its own food for the experimental animals used in breeding and genetic experiments. Beginning in 1926, Pincus published over twenty scientific reports in a three-year period, documenting the inheritance of various physiologic traits such as responses to light and gravity. Harvard awarded Pincus a master's degree in science and the Sc.D. degree (the doctor of science degree is equivalent to a Ph.D, doctor of philosophy, the more commonly awarded degree today). His thesis, basically a study of the inheritance of coat coloring in rats, was entitled: I. A Comparative Study of the Chromosomes of the Norway Rat and the Black Rat; II. A Study of the Genetic Factors Affecting the Expression of the Piebald Pattern in the Rat." Goody's parents, sister Sophie and brother Alex attended the graduation ceremony in Cambridge in June 1927.[4]

Gregory Pincus, Assistant Professor, Harvard

Pincus lived in a Cambridge apartment with his brother Bun and Leon Lifschitz, his Morris High School classmate, enduring friend, and a student at the law school.[5] Later, when he practiced law in New York City, Leon changed his family name to Leighton. Leon and Bun had opened a bookstore, "The Alcove," to meet their expenses, where Goody and later, Lizzie, worked part time.

In the summer of 1925, his second year at Harvard, after Goody married Lizzie, she came to live with him in the same apartment shared with Bun and Leon, horrifying Mother Lizzie.[6] Brother Alex visited Goody and Lizzie shortly after their marriage, observing that their Cambridge apartment hosted a book collection dominated by the works of Havelock Ellis, Richard von Krafft-Ebbing, August Forel, "and a few other encyclopediasts of sexology."[7]

Goody told Lizzie that he planned to spend the summer of 1926 again running a Boy Scout camp in New Jersey, and that she should spend the summer with her family in Montreal. A pregnant Lizzie's stern response came with an ultimatum. If she went to Montreal that would be the end of the marriage; she would never come back.[8] Goody found a summer job at Harvard with Professor William.E. Crozier. Alex John Pincus, known as John, was born in Cambridge on September 14, 1926.

John Pincus was admitted to Yale University at age sixteen, but after one year he left for the army. He finished his college education at Colby and received a Ph.D. from Harvard in economics, specializing in agricultural and international economics. John worked for the Rand Corporation until his retirement. After his retirement, already fluent in French, he learned Spanish and worked as an interpreter in the courts. John's sister, Laura Jane Pincus, was also born in Cambridge, on May 6, 1935. She graduated from Radcliffe, worked on the oral contraceptive clinical trial in Puerto Rico, then with Planned Parenthood in Chicago. For eighteen years, Laura was a major fund raiser for Tufts University, with an emphasis on international contacts.

THE SUMMER job in 1926 with Crozier sparked a new research interest, this time forced by Lizzie. Working in a laboratory in the basement of the Peabody Museum on the edge of Harvard Yard, Pincus published ten scientific reports with Crozier from 1926 to 1930, mostly dealing with behavioral responses of rats to stimuli like light or heat (tropism).

Following graduation, Pincus received a fellowship from the National Research Council for three years (1927–1930) of postdoctoral

Gregory Pincus — 1929

research with an annual salary of $2,800, which supported him for two years at Harvard and one year divided between The University of Cambridge in England with John Hammond, a reproductive physiologist, and the Kaiser Wilhelm Institute in Berlin with R. Goldschmidt, a noted geneticist.[9] While in Europe, Pincus published "Observations on the Living Eggs of the Rabbit," detailing his first thoughts of another new direction for his research, a direction he pursued for the next six years as an assistant professor at Harvard. [10]

Upon his return from Europe in 1930, Pincus was met at the dock in New York by his whole family who then gathered at Aunt Annie's on Ninety-Fourth Street. Unfortunately Goody left his suitcase in his taxi; it contained all of his notes and fruit fly specimens. Goody wryly remarked, "Now the world would not find out what determined sex."[11]

The next six years at Harvard were unquestionably successful, reflected by multiple publications, national attention in magazines and newspapers, and a widely acclaimed 160-page monograph summarizing his work, published by The Macmillian Company in 1936, *The Eggs of Mammals.*[12] The book was dedicated to his two mentors, W.E. Castle and W. J. Crozier, and the research was supported by the National Research Council Committee for Problems of Sex and the Josiah Macy Jr. Foundation. Years later, M-C Chang wrote, "The mammalian egg was the first love of Gregory Pincus, as he often said. It is such a pretty thing. . . . In the book, *The Eggs of Mammals,* by Pincus, it shows how much pleasure he must have derived from the study of eggs."[13]

When Pincus turned his attention to reproductive physiology, the sex hormones had been identified and isolated, fertilization and ovulation in mammals had been described, and the relationship between the brain and the ovary was understood. The general concepts were recognized; however, the details were not known; for example, hormones could not be measured in blood and the daily levels and pattern of hormones during a menstrual cycle were still a mystery. The complexity of the female reproductive system can be appreciated by reading the present-day review of the endocrinology of female reproduction in the Appendix. In addition to the limited knowledge in the 1930s, the sex hormones were not generally available for scientists to administer to experimental animals. Pincus developed methods to make an ovary produce a batch of mature eggs and perfected the collection and maintenance of viable eggs. Ultimately, he reported the delivery of normal rabbits from eggs induced to develop without fertilization (parthenogenesis). This work was not only controversial; it was extraordinary and ground-breaking: the beginning of the foundation upon which human in vitro fertilization is based.

Pincogenesis

Goody returned to Harvard in 1930 at age twenty-seven as an instructor in the department of general physiology; a year later, he was appointed assistant professor of biology. Pincus was significantly influenced by his department chairman, William J. Crozier. Crozier was only thirty-two in 1930, the youngest associate professor at Harvard, and a magnet who attracted young scientists like Gregory Pincus, Hudson Hoagland, and B.F. Skinner. Anyone who knew Pincus for an extended period of time became his good friend; in later years, Crozier wrote Goody many letters and signed them, "Affectionately, Bill and Louise."

Crozier's hero was Jacques Loeb who had induced parthenogenesis working with sea urchin eggs. Most importantly, Loeb, who died in 1924, was a strong believer in applying science to improve human life. Crozier, influenced by Loeb, taught Pincus, Hoagland, and Skinner—respectively, in reproductive biology, neurophysiology, and psychology—to apply science to human problems. This was to be the foundation of Pincus's own scientific philosophy. Beginning in 1930, Pincus turned to his lifelong focus on reproduction. Pincus continued to produce an impressive number of publications with Crozier, but at the same time he published significant research detailing fertilization in rabbits, largely with E. V. Enzmann, and in 1939, Pincus claimed success in producing a parthenogenetic rabbit. But by then he was no longer at Harvard.

In 1937, Pincus was granted a sabbatical and a research grant from Harvard allowing him to return to the University of Cambridge; however, at the same time he was informed that at the end of the year he would not be reappointed, despite the fact that his work had been cited by the university in its list of greatest scientific achievements in its history.[14] Whether the end of Pincus's time at Harvard reflected the politics of reactions to his work, anti-Semitism, or the reorganization of the department, and most likely, a combination of all three factors, will never be resolved.[15]

The termination of Pincus's faculty appointment was probably affected by the elimination of the department of physiology. James Bryant Conant, who became president of Harvard in 1934, engineered a restructuring of the university aimed at greater efficiency and use of financial resources. A single department of biology was created, and Pincus's two mentors were no longer influential. With the closing of the Bussey Institution and upon reaching retirement age, Castle moved to the University of California. Crozier remained at Harvard, but he became a research professor with no teaching duties and no administrative role.[16]

According to his brother Alex, Pincus had no doubt that the decision regarding his promotion was "political."[17] He believed that senior colleagues resented the national publicity that followed his reports in 1934–1936 of activation and embryonic development of rabbit eggs. In 1934, under the headline "Rabbits Born In Glass," Pincus was quoted in *The New York Times* saying, "We believe that this is the first certain demonstration that mammalian eggs can be fertilized in vitro."[18] In 1935, *The New York Times* headlined "Bottles Are Mothers."[19]

Pincus did not seek publicity; it found him. William L. Laurence, a reporter from *The New York Times*, was in the audience when Goody presented his work at the annual meeting of the Federation of American Societies for Experimental Biology in Washington, D.C.

Under the headline "Life is Generated in Scientist's Tube," Laurence wrote on March 27, 1936: "'Bottle babies,' predicted by Aldous Huxley for the distant future in a 'brave new world,' where children will be born in test tubes, have been brought at least part way toward actuality by Dr. Gregory Pincus at the Harvard Biological Institute."[20]

The article emphasized that Pincus achieved fertilization outside the body in a test tube, but Pincus went "an important step further." An early embryo was observed to develop subsequent to fertilization. The reporter went on to speculate that the possibility was raised of human children being brought into the world by a host mother not related by blood to the child, and that eventually women might hire other women to bear their children for them. Even more inflammatory was the statement that advocates of "race betterment" might urge such procedures for men and women of special aptitudes, physical, mental, or spiritual. The reporter interviewed Pincus who pointed out that he had accomplished embryonic development by a strong salt solution and exposure to a high temperature, and that these embryos were also transplanted into host rabbits, although the pregnancies were terminated early to assess the results. Pincus said that all such offspring would be "fatherless" females.

The New York Times followed with an editorial entitled "Brave New World."[21]

> Dr. Gregory Pincus of Harvard is not exactly a novelist's Bokanovsky (Director of Hatcheries and Conditioning in *Brave New World*), but he has gone far toward realizing Huxley's social order by developing rabbits' eggs in glass with the aid of nothing but strong salt solution or high temperature.
>
> … our sense of unity with lowly forms is heightened. The higher animals, man included, are now more closely linked than ever with such creatures as water-fleas, bees, moths, frogs, all of which sometimes come into the world half-orphans under some conditions.
>
> The social implications of Dr. Pincus's advance are not easily grasped. Parenthood is still associated with love. Much of the lyric poetry of the world deals with the wooing of maids, and much of the music and painting that have been given to us by great artists are but expressions of the urge that makes grass sprout and lilacs burst forth in the Spring.
>
> The more imaginative biologists are not dismayed by the prospect of looking affectionately at a glass vessel and saying: "That's my mother." Serenades will still be strummed on guitars, Romeo and Juliet will still part reluctantly on the balcony, Leander will still swim the Hellespont to his Hero. Love will simply be divorced from parenthood if the biologists are right. … The species will be more important than any individual. A new kind of sacrifice will be demanded, a new kind of joy reaped. But love—that will never die.

This publicity might have been ephemeral but the story was picked up by other newspapers. The Ames, Iowa, *Daily Tribune and Times*, for example, featured the story and a picture of Pincus on its front page,[22] and even more attention followed with a story in *Collier's*, a popular magazine with a countrywide circulation that far surpassed that of *The New York Times*. Brother Alex recalled that, according to Lizzie, when the *Collier's* writer showed up at Goody's laboratory, Goody turned him away saying that a good scientist does not seek or want publicity. He then had a phone call from the president's office commanding him to give the interview.[23] The article appeared in *Collier's* on March 20, 1937, entitled "No Father to Guide Them."[24]

> It's a biologist's business to know life; young Mr. Gregory Pincus of Harvard has got on so well that he can now play tricks with it. Witness his fatherless bunnies. And will there be fatherless babies presently? You

may speculate as much as you please; young Mr. Pincus is not going to say.

In the huge Biological Laboratory—a building which represents several of Harvard's fifty-two million dollars' worth of real estate—a 33-year-old scientist leaned over a microscope. His name might have been borrowed from a cop in a detective novel: Gregory Pincus. But what he saw has possibilities more thrilling than anything a detective-story writer ever imagined: a world in which woman would be a dominant, self-sufficient entity, able to produce young without the aid of man. The father of that initial growth was not a healthy buck rabbit. It was nothing more than a tube of extremely salty water.

Pincus walked out of his severely neat laboratory.... In his own private animal room he looked over his experimental subjects: 60 rabbits, 1,000 mice, and 1,000 rats. Working with his slender, almost feminine hands, Pincus removed an ovum from the plump female rabbit that he selected. As of this article, Pincus had not allowed any implanted embryo to fully develop.

Since, as we have said, there is little difference between the process of reproduction of men and rabbits, there is every reason to suppose his finds could be applied to human beings. In the resulting world man's value would shrink. It is conceivable that the process would not even produce males. The mythical land of the Amazons would then come to life. A world where women would be self-sufficient; man's value precisely zero.

No one need have the fears that assailed two maiden ladies summering at Woods Hole, Massachusetts. Hearing of Pincus' work, they inquired at the biological station if it were quite safe for them to go swimming in the Atlantic.

He has, for example, extracted an ovum from one rabbit, fertilized it in a test tube with sperm borrowed from a male and then installed it in the body of a third rabbit. Forty-five of these ova have developed into normal, healthy bunnies in their host mothers...Apparently there is little reason why the rabbit findings cannot be applied to human beings in the near future.

[The article quoted, Alexis Carrel, the 1912 Nobel prize winner in physiology or medicine from the Rockefeller Institute in New York, who said] "It would be the ruin of women. Healthy women develop tremendously after they have had children. Their nervous systems are much improved—somewhat after one child, more after two, but more yet after three or four. And their looks are improved too."

When objections to his work are raised "Pincus snaps with annoyance. I am not interested in the implications of the work."

The article in *Collier's* apparently caused a palpable negative reaction at Harvard. Pincus's brother Alex alleged that Goody received a letter from the president of Harvard giving two reasons for not granting tenure: the sensationalism of Goody's work on fatherless rabbits and the fact that he was Jewish.[25] The sensationalism arose from the article in *Collier's* with what Alex called "the huge, ugly photo," a picture of Goody, smoke curling up from a cigarette dangling from the middle of his mustachioed mouth to his dense, black thatch of hair, as he looked down with hooded eyes at a rabbit held in his arms. He looked more like a gangster than a distinguished scientist.

Pincus's work should be understood in the context of the times. His harvesting and manipulation of rabbit eggs occurred at a time when the endocrinology of ovulation was largely unknown. For this reason, it was difficult to reproduce his results, a requirement for scientific credibility. Detractors pointed to this difficulty and refuted his claims for embryonic development. However, Pincus's publications clearly indicate that he believed that the initiation of egg development in vitro was the result of parthenogenesis and not fertilization with sperm. Until 1939, Pincus never produced a fully developed fetus or newborn, sacrificing the living rabbit recipients of his activated eggs in order to retrieve embryos, because his focus was on egg development, not on producing cloned individuals. It was not until he left Harvard that Pincus reported in 1939 the production of offspring from rabbits by artificially activated eggs.[26]

In achievements not to be underrated, Pincus was deservedly recognized for drug-induced multiple ovulations, the in vitro growth of retrieved ova, and the successful implantation of those ova into host-mothers. Lizzie once told an interviewer that Pincus "used to say in response to criticism, 'Take it easy, baby, it can't hurt me, you do not understand the human ego, it is irrepressible.'"[27]

The New York Times reporter, William L. Laurence, followed Pincus's progress and dutifully reported his presentations at scientific meetings. In April 1939, at a meeting of the Federation of American Societies for Experimental Biology in Toronto, Pincus reported the activation in vitro of immature human ova, and the newspaper account headlined "First Step Shown in Human Creation."[28]

In reporting his pioneering experiments, which may lead to a new stock of fatherless human beings, given birth by women not actually their mothers, Dr. Gregory Pincus of Clark University flashed on the screen in a darkened room pictures that revealed mysteries of the outset of human life.

Amid a tense silence, the several hundred biologists present saw the immature human egg, a tiny microscopic bit of protoplasm less than one two-hundredths of an inch in diameter, take its first step toward becoming a potential human being, leaving the ovary for its relatively brief receptivity to fertilization.

Dr. Pincus obtained 144 immature ova from women who had undergone surgical operations at the Free Hospital for Women at Brookline, Mass. ... Dr. Pincus emphasized in an interview that his experiments were "distinctly not attempts to obtain human offspring artificially without fathers," but were "simply studies of the maturation of human ova." Nevertheless, the fact remains that such experiments performed on rabbits by Dr. Pincus three years ago were responsible for several litters of rabbits born out of eggs that had been implanted in host-mothers.

This was heady stuff. How many scientists have their work stimulate editorials in *The New York Times*? Unfortunately when the Associated Press transmitted the report from Toronto to its New York office for dissemination to newspapers, one important word, "not," was omitted. The dispatch said that Gregory Pincus was "planning to find out whether test tube babies can be made." The mistake was corrected, but not before many newspapers printed the original statement. Follow-up stories relayed Pincus's words that the episode caused him "some of the most embarrassing moments ever inflicted upon a scientist" and that he emphatically "is not planning to carry it on to find out whether human babies can be made by test tube methods."[29,30]

A few months later, Pincus presented an exhibit at the New York Academy of Medicine, earning him an article in *Time* magazine entitled "Pincogenesis." Laurence was once more present at the meeting to report on November 2, 1939, in *The New York Times*, with the headline, "Mammal Created Without a Father."[31]

The first mammalian creature to be brought into the world as a result of synthetic parthenogenesis (fatherless birth), regarded by many of the distinguished physicians who viewed it as a modern miracle heralding the "brave new world" forecast by Aldous Huxley, in which human beings may be brought into the world by "glass mothers," was the feature of the exhibit on the progress made in recent years in the research on the glands of internal secretion. ... The first "synthetic" rabbit, a large lively chinchilla, whose live incubator "mother" was a pure albino, was shown by Dr. Gregory Pincus of Clark University, who began his epoch-making work at Harvard.

Since it is the so-called Y-chromosome that determines the sex of a mammal, and since this chromosome is supplied by the male, Dr. Pincus explained, animals born without benefit of a male must necessarily be all females.

The fatherless rabbit, Dr. Pincus revealed, already has been mated normally and has recently given birth to a normal litter, the first animal of a higher order that never had a grandfather, nor even a grandmother in the usual sense of the word.

This report was relayed by news services to newspapers throughout the U.S. and Canada. Another editorial appeared in *The New York Times* the very next day after Pincus's presentation.[32]

... Now Dr. Pincus outdoes himself. He exhibits his latest success at the New York Academy of Medicine and says in effect: "Lo, a fatherless rabbit." And this rabbit, which has only a temperature of 113 degrees F. for a father, is the mother of a normally produced litter.

Pincus's last presentation on his rabbit experiments took place on April 29, 1941, in Washington, D.C., at the annual meeting of the National Academy of Sciences, again reported by Laurence in *The New York Times*.[33]

Test Tube Babies Come Step Nearer

Dr. Pincus made it clear that his experiments were not being conducted for the purpose of making possible "test tube babies." They are aimed primarily at gaining more intimate knowledge of the physiological process involved, in the hope that such knowledge will yield means for bringing into the world physically and mentally healthier children.

His studies consisted in adding various chemicals to the nutrient media in the test tubes and watching their effects. About 3,000 to 4,000 rabbit eggs were employed in the experiments.

By the use of these chemicals, Dr. Pincus reported, he succeeded in keeping rabbit embryos developing in the test tube for a period of seven days, bringing them through the critical period in the early stages of embryonic development. The experiments were discontinued at this point to permit more detailed checking.

WHEN PINCUS DIED IN 1967, no one had duplicated his reports of parthenogenesis in mammals. For this reason, skeptics criticized the work, and in a derogatory fashion adopted *Time* magazine's term, referring to it as "Pincogenesis." Nicholas Werthessen objected to this treatment, exclaiming "I was there, I *helped* make it happen."[34]

Werthessen first met Pincus when he was a sophomore at Harvard in 1931. Forty-three years later, he still claimed that Pincus's course in physiology was the best he ever took; he was one of only a few undergraduate students in the class.[35] After graduating, Werthessen worked with Pincus for six years, while earning his Ph.D.

During his years as an assistant professor, Pincus, together with E. V. Enzmann, studied rabbit eggs in vitro. The success of fertilization and development of eggs in vitro hinged on transplanting the eggs into a female and obtaining rabbit fetuses. Initially Pincus reported that his

manipulated eggs failed to produce embryos.[36] Finally in 1934, Pincus and Enzmann reported seven fetuses in one New Zealand doe and two fetuses in an albino doe, the first demonstration with certainty that mammalian eggs could be fertilized in vitro.[37] This early work was summarized in great detail in a series of four publications from 1935 to 1939.[38-41]

The Pincus laboratory made several important conclusions: eggs removed from rabbits can be fertilized in vitro, parthenogenetic activation and development can be observed, biochemical factors that favored or inhibited the development of rabbit eggs were delineated, methods of superovulation producing up to 110 eggs per rabbit were described, the time course of developmental events after fertilization was recorded, sperm obtained from other animal species could not penetrate rabbit ova, and finally, three of nineteen females receiving artificially activated ova produced young at the end of normal gestations.

Choosing the rabbit was a clear-cut decision. A rabbit could be put into a cage, easily assessed for vaginal signs of ovulation, and a foundation of knowledge had established the time sequence of transportation and implantation of a fertilized egg. Pincus's experiences with William E. Castle at Harvard and with John Hammond at Cambridge gave him a thorough knowledge of the reproductive physiology of the rabbit.

Pincus took Werthessen with him to Cambridge in 1937 to work with John Hammond and with F. H. A. Marshall, supported by grants from Harvard and the Josiah Macy, Jr., Foundation. Pincus and Werthessen demonstrated in rabbit experiments carried out at Hammond's Animal Research Station that progesterone alone was the required hormone of pregnancy.[42] In addition, they wished to produce "a live birth that was unquestionably due to an artificially activated egg."[43] Hammond's laboratory had developed inbred strains of rabbits, and parenthood could easily be identified by coat colors. Each evening, Werthessen was responsible for putting a vasectomized male into the female cages, male rabbits that Werthessen personally sterilized and used in many matings, and thus of known sterility. The proof of sterility hinged on the many matings, but skeptics were wary that the very next mating could contain a sperm.

Pincus and Werthessen had already learned that a female rabbit treated with gonadotropin could maintain an embryo just as effectively with the same time course of events as normal mating.[44] In 1937, a commercial preparation of human chorionic gonadotropin, the gonadotropin made by the human placenta, became available. A placental gonadotropin is a hormone that maintains pregnancy by stimulating ovarian production of progesterone. Using this gonadotropin in host rabbits and sterilized male matings to obtain eggs in donor animals (mating induces ovulation in the rabbit), the two men produced offspring from host mothers using activated eggs. At the end of the year, a large crate of labeled rabbits was prepared for shipment to the U.S.

But by spring of 1938, the lasting effects of the depression were being felt everywhere, and grant money disappeared. Pincus and Werthessen had no prospects for salaries, yet alone research money. Pincus, Lizzie, and three-year-old daughter Laura returned to the U.S. Werthessen, his wife, and Pincus's son, twelve-year-old John, visited Werthesen's relatives in Luxemburg. Werthessen sent John back to New York, and soon followed, arriving in Boston to find they were going to Worcester, Massachusetts. Werthessen subsequently became Pincus's assistant in his laboratory at Clark University at a salary of $25 per week.

The rabbits showed up in Worcester, along with the news that John Hammond had found sperm in one of his vasectomized male rabbits. Because parthenogenesis produces only females, he was prompted to investigate when a male offspring unexpectedly turned up in a host mother. Werthessen pointed out that in the 1939 articles by Pincus[45,46] three rabbits delivered young from eggs retrieved from a foster mother treated with chorionic gonadotropin; *no mating was involved,* and he, as well as Pincus, concluded that the young females had to be parthenogenic.

In 1939 and 1940, the Pincus group at Clark University produced eggs by ovulation without mating, induced development by cooling, and produced embryos in host mothers. One host rabbit out of sixteen produced a live female rabbit.[47] Pincus believed, therefore, that parthenogenic full-term rabbits were born in two different locations; Cambridge, England, and Worcester, Massachusetts—from host rabbits with normal gestations and young that were produced without mating. In a monograph published in 1957, R. A. Beatty from the University of Edinburgh concluded that Pincus's reports of parthenogenic offspring were accurate.[48]

Yet, the "Pincogenesis" controversy continues today. Contemporary physiologists believe that birth and survival into adulthood from artificially-induced parthenogenesis were first demonstrated in mammals in 2004 by a team from Tokyo and Seoul that obtained the eggs used in the experiments from genetically-altered female mice.[49] Only ten live pups survived from a total of 371 parthenogenic embryos. Prior to this report, it had been generally accepted that all previous attempts produced incomplete and abnormal embryonic development. It is argued that an essential contribution in mammals comes from males that affects genetic expression, and in the absence of that paternal input, parthenogenetic full development is not possible.[50] Recent reports in the scientific literature on parthenogenesis in mammals do not contain the Pincus publications amongst the references. Does the failure to cite Pincus simply mean that his work is so far back in history, it is forgotten, or does this neglect indicate a continuing reluctance to accept that Pincus accomplished mammalian parthenogenesis?

Queries to respected scientists in the field produced responses that indicate an on-going disbelief that Pincus achieved mammalian parthenogenesis.[51,52] There is a persistent conviction that an unknown mating occurred with a fertile male rabbit. The controversy remains.

According to Werthessen, the work with parthenogenesis ceased because no one was interested in funding such work. It was the time of World War II; money was diverted to subjects of military interest. Thus, Pincus turned to steroids. Pincus planned on returning to parthenogenesis, but he never did as his time became totally consumed in his new direction. Twice new laboratories were constructed for work on parthenogenesis, but Pincus was too busy and the labs were reworked for someone else.[53]

PINCUS'S FRIENDS AND COLLEAGUES, especially Castle and Crozier, tried to find a position for him in 1938, but to no avail. The threat of a new war was easily perceived, Crozier going so far as to advise that the Pincus family should move in England as far away from Germany as possible. With World War II threatening, Goody resolved to take any offered appointment. Brother Alex recalled that "Lizzie went into hysterics about her children being bombed."[54] However, Goody had zero offers. Seymour Lieberman remembered that Pincus "once told me himself that there was a period where he had two kids and he didn't know where his next meal was coming from."[55] Upon returning to the U.S., Goody even visited Albert Einstein at Princeton, and he begged his wealthiest cousins to help him.[56] But only his friend Hudson Hoagland, now chairman of the department of biology at Clark University, came through.

Lizzie, Laura, John, and Goody Pincus, Passport Photo — 1937

CHAPTER SIX

IT'S NOT EVEN IN WORCESTER: THE WORCESTER FOUNDATION FOR EXPERIMENTAL BIOLOGY

THE STORY of the Worcester Foundation for Experimental Biology is unique. Its creation as an independent research institute, initially without hospital or university affiliations, was an innovation in American science. The establishment of the Foundation in 1944 can be attributed directly to Hudson Hoagland and Gregory Pincus, their enduring friendship for each other, their confidence, enthusiasm, ambition and drive. It was their spirit that turned many citizens of Worcester, Massachusetts, into financial supporters of biologic science. Hoagland and Pincus accomplished what they set out to do: they created and sustained a vibrant, productive scientific institution where it was a pleasure to work, unencumbered by academic rules and regulations or faculty competition and bickering.

Hudson Hoagland

Hudson Hoagland was born in Rockaway, New Jersey, on December 5, 1899. He came from a wealthy family that got richer by repeatedly marrying members of other wealthy families. The Hoagland family came from Holland in the seventeenth century and settled on a farm on a site in New Amsterdam now occupied by Columbia University.[1] The Hoaglands moved to a farm near Rockaway, New Jersey, and when it was discovered that the land was rich with iron ore, the family developed a foundry, machine shop, and a company that manufactured rolling mill machinery. After a century of profits, the company was liquidated prior to World War II.

Lying about his age, Hoagland enlisted in the Army in 1916. He fell victim to the 1918 influenza epidemic, and World War I ended before Hoagland could travel overseas. During this time, Hoagland, only seventeen years old, fell in love at first sight, and three days later became engaged to Anna Plummer.[2] Three years later, in 1920, they married, a marriage that would last fifty-three years until her death in 1973. Anna's parents died when she was only a year old; at age six she was placed in the Catholic Convent of the Sacred Heart in New York City.[3] Seven years later she was adopted by Wendell T. Bush and his wife, a first cousin of Anna's father. Bush and his wife both came from very wealthy families; Bush was a professor of philosophy at Columbia University.

At war's end, Hoagland took advantage of Columbia University's new admitting policy for veterans. He had not finished high school, but successfully passed Columbia's aptitude tests and was admitted. He graduated in 1921 in three years time, went to the Massachusetts Institute of Technology, and earned a master's degree in chemical engineering in 1924. His plan was to enter the family's manufacturing business. However, Hoagland's father-in-law, Professor Bush, steered him toward an academic career in science. Hoagland became interested in the physiology of the nervous system, combining his engineering training with his new interest in basic science.

Hoagland enrolled at Harvard as a graduate student in experimental psychology, earning a Ph.D. in 1927 under the direction of William J. Crozier, the chairman of the Department of General Physiology and Pincus's mentor. From 1927 to 1930, Hoagland was a research fellow in Crozier's department and an instructor in physiology and biology at Harvard and Radcliffe. During this time, the Hoaglands, supported by their wealthy families, had their four children. The birth of Mahlon, their eldest, was assisted by John Rock, the famed Harvard obstetrician-gynecologist who would later work with Pincus to develop oral contraception.[4] At the time, Rock had just finished his training and was called on to administer anesthesia for the birth.

In 1930, Hoagland extended his studies of the nervous system, working under E.D. Adrian at The University of Cambridge in England. Hoagland was well known at Clark University in Worcester, Massachusetts, having taught seminars there in 1929. Prior to leaving for England, Hoagland, now thirty years old, accepted a position as professor and head of Clark's department of biology. The administration hoped that Hoagland's interest in neurophysiology would complement the already strong department of psychology.

Clark University was founded in 1887 by Jonas Clark who made a fortune selling equipment to miners during the California gold rush.[5] He returned to Worcester with an aim to provide a college education for boys who couldn't afford it. Clark hired G. Stanley Hall as the first president of the university; Hall's Ph.D. from Harvard was the first in the U.S. granted in psychology. However, Hall had a different agenda in mind. He was committed to the Johns Hopkins model, with an emphasis on research rather than teaching. Despite the philosophical conflict with the university's founder, Hall succeeded in attracting to the faculty a group of young men, many of whom would go on to substantial careers in science. Eventually the contention between Jonas Clark and Hall proved demoralizing. Faculty members were disgruntled over low salaries and worries about their future security. At this time in 1893, John D. Rockefeller established the University of Chicago, and its first president raided Clark, especially the department of biology, for his new faculty.

In 1920, G. Stanley Hall retired and Wallace W. Atwood was named the new president of Clark University. Atwood was a professor of geography at Harvard, an authority on the Rocky Mountains, and author of a popular text used by public schools throughout the U.S. Atwood built a new geography section, siphoning available funds from other established departments, causing another faculty exodus. The head of the physics department was Robert Goddard, America's rocket propulsion pioneer. Goddard, with funding from the Guggenheim Foundation, moved to New Mexico; besides the lack of funds

at Clark, his rocket testing was deemed hazardous in the populated environs of Worcester.

When Hoagland accepted the offer to be the new head of biology, there was only one other faculty member in the department, David Potter, currently working on his Ph.D. at Harvard (later to chair Clark's department of biology for many years), and his assistant Charles Pomerat, who would remain a member of the Clark faculty for the rest of his academic life. The bulk of the undergraduate teaching responsibilities fell on Potter and Pomerat. Hoagland was interested only in research and graduate students.

Hudson Hoagland — 1940

Hoagland began his Clark years with $2,000 grants from the Rockefeller Foundation and the Josiah Macy, Jr., Foundation, studying impulses in the nerves of frog skin. In 1935, Hoagland published a book summarizing his work on "pacemakers," the regulation of rhythmic events such as breathing and the beating of the heart.[6] Beginning in 1934 and into the 1940s, he was one of the first to study brain waves recorded by an electroencephalogram, for example, in schizophrenic patients during insulin shock treatments, and most notably, the response of the brain to stressful stimuli. Hoagland established a laboratory for these studies at the Worcester State Hospital.

Hoagland still hoped Harvard would call. He had been led to believe by Crozier, his mentor, and the dean of the graduate school that they would offer him a position as associate professor after a few years at Clark. Indeed, in 1935, Hoagland was notified that the department of general physiology had voted to grant him this appointment. However, at this time a major upheaval took place at Harvard. A new president, James Bryant Conant, a professor of chemistry, reorganized the three departments of botany, zoology, and general physiology, amalgamating them into one department of biology. It was the time of the depression, and a major reason for the reorganization was financial, but Hoagland believed Conant was also reacting to jealous competition among the biologists.[6] All of a sudden, Hoagland's mentor was cast aside; Crozier was made a research professor and lost his teaching and administrative responsibilities. Hoagland's Harvard appointment withered without action.

Rebounding from the Harvard rejection, Hoagland accepted an offer from Columbia University to be a full professor and associate director of the Neurological Institute, with an understanding that he would succeed the current director who was soon to retire. Hoagland set a date to leave Clark in six months, and was about to purchase a house across the river from Columbia in New Jersey, when Columbia rescinded his appointment. Columbia's dean told him that insufficient funds would preclude his new appointment, although later Hoagland heard that faculty members had objected to the fact that Hoagland was not a clinically-oriented M.D., an objection that even Hoagland agreed was reasonable.[8] Fortunately, Clark University agreed to take Hoagland back.

Goody Comes to Worcester

Hoagland and Pincus met as graduate students at Harvard, both receiving their doctorate degrees in 1927. Although Pincus's work was under the direction of William E. Castle, he spent much of his time with Hoagland in Crozier's laboratory.

As described in Chapter 5, Pincus returned to Harvard in 1930 as an instructor, the lowest level in the academic hierarchy, and proceeded to make national headlines with his work on parthenogenesis. Harvard, as did many schools, had a tough up-or-out promotion policy. An assistant professor could be appointed only for two three-year terms, after which he or she had to leave if not promoted to associate professor. As detailed in Chapter 5, Pincus was informed that he would not be promoted after his second term as assistant professor expired in 1938. Pincus left Harvard to spend the last year of his appointment working at the Strangeways Laboratory in Cambridge, England.

Hoagland learned of Pincus's situation while Pincus was in England. He attributed the lack of promotion to a combination of academic politics, including dislike of Crozier who routinely antagonized many of his colleagues, and "some anti-Semitism."[9] Joseph Goldzieher believed that anti-Semitism was a critical influence on Pincus's career. "He was a person who had been made an individual because of anti-Semitism, I'm sure. He ran into that at Harvard, and I think that kept him from embracing the academic environment, and that was the best thing that ever happened to him because he was not the kind of person who would be comfortable in territorial arguments and degrees of professorship and stuff like that. I think he would have considered that trivial."[10]

When it became clear that Pincus was without a job, Hoagland resolved to bring him to Clark University. Because no Clark funds were available, Hoagland offered Pincus the title of Visiting Professor of Experimental Biology. Hoagland wrote to Pincus in May 1938, "You must recognize that money is very tight. We are back in a major depression and it is simply impossible to hope to be financed on the ideal scale or the one that you had at Harvard."[11]

Hoagland's multiple attempts to find funding were unsuccessful, prompting him to say with disappointment, "Under the circumstances I feel it best for you to stay in England if you possibly can."[12] Even Pincus's Harvard mentor, W.E. Castle, now at the University of California, Berkeley, with Goody's uncle Charles Lipman, could not offer a salary or even an honorary appointment without funding.[13] Pincus's initial funding came from his fellow investigator at the Strangeways Laboratory at The University of Cambridge, Lord Nathaniel Rothschild, an English baron who in May 1938 provided $2,500 for salary support.[14] Finally, the Pincus family in New York City arranged for a rabbi to introduce Hoagland to Henry Ittleson, a wealthy businessman.[15] Ittleson agreed to provide funds to Clark to partially support a salary for two years.

This funding success impressed the two men, especially Hoagland, planting the idea that it would be possible to support research with private money. The total amount included $5,000 for salaries (Pincus and an assistant) and $1,000 for research expenses. With enough money in hand to support one year of work, Pincus moved to Worcester in the summer of 1938. Hoagland had a small grant from the G.D. Searle Company, studying new anticonvulsant drugs in animals. He requested that this grant be transferred to Pincus, and thus began a long relationship between Pincus and Searle.[16]

Nearly penniless, Goody, Lizzie, and three-year-old daughter Laura, moved into Hudson Hoagland's house on Downing Street across from Clark University, while the Hoagland family was away for the summer.[17] From there, they moved to an apartment at 60 Downing Street, a block or two from the Hoaglands. Son John, age twelve, arrived from Europe in time to start school in fall 1938.

The reputations of Hoagland and Pincus rapidly attracted young scientists who wanted to work with them. Herbert Shapiro, Mark Graubard, and Nicholas Werthessen joined Pincus, working in the basement of a Clark building, a site contaminated by coal dust from the nearby coal bunkers. Graubard was a chemist, a writer of popular science books, and fired (justly, according to him) from Columbia University for neglecting his teaching and research because of his commitment to the Communist Party.[18]

He went to Russia, intending to spend his life there, but became disillusioned. Nevertheless, he preferred Stalinist communism to Hitler's fascism. He accepted a Russian assignment to go to Germany and spy. Pincus's brother Alex, recalled that Graubard met "an officer in the SS at the officer's club (What safer place, he told me) to carry messages back and forth."[19] But Graubard was betrayed by the Russians, and he made his way back to the U.S.

Ray E. Umbaugh, a former Foundation scientist, was trying to improve the quantity of purebred cows by obtaining fertilized ova from superovulated pedigreed cows and implanting them into ordinary cows.[20] His work in Texas was supported by Tom Slick, a wealthy cattleman and oilman. Umbaugh was convinced that the world was entering a period of severe food shortages. His solution was to cause cows to have twins at every birthing. Graubard joined the Pincus group wanting to know what caused twinning. Pincus cautioned that this would take years of research, but he helped Graubard to find a nearby farm for his work, and Pincus initiated and maintained a close friendship with Tom Slick who provided the cattle for the studies.

Tom Slick was a remarkable individual.[21,22] Following his father's footsteps, he managed the family oil company in Texas that had already achieved great success to even greater riches. He founded the Southwest Foundation for Biomedical Research in San Antonio in 1941, where Joseph Goldzieher would perform some of the first American studies with oral contraceptives. Slick opened another research facility eight miles outside of San Antonio in 1947, the Foundation of Applied Research and Institute of Industrial Research, deliberately modeled after the Worcester Foundation.[23] Slick called on his friend, Goody Pincus, who as chair of the board of trustees was present at the opening ceremony, to recruit scientists to Texas.[24] Slick was a world explorer, searching for Bigfoot, the Loch Ness Monster, and Yeti, an adventurer, an inventor, and an author, writing mostly about his vision and plans for world peace. Only forty-six years old, Slick died in a plane crash in 1962.

But in 1938, the Worcester Foundation was not even a dream. Pincus and his young scientists moved into a barn. It was a nice barn, actually a carriage house belonging to the Victorian house owned by Clark University and rented to Hoagland. It had three stories with carriage rooms, horse stalls, and living quarters for a coachman and his family. Hoagland raised money from friends in the Worcester community to convert the barn into laboratories. This building became the physiological laboratory of Clark University, the nucleus from which the Worcester Foundation for Experimental Biology emerged.

During World War II, Hoagland and Pincus received significant financial support from the military. In the summer of 1940, Hoagland visited the naval air base in Pensacola, Florida, to apply his electroencephalogram expertise to the question of what could explain which candidates succeeded or failed as pilots. The technique turned out not to be helpful, but Hoagland and Pincus then conceived of studies to assess adrenal cortex responses to stress. It was already known that the adrenal cortex was instrumental in meeting various stressful experiences. Hoagland and Pincus set out to study pilot fatigue.

Gregory Pincus —1940

Using an apparatus designed to mimic flying, the group at Clark University linked adrenal cortex responses to pilot performances. Hoagland and Pincus expanded these studies to factory workers in Worcester and to mentally ill patients at the Worcester State Hospital. They believed that performance was improved by the administration of pregnenolone, a precursor of steroid hormones, provided to them along with financial support by the G. D. Searle Co. Pincus summarized this work in his presentation to the Laurentian Hormone Conference in 1945, but these preliminary results never could be substantiated.[25]

About this time, Hoagland endured yet another rejection. Hoagland and Pincus visited Washington, and specifically failed to attract financial support from the Air Force. Undaunted, they sent a progress report to the Office of the Air Surgeon. In an accompanying letter, Hoagland made a few sarcastic comments about the initial refusal by the Air Force.[26] Hoagland was then invited to join the Operations Analysis Group of the Air Force overseas with the Eighth Air Force. This time, he obtained a leave of absence from Clark. After a goodbye party, he traveled to Washington where he was greeted with another shock. The Air Surgeon's office had ordered

Hoagland and Pincus — 1945

that Hoagland not be included in the group because he had been insubordinate, carrying out a study on Air Force personnel without the permission of the Air Surgeon. Humiliated, he isolated himself for a few days, then returned to Worcester and announced "debonairly as possible that I had come back from the war."[27] Hoagland had been scheduled to fly to Lisbon, there to board a flight to London. That plane to London was shot down over the English Channel, killing all aboard, including the movie actor, Leslie Howard.

Meanwhile, Pincus was measuring steroid hormones in cancer patients using newly developed methods, after establishing normal values in about 600 people.[28] Hoagland obtained a Guggenheim Fellowship and retreated totally into research. Pincus and Hoagland proceeded to investigate adrenal gland function in schizophrenic patients at the Worcester State Hospital. Pincus had purchased a duplex house at 68 South Lenox Street in Worcester, and prior to moving in, the family lived for a few months in a small apartment at the Worcester State Hospital.

Laura, Lizzie, Goody, Passport Photo — 1947

Lizzie enjoyed answering the question how was it to live in a mental hospital by responding, "It's like living in a madhouse."[29] At the State Hospital, Pincus and Hoagland were measuring adrenal steroids and sex hormones in urine, and comparing normal men to normal women, and normal to schizophrenic patients; but their work ultimately yielded no insights into the mechanisms or treatment of schizophrenia.[30,31]

The work at the Worcester State Hospital was primarily funded by Katharine McCormick. In 1927, she had been instrumental in funding the Neuroendocrine Research Foundation at Harvard in hopes of finding an effective treatment for schizophrenia, diagnosed in her husband Stanley McCormick two years after their marriage in 1904. Although this Foundation was headquartered at Harvard, its activities took place at the Worcester State Hospital under the direction of Roy G. Hoskins. Hoagland had collaborated with this group throughout the 1930s, and now Pincus became involved as well. One day, years later, Katharine McCormick talked with Hudson Hoagland about her interest in contraception. Hoagland described to McCormick the work of Pincus and Min-Chueh Chang.[32] McCormick shared the information with her friend and birth control activist, Margaret Sanger, leading to the pivotal meeting of Sanger with Pincus described in Chapter 9.

The Worcester Foundation for Experimental Biology

In the midst of their work at Worcester State Hospital, reflecting on their experiences in which both men had been traumatized by academic rejections, Hoagland and Pincus began to joke about independence. The joke became a dream that turned into reality. Their goal was a research institute free of academic rules and regulations.

By 1943, Clark's department of biology numbered fifteen out of a total faculty that varied from fifty to sixty, and only Hoagland had an academic appointment. The group felt like second-class citizens, even though they operated on an impressive budget of $100,000, all from grants. Pincus was already a paid consultant for the G.D. Searle Company. President Atwood became contentious, believing the department of biology was too large, too strong, too exasperating. Hoagland and Pincus "welcomed the idea of freedom from bickering faculty meetings, futile committees, jealous colleagues and teaching prescribed credit courses to often indifferent students."[33] Hoagland's son recalled that his father "raged at the academic system in general and at Atwood in particular."[34] Hoagland and Atwood were complete opposites: liberal vs. conservative, outgoing vs. secretive, consensus-building vs. private decision-making.[35]

Both Hoagland and Pincus were in their early forties, still young enough to be vigorous and adventuresome. John McCracken, a Foundation scientist from 1964 to 1998, observed that "Even though they came from different backgrounds, they were 'two birds of a feather' and extremely close."[36] In 1944, they, as co-directors, established the Worcester Foundation for Experimental Biology, a tax-exempt, nonprofit research institution. Hoagland said, "This name was selected because, while we had no money to justify calling ourselves a foundation, we hoped to rectify that situation, and 'foundation' had a strong and substantial sound. I rather preferred 'institute' for 'foundation,' but Worcester had its well-known Polytechnic Institute, and we called it the Worcester Foundation because of our desire for support from friends in the community."[37] Hoagland came to believe the choice of name was unfortunate. After 1944, it wasn't even located in Worcester. The name implied a grant-giving organization, an impression that would turn back potential donors, and "the name was long, hard to remember and write on checks."[38]

The early studies of Hoagland and Pincus on the physiology of stress directed them to a newly perceived problem, the emotional status of traumatized men returning home from World War II. Although the study of these men was the research agenda proposed at the first organizational meetings of the Foundation, a large and diversified research program rapidly followed this initial focus on human stress and mental illness.[39]

The Foundation was incorporated in February 1944. The president of the board of trustees was Hoagland's old friend, Harlow T. Shapley, a distinguished astronomer; the vice-president was Rabbi Levi Olan, and the Board included three Nobel laureates and a group of Worcester businessmen. Hoagland resigned from Clark, and the Foundation scientists worked at the Worcester State Hospital. Over the next year, Hoagland and Pincus recruited an impressive collection of young scientists, among them Min-Chueh Chang, William Pearlman, Oscar M. Hecter, Ralph Dorfman, Clara M. Szego, Robert P. Jacobsen, and Sydney Roberts. A relationship was established with Tufts Medical School with courtesy appointments making it possible for graduate students, such as Eli Romanoff, to work at the Foundation in pursuit of Ph.D. degrees. Later, a similar program was instituted with Boston University.

Because of his background, Hoagland traveled among the wealthy members of Worcester society. Hoagland and Pincus organized a lecture series inviting "well-disposed people," and made the rounds of clubs, church groups, and civic organizations.[40] They created a system whereby individuals were invited to join the Foundation,

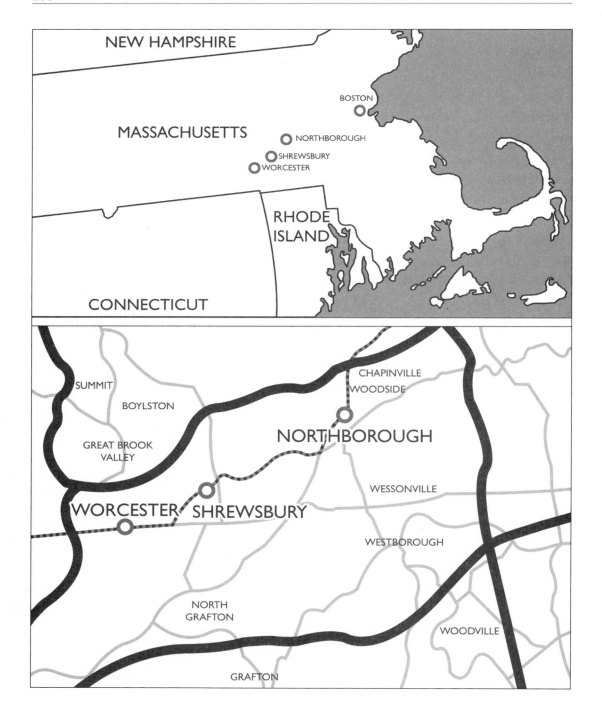

with annual membership fees that ranged from $5 to $1,000. Ten years later, there were 1,403 members.[41] This provided no strings-attached money that, unlike grant money directed to specific purposes, could be used for various, essential expenses. In these early days, Hoagland and Pincus were operating on a shoestring; in fact much of the early support came from the man who held the patent for the hardening at the end of shoestrings.[42] When money was short, Hoagland used his own personal funds to meet the payroll.[43]

Hoagland's son, Mahlon, wrote, "They were the two musketeers; full of humor, confidence, pride, and brazenness—ready to take on anyone and anything. To those men and women who came to share their ambition as colleagues, trustees, and supporters, the two men radiated an irresistible enthusiasm and commitment. They turned many of the enlightened members of Worcester society into a cadre of biology boosters."[44]

Hoagland and Pincus immediately began searching for a permanent location and facility. A residential estate owned by Harry P. Hovey, an executive of a laundry business, was for sale, across Lake Quinsigamond, in the small town of Shrewsbury, named in 1722 after Shrewsbury in England, which honored the Earl of Shrewsbury.[45] There were twelve acres of lawns and gardens with a Georgian-style fifteen-room, brick house

and a large garage, built in 1913. The price was $25,000, quickly raised among the trustees and friends in the community. Another $25,000 was acquired to convert the buildings into laboratories, and the Worcester Foundation for Experimental Biology occupied its new quarters in June 1945.

From 1945 to the death of Pincus in 1967, the staff grew from twelve to 350 scientists and support people, thirty-six of whom were independently funded and forty-five were postdoctoral fellows. The annual budget grew from $100,000 to $4.5 million. One hundred twenty-nine acres of the adjoining land owned by Howard D. Brewer were acquired in 1962, and the campus grew to eleven buildings. In its first twenty-five years, approximately 3,000 scientific papers were published.

Pincus was an effective recruiter, best exemplified when in one massive stroke he resolved a crisis when a large group of steroid chemists left the Foundation to join industry in 1964. Pincus went to England and convinced thirty-five-year-old Ian Bush, an upcoming steroid scientist, to emigrate. Bush, in his early twenties, had developed the system of paper chromatography for the separation and isolation of steroids. The technique was so widely known, it was called the Bush System. Not satisfied with Bush alone, Pincus encouraged most of Bush's department to

The Hovey estate — 1939

The Worcester Foundation for Experimental Biology — 1949

join in the exodus. Nine new scientists and five technicians arrived at the Foundation, prompting a major reaction in Europe, raising an alarm about a "brain drain" and directly leading to an increase in funding for English scientists. John McCracken was one of the scientists, and he remembered that "All hell broke loose. On Monday morning the department was filled with reporters from all over Britain, all over Europe, including English and American television stations."[46]

Pincus was hoping that Ian Bush would be the successor, to become the director of the Foundation, but Bush didn't have the personality for leadership, and it wasn't long before he left.[47] McCracken pointed out that "One of Pincus's great assets was his ability to pick good people, but he could also pick people who were slightly off-center, and he would take a gamble on folks."[48] Seymour Lieberman, a noted biochemist at Columbia University, said, "Pincus could tolerate people who were a little strange or a little different. He had sufficient self-control that he wasn't threatened by any of those guys."[49]

Hoagland and Pincus were committed to graduate education. Over the years, hundreds of college and graduate students spent their summers at the Foundation in programs designed to stimulate an interest in science. Ph.D. candidates from Clark University, Tufts University, Boston University, and Worcester Polytechnic Institute performed their experimental thesis work in the Foundation laboratories. For eleven years, a Fellowship in Reproductive Physiology program, funded for foreign students by the Ford Foundation, trained clinicians and scientists to return to teach in their own countries. Katharine McCormick provided the funds to house the students in a Worcester motel (about $10,000 per year), even paying for furnishings obtained by Lizzie shopping in Copenhagen.[50,51] Goody reassured Katharine that the prices were better than what could be obtained in the U.S., undoubtedly true in those days.

The estate garage, remodeled and enlarged for Pincus's office and laboratories

For fourteen years, a Training Program in Steroid Chemistry, supported by federal grants, taught the science of hormones to doctors of medicine and science. I was a fellow in the Training Program in Steroid Chemistry in 1968–1969, and my experience was a testimony to the vibrant spirit of the Foundation. Young students mingled in a friendly atmosphere with accomplished scientists. We took our training seriously and appreciated and respected our teachers, but the spirit also spilled over into parties hosted by junior and senior scientists. I missed knowing Pincus by one year, but I remember well trying to understand the inscrutable M-C. Chang in the lecture room as well as in individual conversations in a laboratory. Everything that has been written about the Foundation in the way of admiration and praise was strongly evident in my days there.

The Foundation was a pleasant place to work. The scale and pace were comfortable; one never had to deal with a congestion of large buildings or a high density of people. The brilliant New England seasons could be appreciated just by walking the well-kept grounds, breathing the clear air of a small town in the country. Everyone called each other by first names, except, of course, Chang. It was a bastion of science in the midst of warm interactions, a source of good memories and good friends.

Manuel Neves e Castro, at the end of his fellowship, threw a farewell party on a Saturday late afternoon, timed to precede other evening obligations held by many of the staff.[52] His parents were visiting from Portugal, and his father was assigned the task of preparing a typical Portugese punch. The punch was a great success, requiring new batches to be made. By evening, the guests decided the party was too good to leave. Around midnight, Goody and Lizzie, lying on the lawn, stood up to make their departure. But Lizzie did not know where she had left her shoes. Everyone pitched in to find the shoes knowing they couldn't leave before the Pincuses.

One of the events that everyone looked forward to was the annual Foundation party for the entire staff, a grand affair held at places like the White Cliffs Restaurant in Northborough or the Pleasant Valley Country Club in Sutton. Another popular event was the Biology Ball, a black tie annual party sponsored by the Women's Auxiliary of the Foundation. These events fostered a sense of belonging for the staff and promoted good relationships with the community.

IN THE FIRST TWO YEARS of the Worcester foundation, a little over 25 percent of the total research budget of around $160,000 came from Searle. Besides Pincus, whose salary was $4,500 per year, this money supported five investigators and four technicians.[53,54] By 1970, the Foundation derived its money from federal government grants and contracts (69 percent), private foundations (22 percent), pharmaceutical companies (5 percent), and endowment (4 percent).[55]

But in the early years, Pincus was the animal keeper, Mrs. Hoagland the bookkeeper, M-C. Chang was the night watchman, and Hoagland mowed the lawn using a donated motorized lawnmower. "One very hot day in summer, stripped to the waist, I was dashing along behind my lawnmower when there arrived a friend who had just become a trustee, Aldus Higgins, then president of the Norton company. He was shocked

The Worcester Foundation for Experimental Biology — 1976

to see me, whom he called an eminent scientist, spending my time cutting the grass and he was so emphatic about it that he contributed a salary to enable us to hire our first groundskeeper."[56]

Pincus was usually in his office before most of the staff arrived. The only time he was seen not wearing his suit coat was when he put on a white laboratory coat for a picture.[57] Like many in those years, both Goody and Lizzie were heavy smokers, and his office was impregnated with the smell. When the studies linked cardiovascular disease and lung cancer to smoking, Goody quit smoking a few years before his death.[58]

Jackie Foss, his secretary for many years, recalled that everyone called him Goody.[59] After a few years, she did as well. She smiled when she said, "I don't think there was an arrogant thing about Goody."[60] She remembered that although he didn't laugh frequently, he smiled a lot. He would dictate across his desk, turning on his swivel chair, and playing with his mustache. When he turned too far, she had to remind him, "Goody, I can't hear you!" If he came home from a trip on a Friday night, he expected his secretary to be there for a full work day on Saturday.[61]

Chang was convinced that Pincus could think simultaneously along two different tracks. Chang even thought he knew when it was happening. While involved in an activity or conversation, but thinking about something else altogether, Pincus would begin pulling at his mustache.[62]

Weekly conferences were held for the fellows in the training programs. Burton Caldwell, a former fellow, said, "It was well known that the talk was never over until Gregory got up. Often the fellows made the presentations. You would get all sorts of plaudits, and there would be all sorts of questions from the audience, but you never knew how you really did. Gregory would get up and he would ask the one question that everybody else in the audience should have asked and would make the one suggestion necessary for the next step."[63]

Goody was a very astute man, according to John McCracken: "He knew his way around with people, and with science, and with funding institutes."[64] McCracken went on to say that "He was impressive and formidable, but at the same time he was very warm. He made you feel relaxed, and you didn't feel under stress talking to him. He had a very good sense of humor. As you got to know him better, he would occasionally come up with a pretty nice story, mostly reproductive in nature. He didn't pussyfoot around; he just spoke quietly and made his opinion known"[65] Pincus would look you straight in the eyes with a warm feeling that was unanticipated.[66] Manuel Neves e Castro always offered a "Good morning, Doctor Pincus," as most days he passed by Goody's open office door on the way to the laboratory. Pincus would call out, "Good morning Manuel, how are you? Are you enjoying your stay here? Come in, have a sit and talk a bit about yourself."[67]

Goody was neither modest nor arrogant. He carried himself between the two extremes with the self-confidence, but without the cockiness, of an exceptional athlete. Burton Caldwell remembered him from his fellowship days in 1966. "He even had the walk. It's like a professional golfer. When they walk, they don't walk like a regular person. They look like they belong there. He always looked like wherever he was that he belonged there. He was a little bit above normal life. He was this man who changed our field in many ways, but he didn't disappoint. He is one of those people who actually met his legend straight on. He really measured up to what we thought he would be."[68]

Anne Merrill was Goody's chief assistant and technician; he always considered her to be more than a technician, even listing her as a co-author on some of his publications. She came to work at the Foundation in 1949, and remembered Goody as a tough man, but open and friendly. "It didn't matter where you fit in the scheme of things, he knew just as much about the family of the second lowest person in the maintenance department as he did about you or me or anyone else. He treated us all the same."[69] One of his young scientists remembered, "Goody with his personality could project authority without being harsh or anything of the kind."[70]

Fernand Péron, a Foundation scientist, said, "Dissatisfaction with one's work or the workplace could always be discussed with the Boss, and if there was an impasse, Gregory would open a drawer in his desk to reveal files of 'contacts' which he could communicate with and offer a job to the person who wanted to 'leave.' … Nevertheless, to show how fair he was, I recall that on a day when a colleague and I were preparing an experiment, his secretary asked me to go to Pincus's office to which I replied that I couldn't go because I was 'busy.' Moments later when we were dissecting tissue, who comes in our lab with 'ruffled feathers' but Pincus himself. He immediately took stock of the situation and instead of an expected 'explosion' he just mentioned to see him later and walked out."[71] The Foundation was a big family and Pincus was the patriarch. When people complained about this or that, he would invite them to his office and use his "drawer method." John McCracken remembered the method: "He would pull out a file and say, 'Now this looks like a very interesting job.'"[72] The implication was always clear, but he was not autocratic. He was very sympathetic and understanding. McCracken was emphatic: "I don't know of anyone who disliked him. He was a good guy. He was very fair."[73]

Pincus did everything he could to help young scientists, especially those training at the Foundation.[74-77] Burton Caldwell recalled the time when he was about to leave the Foundation for a year of study in Cambridge, England.[78] Pincus dropped by the lab and said, "When you go over there, would you please give this note to Thaddeus?" Caldwell had no idea who Thaddeus Mann was, let alone that he was the director of the Agricultural Research Council Unit of Reproductive Physiology and Biochemistry where Caldwell was to study for a year. "No one ever got to see Thaddeus. With my letter in hand from Gregory Pincus, I got to see Thaddeus in the first week, and I didn't think of it at the time, but it was a very big thing for Pincus to do, giving me an introduction to the man who was the boss. This was the type of thing he would do. He treated you in a personal way. He would do whatever he could to ensure that members of his team had the best chance."

GOODY'S MAIN FORM of exercise was swimming. Sometimes, he took his assistants with him when he visited a nearby pool.[79] When visiting the ocean in the summer, he would swim as much as a mile straight out from the beach.[80] His daughter Laura recalled, "The people on the beach asked my mother to do something about it. So my mother told him

that he was going to have to swim parallel to the shore and not a mile out."[81]

"He was an omnivorous reader from childhood; his literary interests later in life included the 'escape' variety and he went through mystery and spy stories by the hundreds."[82] Goody and his son John enjoyed listening to Boston Red

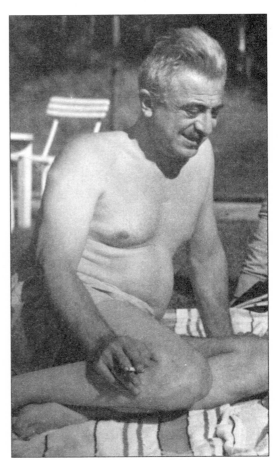

Gregory Pincus —1958

Sox games on the radio, but he really liked to play gin rummy and Scrabble, and hated to lose. Goody's daughter said, "He and my brother would have terrible fights over Scrabble, but my father always won."[83] Son John said, "The competitiveness sometimes made it a bit difficult for children and grandchildren, as he preferred to win games, no matter what the age of his opponent."[84] When playing Scrabble, he kept the large and thick unabridged version of Webster's Dictionary at his side. In 1963, Pincus lectured on the challenges and dangers of modern biology at his daughter's school, the Putney School in Vermont. He returned his honorarium as a donation to the school, and he wowed his host family with his prowess in Scrabble.[85] After Pincus died, Lizzie asked Anne Merrill if she wanted any of his personal things as a memento. "I said I wanted that great big dictionary. She said that's his Scrabble dictionary. He played all the time at home, and used one of those huge dictionaries that they have like in the library, and you need a special table to put it on."[86]

Pincus learned to drive in 1944 when he was forty-one years old. Later, he drove a car that was shipped from France in September 1958 for 903,000 francs (about $1,800), "a car that was often the subject of conversation. The turtle or squatter as it was called was a pale yellow French Citroen which indeed slumped down on its axles when the ignition was turned off and the motor

at idle. With the ignition on, the car would sort of jump up to traveling position. Pincus, who liked a smooth and soft ride, could adjust the height of the car to get the proper effect."[87] Pincus sold his Citroen in 1967 for $500.[88]

THE PINCUS FAMILY moved to 30 Main Street in the small town of Northborough in October 1954, about five and one-half miles due east from the Foundation. The house, just one hundred yards east of the town center, was built in the mid-nineteenth century of red bricks from a Northborough brickyard. It is a large house, with ten fireplaces; the main entrance opens to a central hall with a graceful, curving staircase to the second floor. There are three large rooms on the first floor, four on the second floor, and several small rooms in the attic-like third floor. In addition, there was a living space in the basement that often housed young scientists. The house was flanked by the old Northborough library on the east side and the town's first bank on the west side. The house was built by a physician, Stephen Ball, who practiced in Boston. In 1927, the house was acquired by Orello Buckner, president of a successful company that manufactured abrasives; Buckner sold the house to Pincus for $30,000 in 1954.[89] Lizzie sold the house in 1969 to a local physician, Robert T. Bush. Today, the building houses a book store and a coffee shop.

Pincus House in Northborough

Laura Pincus Bernard remembered that their house had eight functioning bedrooms.[90] The two on the third floor were unfinished; the second floor had three guest bedrooms and Goody's study. Goody and Lizzie slept in a large bedroom a few steps up from the first floor. Lizzie decorated the house in Northborough with oriental furniture and art, acquired over the years on their extensive travels. Family pictures reveal elegantly furnished rooms that provided a perfect venue for hosting the many scientists and dignitaries who visited the Pincus home over the years. A wine collection filled two temperature- and humidity-controlled basement rooms. The wines were personally selected by their son John who had become a French oenophile. It was a fine house for parties, with a large kitchen for Lizzie's excellent cooking.

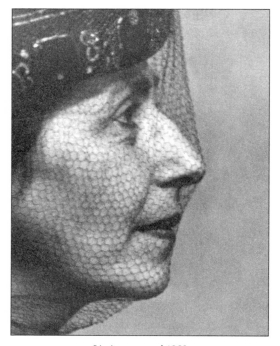

Lizzie — around 1960

A former colleague said, "We always felt he considered us as colleagues rather than employees. On quite a few occasions we were his guests at his home. A perfect host with 'Liz' his wife who was in charge of the menu (always good food and excellent wines). Scientific or more banal discussions were always the fare of après-diner. Our wives who accompanied us were cause for much attention."[91] John McCracken remembered that Lizzie "was always fussing about making sure everybody was happy. Pincus was more into discussing things about science."[92] Celso-Ramón Garcia, who worked with Pincus on the development of oral contraception, said, "Dinner at his house was a wonderful experience. He and his wife were gourmets, and the combination of her cooking and their warmth and hospitality was memorable."[93] After Goody died in 1967, an inventory of the Pincus wine cellar revealed 313 bottles of French wines with values that ranged from $2.00 to $12.00 per bottle.[94]

Min-Chueh Chang

Min-Chueh Chang is an integral part of the Worcester Foundation story. Recruited by Pincus

Hoagland and Pincus — 1960s

in 1944, he remained a Foundation scientist until his death in 1991. Chang was born in Tai Yuan, China, on October 10, 1908. In 1933, he earned a bachelor's degree in animal psychology from the Tsing Hua University in Peking, and stayed at the university as a teacher.[95] Chang won a national competition in 1938 that funded study abroad. He chose to study agricultural science at Edinburgh University. After one year, he was pleased to receive an invitation from Arthur Walton to study the physiology of sheep sperm at The University of Cambridge, and he promptly accepted.

Chang received his Ph.D. in animal breeding under the direction of Walton and Sir John Hammond at the University of Cambridge in 1941. It was virtually impossible to leave England during the early years of World War II, and Chang continued to work at the University. In 1944, Chang planned to return to China, but first he wanted to spend a year in the U.S. He wrote three letters to American scientists, and only Pincus answered, offering a fellowship at Clark University.[96] Chang mistakenly assumed that a fellowship in the U.S. was the same as at the University of Cambridge where a Fellow was assured of a lifetime income.

In March 1945, Chang came to the newly established Worcester Foundation. On his first day he found that Pincus was traveling in California, so he went to visit Hoagland who on that day was at the Worcester State Hospital, the site of his studies on schizophrenia. Chang recalled, "When I got there, the people thought I was a

M-C. Chang — 1933

Chang — 1941

patient of Dr. Hoagland."[97] Hoagland arranged for a room at the local YMCA. Goody and Lizzie helped Chang get settled in Worcester. At one point in Chang's first days, this interchange occurred:[98]

Pincus:	You must be tired.	
Chang:	Yeah, very tired.	
Pincus:	You must be hungry.	
Chang:	Oh yeah, very hungry.	
Pincus:	Why don't you come over to dinner with us tonight?	
Chang:	(a puzzled, confused look on his face)	
Pincus:	(repeating) Why don't you come over to dinner with us tonight?	
Chang:	(rubbing his forehead) I don't know why I don't come to dinner with you.	

Until Pincus had his own automobile, Pincus and Chang often waited for the bus together to return home. For a while, Chang lived with the Pincuses, then later, he moved to an apartment at the Foundation which was convenient for his duties for more than a year as night watchman.

When Marcel Gut came to the Foundation from Switzerland, he was received with a warm hospitality that became a Foundation tradition. John McCracken enjoyed telling this story. Gut decided he would look out for Chang. After enjoying dinner, Gut and Chang went to the Worcester Auditorium for a ballet performance. "The usherettes had decided to dress themselves in tutus … and this young usherette with the tutu on took it upon herself, for whatever reason, to come along to take a shortcut along the row where Chang and Gut were sitting. Just as the young lady approached the two of them, Marcel Gut looked down and said to Chang, 'Your fly is open.' Just as the young lady went past Chang, he zipped up his fly, and he zipped up the young lady's tutu in his fly, and the lights went out. Chang ended up with the young girl nearly sitting on his lap, but Gut came to the rescue and took out his faithful Swiss Army knife, and he cut the young lady's tutu off of Chang's fly, and she escaped from the clutches of Chang. … I said to Marcel, 'Marcel, you made that story up didn't you?' And he looked me straight in the eye and said, 'John, my imagination is not that good.'"[99]

Fortunately Chang did have a sense of humor because he often seemed to forget to zip up his fly. Gabrial Bialy, at one time a Foundation scientist and now the deputy director of the Center for Population Research at NIH, and his wife were walking through the famous Piazza in Venice, and "there was M-C. Chang sitting by himself at one of the tables. The restaurants were not open, but he was sitting there with his fly open. I said to him, 'M-C., your fly is open.'

He said, 'Well, you never know when a pigeon might land on it.'"[100]

PINCUS PUT CHANG to work with Nicholas Werthessen superovulating cows, obtaining the eggs for fertilization in vitro, then transferring fertilized eggs to other cows on a Texas cattle ranch. This was Ray Umbaugh's project funded by Tom Slick, and it provided half of Chang's salary.[101] In Massachusetts, Chang was to assist in the new technique of perfusing ovaries using the system created by Pincus and Oscar Hechter. But Chang remembered Pincus's early work with in vitro fertilization of rabbit eggs, and that was his interest as well. Pincus allowed him to pursue this interest. Chang's early fertilization studies were unsuccessful, including an attempt to repeat Pincus's experiments with rabbit eggs. In 1947, he reported the successful delivery of normal rabbits after storing fertilized eggs in his

Chang — 1946

kitchen refrigerator, then transferring them to other rabbits.[102] This work was the subject of his first presentation at an international meeting, in Milan, Italy, in 1948.

"After submitting a paper in 1950 on fertilization of rabbit eggs to the American Sterility Society [later the American Fertility Society, and now the American Society of Reproductive Medicine], they awarded me $1,000, which I used to buy my first car."[103] By 1951, Change had reported his decisive work on the capacitation of sperm in the female reproductive tract, a transformation that occurs during an incubation period in the female and that is required in order for sperm to be capable of penetrating eggs. When Chang wrote his paper on sperm capacitation, he asked Pincus to join him as an author. Chang reported that to his credit, Pincus replied, "No it wasn't his work. You are a sperm man and I am an egg man."[104] During this same time, Pincus and Chang started their work on the effects of synthetic progestins on reproduction.

Chang tried a lot of things: crossing hares and rabbits, minks and ferrets, transferring eggs from one species to another. He attracted young scientists to work on his various projects. Yanagimachi, working in Chang's lab, reported the fertilization of hamster eggs in vitro in 1963. In 1969, Stella Pickworth succeeded in fertilizing Chinese hamster eggs in vitro, and Iwamatsu

Chang — 1969

Chang — 1970

fertilized mouse eggs in vitro with epididymal sperm; in 1973 and 1974, Miyamato and Toyods fertilized rat eggs in vitro; and in 1978, Hanoda, Fukuda, and Maddock reported the in vitro fertilization of deer mouse eggs. Chang said, "They did the work but I wrote the papers."[105]

Chang's philosophy towards students and fellows was Darwinian; leave them alone to sink or swim. He learned this from his Ph.D. studies in England when Hammond, his supervisor, was fond of saying, "If a chap is going to be any good for research, he does not need spoon feeding."[106] The work on in vitro fertilization in Chang's laboratory extended the early work of Pincus and became the foundation that made human in vitro fertilization possible.

"When I reported producing young rabbits by transfer of eggs fertilized in vitro with in vivo capacitated sperm at the West Point meeting in 1959, they gave me a standing ovation at the final banquet"[107] Indeed, Chang earned international respect and fame as a reproductive scientist with his work apart from that which led to oral contraceptives, providing training and guidance for about 100 research fellows coming to Massachusetts from all parts of the world.[108]

In 1962, Chang, encouraged by Pincus, applied for and was granted a Career Research Award from the National Institutes of Health. This support (the highest salary provided was $25,000 per year) persisted until 1982. After Pincus died, Hoagland requested that Searle provide Chang with financial support. Chang recalled, "I also understood that the Searle Company asked him, 'Who is M-C. Chang? Never heard of him.'"[109] This despite the fact that in 1955, 1959, and 1967, Chang was featured in presentations in Tokyo, New Delhi, and Santiago, sponsored by the International Planned Parenthood Federation. His place in science was eventually secured by multiple awards, including election to the National Academy of Sciences in 1990.

CHANG was a classic workaholic, tenaciously pursuing his goals. He liked to joke that he lived in the laboratory, producing the rumors among neighbors that the mad scientists at the Foundation kept a Chinaman chained in the basement.[110] His wife said, "I know how often he went to the lab. He went seven days a week and after meals. He might as well have gotten a cot there; he lived there."[111] The description of capacitation took six years of work; in vitro fertilization in mammals required fourteen years.[112] At one point in time, he was publishing nineteen research reports annually, a prodigious output by any standard.

He was a stern disciplinarian who maintained male dominance in his marriage.[113] At one point, Chang asked Goody and Lizzie to find a wife for him.[114] Then through friends at Yale University, early in 1948 he met Isabelle Chin, an American-born Chinese woman. Isabelle was a student in the Yale graduate school of oriental studies, learning Mandarin, which Chang spoke. Chang traveled by bus to Union Station in Worcester and took the train to New Haven every weekend. Isabelle remembered "Of course, I had to meet Mrs. Pincus. Mrs. Pincus had to pass judgment."[115] Isabelle and Chang married in May 1948 and had two daughters and a son. A graduate from Simmons College School of Library Science, Isabelle worked at the public library in Shrewsbury and then as the media coordinator for the Shrewsbury schools. She published a Chinese cookbook and a children's book of Chinese fairy tales.

Chang had a special relationship with Lizzie Pincus. Isabelle said, "Lizzie Pincus smoked like a chimney, and her brand was Philip Morris. Of course, Chang had to start smoking Philip Morris."[116] But Lizzie and Isabelle never did get along. Lizzie Pincus told Isabelle, "Don't ever forget which side your bread is buttered on," prompting Isabelle to think, "And here is the mother-in-law I never had."[117]

Chang had another family. To everyone's shock, one day in the 1950s, Chang's oldest daughter arrived at the Foundation seeking her father. From that moment on, the Foundation people knew that when Chang left China for Edinburgh in 1938, he left behind a wife, named Li, and Yan Lin, his daughter.[118] This was not an unusual circumstance for Chinese emigrants in those days, and Chang informed Isabelle Chin of his other wife and daughter when he asked her to marry him. Over the years, Chang and Isabelle sent money and gifts to the family in China.

Chang was a slim, friendly, energetic man whose wit was obscured by his mumbling difficulties with English. Called "Chang" by almost everyone, including his wife Isabelle, he always seemed modest and humble, but at the same time, he and his family were proud of his accomplishments. At times Chang believed that his role in the development of the oral contraceptive seemed slighted, but Roy Greep, in his biographical memoir of Chang, said, "It is much to Chang's credit that he never wavered in his admiration and respect for his benefactor, Gregory Pincus."[119] At least publicly that was so, because privately he did complain of not receiving his just due, that he had been taken advantage of, and he was resentful.[120-122] As the years went by, the negative feelings abated and he grew to appreciate the positive influence Pincus had on his life. Pincus in turn, when citing his collaborators, said of Chang,

"Among them is Dr. M-C. Chang whose brilliant and illuminating animal experimentation is the product of an original mind which continues to stimulate all who talk and work with him, including myself."[123]

Chang wrote in 1985, "I have had a very pleasant and comfortable life during the past forty years at the Worcester Foundation, because the directors, my co-workers, the maintenance personnel, and other friends have all treated me kindly and nicely. I am a timid and peace-loving soul, who hates to fight and to grumble, and so I like to have a peaceful life, doing the things I like to do.[124] When asked whether he had achieved what he had planned for his life, Chang responded, "I achieved more than I wished for, so I should be very happy in my old age."[125]

Chang died on June 5, 1991, at the age of eighty-two. A heavy smoker all his life, he struggled with emphysema that caused him to be hospitalized during a trip to Italy. About one week after returning home, Chang suffered a stroke that left him unresponsive in a hospital until he died sixteen days later.[126] He is buried, as is Gregory Pincus,

*Pincus, Sir John Hammond, and Chang, presumably at an
international meeting, unknown date*

in the Mountain View Cemetery in Shrewsbury, Massachusetts. Chang's wife, Isabelle, installed a stone monument that designated Chang as the father of the birth control pill.

The Foundation after Pincus

Hoagland and Pincus settled into their roles. Hoagland kept an eye on day-to-day operations, and willingly assumed the responsibility of promoting the Foundation to the public and donors. Pincus focused on his science and research grants and eventually the academic and public acclaim associated with the birth control pill. His initial official title was Director of Laboratories,

and then after 1955, Research Director. Hoagland planned to retire in 1967 when he was sixty-seven. The plan was for Pincus, three years younger, to serve as director until 1970. Pincus's brother Alex recalled, "Months before Goody died I visited the Foundation and asked Hudson about plans for retirement. Hudson complained that he had not been able to get Goody to discuss their joint retirements, and he exclaimed, 'Goody thinks he is immortal.'"[127]

In 1967, Hoagland and Pincus recruited Mason Fernald from his position as director of a large pharmaceutical laboratory to be the administrative director of the Foundation,

expecting him to succeed Pincus in 1970. Pincus died only two months after this agreement was reached. Hoagland stayed on for another year, but Fernald struggled with low morale and reduced federal research funding. The Foundation leaders decided a new director was needed, a distinguished scientist who could take the Foundation in a new direction.

Hudson and Anna Hoagland had two boys and two girls. In early 1970, Hoagland's elder son Mahlon Bush Hoagland accepted the offer to be the new director of the Foundation. Mahlon was a graduate of Harvard Medical School and had followed an academic career in molecular biology, noted for the co-discovery of transfer RNA, a molecule responsible for translating the DNA code into protein. He was on the road to becoming a surgeon but he contracted tuberculosis while a medical student. Two years later, recovered, he completed his medical training but, finding himself still not up to the physical demands of surgery, he turned to biochemistry. By 1967, he was the chairman of the department of biochemistry at Dartmouth Medical School.

Pincus had tried to persuade Mahlon to move to the Worcester Foundation in 1965.[128,129] Mahlon Hoagland recalled that meeting: "Gregory Pincus came to visit me with purpose written on his face. A decade had passed since his immortality had been assured by his commitment to the birth control pill and its powerful social implications, and he would have only two more years until his death. My relationship with Pincus before this visit had been that of a young man with a benevolent, kindly uncle. As my father's lifelong friend, Pincus had always been to me gentle, attentive, amusing, and understanding. While some of his colleagues saw an aggressive scientific entrepreneur, I saw a sort of family Einstein: a head full of wisdom, with penetrating kindly eyes and topped by a surprised mass of hair."[130]

In this last conversation between Mahlon and Goody, Pincus was looking into the future and was concerned that molecular biology was not being pursued at the Foundation. And Pincus offered the solution: Mahlon Hoagland should establish his research program at the Foundation. Implied was Mahlon's succession after his father's retirement. But Mahlon was concerned by the lack of endowment at the Foundation, and he did not see either of these two vigorous men giving up their leadership roles in the near future—he declined.

After Pincus died in 1967, a search committee of prominent scientists again approached Mahlon Hoagland, but again he declined to disrupt his current position and work. The committee went back to the drawing board; however, Mahlon had a change in heart. The need of the Foundation in a difficult time pulled at his family connection, and this combined with the opportunity to take the Foundation in a new direction emphasizing molecular biology convinced Mahlon to take the job. Mahlon arrived at the Foundation as its new president in the summer of 1970.

Mahlon Hoagland recruited Thoru Pederson, a noted cell biologist, to join the Worcester Foundation in 1971, and in 1985, Pederson became the president and director of the Foundation. In 1995, the name of The Foundation changed its name to the Worcester Foundation for Biomedical Research and two years later, Pederson and the Board of Trustees organized a merger with the University of Massachusetts Medical School, located just across Lake Quinsigamond in Worcester. Pederson is now professor of biochemistry and molecular pharmacology at the University of Massachusetts Medical School in addition to his directorship of the Foundation. The majority of the Foundation's scientists received academic appointments at the medical school, and the Foundation's legacy programs continue. These include the Hudson Hoagland Society, an annual donor group whose gifts make possible innovation grants to young scientists, the prestigious Gregory Pincus Medal that recognizes pioneers in the fields of endocrine and reproductive biology, as well as lectureships in honor of Min-Chueh Chang, Mahlon Hoagland, and Eliahu Caspi. In addition

the campus in Shrewsbury has been named the Worcester Foundation campus and all the buildings have been modernized for a variety of scientific and educational programs operated by the medical school, many of which are located in the Hoagland-Pincus Conference Center, an elegant building designed by the renowned Architects Collaborative of Cambridge, Massachusetts, and dedicated in 1968.

Anna Hoagland died on May 23, 1973, a long time sufferer from a consequence of smoking, emphysema; the auditorium at the Hoagland-Pincus Conference Center bears her name. In the early 1950s, Anna developed the skill of transcribing books into Braille for the blind. She produced over 200,000 pages over twenty years, concentrating on college textbooks, and received many awards for her work.

Hudson Hoagland died in 1982, dedicated to science to his last day. Hoagland labeled himself as a "chronic liberal."[131] Neither he nor his wife Anna were religious, but both were highly ethical individuals. Hoagland wrote, "The scientist has a high regard for truth and spends much time in trying to ascertain it, and the fraternity of scientists transcends national boundaries and class and color restrictions. ... a scientist can be wrong without being wicked, in contrast to thinking in spheres that are dominated by authoritarianism in religion and politics. ... I believe that life can be rational and that reason and loyalty to our historically tested values, derived by the struggles of free men over the centuries, can do more than anything else to resolve the tragic problems of our generation. This is not an easy road, but I know of no short cut."[132]

THE 1950s AND 1960s saw the halcyon days of the Worcester Foundation. The timing of the emergence and success of the Foundation couldn't have been better for the development of oral contraception, placing it in the perfect position to provide an enabling environment, the capability to interact with industry, and the freedom for Pincus to exercise his entrepreneurial energy and drive.

Hudson and Anna Hoagland — 1970

CHAPTER SEVEN:

THE LAURENTIAN HORMONE CONFERENCE

THE LAURENTIAN HORMONE CONFERENCE was a prestigious annual meeting where for sixty years scientists and clinicians gathered by invitation to discuss the cutting edge developments in endocrinology. This conference, and its published proceedings, became another noteworthy contribution by Gregory Pincus, but it also provided a stage where he performed brilliantly.

It all started when the American Association for the Advancement of Science sponsored a conference on hormones in the spring of 1943 on Gibson Island, in the Chesapeake Bay near Baltimore. It was a small crowd, about thirty in number, but a group of scientists already distinguished by their work. What happened at this conference had a long-lasting impact on Gregory Pincus, and indeed, the entire field of endocrinology.[1]

The organizers of the Gibson Island conference were Hans Jensen working at the Upjohn Company and Fred Koch who was at the University of Chicago. Gibson Island, the venue chosen for the conference, was a private club. Percy Julian, a highly admired African-American chemist, was invited to the conference but was refused admittance. Seymour Lieberman remembered, "At the very first meeting, Fred Koch stood up and said, 'There's something I want to say to the assembled group. There's a man who wants to attend this meeting, and he's cooling his heels in Baltimore because they won't allow him on this island, and the reason that they don't is they only allow black waiters on the island, and he is black.'"[2]

Gregory Pincus led a protest that lasted three days before management allowed Julian to join the conference. At the end of the conference when it came time to discuss meeting again, the participants were unanimous in their refusal to return to Gibson Island. Pincus, Robert Bates, and Samuel Guerin were elected to arrange next year's conference. For some reason, forty-year-old Pincus failed to make the committee meeting, so Bates and Guerin notified him that he had been elected chairman, a position he held until his death twenty-four years later.[3] The Montreal Physiological Society extended an invitation to hold the meeting in the Laurentian Mountains at Mont Tremblant Lodge, about ninety miles north of Montreal, and the Laurentian Hormone Conference was born in 1944.

At the second meeting at Mont Tremblant, the participants voted to call the annual get-together, "The Laurentian Hormone Conference." Unfortunately, anti-Semitism was encountered in the person of the owner of the resort. Once again, the group stayed true to principle, and the meeting did not return to Mont Tremblant until six years later when the owner died.

Gregory Pincus was chairman of the Committee on Arrangements from 1944 to 1967, a group that varied from three to seven individuals over the years. Pincus's skill at organization and management gradually came to be appreciated

and admired. Sir Alan Parkes from the University of Cambridge wrote, "… there was no doubt about the source of the inspiration and driving power. Everything seemed to hinge on Pincus."[4] He arranged the program, edited the proceedings, and his office handled all the logistics. The number of participants was deliberately kept small, 150 to 200, to enhance interaction and discussion. It wasn't long before *not* being selected to attend became a problem.

Attendance at the meeting required application, and demand soon outpaced the accommodations. Stung by criticism that he was making biased decisions that favored his friends, Pincus established an anonymous committee of three individuals (one biochemist, one physiologist, and one clinician) to process applications, and made sure that those who were passed by once or twice received priority treatment. After a few years, an "old guard" list of about eighty people was created (those who had attended every meeting), and these individuals were guaranteed attendance.[3] The list gradually diminished in size over time as those who failed to attend two years in a row were dropped, as well as those who aged and retired.

Dwight Ingle, a scientist at the University of Chicago, wrote "These criticisms were not deserved. Gregory was never overtly distressed by criticism or hostility but those close to him knew

Gregory Pincus — 1950

that he was hurt by accusations of partiality."[6] On the other hand, Seymour Lieberman had a different memory. "He controlled who came there and who was there to speak, and if you don't think that's powerful, you don't know science. In my judgment, there was a time when people couldn't get jobs unless Pincus gave his approval. There was nobody with the stature and influence that Pincus had at the time he was ruling, let's say between 1950 and 1967 when he died, the equal of Pincus then or now or since, particularly in the field of endocrinology."[7]

In the early days of the Laurentian Hormone Conference, Lieberman was one of the three scientists reviewing applications for attendance. He was the third (the last) viewer and would return the applications to Pincus. "So I could see when I got to the Laurentian Hormone Conference those people who had applied and those people who had gotten in without applications. … And of course the careers depended on whether you got invited to speak, so you can see where his power was derived."[8]

The Laurentian Hormone Conference quickly became the premier academic event in the world of endocrinology, not just in the U.S., but worldwide. It was a place where reputations could be made. The site was away from a city, a ski resort without snow, forcing close interactions at the meetings, meals, and cocktail parties. Science at the Laurentian Hormone Conference was well-served by an open exchange of ideas, and friendships were made that often led to collaborations among academicians and new endeavors in industry. The Laurentian Hormone Conference was a major reason almost every endocrinologist in the world knew each other. And Pincus knew everyone. The conference provided a power base for Pincus, making him known to all in endocrinology, from already distinguished scientists to beginning graduate students.

Scientists and academic clinicians generally learn to know most of the people in their specialized field. But hardly anyone crosses disciplines like Goody did. He saved every letter he received and carbon copies of every letter he ever dictated. The collection of his letters in the Library of Congress reads like a who's who, with prominent names from multiple clinical and scientific disciplines all over the world, plus researchers and administrators in the pharmaceutical industry. Even students at all levels were not neglected. Goody responded with advice and recommendations to junior academicians, graduate students, and even high school students. Goody never hesitated to write letters of support or to enquire of his many friends of possible job opportunities, not only for his relatives, but for his many friends.

Seymour Lieberman stressed that "For Pincus it

was his road to fame to be not only the organizer of the Laurentian Hormone Conference, but also the editor of the conference reports."[9] In 1953, the Conference was incorporated in the Commonwealth of Massachusetts as a nonprofit organization, with Pincus as president.

ELWOOD JENSEN is a good example of Goody's impact on science and scientists. Jensen, a pioneer in the studies that established the existence of a specific receptor for estrogen that opened a new era in endocrinology, recalled many years later that it was Gregory Pincus who gave his work a stage at a time when others were disbelieving.[10] Jensen's early studies were presented at the 1961 Laurentian Hormone Conference, and in 1965, Pincus invited Jensen to participate in an international conference in Tokyo at which for the first time the word "receptor" was introduced.[11] The proceedings from both meetings were published in books edited by Pincus.

In his biographical memoir of Pincus, Dwight Ingle said, "He was not a modest man but neither was he haughty nor was he intolerant of the limitations and foibles of others. It was characteristic of Gregory Pincus to be unobtrusive; he spoke briefly to open each conference and to set the tone of informality and good humor."[12] Joseph Goldzieher remembered Pincus opening the meeting on the first day by saying, "Everybody is hereby introduced to everybody else."[13] Pincus wrote of the conference, "However able as ears, eyes, and hands a Conference Committee may be, the speakers and membership are mouth, head, and heart. Working with us there have been wise heads, warm hearts, and eloquent mouths."[14]

Pincus always wore a suit except when he was at the Laurentian Hormone Conference. In fact, he often wore a red shirt to the meetings to establish the concept of relaxation, but partly, according to John McCracken, because "he wanted to be identified as the number one man."[15] But he didn't rub people wrong; there were "never any ill thoughts or ill acts against anyone. I never heard him speak badly of anyone."[16] Abraham White, Professor and Chairman of Biochemistry at Albert Einstein College of Medicine, wrote after Pincus died, "His concern for his colleagues and their problems extended to their families; his gentleness and warmth were appreciated by everyone who knew him, and were readily discerned by children, who quickly came to love him."[17]

When asked how Pincus behaved, a friend and colleague said, "Like a king!"[18] Individuals who described Pincus in exalted, royal terms did so without rancor, jealousy, or bitterness. They hastily pointed out that Pincus earned his position and maintained it with grace, charm, and warmth. Even though he may have been spoiled by royal treatment, especially in foreign countries, he was never arrogant or condescending. Instead, he made lifelong friends.

Another colleague noted that Lizzie Pincus assumed a "Queenly" role at the Laurentian conferences.[19] Goody's secretary referred to her as "Madame Pincus."[20] Seymour Lieberman said, "I think she was an extremely good wife for Pincus. I can't talk about their intimate relationship, but I thought she was meant for somebody like him, and she obviously was very important in his career and his advancements. She had sufficient self-esteem and that may be what's called 'toughness.' She wasn't a delicate wallflower. To a certain extent she could take care of Pincus. She could tell him off. On the other hand, she was a good wife for him."[21]

THE CONFERENCE met for five days either before or after the first Monday in September. An hour was allotted for each presentation and an hour for discussion. There were two presentations each morning and one each evening except Wednesday. Wednesday evening was reserved for a cocktail party and dinner dance. Spouses and children were encouraged to attend, and many did.

Most of those in attendance at the Laurentian Hormone Conference slept in cabins. The Pincus cocktail party in their personal cabin, with a more formal dress code, was an important occasion. Seymour Lieberman said, "To be invited to that cocktail party was the height of recognition of acceptance, of honor, because of the several hundred people who were attending the meeting, only forty or fifty were invited to the party. Of course they had other parties where everybody was invited obviously, but to be recognized by Pincus as being worthy of getting an invitation to his party, that really made you a member of the elite."[22]

As was his habit in every conference he attended, Goody Pincus sat in the front row, fondling his mustache, listening politely, but with great intensity.[23] Scientists making presentations could feel his presence and awaited his question or query with nervous anticipation. However, Pincus never asked a question or made a statement in an aggressive, rude manner. He was always genuinely interested in the material and truly interested in seeking or making a clarification. He asked a lot of questions, always relevant and thoughtful, never nasty.[24] Sheldon Segal recalled attending the Laurentian Hormone Conference when he was a young investigator. "Total membership was just a few hundred, and I met this very fearful looking man, dark eyes and mustache, sitting in the front row where he always sat at every meeting, listening intently, stroking his mustache. In fact, I had in those early years a recurrent dream that I was going to give a paper someplace and I had left my slides behind, and there in the front row was Goody Pincus, sitting, waiting for this talk to be given, and *I didn't have my slides!*"[25]

Sir Alan S. Parkes, Professor at the famed Physiological Laboratory in Cambridge, England, said, "... I never failed to be impressed by the breadth of knowledge and capacity for making a point effectively which he displayed in discussion."[26] In 1964, Pincus chaired a meeting convened by the World Health Organization, entitled *The Mechanism of Action of Sex Steroids and Analogous Substances*, and Sir Parkes commented, "... I have never seen a meeting dominated so completely, pleasantly but effectively, by its chairman."[27]

After the first year in Canada, the proceedings, edited by Gregory Pincus, were published in an annual volume entitled *Recent Progress in Hormone Research. The Proceedings of the Laurentian Hormone Conference*. The volumes contained important, often referred to, reviews by the conference speakers who were usually scientists who had already accomplished a considerable body of work or sufficient work in a new and exciting area. Pincus added after each manuscript the comments from the question and answer sessions following each presentation, bringing new insights and personalities to wide attention. Pincus made sure the discussion was immediately typed from the recordings, for review and editing by the discussants before the end of the meeting.

Pincus wrote in the Preface to the first of the twenty-three volumes he would edit: "The spirit of inquiry dies without criticism and discussion, and it is largely the purpose of these conferences to nourish that spirit. The hormones are often regarded as regulators of the rates of numerous vital processes. We hope that these papers will act as hormones to the creative processes of students and scholars in this far-flung field."[28]

There are scientists and there are scientists. There are scientists who do their work to a significant degree motivated by their own selves, their own ego, their own self promotion. Pincus seemed to be genuinely devoted to science. John McCracken opined, "Some philosopher guy said that for every thousand that can talk, only one can write, and for every thousand that can write, one can see. Pincus could see. He was a very discerning individual.[29] Celso-Ramón Garcia, Goody's colleague, observed that "His mind was encyclopedic, his retentive and recall abilities legion."[30]

I was fortunate to be able to attend two Laurentian Hormone Conferences. On each occasion, the director of one of my two research fellowships was presenting his work. Having made a small contribution to the work, I was invited as a guest of the principal scientist. By this time my mentors were accomplished and respected, yet in the preparation in the days before the conference, each exhibited the nervousness of a very junior academician about to discuss his work with a Nobel Prize winner. In my experience, the conferences were everything ever said about them. I met new people in my fields of interest; I was introduced to individuals who were in my view "famous names;" I enjoyed the challenges issued forth during the discussion sessions; and I was awestruck at this early stage in my career to mix with pure scientists and renowned clinicians at the parties.

PINCUS DIED IN 1967 just before the Laurentian Hormone Conference. A week before his death, Dwight Ingle received a letter from him asking him to chair a session at Mont Tremblant. The conference took place only days after his death. "His secretary said that in lucid moments prior to death he asked that the hormone conference be held as planned."[31]

Alex, Goody's brother, remembered that when the scientists heard that he was hospitalized, most were panicked at the thought of losing his leadership. "I recall one famous scientist who was about Goody's age actually crying that he was 'losing a father.'"[32] Robert Bates wrote in the Preface to the proceedings of that year's conference, "He was an ambassador-at-large for the world of endocrinology. He was not the domineering salesman type. He was a good listener who knew how to evaluate what he heard. Hence his rapport with others was such that he made friends wherever he went. Few men in the world today have done as much for their friends, for the field of science, and for the world as Gregory Goodwin Pincus did in his quiet, unobtrusive way."[33]

THE LAURENTIAN HORMONE conference spawned many others of its ilk, and the competition eventually made it unsustainable. The Endocrine Society became responsible for the conference, moving the meetings from site to site in the U.S. and Canada. The Gregory Pincus Memorial Lecture at the Laurentian

Hormone Conference was established in 1968. Neena Schwartz was honored to make the first presentation.[34] The last and fiftieth annual meeting was held in Puerto Rico in 1993, and the last Gregory Pincus Memorial Lecture was delivered by Carl Djerassi.[35] Publication of *Recent Progress in Hormone Research* ended in 2004 with volume 59, but the tradition lives on. An annual special issue of the Endocrine Society publication *Endocrine Reviews* is dedicated to the Laurentian history, with invited manuscripts from investigators with a history of accomplishment in their fields. Gregory Pincus would be pleased.

CHAPTER EIGHT:

RUSSELL MARKER SOLVES A PROBLEM

T HE EXISTENCE of hormones (chemicals formed in one part of the body and carried in the blood to a target tissue in another part of the body) was unknown two hundred years ago.[1-5] In the last half of the nineteenth century, a scattering of chemists and physiologists began to produce hormonally active extracts from glands, bile, and urine of animals. Adventuresome clinicians used these extracts to treat patients, for example supplying thyroid hormone to treat severely hypothyroid individuals, and the specialty of endocrinology was born. The word "endocrine" was adopted to designate the "glands of internal secretion," the multiple sources of hormones.

Charles Edouard Brown-Sequard, the son of a French woman and an American sea captain, was born on the island of Mauritius. Speaking fluent English and French, he practiced medicine and lectured in London and New York before settling in Paris. Brown-Sequard reported in 1889 that he was rejuvenated by the self-administration of extracts from dog testicles, most likely a placebo effect considering the scant amount of testosterone he could have extracted using his aqueous method, and he suggested that ovarian extracts would have the same revitalizing effect in women. Efforts to treat women around the turn of the century were largely unsuccessful, but in 1897, ovarian extract was reported to be effective for menopausal hot flushing.[6]

The ovarian hormones were not isolated until the 1930s. Edgar Allen and Edward Doisy were the first to isolate the ovarian hormone, estrogen. Allen was born in Colorado, educated at Brown University, and served in France during World

War I. In 1933, he became the chairman of the Department of Anatomy at Yale University. He died of a heart attack while on patrol off Long Island for the U.S. Coast Guard in February 1943. Doisy was born in Illinois and educated at the University of Illinois and Harvard. During World War I, he was assigned to the Rockefeller Institute in New York City and then to the Walter Reed Hospital in Washington. Doisy was the first chairman of biochemistry at the St. Louis University School of Medicine. He received the Nobel Prize in Medicine, along with Henrik Dam, in 1943 for his isolation and synthesis of vitamin K. Doisy died in 1986 at the age of 92.

In 1919, Allen and Doisy, both discharged from the army after World War I, joined the faculty at the Washington University School of Medicine in St. Louis. They became friends playing on a faculty baseball team and planned their first experiments while driving to work together. In 1922, Allen moved to the University of Missouri to be Professor of Anatomy, and Doisy went to St. Louis University, but they continued their collaboration. Doisy prepared ovarian extracts and mailed them to Allen for experiments. In 1923 and 1924, Allen and Doisy reported the isolation from pig ovaries and the administration to animals of "an ovarian hormone."

In 1926, Sir Alan S. Parkes and C.W. Bellerby coined the basic word "estrin" to designate the hormone or hormones that induce estrus in animals, the time when female mammals are fertile and receptive to males. Doisy and his students Veler and Thayer in St. Louis isolated a few milligrams of estrogen in crystalline form in 1929 from large amounts of urine from pregnant women. The terminology was extended to include the principal estrogens in humans, estrone, estradiol, and estriol, in 1932 at the first meeting of the International Conference on the Standardization of Sex Hormones in London, although significant amounts of pure estradiol were not isolated until 1936. At this same meeting, the pioneering chemists were bemoaning the problem of scarcity that limited supplies to milligram amounts when a relatively unknown biochemist, A. Girard from France, offered twenty grams of crystalline estrogen derived by the use of a new reagent to treat mare's urine.[7]

In the 1920s, George W. Corner at the University of Rochester invited Willard Myron Allen, an organic chemist who was then a medical student, to join him in the study of the corpus luteum, the structure in the ovary that after ovulation makes progesterone, the hormone that sustains pregnancy. Within two years, they had a pure extract, but it was not until 1934 that crystalline progesterone was isolated almost simultaneously in several countries. It took the corpora lutea of 50,000 pigs to yield a few milligrams.

At the Second International Conference on Standardization of Sex Hormones in London, Corner and Allen proposed the name progestin. Others proposed luteosterone, and, at a cocktail party, the various biochemists agreed to call the chemical progesterone.[8]

Hormones were being administered to patients in the 1940s, but supplies were very limited. And with a scarce supply, hormones were incredibly expensive. Progesterone, for example, cost $200 per gram. "To secure barely enough androsterone to cover the head of a pin, Adolph Butenandt had had to start with nearly four thousand gallons of urine; to obtain less than one hundredth of an ounce of pure testosterone crystals, Ernst Laqueur had had to process nearly a ton of bulls' testicles. It took a full ton of cholesterol, from the spinal cords or brains of cattle or from the grease of sheep's wool, to yield just twenty pounds of the starting material from which progesterone ultimately could be obtained. Edward Doisy had had to process the ovaries of more than eighty thousand sows to get just twelve thousandths of a gram of estradiol."[9] Russell E. Marker would solve this problem of supply.

Russell E. Marker

Beginning in 1920, Ludwig Haberlandt, professor of physiology at the University of Innsbruck, Austria, demonstrated that ovarian extracts given orally could prevent fertility in mice. Haberlandt is acknowledged as the first to perform experiments with the aim of producing a method of hormonal contraception; he called it "hormonal sterilization."[10] In the 1920s, a Viennese gynecologist, Otfried Otto Fellner, conducting experiments in his spare time, and administering ovarian and placental extracts to a variety of animals, also reported hormonal sterilization.[11] By 1931, Haberlandt proposed the administration of hormones for birth control. An extract named Infecundin was produced in collaboration with the Hungarian pharmaceutical company Gideon Richter, but Haberlandt's early death of a heart attack in 1932, at age forty-seven, brought an end to this effort. Fellner disappeared after the annexation of Austria to Hitler's Germany.

The concept was annunciated by Haberlandt, but steroid chemistry wasn't ready. Scientists throughout the world were aware that the extraction and isolation of a few milligrams of the sex steroids required starting points measured in gallons of urine or thousands of pounds of organs. The supply problem was solved by a cantankerous iconoclast, Russell E. Marker, who completed his thesis, but not the course work, for his Ph.D.[12-16] The following story is derived from Marker's own words, in an autobiographical article and from a two-hour interview for the oral history archives of the Chemical Heritage Foundation in Philadelphia.[17,18]

Marker, born in 1902 in a one-room log cabin on a farm near Hagerstown, Maryland, received his bachelor's degree in organic chemistry and his master's degree in colloidal chemistry from the University of Maryland. Although he had completed his work for a Ph.D., his supervisor, Morris S. Kharasch, announced that Marker still lacked some required chemistry courses. Considering the courses a waste of time, Marker said, "The hell with it," and abruptly left.

After leaving the University of Maryland, Marker worked first in the laboratory of the Naval Powder Factory, then with the Ethyl Gasoline Corporation, where in 1926 he developed the system of octane rating of gasoline. Frank Whitmore, dean of Pennsylvania State College, now Pennsylvania State University, visited Marker at Ethyl. Impressed with his work, Whitmore said, "If you're ever looking for a job, let me know."

From 1927 to 1934, Marker worked at the Rockefeller Institute, publishing a total of thirty-two papers on configuration and optical rotation as a method of identifying compounds. He became interested in steroid chemistry, but he was told to continue with his work in optical technology. Instead, Marker called Dean Whitmore at Penn State.

In September 1935, Marker moved to Penn State at a reduced salary, from $4,400 per year at Rockefeller to $1,800, but with the freedom to pursue any field of research. His work was supported mainly by research grants from the Parke-Davis pharmaceutical company. At that time, it required the ovaries from 2,500 pregnant pigs to produce 1 mg of progesterone. Marker decided to pursue the goal of an abundant and inexpensive supply of progesterone, and for several years he concentrated on urine from pregnant animals. Then in 1939, Marker devised the method, called the Marker degradation, to convert a sapogenin molecule into a progestin.

Marker was convinced that the solution to the problem of obtaining large quantities of steroid hormones was to find plants in the family that includes the lily, the agave, and the yam that contained sufficient amounts of diosgenin, a plant steroid, a sapogenin, that could be used as a starting point for steroid hormone production. He discovered that a species of *Trillium*, known locally as Beth's root, was collected in North Carolina for the preparation of Lydia Pinkham's Compound, popular at the time to relieve menstrual discomfort. A principal ingredient in Beth's root was diosgenin, but the rhizome was too small to provide sufficient amounts for commercial production.

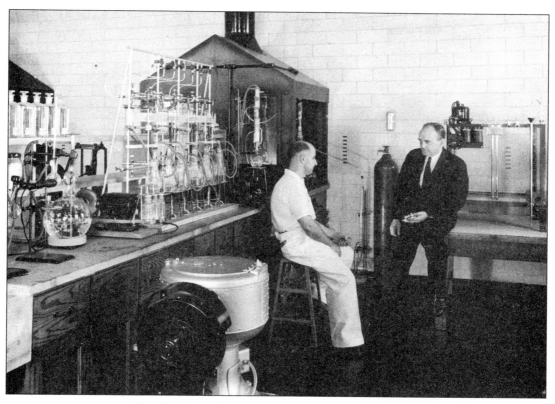

Russell Marker and Dean Frank Whitmore at Penn State — 1939

Marker's search for an appropriate plant took him to California, Arizona, and Texas. Spending his summer vacations in the Southwest and Mexico collecting sapogenin-containing plants, Marker's laboratory analyzed more than a hundred thousand pounds of over four hundred different species of plants.[19] Marker discovered that the roots of the *Dioscorea* plant (a wild yam) were the richest source of sapogenins.

On a visit to Texas A & M University, Marker found a picture of a large *Dioscorea* (*Dioscorea mexicana*) in a book that he just happened to pick up and browse through while spending the night at the home of a retired botanist who was helping him collect disogenin-containing plants. After returning to Pennsylvania, he traveled by train for three days to search for this *Dioscorea* in Mexico.

Marker first went to Mexico City in November 1941, but his effort was blocked by the lack of a plant-collecting permit from the Mexican government. He returned in January 1942,

Russell Marker

and the American Embassy arranged for a Mexican botanist who had a collecting permit to accompany Marker to Veracruz. Marker rented a truck with a driver, and when the botanist arrived at Marker's hotel, he was accompanied by his girlfriend and her mother, who served as the girl's chaperone. Marker was forced to take the entire group. They covered eighty miles the first day, staying overnight in Puebla. The next day, the drive to Tehuacan was a shorter trip, but the botanist insisted on a two-day stay devoted to his own collection of specimens. Then next morning, the botanist refused to go any further, claiming that the natives had discovered Marker was American and wanted nothing to do with him. They turned around, managed to overcome a breakdown of the truck near Puebla, and made it back to Mexico City five days after starting, with nothing to show for the trip.

The next day, a Monday morning, Marker reported to the American Embassy and was advised to leave Mexico. It was just after Pearl Harbor and Mexico was being courted by Germany. The Embassy was concerned for the safety of Americans traveling in Mexico. Instead of returning home, Marker took an overnight bus to Puebla, arriving after midnight, and boarded a second bus that already held pigs and chickens in addition to a few passengers. He arrived in Orizaba the next morning, and fortunately there was a small hotel next to the bus terminal. Marker remembered that the botany book in which he first read a description of *Dioscorea mexicana* indicated that the plant, a wild yam vine that grows up trees in the mountains of southern Mexico, could be found along a stream that crossed the road between Orizaba and Cordoba. He climbed aboard the local bus to Cordoba, which he stopped and disembarked when the bus drove through a large stream crossing the road about ten miles after leaving Orizaba. He found a small country store next to the road, owned by an Indian named Alberto Moreno.

Moreno did not speak English; Marker did not speak Spanish. But somehow, Marker conveyed his desire to obtain the *Dioscorea* that was known locally as "cabeza de negro," black tubers. Moreno in turn somehow made Marker understand that he should return the next morning. And there in the store, the next morning, were two plants, each in a bag that Moreno placed on the roof of the next bus back to Orizaba. Each tuber was nine to twelve inches high and consisted of white material like a turnip; it was used by local Mexicans as soap and as a poison to catch fish. When Marker got off the bus in Orizaba, both bags were missing. A policeman was there, but it became apparent he was there to collect a fee for the return of the bags. Marker gave him what he had, a ten-dollar bill, but that only retrieved one bag, which he managed to smuggle back to Pennsylvania.

Marker used only a portion of the plant to isolate diosgenin. In February 1942, he took the remainder to the Parke-Davis chemists in Detroit. Demonstrating his process for obtaining diosgenin, Marker convinced the director of research, Oliver Kamm, that he was on to something, a source for raw material that could provide for the commercial production of hormones. Unfortunately, they could not convince the president of Parke-Davis, nor could Marker convince anyone at several other companies.

Unable to obtain support from the pharmaceutical industry, Marker, drew on half of his life savings and returned to Mexico in October 1942. He arranged with Albert Moreno to collect the roots of the Mexican yam. Marker paid Mexican medical students to collect the yams. The students were arrested when farmers reported that their yams were being stolen, but not before Marker had enough to prepare a syrup.

Back in the U.S. with his syrup, Marker arranged to work in the New York laboratory of a friend, Norman Applezweig, an organic chemist involved in steroid research, in return for one-third of whatever progesterone his syrup could yield.[20,21] He isolated diosgenin and synthesized three kilograms of progesterone, the largest lot of progesterone ever produced. United States pharmaceutical companies still refused to back Marker, and even his university refused, despite Marker's urging, to patent the process.

Before Marker left Mexico, he looked through the yellow pages in a Mexico City telephone directory and found something he recognized, a company called "Laboratorios Hormona," owned by a lawyer who was a Hungarian immigrant, Emeric Somlo, and a German immigrant who had both a medical degree and a Ph.D. in chemistry, Frederick A. Lehman.

> ... when the phone rang. A distant voice asked in barely comprehensible Spanish if he [Frederick Lehman] spoke English.
> "Yes, of course."
> "I found your company's name in the telephone book, since I recognized two words, 'Laboratories' and 'Hormones.' I have something you may be interested in: a cheap source for progesterone."
> "Who are you?"
> "I am Marker, a steroid chemist."[22]

Visiting the company, Marker met Lehman, the minority owner of Laboratorios Hormona, who had the good sense to see where this was going. From his reading of the literature, he knew who Marker was; he knew the value of steroids; and he was a businessman. Lehman called his partner who was visiting New York and convinced him to return as soon as possible. The three men agreed to form a Mexican company for the production of hormones, and Marker returned to the U.S., leaving behind a list of equipment and chemicals to be ordered.

Marker returned to Mexico in spring 1943 to collect plants and to check on progress at Laboratorios Hormona. He just happened to mention to Lehmann that he had two kilograms of progesterone. As soon as Marker returned to Pennsylvania, he received a phone call from Somlo who said that if Marker still had those two kilograms of progesterone he sure would like to see it; could he meet him in New York? Over dinner at the Waldorf-Astoria, Somlo offered Marker 40 percent of their new company in exchange for the progesterone, with a share in future profits. Marker arranged for a friend to deliver the progesterone to Somlo in New York.

Somlo had a small company in New York called Chemical Specialties, and in the early years of Pincus's work, he obtained progesterone through this Syntex subsidiary.

In December 1943, Marker resigned from Pennsylvania State College and went to Mexico where he collected the roots of *Dioscorea Mexicana*—ten tons worth! Marker chopped them up with a machete, and left the pieces to dry in the sun across from Moreno's store in a

small structure for drying coffee. It took two months of work in an old pottery shed in Mexico City to prepare several pounds of progesterone, worth $160,000, with the help of several young women who had little education and spoke no English.

Somlo suggested calling their new company Synthesis, but Marker insisted on some link to Mexico, and the three partners formed Syntex (from *synthesis* and *Mexico*), incorporated in

Marker and the "Cabeza de Negro"

March 1944. Marker moved into a new four-room laboratory, and over the next year, produced over thirty kilograms of progesterone and ten kilograms of dehydroepiandrosterone. The price of progesterone fell from $200 to $50 a gram.

During this time, Marker received expenses, but he was not given his share of the profits or the 40 percent share of stock due to him. In March 1945, Somlo claimed there were no profits, but then admitted that the profits had been paid to the two Mexican partners as salaries. Failing to reach a settlement, Marker left Syntex in May 1945, took some of his young female workers with him, and started a new company in Texcoco, called Botanica-Mex. He changed to *Dioscorea barbasco,* which gave a greater yield of diosgenin, and the price of progesterone dropped to $10 a gram, and later to $5.

> After I broke up with Lehmann and Somlo, I chose a place east of Mexico City (Texcoco), where labor and water were plentiful. I there repeated my simple procedure of converting diosgenin into progesterone. My workers were happy but one day they came to me and said, "We all live on this dry-lake bed, and we come from very far away. If you want us to go on working for you, we need bicycles." "Sure," said Marker, "I'll buy them for you, and you will pay them back from your salary." The workers, happy with this offer, and the image of a white man with promise, celebrated drunkenly one evening. Late at night they went to a nearby quarry where a great effigy of the Aztec rain god was still attached by its back to the bedrock (It wasn't moved to the museum until 1964). They then began chiseling my name over Tláloc's right eyebrow, but were interrupted by angry villagers and had to run away after having carved only the first two letters.[23]

The volcanic stone monolith of Tláloc the rain god was carved in a horizontal position sometime in the period of 400 B.C. to 200 A.D. On April 16, 1964, the unfinished statue was detached and transported on a day's journey to Mexico City, and placed in a vertical position at the road entrance to the Museo Nacional de Antropologia, an imposing 168 tons, twenty-three feet high. I was delighted to see that the initials "MA" can be easily discerned at the right edge of the headdress; Marker's workers obviously intended to place his full name across the entire width. The evening arrival of the rain god was greeted by a crowd of 25,000 people. Despite the fact that it was the dry season, a record rainfall fell on the day the statue arrived![24]

Marker's new company was allegedly harassed, legally and physically, by Syntex, and in 1946 it was sold to Gideon Richter, which moved it to Mexico City and renamed it Hormosynth.

Tláloc, the rain god, at the Museo Nacional de Antropologia in Mexico City

Eventually it came under the ownership of Organon of Holland, which still uses it under the name of Quimica Esteroides. By the 1960s, several pharmaceutical companies were benefiting from the root-gathering operations in Mexico, closely regulated by the Mexican government that imposed annual quotas, about forty-three thousand tons, to balance harvesting with the new annual growth.[25] Mexican yams provided the starting material for the manufacture of oral contraceptives for about fifteen years, giving way to other sources, such as soya beans, methods for total synthesis, or microbial fermentation.[26]

In 1949, Marker retired to Pennsylvania to devote the rest of his life to traveling, and in 1959 he began an association with a French silversmith who had emigrated to Mexico City, and then with his son, Pedro Leites. After 1970, Marker turned to collecting paintings by Mexican artists. The artwork and the replicas of antique works in silver were successful businesses that allowed him, in the 1980s, to endow scientific lectureships at both Pennsylvania State University and the University of Maryland. In 1970, the Mexican government honored Marker and awarded him the Order of the Aztec Eagle; staying true to his irascible nature, he declined. In 1984, Pennsylvania State University established the annual Marker Lectures in Science and, in 1987, the Russell and Mildred Marker Professorship of Natural Product Chemistry. In 1987, Marker was granted an honorary doctorate in science from the University of Maryland, the degree he failed to receive in 1926.

In 1990, Marker was planning on a quiet visit to Mexico to present a plaque made in his honor by Pennsylvania State University to Adolfina Moreno, the daughter of Alberto, the owner of the small country store whom Marker met in 1942. Mexican scientists and pharmaceutical people learned of the visit, and that summer a chartered busload of fifty people retraced Marker's trip from Mexico City to Orizaba.[27] Marker rode in a car with Frederico Lehman's son, Pedro, who had become a distinguished chemist. Meeting in an auditorium at the University of Veracruz, Marker was honored by speeches and an engraved silver tray. After lunch at a local brewery, nearly 100 people made their way to the bridge over the Mezcala River. Marker entered the living quarters behind the store now owned by Adolfina. She tearfully thanked him and pointed to a nearby photo, her marriage picture from fifty years ago, with Marker in the wedding group.[28] At the age of ninety-two, Russell Earl Marker died in Wernersville, Pennsylvania, in 1995, from complications after a broken hip.

The Race for Cortisone

When Marker left Syntex, he took his know-how with him. Fortunately for Syntex, there still was no patent on his discoveries. George Rosenkranz left his native Hungary to study chemistry in Switzerland under the renowned steroid chemist Leopold Ruzicka, who was awarded the 1939 Nobel Prize in Chemistry.[29] On the day Pearl Harbor was attacked, Rosenkranz was in Havana waiting for a ship to Ecuador where the chair in organic chemistry awaited him at the University of Quito. The ship never showed. Rebuffed by the national university in Cuba, Rosenkranz took a job with a local pharmaceutical firm for $25 per week. Because of his success in developing new products, he was soon earning $1,000 per month and directing a research program with Ph.D. candidates from the university. He was also learning how to be a business man; for example, he organized the shark-fishing business in Cuba in order to produce vitamin A from shark liver oil.[30]

The Rosenkranz laboratory was following Marker's published techniques and making small amounts of progesterone and testosterone from sarsaparilla roots imported from Mexico. The news of this activity led to an invitation from Syntex to take over for Marker, with an option of buying 15 percent of Syntex stock, although the company was currently practically bankrupt.

Rosenkranz's task was complicated by Marker's secretiveness. He found reagents labeled with code words; Marker's workers identified solvents by their weight and smell.[31] Rosenkranz gave up on reconstructing Marker's process, and worked out his own commercial manufacture of progesterone and testosterone from Mexican yams, and soon Syntex was making large profits providing the sex hormones as raw material to other pharmaceutical companies. Rozenkranz

Photo staged for Life magazine — Rosenkranz with test tube of cortisone pointing to the Mexican yam; Djerassi in suit on the right.

now had a large active laboratory that attracted a young chemist, Carl Djerassi. These men knew each other, meeting and interacting with each other at the Laurentian Hormone Conference, the annual meeting organized and directed by Gregory Pincus.

THE DJERASSI FAMILY lived in Bulgaria for hundreds of years after escaping Spain during the Inquisition.[32] Carl Djerassi, the son of a Bulgarian physician, was born in Vienna, as was his physician mother. Djerassi, age sixteen, and his mother fled the Nazi Anschluss and emigrated to the United States in 1939. A Jewish refugee aid organization placed Djerassi with a family in Newark, New Jersey. With a scholarship to Tarkio College in Tarkio, Missouri, he was exposed to Middle America, where he earned his way giving talks to church groups about Bulgaria and Europe. His education was further supported

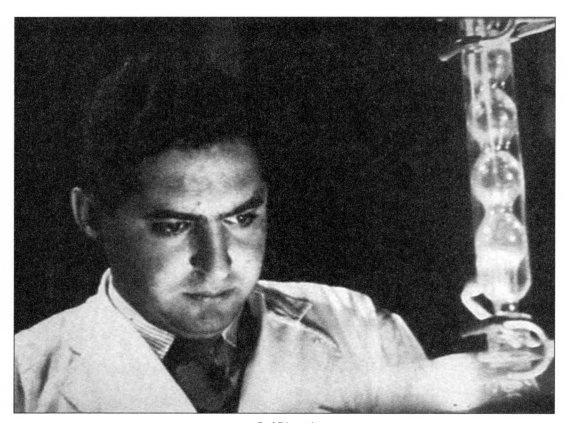

Carl Djerassi

by another scholarship from Kenyon College in Ohio, where he pursued chemistry. After a year working for CIBA, Djerassi received his graduate degree from the University of Wisconsin. Returning to CIBA and being somewhat unhappy, he responded to an invitation to visit Syntex. Rosenkranz proposed that Djerassi head a research group to concentrate on the synthesis of cortisone. Djerassi's initial reaction was that "the location of Syntex in the chemical desert of Mexico made the offer seem ludicrous."[33] But the twenty-six-year-old Djerassi, impressed by Rosenkranz and excited by the challenge to develop a method to synthesize cortisone, accepted the position and moved to Mexico City in the fall of 1949.

Earlier in 1949, Philip S. Hench, a Mayo Clinic rheumatologist, showed a movie at a medical meeting documenting crippled arthritic patients before treatment and the same patients active, even dancing, after daily injections with cortisone.[34] *Cortisone can be converted to the more active cortisol (also called hydrocortisone), the major product of the adrenal cortex. Cortisone is produced by hydroxylation, which converts the oxygen attached at the 11 position to a hydroxyl group by adding a hydrogen.*

Hench had obtained the very expensive cortisone through a biochemist at the Mayo Foundation, Edward C. Kendall, the discoverer of the thyroid hormone, thyroxine, who had been working with Lewis H. Sarett at Merck & Company to determine the structures of compounds isolated from extracts of the adrenal cortex and from cattle bile; cortisone was known as Kendall's Compound E. Hench reported good results in fourteen patients; his movie received a standing ovation,[35] and in 1950, Hench and Kendall were awarded the Nobel Prize in Physiology or Medicine. It was recognized that continuing regular treatment would be necessary, and the race was on to develop an easy and cheap method to synthesize cortisone and related drugs.

In Mexico City, Carl Djerassi was using the plant steroid diosgenin from the Mexican yam as the starting point. In two years time, Syntex achieved the partial synthesis of cortisone, reported in 1951.[36] The Syntex method never reached commercialization, however, because a more efficient process was developed by the Upjohn Company. Djerassi's productivity at Syntex, sixty publications, attracted a job offer from Wayne State University.[37] Wanting all along to be in the academic world, Djerassi moved to Detroit in January 1951. Five years later, he took a leave of absence to return to Syntex, now American-owned and a public company. Syntex's topical corticoid anti-inflammatory products, Synalar and Neosynalar, came from Djerassi's laboratory. Djerassi maintained his laboratory at Wayne State, and in 1959, when W.S. Johnson at Wisconsin moved to head the chemistry department at Stanford University, Djerassi joined him—a professorial position he held for the next twenty-five years.

The Upjohn Company and G. D. Searle & Company joined the competition to synthesize cortisone, with Upjohn, the bigger company, devoting over 150 scientists and technicians to the task.[38] Upjohn leadership assigned a symbol to represent the project, a blow torch, making it clear that this was a heated race they wished to win.[39] G.D. Searle was a smaller company, but its participation in this race would cement a long-term relationship with Gregory Pincus.

G. D. SEARLE was founded in 1888 by Gideon Daniel Searle, a pharmacist in Indiana, to provide elixirs, syrups, and drugs directly to clinicians. Searle's son, Claude, graduated from Rush Medical College in 1898 and developed a large, successful practice in Sabula, Iowa. In 1909, when his father suffered a stroke, the son returned to Chicago to manage the company, setting up a research department that developed new products. His son, Jack Searle, graduated from the University of Michigan with a degree in pharmacy, and succeeded his father as president of the company in 1936. He recruited Albert L. Raymond from the Rockefeller Institute to serve as director

of research, working in new laboratories in Skokie, Illinois. Dramamine, to prevent motion sickness, and Banthine, to treat peptic ulcers, came from these laboratories.

By 1949, Raymond and the G.D. Searle company were supporting steroid research at the Worcester Foundation for Experimental Biology, and Gregory Pincus was a Searle consultant.[40] Pincus and Oscar Hechter had developed a perfusion method, pumping blood, serum, or a serum-like solution through fresh endocrine glands (adrenal glands, testicles, or ovaries) held in a glass apparatus and collecting the perfused fluid. Using the enzymes in the glands, precursors in the perfusing fluid were converted to the final products, hydrocortisone or the sex steroids. This was a method that could be used to produce commercial amounts of cortisone products. Its development revealed the strengths of Pincus.

The round-faced, balding, acerbic Oscar Hechter came to Worcester in 1944 on a fellowship funded by G. D. Searle.[41] Pincus assigned him the task of perfusing adrenal glands, with the aim of identifying the products of adrenal secretion and the hope of creating a system for commercial production. It was five years of work, Hechter and two technicians moving "from one failure to another."[42] There were many things that had to be perfected: the surgical technique of obtaining the adrenal glands, the perfusion apparatus, methods to extract the steroids from the perfused serum, and measurement of the steroids. "Pincus permissively let me explore alternative problems but always drew me back to the problem of adrenal perfusion; he did this by persuasion and by personality. He had fantastic *persistence* and *faith*. … But perhaps most important, in the face of difficulty and uncertainty, he radiated serenity and confidence. Pincus acted as if there were no insolvable problems. And he had the art and power to transmit faith, confidence, and hope to others. If he had problems, worries, and fears—and I knew from other sources that his was a normal human quota—he never revealed them. He projected an image of a man who had freed himself from trivial matters and was indestructible."[43]

Five years later, Hechter presented the first positive results at a conference in Detroit in 1949.[44,45] At that same meeting, Hechter saw Hench's movie and listened to his results.[46] Hechter returned to the Foundation and urged that his project be given top priority. Pincus didn't say much, but the following week all nine of the chemists supported by Searle fellowships[47] were shifted to Hechter's perfusion system. As problems emerged, discussions were held by the entire group with Pincus as chairman. "Only Pincus remained, or appeared to remain, calm. He made few suggestions, listened, and then forced consensus. He consistently supported the innovators; when the new methods turned out to be right, the results obtained convinced the orthodox."[48]

This was no small achievement. The participants were aware fame and fortune might be had. Hechter remembered that "… competition and suspicions among the participants became almost intolerable. … It was a fantastic feat to coordinate the activity of a set of prima donnas, each hungry for fame and fortune. He [Pincus] achieved this by virtue of personality and an ability to use power. He had *charisma*, and this was the power which made it possible for him rapidly and effectively to translate a set of ideas generated by others into a finished scientific product."[49] Pincus often met with the group over lunch. One day he wrote to Al Raymond at Searle, "Today at lunch we calculated that the whale adrenal gland will weigh between 30 and 80 pounds. This means that from a single whale the equivalent of 1,000 cow adrenals is obtainable. Maybe you should start manufacturing on whale ships."[50]

Hechter recognized certain fundamental characteristics in Pincus: "His bulldog persistence, once he fixed a goal; his responsiveness to creativity in his associates, which was independent of personal relationships; his ability to compartmentalize his feelings for a man as a man and as the man as a scientist to a degree I have never seen before or since. … freedom (whether real or apparent) from emotional turbulence in the face of collective emotionalism; an ability to compromise to obtain a working consensus while keeping his goal clearly in mind."[51] He never said anything trivial. "In a complex discussion, he could penetrate instantly to the core issue involved, be it a matter of goal, issue, or strategy, chemistry, biochemistry, or biology. … He made promises infrequently, and then only when he could deliver."[52]

Goody's enduring relationship with Searle that yielded research support and new steroid compounds for almost never-ending testing began in earnest with the race for cortisone and his development of the perfusion system to use animal glands for the synthesis of steroid drugs. The perfusion system was complicated. It required the development of methods to maintain the animal organs, a web of glassware to infuse and collect appropriate perfusing solutions, and the separation and identification of the steroid products. At the moment of its coveted value in 1946, Pincus chose to sell his rights to Searle for only one dollar, allowing Searle to patent the process.[53] In return, Pincus obtained and tested steroids that could yield products for clinical use. In the 1950s, Goody exchanged seven to ten letters per month with Searle officials and attended monthly research

meetings in Skokie, Illinois, with about twenty-five Searle scientists.[54]

RESPONDING TO PINCUS AND HECHTER'S SUCCESS, the Searle company constructed rows of perfusion systems in their Skokie plant.[55] Each contained a periodically replaced fresh beef adrenal gland, producing every few hours a large volume of perfused solution. The long-term plan was to engineer a more economical and profitable system. But in the meantime, Searle was able to provide substantial amounts of cortisone to clinical researchers throughout the U.S.

At the same time, Merck ramped up Sarett's thirty-six step synthesizing process from bile acids,[56] and by the end of 1950, they were selling cortisone acetate to clinicians for a price that had been reduced from $200 per gram to $35. In Kalamazoo, Michigan, Upjohn chemists were pursuing a method based on the process used to make penicillin, conversion of precursors by microbes to the desired product.[57] The work was headed by Durey H. Peterson, the son of Swedish immigrants. Peterson supported his education by playing semi-professional baseball.[58] Early in his career, he developed nylon surgical suturing material as well as "Toni," a product for home permanents to create curly hair. Peterson joined Upjohn in 1946 to work on antibiotics, but he almost immediately became part of the race to synthesize cortisone. Peterson believed that lower microorganisms might possess the same enzymes used by adrenal glands to make cortisone, especially the difficult step of introducing an oxygen molecule to the structure. When told this could not be done, Peterson said, "The microorganisms do not know this."[59]

Using paper chromatography methods developed by Alejandro Zaffaroni, Peterson and H. C. Murray attacked the problem, beginning in 1949. First they needed a microorganism. This they acquired, a fungus of the *Rhizopus* species, by leaving an agar plate on the window sill of the "oldest and dirtiest laboratory at the Upjohn Company."[60] In one year's time, the two chemists proved the value of microorganisms in chemical synthesis. Their method used *Rhizopus nigricans* to covert progesterone to 11-hydroxyprogesterone, that could in turn be processed into hydrocortisone, also called cortisol, the major corticosteroid secreted by the adrenal cortex.

By 1955, Upjohn had become the market leader, and Searle shut down its perfusion cells and quit the race. Upjohn's commercialization of the methods developed by Peterson and Murray led to popular and successful products. But the Searle people had gained valuable experience that would eventually pay off with other synthesized hormones and products.

The Upjohn method used progesterone as the starting point, available in the early 1950s only from Syntex. George Rosenkranz's laboratory at Syntex was also pursuing the industrial synthesis of cortisone, and in July 1951, Syntex was about to sign a contract with a large chemical firm to begin production. This never happened because of a phone call. Rosenkranz told the story: "I received a phone call from Upjohn asking me whether we would be able to accept an order for ten tons of progesterone at forty-eight cents a gram."[61] The quantity was unheard of, and Upjohn's order remained a puzzle until the microfermentation method was published. Rosenkranz accepted the order, and Syntex found itself as the key supplier of progesterone to other companies.

The Synthetic Progestational Drugs, Norethindrone and Norethynodrel

Djerassi and other Syntex chemists turned their attention to the sex steroids. They discovered that the removal of the 19-carbon from yam-derived progesterone increased the progestational activity of the molecule. The clue for this work came from Maximilian Ehrenstein at the University of Pennsylvania, who reported in 1944 that a potent progestational compound he had produced appeared to be progesterone without its carbon at the 19 position; henceforth the 19-nor family of compounds indicated steroid chemical structures without the carbon atom at the 19 position.[62] Chemists at Schering A.G. in Berlin had produced orally active versions of estradiol and testosterone in 1938, by substituting an acetylene group in the 17-position of the parent compounds. The resulting ethinyl estradiol later became the estrogen component in oral contraceptives. The ethinyl testosterone product was known as ethisterone, marketed in 1941, and the Syntex chemists reasoned that removal of the 19-carbon would increase the progestational potency of this orally active compound.

Djerassi pointing to norethindrone, Zaffaroni on the left, Rozenkranz on the right

On October 15, 1951, norethindrone was synthesized at Syntex; the final steps were performed by Luis Miramontes, working on his undergraduate thesis in chemistry under Djerassi's supervision.[63,64] The patent application was filed six weeks later on November 22, 1951, and the work was presented in April 1952 at the annual meeting of the American Chemical Society and published in 1954.[65,66] The greater potency of norethindrone, achieved by removing the 19-carbon of ethinyl testosterone, compared with progesterone was demonstrated in monkeys and then four women at the National Institutes of Health, reported in 1953, 1956, and 1957.[67-69] Syntex supplied norethindrone to many investigators, including Gregory Pincus. Edward T. Tyler first reported its clinical use in 1955 for the treatment of menstrual disorders.[70]

Frank Colton, a chemist at G.D. Searle & Company, filed a patent for norethynodrel, a compound closely related to norethindrone, differing only in the position of the double bond, on August 31, 1953. The Polish-born Colton received his Ph.D. in chemistry from the University of Chicago. From 1949 to 1951, he was a research fellow working with Edward Kendall at the Mayo Foundation on the synthesis of cortisone. Colton joined Searle in 1951, along with Byron Riegel, to develop steroid drugs, succeeding with Nilevar, the first commercial anabolic agent marketed in 1956 and Aldactone, the anti-aldosterone anti-hypertensive agent introduced in 1959.

Norethynodrel was the result of a deliberate and planned program to create orally active agents with progestational activity. Later, Colton pointed out that although the Syntex and Searle chemists followed a similar path, they were independently pursuing the trail blazed by previous scientists.[71] Along the way, hundreds of compounds were sent to Pincus at the Worcester Foundation to test for ovulation inhibition in rabbits. Their best drug, norethynodrel, assigned the number SC-4642, was synthesized at Searle in a process that was considered to be significantly different from the Syntex method.[72]

Djerassi urged legal proceedings for patent infringement, claiming that norethynodrel was converted to Syntex's compound, norethindrone, by gastric acid, but Parke-Davis, the American company licensing norethindrone, did not want to make waves presumably because Parke-Davis was supplying the antihistamine component of Searle's best-selling product for motion sickness, Dramamine.[73] Pincus would ultimately choose the Searle compound, norethynodrel for clinical testing as an oral contraceptive, and Syntex, not having marketing capability, licensed norethindrone to other pharmaceutical companies. Norethindrone was tested as a contraceptive by Edward Tyler in Los Angeles and Joseph Goldzieher in San Antonio, Texas, but Parke-Davis chose not to pursue government approval, probably fearing religious reactions. Subsequently, Syntex turned to the Ortho division of Johnson & Johnson. By 1964, Ortho, Parke-Davis, and Syntex (now in California) were marketing oral contraceptives containing norethindrone or its acetate.

> The creation of norethindrone and norethynodrel by the chemists was essential in the development of oral contraception because the natural hormone progesterone is relatively impotent given orally, requiring very large doses that even then do not achieve a uniform response. The synthetic progestational agents are very active when administered orally, producing reliable effects with small doses.

A WALL STREET ENTREPRENEUR, Charles Allen, acquired Syntex in 1956 for $2 million cash and a loan of $2 million to be paid from future profits.[74] Rosenkranz became president and CEO, Alejandro Zaffaroni, an Italian who emigrated from Montevideo, Uruguay, executive vice president. Zaffaroni obtained his Ph.D. in 1949 in biochemistry from the University of Rochester, developing a paper chromatography system that soon became a principal method of studying steroid hormones.[75] Rosenkranz met Zaffaroni at the Laurentian Hormone Conference in 1951. Their aim was to develop a pharmaceutical company on a foundation of research. Carl Djerassi, who had left for an academic position at Wayne State University, was recruited back to the company. Rosenkranz said, "We were the brilliant amateurs with a 'can do anything' attitude. We were like stem cells (though then none of us really knew the concept). We could differentiate into anything we desired. Production, finance, sales, marketing—all held no fear for us."[76]

In 1961, the company moved to Palo Alto, California, influenced by Djerassi who was teaching at Stanford University. The growth of the company was meteoric, with blockbuster hits like Synalar, a topical corticoidsteroid for the treatment of psoriasis, and Naproxen, a nonsteroid, anti-inflammatory drug. Much of this success was to an innovative philosophy in the pharmaceutical business, "patent and publish."[77] The Syntex scientists were encouraged to promptly publish their results, gaining the peer recognition that is such a motivating force for basic scientists. In 1994, Roche Holdings acquired Syntex for $5.3 billion.

Djerassi eventually left Syntex to become a full-time professor at Stanford University, and is now a playwright and novelist living in San Francisco. Zaffaroni started his own company in 1968, ALZA (after his own name), dedicated to new methods of drug delivery, such as a skin patch. ALZA was acquired by Johnson & Johnson in 2000.

THIS WAS A LONG STORY, but one of inexorable progression as succeeding scientists built upon the discoveries and innovations that preceded them. It is remarkable that the scientists involved all knew each other, to a large degree because of their faithful attendance at Pincus's Laurentian Hormone Conferences. The supply problem was solved; orally active, potent progestational drugs were now available. The next stage in the development of an oral contraceptive would be the crowning achievement of Gregory Pincus.

CHAPTER NINE:

THE SAMURAI AND THE DOWAGER

On A WINTER EVENING, no one knows the exact date, in early 1951, forty-eight-year-old Goody Pincus and seventy-one-year-old Margaret Sanger met in the Manhattan apartment of Abraham Stone, in a meeting arranged by Stone.[1,2] Stone was currently the medical director and vice-president of the Planned Parenthood Federation. He and Sanger wanted to impress Goody Pincus with the urgent need to develop an effective method of contraception. They knew that because of his reputation and accomplishments in the field of reproductive physiology, Pincus was an excellent candidate to pursue this mission.

David Halberstam called Margaret Sanger an "American samurai."[3] She devoted her life to fighting for the right of women to control their own bodies. Inevitably, she clashed with organized religion, especially the Catholic Church. Her fundamental belief was that women needed to control their own bodies in order to control their lives, and this included the avoidance of unwanted pregnancies. She coined the phrase "birth control."

Maggie Higgins was born in September 14, 1879,

into a working-class Irish family with eleven children out of eighteen pregnancies.[4] She trained as a nurse in White Plains, New York, where at age twenty-two she met and married Bill Sanger, an architect and socialist. Ordinary life with their three children changed when the family moved to New York City. Margaret Sanger, working as a nurse among the poor, quickly became involved with left-wing politics and labor unrest in Greenwich Village, a setting that nurtured and provided an outlet for her ideas about sexuality, especially birth control.

In 1913 and 1914, Sanger's writings in a radical paper and seven mailings of her own newspaper, *The Woman Rebel,* ran afoul of the postal authorities enforcing the Comstock laws, laws pushed through Congress in 1873 by Arthur Comstock prohibiting the mailing of pornographic materials, loosely expanded to include anything dealing with sex.

The Prevention of Conception
By Margaret Sanger
The Woman Rebel, March, 1914

Is there any reason why women should not receive clean, harmless, scientific knowledge on how to prevent conception? Everybody is aware that the old, stupid fallacy that such knowledge will cause a girl to enter into prostitution has long been shattered. Seldom does a prostitute become pregnant. Seldom does the girl practicing promiscuity become pregnant. The woman of the upper middle class has all available knowledge and implements to prevent conception. The woman of the lower middle class is struggling for this knowledge. She tries various methods of prevention, and after a few years of experience plus medical advice succeeds in discovering some method suitable to her individual self. The woman of the people is the only one left in ignorance of this information. Her neighbors, relatives and friends tell her stories of special devices and the success of them all. They tell her also of the blood-sucking men with M.D. after their names who perform operations for the price of so-and-so. But the working woman's purse is thin. It's far cheaper to have a baby, "though God knows what it will do after it gets here." Then, too, all other classes of women live in places where there is at least a semblance of privacy and sanitation. It is easier for them to care for themselves whereas the large majority of the women of the people have no bathing or sanitary conveniences. This accounts too for the fact that the higher the standard of living, the more care can be taken and fewer children result. No plagues, famines or wars could ever frighten the capitalist class so much as the universal practice of the prevention of conception. On the other hand no better method could be utilized for increasing the wages of the workers.

As is well known, a law exists forbidding the imparting of information on this subject, the penalty being several years' imprisonment. Is it not time to defy this law? And what fitter place could be found than in the pages of the WOMAN REBEL?[5]

Indicted and facing trial, Sanger went to Europe and promptly had an affair with Havelock Ellis, a pioneer investigator and writer about sex.[6,7] About a year later, she returned to face trial because her husband had been arrested and convicted for distributing a birth-control pamphlet. Margaret's trial generated considerable publicity, most of it favorable, prompting the district attorney to drop the case.

Sanger's cause became respectable. Middle- and upper-class women—educated, prominent, and wealthy—enlisted in her campaign. A major speaking tour attracted crowds throughout the country despite threats from authorities and even an occasional arrest. Toward the end of 1916, Sanger and her sister opened the first American birth-control clinic in Brooklyn. They were arrested ten days later, and the two women spent thirty days in prison. But the arrests backfired, bringing publicity and support.

Sanger's battle changed from a personal radical crusade to a public debate and social struggle in 1921 after New York City police carried her out of Town Hall before she could speak at a conference on birth control. By 1925, her Sixth Annual Conference on Birth Control attracted more than a thousand physicians. The prescient Sanger realized that enlisting the medical profession in her cause would be important. Physicians were attracted by the notion that only doctors could provide diaphragms. They would create a powerful political ally that could not be ignored.

Sanger took on the Comstock laws. "I bumped up against this very, very, arrogant, old-fashioned stupid law. … I decided the best way to change it was to break it."[8] In 1931, Sanger's mail order of Japanese diaphragms tested the Comstock laws, and the court ruled that the laws were out of date and inappropriate considering the current understanding and need for contraception. Because of Sanger, it was now legal to sell contraceptive devices through the mail.

In 1920, Sanger founded the American Birth Control League. In 1939 the League merged with the Birth Control Clinical Research Bureau to form the Birth Control Federation of America, which in 1942 became the Planned Parenthood Federation of America. The change from a radical cause to a middle-class movement was aided by a shift from an emphasis on individual benefits to the widespread impact on social health.[9] An important part of Planned Parenthood's philosophy has always been the relationship between poverty and unregulated fertility.[10]

Abraham Stone, born in Russia in 1890, came to the U.S. when he was fourteen years old.[11] He was a urologist who became focused on marriage counseling and family planning, probably because of his marriage to Hannah Mayer in 1917. Hannah was also a physician, a close friend of Sanger, and the medical director of the Margaret Sanger Research Bureau in New York City. Although officially a research arm of the American Birth Control League, the Bureau also functioned as a clinic. Hannah was arrested in 1929 when the police raided the Bureau. The Stones provided marriage counseling at the Community Church in New York. Their very popular 1935 book, *A Marriage Manual: A Practical Guide-Book to Sex and Marriage,* was one of the first books published on marital relations. After Hannah's death in 1941, Stone succeeded his wife as medical director, and eventually became the overall director of the Bureau, now known as the Margaret Sanger Center, expanding its services and becoming the research site for the Planned Parenthood Federation. He became known and admired worldwide for his educational efforts.

The night Pincus and Sanger met in New York City, Stone picked up an old medical journal and said, "Let me read you something Hannah and I wrote fifteen years ago—a sort of prescription. 'The ideal contraceptive still remains to be developed. It should be harmless … entirely reliable … simple, practical, universally applicable, and aesthetically satisfactory to both husband and wife.'"[12] Stone explained that he had invited Pincus to New York to meet Sanger, who for many years had promoted contraceptive research, and to tell him that a small amount of money was available from Planned Parenthood to develop something new. Finally, he asked, "How about it? We can put in a little money.

Will you put up your brains and time?"[13] Pincus smiled and said, "If both of you hadn't talked so long, I'd have said yes twenty minutes ago."[14]

The coveted goal was sexual intercourse without procreation, a method of contraception that would be completely separated from coitus and a method that would be acceptable to nearly all individuals. Stone's adjectives were pertinent for both clinicians and patients: harmless, reliable, easy, simple, aesthetic. A hormonal method was not a new thought. In 1937, Raphael Kurzok, an obstetrician-gynecologist on the faculty at Columbia University, emphasized that sex hormones inhibited ovulation in animals and called for human studies.[15]

The day after the meeting in Stone's apartment, Pincus was driving home, realizing that the $3,100 from Planned Parenthood for 1951 and $3,400 for 1952 would be just a start.[16,17] The money provided $1,000 for Chang and $2,100 for rabbits and supplies.[18] He estimated he would need an additional twenty to thirty thousand dollars for just the first year. It was on this long drive that Pincus supposedly compared the need for contraception to the absence of ovulation associated with the hormones of pregnancy and resolved to test the ovulating-inhibiting properties of progesterone. He reached the Foundation near closing time and gathered Hudson Hoagland and M-C. Chang for a conversation that lasted into the evening.

Gregory Pincus — 1950s

Margaret Sanger knew the level of funding provided by the Planned Parenthood Federation was insufficient, and she turned to Katharine McCormick. In March 1952, she wrote McCormick asking her if she had heard of Pincus's research. In May 1953, McCormick moved from Santa Barbara back to her home in Boston and arranged with Roy G. Hoskins, now a trustee of the Worcester Foundation, to meet Pincus. On June 7, 1953, McCormick, Sanger, and Hoskins' wife visited the Worcester Foundation, and McCormick wrote Pincus a check for $20,000, a level of funding that grew with each rewriting of the Pincus budget.[19] For the rest of her life, McCormick gifted the Foundation from $110,000 to over $150,000 per year, plus periodic contributions for new buildings and laboratories.

Katharine Dexter McCormick

Katharine McCormick was a trained biologist,

an early suffragist, and rich, inheriting millions from her mother and a McCormick fortune from her husband. Her intervention with money, energy, incisive thinking, and persistent dedication was instrumental in the development of oral contraception.

Katharine Dexter was born in 1875, the second and last child of a successful attorney in Chicago.[20] Her great-grandfather served as U.S. Senator and secretary of war under John Adams and of the treasury during the presidencies of Adams and Jefferson. Her grandfather moved to Michigan after his graduation from Harvard in 1812. He founded the town of Dexter, published a newspaper, served as chief justice in the county court, and helped found the University of Michigan. Her father married Josephine Moore, a school teacher from Springfield, Massachusetts. He was a leader in the rebuilding of Chicago after the Great Fire. After Dexter died of an early heart attack, Josephine moved to Boston, into a home at 393 Commonwealth Avenue, across

Katharine Dexter in a laboratory at MIT

the river from the Massachusetts Institute of Technology (MIT).

When Katharine was nineteen years old, her older brother Sam died of spinal meningitis, leaving her as an only child. She and her mother left for an eighteen-month healing trip in Europe. In the small town of Nyons, near Geneva, they discovered the Château de Prangins on Lake Geneva. Josephine purchased the estate from the French Government, which had built the chateau as a summer resort for its royalty; its last occupant twenty years earlier was Joseph Napoleon. Katharine would use the chateau for most of her life, finally donating it to the U.S. government to house employees working at the United Nations headquarters in Geneva.[21]

Against her mother's wishes, strong-willed and independent Katharine intended to be a scientist or a surgeon. She prepared for three years as a special student at MIT to take the entrance examinations. By now, she was fluent in French and German, and had learned Italian. She entered MIT in 1899 and graduated in 1904 with a major in biology, the second female graduate of MIT and the first woman with a degree in science. Her senior thesis was entitled "Fatigue of the Cardiac Muscles in Reptilia."[22] During her student years, she became involved with college women in Boston affiliated with the suffragist movement.

Stanley McCormick, a varsity tennis player at Princeton, courted Katharine during her last year at MIT. McCormick was the son of Cyrus McCormick, the founder of the International Harvester Company. McCormick invented the reaper, a steel cutter and collector of grain, on his father's plantation in Virginia. He patented his invention in 1834, and sought a location for a factory that would be closer to American grain production. In Illinois he found that grain could not be harvested before it decayed within four to ten days because of a lack of laborers. He built his first factory on the mouth of the Chicago River, and by 1860, he was making over 4,000 reapers a year. McCormick was the first to use extensive advertising and to back his product with an unconditional, money-back guarantee.

Katharine's relationship with Stanley McCormick was stormy during the courtship and it became even more difficult after their marriage. Stanley's family was complicated, struggling with multiple behavioral aberrations.[23] Stanley's tyrannical father ignored the children, but his religious, obsessive mother filled Stanley's space. Two children died after birth, three had complex lives involving psychotherapy, and Stanley's schizophrenic sister was hospitalized for most of her life. Stanley was a quiet, introspective young man attracted to artistic life, but he was expected to enter the family business. He was smothered by his mother and unsuccessful during his multiple attempts to work for International Harvester. Indecisiveness, nervousness, and anxiety attacks repeatedly forced him to escape his family and the business world. On one such escape in 1903, an automobile tour of New England, thirty-year-old Stanley encountered twenty-eight-year-old Katharine.

Stanley followed Katharine back to MIT and began an intensive courtship with visits and daily letters. Katharine found him wanting because of his lack of self-confidence and gloomy attitude. Right from the beginning, Stanley's sister and mother did not accept Katharine. Three times Katharine agreed to marriage, and three times she broke the engagement. She was bothered by Stanley's behavioral problems, but unaware of the depth of his mental conflicts. She finally became convinced that away from his family, she could provide the loving attention and guidance that would make a successful marriage. Much later, she would regard her marriage as an "unfortunate venture."[24]

Stanley and Katharine married in 1904 in Nyons, the hometown of the Dexter family chateau on Lake Geneva. This was not to be a happy marriage. Later in life, Katharine completed a series of intensive sessions that lasted nearly a year with a psychoanalyst. She was prompted to do so, not by mental problems, but by her scientific desire to know herself as well as she could. During the sessions, she revealed that the only time the couple had sexual intercourse was early during the honeymoon, and even then she didn't believe that Stanley ever experienced an orgasm.[25] Stanley's impotence reflected his mental illness, his inner conflicts with his mother, and his disturbed reaction to a period of masturbation when he was in college.

Stanley's emotional, erratic behavior escalated. He was diagnosed and hospitalized with schizophrenia only two years after the marriage. In 1908, Stanley was placed on an estate purchased in Santa Barbara, California, cared for by a live-in psychiatrist, servants, gardeners, and musicians, and he was declared legally insane. From this time on, Katharine dressed formally with gloves and a fancy, large hat, but always in the fashion of the period of her marriage, with hemlines that reached the ground.

Katharine was committed by her own sense of obligation to be Stanley's guardian, and the years became filled with conflicts and turmoil, constant bickering and fighting with Stanley's family. Negotiations came to require lawyers and courts for nearly forty years. The description in Katharine's biography reads like a riveting novel.[26]

To help fight her battles, Katharine selected a lawyer she came to know during the suffragette struggle. Newton D. Baker, Jr., was a progressive politician serving as mayor of Cleveland, Ohio, from 1911 to 1915, and as secretary of war under Woodrow Wilson from 1916 to 1921. He returned to Cleveland and his private law practice; the law firm he founded, Baker Hostetler, is today one of the nation's largest. When Baker had a sudden heart attack and died on Christmas day, 1937, his partner, William H. Bemis, assumed Baker's professional relationship with Katharine, an association he maintained until her death in 1967. Bemis always addressed her as "Mrs. McCormick," as did everyone else.[27] Both lawyers were Katharine's staunch allies and personal confidantes in her fights with the courts and the McCormick family, her negotiations regarding the complex tax obligations of her inheritances, and her philanthropic activities.

While her husband was alive, expenditures from the estate had to be approved by the Chicago probate court, limiting Katharine's ability to support her interests with gifts. In 1937, Katharine inherited $10 million, largely Dexter family

Katharine McCormick — about 1910

real estate properties in Chicago and Michigan, when her mother died. Two years later Katharine moved to Santa Barbara to be near Stanley. For over a decade, Katharine maintained her interest in contraception, but from the periphery and with periodic donations to Margaret Sanger and Planned Parenthood.

Stanley McCormick never recovered and died of pneumonia at age seventy-two in January 1947. Katharine McCormick had to fight the McCormick family for control of her husband's estate, worth an estimated \$35–\$40 million, but after five years, assisted by Walter Bemis, she won the legal battle. Fortunately, a probate court clerk discovered in Stanley's safe deposit box a valid will written on a single sheet of hotel stationery dated the day after his marriage, bequeathing his entire estate to his wife.[28]

Katharine McCormick became involved in the woman's suffragette movement in 1909, serving as the treasurer and vice-president of the National American Woman Suffrage Association, later

Katharine McCormick — about 1915

to become the League of Women Voters. She worked for the ratification of the Nineteenth Amendment and with the International Suffrage Alliance. Her family's chateau on Lake Geneva hosted many suffrage meetings as well as the 1927 World Population Conference organized by Margaret Sanger. Sanger's conference failed to influence the League of Nations, but did result in the formation of the International Union for the Scientific Study of Population, the first international association of demographers.[29]

Katharine first met Sanger in 1917, and was one of the many travelers returning from Europe who smuggled diaphragms into the U.S. for Sanger's Research Bureau.[30] It has been argued that McCormick's awareness of inadequate birth-control methods was influenced by her husband's illness; she worried over the possibility of genetic transmission.[30] She began her active involvement with the birth-control movement in 1921, spurred by her presence in the audience when the police carried Margaret Sanger out of Town Hall in New York City. After the suffragette campaign, she was ready for another commitment involving women's rights. In 1923, she was one of twenty-six U.S. delegates to Sanger's Fifth Annual International Birth Control Conference in London.

Margaret Sanger repeatedly corresponded with Katharine regarding contraceptive research beginning in 1928. For about twenty years, their correspondence voiced concern over the prospects for scientific development of an effective method of birth control. They became good friends, and in Sanger's last years, her medical expenses were paid by Katharine.[31]

Katharine McCormick provided considerable funds in a search for a cure of schizophrenia, and this brought her into contact with the Worcester Foundation for Experimental Biology. She established the Neuroendocrine Research Foundation in 1927 at Harvard to explore the relationship of mental illness to the function of the adrenal gland, under the direction of Roy G. Hoskins.[32] The Worcester State Hospital was the site for the clinical research, and in the 1930s, Hudson Hoagland collaborated with Hoskins in treating schizophrenics with adrenal steroids. The Neuroendocrine Foundation moved to Worcester in the 1940s, and Hoagland became the director.

The Neuroendocrine Research Foundation closed after Stanley McCormick's death in 1947. Even though the Foundation's efforts proved unsuccessful, Katharine maintained a high regard for Hudson Hoagland. "One day in the early 1950s, she burst into Hoagland's office demanding to know, 'What are you going to do about it?' Hoagland, eager to encourage a potential donor, assumed she wanted to know about the progress of his schizophrenia work and began to outline a plan of research in the biology of madness, only to be informed that McCormick did not mean *that* problem, but the impending world population crisis! Happily he could call in another expert, Gregory Pincus, to explain what the Foundation needed in order to push forward on population control. One of Katharine's remarkable characteristics was that she was an avid reader of scientific journals, and she already knew about Pincus's work. Apparently her stop at Hoagland's office was just a courtesy call."[33]

M-C. Chang recalled that "In 1950 ... Pincus accompanied two ladies, Mrs. Margaret Sanger and Mrs. Stanley McCormick, on a visit to my laboratory. I remember quite vividly that, after I told them what I was doing, one of the ladies remarked to me, 'I do envy you working in the laboratory; you must have lots of fun.' I answered her rather abruptly, 'Sure enough, but I hope it can be useful!'"[34] What a picture the two women must have presented. Sanger, four years younger, was a slender, small woman full of energy. The older Katharine was taller in size and stately in bearing, but no less intense. Neither one had the time or patience for trivial issues or inconsequential talk.

After Stanley died, half of the estate was liquidated to pay federal inheritance taxes. For this purpose, five residences were sold, including the mansion in Santa Barbara, California, where Stanley was cared for with a staff that included forty gardeners and six musicians.[35] With inheritance taxes almost settled, McCormick wrote to Sanger in October 1950 inquiring about prospects for contraceptive research. "Where do you think the greatest need of financial support is today for the National Birth Control Movement; and what are the present prospects for further birth control research, and by research I mean contraceptive research."[36] Sanger recommended a gift of $100,000 to the National Research Council's new Committee on Human Reproduction. But Katharine discovered that she was saddled with new taxes and could not make this commitment. The Committee folded.

By 1951, with Stanley's estate settled, Katharine was ready to renew her efforts. Pincus had reported to the Planned Parenthood Federation that injections of progesterone in rabbits effectively inhibited ovulation. Inexplicably, the administrators in the Planned Parenthood Federation in the New York office were not excited over Pincus's prospects.[37] This surprised Katharine McCormick and both she and Sanger rapidly became disheartened with the New York office. William Vogt, the director of the New York Planned Parenthood office, thought McCormick's gift of $50,000 for a new animal house at the Worcester Foundation was an unnecessary expenditure.[38] McCormick visited the New York office and left disappointed in the lack of vision and planning.

The Planned Parenthood Federation was struggling with its mission. In 1952, John Rockefeller III financed the founding of the Population Council, a nonprofit organization dedicated to population research. A conference on population problems convened by Rockefeller in June 1952 led to the formation of the Population Council five months later. Frederick Osborn, a demographer, was appointed president, and Warren Nelson, professor of anatomy at the University of Iowa, with a focus on male reproduction, assumed the important position of medical director. A research unit was established under the supervision of Sheldon Segal.

In 1953, Paul Henshaw, Director of Research for the Planned Parenthood Federation of America, was reaching out to Pincus in letters and in personal meetings, promoting the idea of clinical studies under the auspices of Planned Parenthood.[17] However, with the increased activity of the Population Council in research, the New York officers believed that Planned Parenthood should concentrate on education and service clinics.[39] McCormick wrote to Sanger, "It appears to me that no one there ... is really concerned over achieving an oral contraceptive and that I was mistaken originally in thinking they were."[40] McCormick, therefore, chose to deal directly with the Worcester Foundation.

On June 7, 1953, when seventy-eight-year-old Katharine met with fifty-year-old Pincus at the Worcester Foundation and wrote him a check for $20,000; she promised him another $20,000. A week later, Pincus and Hoagland met with Katharine and her lawyer, William Bemis. They signed a contract outlining the goals, the decision-making process, and the timetable.[42] Pincus received a second check for $20,000, and Katharine agreed to fund laboratory improvements, which ended up as the completion of a new building in 1955. She even moved back to Boston to be closer to the action.[43]

Initially most of the funds from Katharine to the Worcester Foundation were routed through the Planned Parenthood Federation,[44] but by 1956, the Planned Parenthood Federation no longer had an active role in the work on an oral contraceptive, a status supported by Pincus who knew that Planned Parenthood had a clause in their grant awards giving them control over patents that might result. Thus Searle could patent the specific steroids developed in its laboratories and used for contraception, and not fear loss of control in a conflict with Planned Parenthood. In fact, Pincus did not encourage McCormick to make her gifts directly to the Worcester Foundation until Searle began supporting Pincus with both drugs and research grants.[45]

Katharine's contract with the Worcester Foundation stipulated that Pincus would provide written reports every two weeks. In addition, Pincus and John Rock, the Boston gynecologist performing the initial oral contraceptive studies in his patients, made many visits to Katharine's home office on Beacon Street across the street from the Harvard Club. Katharine had Miss Sara De Laney, her secretary, take careful notes in shorthand, and at the next visit De Laney read the transcribed notes to her boss so that she would be prepared. Lizzie Pincus described Katharine McCormack: "She was tall and carried herself like a ramrod. Little old woman she was not. She was a grenadier."[46] John Rock said "She was rich as Croesus. She had a vast fortune. Her lawyer told me she couldn't even spend the interest on her interest."[47]

Periodically the principals met at the Worcester Foundation. Katharine peppered Pincus, Chang, and Rock with questions and urged them to stop wasting time. She found Pincus "imaginative and inspirational; Rock was informative and very realistic about medical work."[48] By now everyone was familiar with Katharine's methods. She had earned their respect, and detailed reports on laboratory results, clinical planning, and budgets were immediately forthcoming. Time and time again, Katharine proved that she handled delays poorly, but she approached each meeting with an eagerness that slowly but surely was rewarded with success after seven years and an expenditure

of about $2 million of Katharine's money.

Occasionally, Katharine had dinner with other guests at the Pincus house. Anne Merrill remembered that she "wasn't at all highfalutin. She would drink in public but wouldn't eat in public. So, she was free to talk the whole time. She was delightful and she was telling jokes all the time."[49] They weren't really jokes, but amusing stories from her own experiences. One time she told of traveling to Europe when she was about eighty years old and taking some birth control pills to give to someone. "She put them in something like a box of crackers, and the custom men dumped them out and said, 'What are these?' She said they were birth control pills. They said, 'Good for you, lady!'"[50]

In her last years, Katharine continued to support the work of Pincus and Chang. When testing the hundreds of compounds that yielded the progestational agents in birth control pills, Chang observed that some of them prevented implantation of fertilized eggs in rabbits.[51] From 1962 to 1966, Chang and Pincus were pursuing a drug that could prevent pregnancy with one administration, a day or two after sexual intercourse.[52] With Pincus's death, this project was abandoned. It is not certain whether Chang and Pincus coined the phrase the "morning after" pill, but it is accurate to state that the concept came from Chang. Today the method is available, and it is called emergency contraception, an important method for women to be considered when condoms break, sexual assault occurs, if diaphragms or cervical caps dislodge, or with the lapsed use of any method.

When Katharine learned that a major reason for the enrollment of only a few women at MIT was the lack of on-campus housing, she offered to pay for a female dormitory. It took a while for MIT to get used to her methods. She was there for every planning meeting and for the meetings of the building committee. Stanley McCormick Hall was dedicated on October 7, 1963. Katharine presided at weekly teas for the students; the invitations stipulated that hats were required, gloves were optional. She was amused when the students appeared in a variety of fancy hats and gloves that included baseball gloves, oven mitts, and rubber gloves.[53] A second wing was dedicated a year after Katharine's death.

Dedication of Stanley McCormick Hall at MIT — October 7, 1963

When ninety-two-year-old Katharine McCormick died in her sleep on December 28, 1967, four months after Pincus died, her will provided $1 million to the Worcester Foundation and $5 million to the Planned Parenthood Federation of America, which created the Katharine Dexter McCormick Library in New York City.[54] In addition, she provided $5 million to Stanford to assist women seeking a medical degree.

Katharine's biographer, Armond Fields, said that "Katharine Dexter McCormick was in every sense a pioneer on behalf of women's rights. The many examples of her organizational abilities were remarkable and groundbreaking. If inclined to be single-minded and rigid, she nevertheless possessed an unflagging integrity, an overarching intelligence, and a singular gift for 'getting things done.' She knew all too well the price she paid to crusade for women's equality. Yet she possessed boundless courage and an unshakable belief in her goals. And she never stopped fighting."[55] Katharine McCormick was a woman who probably never had a satisfying sexual experience, and yet she devoted herself to women's rights and a woman's method of contraception. She recognized that her commitment to the needs of women was a means for personal fulfillment and identification.[56]

Hudson Hoagland recalled, "A few weeks before Mrs. McCormick died in 1967 at the age of ninety-two, I visited her in her Boston home, and she said she wanted to thank us for having made it possible for her to spend her money on something so very worthwhile to her as the pill. As one who has begged often in vain for money to support research, it was a new experience to hear our generous benefactor thank us for enabling her to give us two million dollars."[57]

The First Oral Contraception Studies in Massachusetts

Pincus knew that sex steroids could inhibit ovulation, an effect in animals that had been reported many times in the scientific literature since 1900.[58] The current understanding of the hormones involved in ovulation, an outstanding example of biological complexity, is reviewed in the Appendix, emphasizing the vulnerable hormonal communications between the brain and the ovary that allowed the development of oral contraception.

As early as 1932, Pincus had demonstrated inhibition of ovarian growth and development by the injections of an estrogenic extract into young rats.[59] Now Pincus's success depended on the development of orally effective progestational agents, as described in Chapter 8. Pincus was at the focal point of two converging forces: the chemical advances leading to oral progestins and the growing need for new and effective contraception. *When Pincus and Chang began their studies, the focus was on inhibition of ovulation, first by progesterone, and then by synthetic progestins.*

The combination birth control pill, consisting of estrogen and progestin components, is given daily for three of every four weeks. The combination pill prevents ovulation by inhibiting the secretion of the gonadotropins, follicle stimulating hormone (FSH) and luteinizing hormone (LH), the hormones secreted by the pituitary gland that stimulate the ovary. The progestational agent in the pill primarily suppresses LH secretion (and thus prevents ovulation of an egg), while the estrogenic agent suppresses FSH secretion (and thus prevents the emergence of a growing follicle that contains an egg). Therefore, the estrogenic component significantly contributes to the contraceptive efficacy. However, even if follicular growth and development were not sufficiently inhibited, the progestational component usually (but not always) prevents the surge-like release of LH necessary for ovulation.

The estrogen in the pill serves two other purposes. It provides stability to the endometrium, the lining of the uterus, so that irregular shedding and unwanted bleeding can be minimized; and the presence of estrogen is required to increase the action of the progestational agents. The latter function of estrogen has allowed reduction of the progestational dose in the pill. The mechanism for this action is probably estrogen's effect in increasing the concentration of intracellular progestational receptors. Therefore, a minimal pharmacologic level of estrogen is necessary to maintain the efficacy of the combination pill.

Because the effect of a progestational agent will always take precedence over estrogen (unless the dose of estrogen is increased many, many-fold), the endometrium, cervical mucus, and perhaps tubal function reflect progestational stimulation. The progestin in the combination pill produces an endometrium that is not receptive to ovum implantation, a uterine lining with exhausted and atrophied glands. The cervical mucus becomes thick and impervious to sperm transport. It is possible that progestational influences on secretion and peristalsis within the fallopian tubes provide additional contraceptive effects. Even if there is some ovarian follicular activity and an egg is made ready for ovulation (especially with the lowest-dose products), these actions serve to ensure good contraceptive efficacy.

CHANG'S CONTRIBUTION was easy to overlook. Chang worked away in his laboratory, and it was Pincus who was highly visible, raising the money and providing direction.

Chang started by repeating the experiments reported by Makepeace in 1927, documenting that progesterone could inhibit ovulation.[60] "For the records, the first experiment I did was on April 25, 1951. The first paper was written by Gregory Pincus with my name as junior author and was published in 1953," on the effect of progestational drugs on ovulation in the rabbit.[61,62] Chang, perhaps because he was riled to be the junior author, saved the letter Pincus had written after reviewing Chang's notes and data:

July 14, 1953

Dear Chang,

Enclosed is the manuscript of a paper constructed from your data. I thought it best to confine this paper to certain types of compounds only. Others that you have tested really belong in a different class, and I want to investigate some of them more intensively. Please let me know if you think this is satisfactory.

I do hope you are enjoying yourself. [Chang was at Bar Harbor, Maine, that summer] With very best wishes to you and the family, I am

As ever,

Gregory Pincus[63]

In Chang's first experiments, ovulation was inhibited in rabbits receiving 5 mg or more of progesterone. Rats get pregnant quicker, within a few days, and it didn't take long to confirm the effect of progesterone in rats.[64]

In October 1951, Pincus asked Searle's director of research, Albert L. Raymond, to direct Searle's attention to contraception. Pincus was already testing progestational agents supported by the grant from the Planned Parenthood Federation of America, and knew he needed much more funding. But Raymond was skeptical. He complained that Searle's investment in Pincus had yielded nothing. Pincus was distraught. He traveled to Chicago for a personal meeting with Raymond, and later that night wrote an emotional letter on The Stevens Hotel stationery:

Dear Al,

Since sleep escapes me I will try to set down what I think is a fair summary of what you said to-nite as we were driving around. You said: "You haven't given us a thing to justify the half-million that we invested in you (except Alidase, which is a minor item), and the responsibility for this failure is yours. I have cooperated in every way possible, but you have given me data on animals which Winter doesn't trust, and have suggested clinical experimenters who have either proven that your particular pet compounds have no clinical utility or who have wasted time and money. I think that the "profile" study of compounds in patients is probably another such futile waste of money, but I have, because of your wish for it, acquiesced in it. There is, to be fair, still some chance that we may find a utility for the lactones and that the perfusion process will prove useful. But to date your record as a contributor to the commerce of the Searle Company is a lamentable failure, replete with false leads, poor judgment, and assurances from you that were false. Yet you have the nerve to ask for more for research. You will get more only if a lucky chance gives us something originating from your group which will make us a profit. If I had unlimited funds I would undertake a large program in the steroid field, but I do not have such funds and the record to date does not justify a large program."

Taking this as it stands, and attempting to assess it, I feel that the moral is plain. There should be, from a business point of view, no need for further support of a person with such a record. The chances of an eventual recoupement from our few discoveries depend upon factors which are out of my hands. You have the lactones and by adequate clinical trial can ascertain if they in fact have any utility. The mechanics of the perfusion process are yours and you may proceed to the production of materials and their clinical trial. If you wish even to follow the few leads we have presented for synthetic work you have all our ideas and could have adequate personnel for their working out.

I want you to know that I have indeed been embarrassed at the failure to see a paying result. I have done what I could, but it is obviously in your view no good. My attempts have led me into a situation which is rather difficult. First of all my earnings have barely kept pace with the increase in cost of living. I have refused other possibilities in the hope that I might repay the Searle Co. by hard and diligent work. But now at a time when I am just about at the peak of productive activity I see my wife buying $6.95 dresses the way she did when we were first married; she does her own housework despite the fact that she is no younger. And if I were to die I would leave my family not too well provided for. If I were permitted to resign I think I could obtain several consultantships which would aggregate enough to ameliorate this situation.

Furthermore, I have made myself responsible for the employment of a group of workers under your grant. I believe that I could place them elsewhere at this time when the demand for workers in the steroid field is large. I do not think that I can go on with them much longer at the present pay rates — only a loyalty to me and a love of their work has kept them so far.

You realize that this is an attempt to be impersonal, and I need scarcely say that my feeling for you personally is as steadfast and warm as is possible for me. Indeed it is because I feel that you are personally subjected to pressures on my account that I would like to see them withdrawn. I am troubled as to how to do so to your satisfaction. I need your honest counsel, and when I see you again, I'd like very much to have it.

Yours, Goody[65]

Fortunately, Katharine McCormick's support allowed the work to continue. Pincus wrote to all the pharmaceutical companies known to be involved in hormone synthesis requesting progestational drugs to be tested. In the fall of 1953, Chang and Pincus directed the efforts of their team of assistants in testing about 200 compounds in rabbits and rats.[66,67] The Searle chemists, Frank Colton, Byron Riegel, and Albert Raymond, had been pursuing the goal of orally active progestins for about a year. By December, 1952, animal testing by Francis J. Saunders had identified two of the compounds provided by their chemists, norethynodrel and norethandrolone, as potent progestins, in time to respond to Pincus's request.[68] Norethindrone was available from Syntex; Roy Herz had already demonstrated its oral potency in monkeys and women.[69-71]

By December 1953, three synthetic progestins were selected as the most potent and effective in inhibiting ovulation: norethindrone from Syntex, and Searle's norethynodrel and norethandrolone. In 1957, these three compounds were approved for the treatment of menstrual disorders with the trade names of Norlutin, Enovid, and Nilevar, respectively.[72]

The animals used for Chang's experiments were housed in the basement of the main building, the house on the old estate. The space was small, and ventilation was a problem. New laboratories and animal facilities became available in 1955, constructed mainly with funds provided by Katharine McCormick. At first the structure was known as the McCormick Building,[73] but today it is designated as the M-C. Chang Building.

Throughout the 1950s and into the 1960s, Chang's laboratory tested hundreds of Searle compounds for hormonal activity, at the rate of about eight per month.[74]

Pincus summarized the work to date in 1956.[75] He carefully acknowledged his coworkers in Worcester and at the Free Hospital for Women in Brookline, pointing out that in publishing this summary, he was acting as spokesman for the entire group. He detailed the effects of progesterone administration in rabbits and rats, and provided the data from the initial

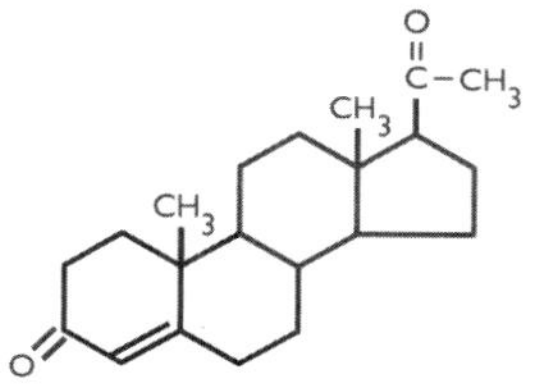

PROGESTERONE

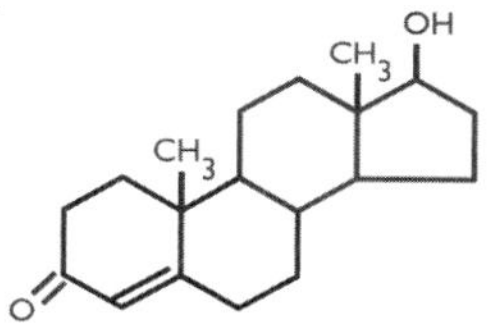

TESTOSTERONE

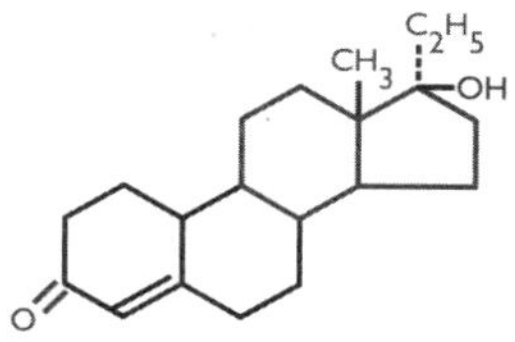

NORETHANDROLONE

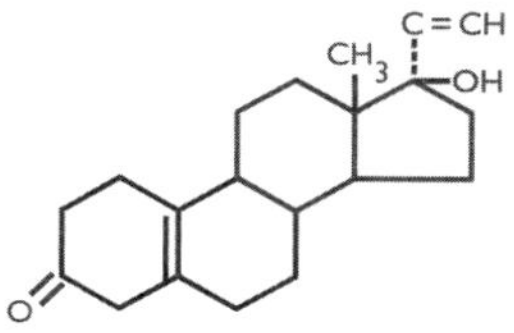

NORETHYNODREL

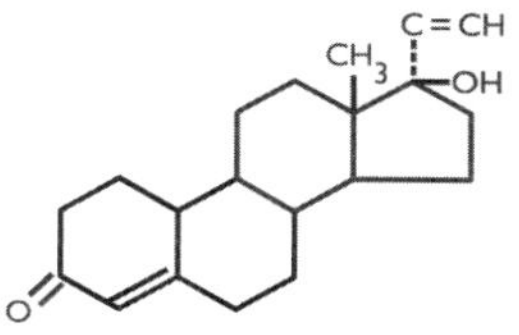

NORETHINDRONE

progesterone studies in women with temperature curves, bleeding patterns, uterine biopsies, vaginal smears, and the measurement in urine of pregnanediol, a metabolite of progesterone. Ten women underwent surgery for infertility, and the presence of corpora lutea, evidence of ovulation, was documented in each (absent in five of the ten women). Four of the women became pregnant after the treatment was discontinued. Pincus then listed fifteen compounds other than progesterone found to inhibit ovulation in the rabbit. From this experience and further testing in rats, norethindrone and norethynodrel emerged as the most potent agents. Relatively high doses of these two progestins, 40 mg of norethindrone and 20 mg of norethynodrel, were each administered to four women. Pincus concluded there was a rough consistency between the animal and human data, but obviously more human testing would be required.[76]

The reports in *Science* by Pincus, Chang, and Rock in 1956 were immensely gratifying for Katharine McCormick.[77,78] She wrote to Margaret Sanger, "I have been very moved and excited over the articles. They are the opening gun in the coming campaign."[79] The animal work was summarized in the scientific journal *Endocrinology* in 1956, but only Planned Parenthood and G.D. Searle & Co. were acknowledged for their grant support.[80] It is unlikely that this bothered Katharine McCormick; she was only interested in results.

The three compounds, norethindrone, norethynodrel, and norethandrolone, were tested in collaboration with John Rock on fifty volunteer women, who although they were ovulating were infertile, for one or more treatment cycles.[81-83] Rock was assisted by Celso-Ramón Garcia and Luigi Mastroianni who would later become chairman of obstetrics and gynecology at the University of Pennsylvania. Mastroianni recalled, "I don't really think I sensed the true significance of what was being done. But I remember the patients vividly and all the people involved in the progestin work. The concept of informed consent that is so talked about now, and is a legal requirement of any research project involving human volunteers, didn't exist then. But Rock practiced it before it was ever defined. There were always long and large discussions of the risk factors. It didn't matter that Rock had no formal guidelines, he set his own and they were high standards, indeed."[84] The progestin doses varied from 5 mg to 50 mg orally given from days five through twenty-five of each cycle. Not one woman ovulated during a treatment cycle, and seven women became pregnant after treatment. Further study determined that the best bleeding results were obtained with a combination of 10 mg of either norethindrone or norethynodrel and a small amount of estrogen.[85]

John Rock was invited in 1956 to present the complete results of this first human study of the new progestins on his fifty volunteers to the famed Laurentian Hormone Conference, which he proceeded to do so with every recorded detail.[86] His presentation emphasized data on tissue effects and patient reactions, down-playing the contraceptive angle. Rock didn't believe it was time to emphasize contraception and stir a religious response.[87] He was careful to point out that Celso-Ramón Garcia had performed "three-quarters of the clinical work . ..."[88]

The first discussant after the presentation was Edward T. Tyler, one of the first to study the new synthetic progestational drugs, who told the audience that he and Pincus had been discussing why Tyler's results measuring pregnanediol excretion, a urinary metabolite of progesterone that would indicate ovulation had occurred, differed when compared to the values reported by Rock, Garcia, and Pincus.

> Dr. Pincus and I discussed this until 2 A.M. last night tying to determine why I failed to find pregnanediol excretion decreased and why his findings showed a consistent decrease. He finally came up with a solution that was so simple I wondered why I hadn't thought of it myself. His explanation was simply that my results were all wrong![89]

Robert B. Greenblatt, a prominent reproductive endocrinologist, stood to say, "One fact which stood out in this study is that Dr. Rock has unwittingly given us an excellent oral contraceptive which may be employed with little untoward effect."[90] In his reply, Rock avoided any mention of contraception, even though he knew very well that a clinical trial had begun in Puerto Rico, as detailed in Chapter 11.

George S. Richardson, a physician at Massachusetts General Hospital, later remembered what happened that evening:

> Rock professed that he was bored with the whole idea of the regular banquet. This may have been a deliberate move on his part to escape from any discussion of oral contraceptives, but it was characteristic of Rock to seek and find what he called "superior forms of entertainment." Without much difficulty he persuaded a group of us to join him. ... At a neighboring establishment, we found just about the only other person in the dining room was a young man eating by himself. Rock proceeded to bear down on this young man in his usual manner—that of an actor trained in Shakespearean roles and drawing room comedies. Like everyone else who has ever been confronted with this affable and yet grandiose presence, the young man

was soon giving his personal psychological and sexual history. Before he knew it, Rock had persuaded him to join us and go on to another resort.

At our next place there was not only a bar but also a capacious dance floor, which we all proceeded to enjoy under Rock's leadership. After cutting in one couple, Rock came back with a detailed report of the sexual problems that these honeymooners were having and his recommendations, which were sure to "clear the whole thing up." His attempt to treat other honeymoon couples in similar fashion was soon modified by his discovery that many of the people were, as he put it, "ladies and gentlemen of pleasure." After all of us—and mostly Rock—enjoyed ourselves hugely, we returned again at breakneck speed to the Lodge. Those who were still talking science on the lawn under the stars were regaled by our evening's finale—the sight of our party plunging nude into the swimming pool. [91]

WHEN THE FIRST ARTICLES were published in *Science* in 1956, Sanger wrote to McCormick, "You must, indeed, feel a certain pride in your judgment. Gregory Pincus had been working for at least ten years on the progesterone of reproductive process in animals. He had practically no money for this work and Dr. Stone and I did our best to get a few dollars for him and I think that that amount we collected went to pay the expenses of Chang. Then you came along with your fine interest and enthusiasm and with your faith and ... things began to happen and at last the reports ... are now out in the outstanding scientific magazine and the conspiracy of silence has been broken." [92]

But Goody Pincus knew the road ahead was still long. A decade later, Pincus reflected about the role of an investigator in contraception research.

Although the physiologist has generally been called upon to undertake research which might lead to easily effective and acceptable means of birth control, his role is indeed a much wider one. The modern-day investigator cannot be satisfied with the invention of a "cunning device." The present accumulated knowledge concerning reproductive processes indicates that the production of gametes, their transport and mating, their fusion, and the fate of the fertilized egg involves an intricate and delicately balanced set of sequential events. Interfering with this sequence at any of a large number of stages may have physiologic consequences that are not apparent on the surface. The research worker is therefore compellingly motivated to arrive at as complete an understanding as possible of the processes involved in the great act of reproduction. Furthermore the understanding which the physiologist seeks must be imparted to others ... .

Under the ivory tower conception of scientific research, much of the foregoing is irrelevant. More simply stated, the job of the scientist is to undertake experimentation and to publish the results of such experimentation. What happens thereafter is allegedly not his business. This concept has been dealt demoralizing blows, particularly during and since World War II. The rapid transition from the research laboratory to the worldwide application of significant discovery has demanded the attention of the scientist to two consequences of his activity. First of all, there is the need for training of fellow scientists, of students, of embryo research workers, of public health servants and so on. Willy-nilly the investigator has had to be also an educator. Secondly, chiefly because of the public alertness to scientific discovery, the research workers' talents have been invoked not only to help in making sure that the public is properly informed and not grossly misinformed, but also to consider questions of policy that are inevitably raised with the application of scientific discovery.[93]

CHAPTER TEN:

JOHN ROCK: A CATHOLIC PROPONENT OF CONTRACEPTION

THE EARLIEST HUMAN STUDIES of oral contraception were supervised by Gregory Pincus's clinical colleague, John Rock. David Halberstam described Rock as " a powerful presence, a doctor of great distinction and originality whose own work and social ideas were taking him ever closer to the work of Pincus and his team. 'If you went to doctors in New England in those days' said Oscar Hechter, 'and asked who was the best obstetrician in the region, you would almost surely be told that it was John Rock—he was a formidable figure.' He was also a man of singular independence. Rock's courage was admired by both Hoagland and Pincus, but they knew he was a brilliant clinician as well, not merely a theorist as they were. … Rock was a man whom they would have invented had he not lived, a bridge from their world of the abstract to a world of real people with real medical problems."[1]

John Charles Rock was born on March 24, 1890, minutes ahead of his twin sister.[2] The Rocks of Marlborough, Massachusetts, were descendants of an emigrant from Northern Ireland. John Rock was the most religious member of his family, faithfully attending the Immaculate Conception Church in Marlborough. Rock left Marlborough during high school, to live on his own in Boston and attend the all-boys Commerce High. After graduating from high school, he worked for a few years as an accountant, an experience that convinced him that he was not cut out for a business life.

Supported by his father, Rock enrolled at Harvard, lettered in track, and performed with Hasty Pudding, the nation's oldest theatrical company, where Rock surely learned techniques that later in his life made him an excellent teacher and an effective communicator. Rock finished his undergraduate courses in three years, and three years later, in 1918, he graduated from Harvard Medical School. Rock completed his training in obstetrics at the Boston Lying-In Hospital and in gynecology at the Free Hospital for Women. In 1922, he was appointed to the faculty at Harvard Medical School, and two years later established a new clinic for infertility at the Free Hospital for Women.

Rock, age thirty-five, married twenty-nine-year-old Anna Thorndike, the daughter of Rachel Sherman, daughter of Tecumseh Sherman, and Paul Thorndike, the chief of urology at Boston City Hospital. Anna grew up in Boston's high society with an independent spirit, majoring in mathematics at Bryn Mawr and driving a Red Cross ambulance in France during World War I. Anna's father sent the couple to an old friend, Cardinal William O'Connell, Boston's archbishop, for a pre-marriage consultation.[3] Cardinal O'Connell married them on January 3, 1925, after solving a last-minute crisis. The day before the wedding, Rock delivered several women by cesarean sections, a method forbidden at that time by the Catholic Church, upholding the belief that pain at childbirth was the price of Eve's fall from grace. Rock's local priest refused to give Rock absolution, a requirement before the wedding. At the wedding rehearsal that evening, Anna's mother explained the problem to Cardinal O'Connell who immediately provided absolution on-the-spot.

The Rocks looked alike. Anna was six feet tall and weighed a compact 180 pounds; John Rock was slim, impeccably dressed, always with a tie or ascot, never an open shirt, and carried his six-feet-one-inch height with a perfectly straight posture. From 1925 to 1933, the couple had five children, and the family lived on Rock's earnings; potentially inheritable estates had been directed to others or used up. Rock never did become wealthy. Good enough to play in tournaments, Anna earned some extra money teaching bridge in her home.

IN THE 1930s, Rock began to draw the ire of the Catholic Church. He was the only Catholic among fifteen Boston physicians who signed a petition in 1931 asking for the repeal of the Massachusetts law forbidding birth control, even teaching about it. In 1936 at the Free Hospital for Women, he opened a clinic to teach the "rhythm" method of birth control, the method that timed intercourse to avoid the fertile period in each monthly cycle in order to avoid pregnancy. Rock said, "I separated biology from theology quite early in my life and never confused them again."[4]

John Rock

The rhythm method, also called natural family planning, depends on periodic abstinence. The method must take into account the viability of sperm in the female reproductive tract, two to seven days, and the lifespan of the egg, the ovum, one to three days. Because of the variability in the timing of ovulation, the period of abstinence must be relatively lengthy. The period of maximal fertility begins five days before the day of ovulation and ends on the day of ovulation. The probability of conception plummets the day after ovulation; however, conception occasionally occurs more than six days before ovulation or immediately following ovulation. Adherence to this method requires commitment from both partners; it becomes a way of life. Unsuccessful use can be predicted in couples who are unable to part with sexual spontaneity, women with irregular menses, disorganized people who cannot keep good records, and because changes in cervical mucus are used to detect the fertile period, women with chronic problems of vaginal or cervical infection that could affect the secretion of normal cervical mucus. If used perfectly, the method is very effective, but the method is extremely unforgiving of imperfect use. Typical use of this method today is associated with a failure rate of about 25 percent per year.

In 1949, Rock and David Loth, director of public information for the Planned Parenthood Federation of America, published *Voluntary Parenthood*.[5] This was a book directed to the public, and it was a remarkable book for the times. In a very readable style, the book clearly and intelligently discussed subjects that were not talked about publicly. The first sentence in the book said, "A blueprint of the knowledge which civilization has been able to amass on the subject of having and raising a family resembles reality about as closely as a mediaeval map of the world resembles a modern globe."[6] The book articulated Rock's philosophy of family with an emphasis on providing the maximal education and opportunity for each child. It provided a history of contraception and explained in detail the use of barrier methods and the rhythm method of contraception.

Rock was a work in progress. Initially a traditional conservative, "He argued against the admission of women to Harvard Medical School and often told his own daughters that he did not think women were capable of being doctors."[7] In his mid-forties, he began to teach contraception to Harvard medical students. He began to fit some of his patients with contraceptive diaphragms. Rock continued to attend daily mass, but he was now concerned about overpopulation, and he began to promote small families.[8] Rock was a firm believer in the Malthusian Hypothesis.

Thomas Robert Malthus, an English political economist, published six editions of his famous book, *An Essay on the Principle of Population*, between the years 1798 and 1826. The Malthusian

WORLD POPULATION

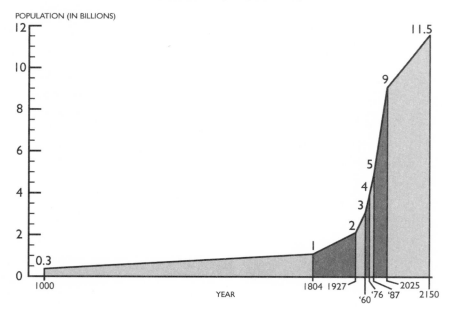

Hypothesis can be expressed very simply: the human population will outgrow the world's resources needed for its support. Malthus argued that population could be controlled only by a high death rate or a low birth rate. But because he didn't approve of birth control, he concluded that a high death rate would be necessary, caused by misery, in the form of wars, famine, and disease, and vice (contraception was in this category, along with murder). Without misery and vice, overpopulation, therefore, would lead to poverty, an animalistic competition for food, and a general loss of civilization. Even a century later, this dim prospect was a major motivating factor in the drive for effective contraception, as expressed by John Rock and the Planned Parenthood Federation.

The Malthusian Hypothesis has been resurrected in recent times. There is a growing awareness that our planet is running out of clean air, potable water, and specific agricultural and mineral commodities. Optimists look to the power of technology and human creativity to solve this Malthusian problem, but the acute need for effective contraception cannot be ignored.

Contraception is a universal requirement, both in the developed world and in developing countries. In the U.S. approximately half of all pregnancies are unintended, resulting in births that are unwanted and an induced abortion rate that is higher than desired. These are problems that add to the consequences of excessive consumption of resources in affluent societies.

It wasn't until after World War II that the problem of a growing world population began to be widely appreciated and contraception's role in population limitation emphasized. Since then, effective contraception has become commonplace in the developed parts of the world. The world population is expected to stabilize at between 11 and 12 billion around 2150, with a fertility rate of 2.1 children per woman.[9] Today, the fertility rate is less than 2.1 children per women in China, Eastern and Western Europe, North America, Japan, Australia, and New Zealand. In 2001, the fertility rate in the U.S. reached a low of 2.03. Approximately 96 percent of the population growth now occurs in developing countries, so that by 2100, 13 percent of the population will live in developed countries, a decrease from the current 25 percent. Some time after 2020, *all* of the growth in global population will occur in developing countries. An estimated 120 million married women in developing countries are not receiving needed contraception.

The control of population growth is a special challenge in the developing world. The 76 percent of the world's population living in developing countries account for: 85 percent of all births, 95 percent of all infant and childhood deaths, and 99 percent of all maternal deaths.

The ability to regulate fertility has a significant impact on infant, child, and maternal mortality and morbidity. A pregnant woman has a 200 times greater chance of dying if she lives in a developing country rather than in a developed country. The health risks associated with pregnancy and childbirth in the developing world are far, far greater than risks secondary to the use of modern contraception. To meet the projected growth in the world's population, the number of women using family planning will need to increase substantially; for example, 40 million more women in India will need to use some method of contraception! At the same time, the socio-economic need for large families must be addressed, reducing the need for the support provided by a family's children. When John Rock was practicing medicine, however, the impact of contraception had yet to be experienced in the U.S., and Rock was one of the few academic clinicians to perceive the need.

IN 1944, after surviving the first of the six heart attacks that he would endure, Rock gave up obstetrics. By then he was being recognized as a clinical scholar, attracting young physicians from all over the world to work with him. Besides maintaining his full gynecologic practice, Rock formulated questions and answered them. What is the purpose of menstruation? How can the time of ovulation be pinpointed? After adoption, do couples have an increased chance of a spontaneous pregnancy? (The answer is no, infertile couples do not get pregnant at a greater rate after adoption.) At the same time, he was perfecting techniques to treat infertility amenable to surgery. He refined the procedure of artificial insemination with frozen sperm. And in his seventies, Rock was treating women with new fertility drugs.

Beginning in the mid-1930s, Rock began to collect eggs from the ovaries of his patients undergoing surgery. These were the Harvard days when Pincus was establishing himself as an expert on mammalian eggs. For a time, Miriam Menkin, who would spend many years as Rock's assistant and collaborator, worked with Pincus. Rock would send ovarian tissue from Boston to Cambridge where Pincus tried without success to collect viable human eggs.[10]

Later, with careful timing, Rock would succeed in providing fertilized eggs to Arthur Hertig, the pathologist at the Free Hospital for Women. It required fourteen years to collect thirty-four fertilized eggs from 210 women who were undergoing surgery and didn't know they were pregnant.[11] The award-winning, published descriptions of these eggs in the 1950s are an enduring classic, and now, with the availability of sensitive pregnancy testing, an exercise likely to never be repeated.[12]

Arthur Hertig recalled, "In the first place, he was fun to work with. He was always excited about what he was doing and that kind of animation was infectious for all of us. The whole problem with fertility and infertility was a big thing and we had a sense that what we were doing was really important. I thought it was great fun to work under him. He was enthusiastic and stimulating and outgoing. He had true charisma."[13]

In 1944, after six years of trying with nearly 800 isolated eggs and 138 eggs exposed to spermatozoa, Rock and Menkin successfully achieved the fertilization of three human eggs in vitro.[14] They used an incubation technique developed by Pincus when he was at Harvard working with rabbit eggs. Every now and then, Pincus and Menkin would talk about the work over the telephone. The published report was highlighted by newspapers throughout the country.

FOR OVER A DECADE, before their collaboration on oral contraception, Pincus and Rock knew each other and shared their research experiences. Rock believed that some cases of infertility were due to a lack of development of the uterus and perhaps the fallopian tubes, and that pharmacologic hormone supplementation would correct this problem; it is now known that this is not a cause of infertility. Rock offered eighty of his infertile patients an experimental treatment. For three months they ingested large doses of diethylstilbestrol, a synthetic and very potent estrogen, and progesterone. After suffering with the drug-induced and exaggerated traditional symptoms of pregnancy, thirteen of the women became pregnant within four months after discontinuing treatment, prompting Rock to believe in his hoped-for "rebound" reaction.[15]

In 1952, forty-nine-year-old Pincus and sixty-two-year-old Rock attended the same scientific conference and were soon exchanging their latest thoughts.[16] Pincus suggested that Rock try progesterone without estrogen. In April 1953, Pincus asked Paul Henshaw, research director of the Planned Parenthood Federation, to invite Rock's participation in the study of progestational agents for contraception.[17]

In their first collaborative study, Pincus and Rock administered oral progesterone, 300 mg per day. Pincus suggested a twenty-day regimen beginning on day five of the menstrual cycle.[18] He had two reasons for choosing this regimen: (1) it covered the time period during which nearly all, if not all, ovulations occurred, and (2)

John Rock

the withdrawal menstrual bleed at the conclusion of the treatment period would mimic the timing of a normal menstrual cycle and reassure the women that they were not pregnant. The first study involved thirty-three volunteers who ovulated regularly but had been infertile for two years. The women were treated for one to three cycles after a baseline control month. About 85 percent of the treated women did not ovulate during the treatment cycles.[19] Not one became pregnant during treatment, pleasing Pincus who all along was aiming for contraception, and four became pregnant after treatment, pleasing Rock who initially was motivated by his pursuit of the "rebound" phenomenon for the treatment of infertility.

Pincus presented these results at the Fifth International Conference on Planned Parenthood in Tokyo in 1955, as described in the Prologue. It was immediately apparent that progesterone had disadvantages. The required dose was very large, ovulation occurred in some cycles, and breakthrough bleeding during the days of treatment was experienced in 18 percent of the women. While this study was in progress, Pincus and Chang were completing their laboratory investigations of synthetic progestational drugs (Chapter 9).

Pincus and Rock realized that what was needed was an orally active, inexpensive progestational agent that could be administered in small doses. In September 1953, Pincus requested from the major hormone-producing companies samples of their progestins for him to test in the laboratory and clinically in collaboration with Rock. Pincus overcame Margaret Sanger's objection that Rock "would not dare advance the cause of contraceptive research and remain a Catholic."[20] Katharine McCormick also argued that Rock's religion would not interefere. Finally, Sanger admitted, "Being a good R.C. and as handsome as a god, he can just get away with anything."[21]

"When the Pill first came out, Rock received an angry letter from a Catholic woman who excoriated him for his role in its development. She told him, 'You should be afraid to meet your maker.' 'Dear Madam,' he wrote back, 'In my faith we are taught that the Lord is with us always. When my time comes, there will be no need for introductions.'"[22]

UNLIKE GOODY PINCUS who died relatively young, at the peak of his career, John Rock had to endure his wife's fight with cancer, attempts to excommunicate him from the Catholic Church, and worries over insufficient income. Practicing physicians and clinical professors in the field of obstetrics and gynecology, including myself, who were aware of and had great respect for Rock's academic stature, were repeatedly surprised to learn of his meager finances. In the last years of his professional life, his beloved alma mater, Harvard, turned its back on him.

John Rock was appointed to the Harvard Medical School faculty in 1922. He practiced obstetrics at the Boston Lying-In Hospital and gynecology at the Free Hospital for Women and the Massachusetts General Hospital. As Rock's reputation grew, his practice focused mostly on infertility. Beginning in the mid 1950s, Rock's office and outpatient practice were on the grounds of the Free Hospital, in a building remodeled and enlarged from 1955 to 1957 by funds from Katharine McCormick. This building at 77 Glen Road housed the Rock Reproductive Clinic with clinical care on the first floor, research space and a laboratory on the second floor, and a record room and library on the third floor. But, Rock found it increasingly difficult to obtain money for research and to support young doctors wishing to train under him. Rock dipped into his own funds, which were limited to begin with, to pay for his research and his assistants.

After his wife died of cancer in 1961, Rock rented out the downstairs part of his home in Brookline, and lived on the third floor. Then he sold the house and lived in his clinic building. Rock shared the proceeds from the sale of his house with his daughters. One used the money to buy a small house with nine acres of land in Temple, New Hampshire, later purchased from her by her father and where Rock would live the last thirteen years of his life.

Rock hoped that Harvard would take over his clinic and maintain its name in perpetuity.[23] But it was not to be. In 1966, the Boston Lying-In and the Free Hospital merged into the Boston Hospital for Women. Budget problems, disagreements over Rock's successor, and Harvard's covetous eyes on Rock's patients all conspired to bring the Free Hospital and Rock's clinic under Harvard's control. Rock was evicted from his own clinic at the end of 1966.[24] Three years later, in 1969, Rock sold his practice to a young colleague. His retirement pension from Harvard was only $75 per year; his social security income amounted to about $4,000 per year. Fortunately and appropriately, G.D. Searle came to Rock's rescue, continuing to provide a stipend of $12,000 per year to serve as a research consultant, evaluating data from the oral contraceptive studies. In 1972, Rock, now eighty-two years old, retired to his farmhouse in New Hampshire, only a two-hour drive from Boston.

CHAPTER ELEVEN:

THE CLINICAL TRIALS IN THE CARIBBEAN

GREGORY PINCUS was a basic scientist most of his life. He had no training in clinical medicine or clinical investigation, but his intelligence and common sense allowed him to effectively transition from the laboratory to the requirements and nuances of clinical studies. Pincus had been thinking all along about the questions that had to be answered by a clinical trial of oral contraceptives:

Would women not motivated by their infertility, like Rock's patients, and who simply wanted contraception be willing to take a regimen of pills?

Would women choose pills over other contraceptive methods?

Would women adhere to the pill-taking regimen for many months, even years?

Would women without higher education be able to follow the pill schedule?

What would be the consequences of skipping a pill, or several pills?

What would be the rate and pattern of side effects, and how would this affect continuation?

Would there be any serious side effects, adverse effects on general health and body function?

Would the method be appropriate for all women or would there be a group of

> women who should not be allowed to use the pills?
>
> Would fertility return promptly and at a normal rate after many months of use, and would the children subsequently born be normal?

But these questions could not be answered in Massachusetts; contraception in Massachusetts was illegal until 1973! Years later, John Rock observed that "It must have amused some citizens of the Commonwealth of Massachusetts, with its rigid law against birth control, to discover that the first breakthrough in contraceptive technology in seventy-five years suffered and survived its labor pains in the environs of Worcester and Boston."[1]

Pincus needed a general population of women of all educational levels in an area where contraception was not illegal. The women of Puerto Rico struggled with a high birth rate and low socio-economic conditions, and the island location ensured that few would be lost to follow-up in a clinical trial. Puerto Rico was close enough to allow efficient transportation of personnel and biologic specimens for laboratory testing. Pincus decided to go to Puerto Rico.

Pincus visited Puerto Rico in February 1954, lecturing on steroid hormones.[2] He was the guest of a colleague from the earliest days of the Worcester Foundation, David Tyler, who was now the chairman of the department of pharmacology at the University of Puerto Rico. Goody had time to talk with local public health physicians about birth control, and he learned enough to convince himself that a clinical trial would be possible in Puerto Rico. This was two years before the effects of the new oral progestins in animals were published in *Science;* Pincus was obviously thinking ahead. As soon as Pincus returned to the U.S., he consulted with John Rock and secured his agreement. In addition, Katharine McCormick, their principal funder, was kept informed of all particulars with written reports and during the frequent visits to Katharine's home by Pincus and Rock, and during Katharine's meetings at the Worcester Foundation. Katharine kept Margaret Sanger up-to-date with detailed letters every week or two.

Katharine's letters were mostly typed by her personal secretary, but occasionally she wrote in longhand, on plain paper that, although unruled, contained her sentences in perfectly straight and uniform lines with elegantly formed letters that had flat bottoms as if she held a ruler on the paper as she wrote. Her letters were always formally signed "Mrs. Stanley McCormick;" however, above that title she would write "Katharine Dexter McCormick" or "K.D. McCormick."[3] When Katharine left Boston, especially for travels to Europe, Pincus was not free of his obligation to communicate. Katharine wrote, "I shall be interested to know of any developments in our vital research program, and I hope you will not hesitate to write me if any problems arise with which I can be of assistance, or if you have any suggestions for changing or improving the research program we have discussed."[4]

THE FIRST STUDY in Puerto Rico was aimed at determining the optimal dosage of progesterone. Pincus obtained a plentiful supply of progesterone from Chemical Specialties, the New York subsidiary of Syntex. Moving rapidly, Pincus and Tyler planned the design of the clinical trial during the summer of 1954. Government, hospital, and medical school officials pledged their enthusiastic support, and Pincus even obtained a promise of cooperation from the Mayor of San Juan.[5] Pincus concluded that the clinicians he would have to work with were well-trained and trustworthy. For those who struggled with their Catholic consciences, the initial project was to be billed as a study of the physiology of progesterone in women.

Problems cropped up immediately with the initial four-month pilot study. The Puerto Rican study director resigned his academic position less than two months after traveling to Worcester to talk with Pincus and Rock. But this turned out to be a stroke of good fortune. The project was reassigned to the department of obstetrics and gynecology, and the chief clinical investigator would be Celso-Ramón Garcia.

The second problem proved to be more serious. The medical school faculty intended to recruit subjects for the study from patients, hospital staff, and students, but entering and retaining women in the study proved difficult. By March 1955, only twenty-three women had entered the study; three months later only thirteen were still enrolled. The study made great demands on the participants. It required a daily morning temperature, a daily vaginal smear on a glass slide, a forty-eight-hour urine sample once a month and a biopsy of the lining of the uterus once a month. Those who remained in the study often failed to fulfill the requirements. Out of desperation, Tyler went so far as to threaten the female medical students with poor grades.[6]

The pilot study struggled; recruitment failed. Only one medical student volunteered, and not a single nursing student agreed to join the study.[7] The research staff even tried prisoners at the Women's Correctional Institute; this too failed. E. Harold Hinman, the dean of the medical school, decided that the project would have to be dropped, and unused funding was returned to Pincus.[8,9] Out of this came a conflict between the dean and David Tyler that would last several years. Tyler finally left Puerto Rico and eventually went to work as an administrator for the National Science Foundation in Washington, D.C.

This delay turned out to be fortuitous, giving time for Chang's animal experiments to demonstrate that the synthetic progestational agents, norethindrone and norethynodrel, were the most effective of the tested drugs in preventing pregnancy. Indeed, Chang's work was so successful, that Pincus insisted on reporting the results in October 1955, at the Tokyo meeting of the International Planned Parenthood Federation, despite Rock's objections. Rock worried quite appropriately that the results were preliminary, and that a meeting of birth control advocates was not the best forum for a presentation. Rock's

hesitancy later gave way to enthusiasm when norethindrone and norethynodrel seemed to work very well in a small number of his patients. Margaret Sanger and Katharine McCormick eagerly supported Pincus, urging him to go to Tokyo. Expenses for Pincus, Chang, and their wives were provided by McCormick, but Isabelle Chang had just delivered their second son and didn't go.[10-12] Travel and expenses to Japan for Goody and Lizzie came to $6,193.78.[13] Even Pincus's daughter Laura went to Tokyo, taking a break from college and working for Planned Parenthood as a typist.

Katharine told Pincus, "Dr. Pincus, it is time to begin our campaign to make it known what we are

Goody and Lizzie, Passport Photos —1955

doing."[14] A week before the meeting, Margaret Sanger was giving enthusiastic, but imprudent, interviews that were printed in American newspapers, stating that Gregory Pincus had almost perfected an oral contraceptive that can be eaten like candy, a discovery that "may revolutionize the world."[15]

AROUND THIS TIME IN 1955, efforts to speed up oral contraceptive development produced plans to start studies in Japan and the Margaret Sanger Clinic supervised by Abraham Stone in New York City.[16] Neither study got off the ground. Stone, funded with $5,000 from Katharine McCormick, gave progesterone and later norethynodrel to only a small number of women at the Margaret Sanger Research Bureau in New York.[17] Despite trips to multiple cities in Japan by Pincus in 1955 and 1959, great interest on the part of Japanese scientists and academicians, and spirited encouragement from Katharine McCormick, the Japanese Ministry of Health and Welfare effectively blocked development and approval of oral contraception. Condoms and abortion remained the main methods of family planning in Japan until oral contraceptives were approved in 1999.

Pincus began to give the new progestational drugs to male and female mental patients at the Worcester State Hospital. By 1957, Pincus had administered norethynodrel to seven psychotic women and a combined estrogen-progesterone regimen to five patients, studying the effect on their menstrual cycles, ovulation, hormone excretion in the urine, hormone levels in the blood, and the lining of the uterus.[18] Two years later, some of the patients had been under study for three years. Norethynodrel was also administered to psychotic men, measuring urinary hormone levels and obtaining testicular biopsies. Never published, the results were presented at a symposium held at the Searle Research Laboratories in 1957. Until he died, Pincus continued to perform research studies with patients at the Worcester State Hospital, assessing the metabolic effects of dozens of Searle compounds, and even giving paid volunteers lysergic acid diethylamide (LSD) to see if hormones would counter the effects.[19] The studies were funded by Searle and Katharine McCormick. It is unlikely that similar clinical experiments could be performed today.

Searle officials were still uncomfortable with any publicity at this stage. But statements from various presentations about the development of an oral contraceptive, such as those at the Searle Symposium in 1957, did appear in newspapers. John Rock mollified Irwin Winter, Searle's Director of Clinical Research, "I daresay, if the dreadful screed does Searle any harm, which I pray it will not, the company will live through it, too. I'm sorry it caused you any discomfort."[20]

These projects were all funded by Katharine McCormick. In mid-1956, $49,400 was directed to the laboratories at the Foundation and to John Rock, $12,870 for expenses in Puerto Rico, and $13,930 for the studies at the Worcester State Hospital—a total of $76,200 funneled through the Worcester Foundation.[21,22] Only $1,000 was assigned as salary support to Pincus, which increased to $4,000 in 1960.[23] A year later, the total annual expenditure from McCormick grants increased to $114,121; Rock and Garcia were now receiving almost full salary support, $12,000 for Rock and $10,000 for Garcia.[24,25] By 1959, Katharine was providing $115,000 to $140,000 per year.[26,27] As the years went by, Katharine was joined by others in funding. The 1965 budget for all Worcester Foundation projects in reproductive physiology, not just the clinical studies in the West Indies, totaled $391,296, divided among the following sources (It should be noted that only a small percentage came from the pharmaceutical industry):[28]

Katharine McCormick	$125,300
American Cancer Society	$95,250
The Population Council	$70,942
Andre Bella Meyer Foundation	$40,000
G. D. Searle	$31,304
Mrs. James Faulkner	$25,000
Ciba Pharmaceutical	$3,500

Research grant support is always given in response to a detailed, written application that describes a specific project with a budget that provides only for that project. Katharine McCormick's support was unique. She was always open to negotiations for alterations, a change in direction, or a request for additional funds. Pincus was very much aware of this fortunate and exceptional arrangement. He repeatedly expressed his gratitude to Katharine, pointing out that "We continue to depend upon the special latitude which your grant gives us for what might be termed the basic program in fertility control research."[29]

Pincus could foresee the feasibility of an oral contraceptive, and he urged Searle to support the project.[30] Francis Saunders, chief chemist at Searle, opposed this direction, arguing that any drug that interrupted the normal cycle would prove unacceptable for use by healthy women. Pincus countered that the three-week regimen allowed menstruation, that doses were relatively low, although in retrospect they were not, and that Rock, a respected academician and clinician, would not be supportive of a treatment if he considered it dangerous or unacceptable. Searle agreed to proceed and to provide the drugs, but requested Pincus to avoid publicity.[31] Fortunately, Katharine McCormick was part of the team.

When a budget was proposed for the next period of study, a simple nod of Katharine's head to her lawyer, William Bemis, was the signal of approval, often requiring Bemis to sell shares of International Harvester.[32] Katharine also assigned shares of International Harvester to the Foundation, to be sold when cash was required.[33] What at first must have been uncomfortable meetings viewed with a sense of obligation by Pincus and Rock, rapidly became an interchange of ideas and thinking that traveled in both directions, earning Katharine the respect of the

scientists and clinicians, establishing her rightful place as a true collaborator.

IN DECEMBER 1955, Pincus informed David Tyler in Puerto Rico that he had chosen norethynodrel for further study. There is no doubt that the relationship of Pincus with Searle influenced the decision to use the most

Gregory Pincus — 1955

potent Searle progestin for clinical testing. Norethynodrel also lacked the mild androgenic activity (stimulation of male characteristics, like the growth of facial hair) present in the other compounds, especially Syntex's norethindrone. This androgenic activity was observed with high doses in animals and may have influenced Pincus; however, the doses of norethindrone used later in oral contraceptives had insignificant male hormone effects.

Edris Rice-Wray, an American-trained physician had worked in Planned Parenthood clinics when she was in private practice in the Chicago area. She was now on the faculty of the University of Puerto Rico Medical School, and also the medical director of the Family Planning Association in Puerto Rico (Associación Puertorriqueña Pro Bienestar de la Familia) and director of the public health unit in Rio Piedras. Most importantly, she was willing to be the on-site supervisor of a clinical trial.

Pincus had met Edris Rice-Wray during his visit in 1954, and he suggested to Tyler that the birth control clinics supervised by Rice-Wray would be the best setting for a clinical study. Thus, a low-income housing development in Rio Piedras, a suburb of San Juan, was selected to be the site of the first significant clinical trial. Pincus wrote to Rice-Wray in January 1956, announcing his intention to visit her in San Juan to discuss a new oral contraceptive trial. He emphatically said, that he and Rock had "an answer, if not *the* answer to their quest."[34]

The first major clinical trial was organized in February 1956 when Pincus visited Puerto Rico. Rice-Wray and her team of workers began to recruit women in Rio Piedras in March 1956. The rate of organization and implementation, occurring only months after Pincus's presentation in Tokyo, surely is a tribute to Pincus's skills. Celso-Ramón Garcia was assigned to assist Rice-Wray. After two weeks, Garcia wrote to Rock asking if he could come to Boston and work with him, and so it became a quartet: Pincus, Rock, Chang, and Garcia.[35]

Actually it was a quintet because Katharine McCormick deserved to be counted as a member of the group. Katharine was seventy-eight years old when she first met Pincus. For the next decade she dealt with men who were twenty to thirty years younger than she. At first the interaction was one of respect given to an elderly donor. Her questioning, prodding, and suggestions must have initially seemed like the fixed ideas of an old lady. But it wasn't long before her intelligence, insight, and drive gave her a status on the project that went beyond the position earned by her money. The five individuals became a team with a harmonious relationship rooted in deep respect.

Garcia, Pincus, Rock

CELSO-RAMÓN GARCIA graduated from Queens College with a major in chemistry, then completed medical school in 1945 at the Long Island College of Medicine (now SUNY-Downstate).[36] After two years in the U.S. Army, Garcia completed a year of training in pathology, then transferred to obstetrics and gynecology at Cumberland Hospital in Brooklyn. Looking for academic opportunities, Garcia, fluent in Spanish, responded to an advertisement for an assistant professor of obstetrics and gynecology at a new medical school, part of the University of Puerto Rico. He arrived in 1953, and a year later met Pincus.

Thirty-one-year-old Garcia remembered his first meeting with Pincus, who was nineteen years older, at the School of Medicine in Puerto Rico. "His warmth, kindness and sincerity were soon apparent, as was his ability to assess people and situations promptly and accurately. This meeting led to a friendly association and later a very warm relationship among all members of our families. He was never too busy to see his colleagues and their families, and was sincerely interested in their lives and their children's."[37]

Pincus introduced Garcia to Rock. A fellowship was available in infertility and gynecology at the Free Hospital for Women in Brookline, Massachusetts. Rock was a one-man selection committee, interviewing candidates over breakfast in his hotel room at the annual meeting of the American College of Obstetricians and Gynecologists. Garcia's intelligence, diction, and elocution passed Rock's muster.[38] In 1955, Garcia joined Luigi Mastroianni, Jr., another young obstetrician-gynecologist beginning his academic career, to assist John Rock in the next round of testing. Fifty of Rock's infertile, but ovulating, patients were selected to each receive one of the three progestins, designated by Chang's work, from the fifth through the twenty-fourth day of each cycle. The doses ranged from 10 mg to 100 mg daily. During two or three cycles, total inhibition of ovulation was demonstrated, and seven became pregnant in the months following discontinuation. The Pincus-Rock-Garcia team was now ready for definitive clinical testing. At this point, five years had passed since Pincus received his

initial funding, and the cost had reached more than $300,000.[39]

After Garcia moved to Boston to work with Rock and to hold a faculty position at Harvard Medical School, he continued to be involved in the oral contraceptive trials, commuting to Puerto Rico.[40] The Free Hospital for Women refused Garcia a full-time appointment causing Rock and Garcia to move their practice to the Faulkner Hospital. The two men returned to the Free Hospital when, in 1955, Katharine McCormick gave Rock $100,000 for an addition and renovations to the building, the Rock Reproductive Study Center across the street from the Free Hospital for Women. She said, "I do dislike to put money into bricks and mortar rather than into brains and experiments, but in this exceptional case it appears necessary."[41]

Pincus recruited Garcia to the Worcester Foundation in 1960 as the director of the Training Program in Physiology of Reproduction supported by the Ford Foundation and the National Institutes of Health. Garcia continued his rise up the academic ladder with an appointment as chief of the infertility clinic at Massachusetts General Hospital in 1962. During this time, Garcia maintained his visits to Puerto Rico performing follow-up examinations of the study participants, a role not required of him by the study protocol, but

Celso-Ramón Garcia

one he made a personal mission because of his desire to monitor the women for long-term side effects.[42]

When Luigi Mastroianni became chairman of obstetrics and gynecology at the University of Pennsylvania, he recruited Garcia to the faculty. During the rest of his career in Philadelphia

until his death in 2004 at age eighty-two, Garcia devoted himself to the development of reproductive surgery, the psychology of infertility, and studies on menopause. He held many distinguished positions, such as president of the American Association of Planned Parenthood Physicians, chairman of the Board of Directors of Planned Parenthood of America, founding president of the Society of Reproductive Surgeons, and president of the American Society of Reproductive Medicine.

IRIS RODRÍQUES, who had been a social worker with the Housing Authority, joined the study at an annual salary of $4,200, and she and Rice-Wray began recruiting married mothers of proven fertility in the spring of 1956.[43,44] When the word spread that there was a pill that could prevent pregnancy, the pool of applicants far exceeded the desired number. Celso-Ramón Garcia gave each applicant a complete physical examination.

Each woman accepted into the trial was given a small bottle containing twenty pills, and instructed to begin on the fifth day of her cycle. Each pill contained 10 mg norethynodrel plus an estrogen component that consisted initially of 0.220 mg mestranol and then progressively lower estrogen doses of 0.180 mg, 0.150 mg, and 0.08 mg.[45] After each treatment period, the women had to return to the clinic to obtain the pills for the next month; however this was rapidly replaced by home visits from trained social workers. A treatment group of 100 women and a comparison group of 125 women began the study in April 1956. The women had been using barrier contraception provided by the family planning clinic, and each had at least two children.

Within weeks, a reporter from one of the local newspapers, *El Imparcial*, questioned the secretary of health regarding the Rio Piedras contraceptive program. Rice-Wray was immediately called on the telephone by the secretary, and the issue was resolved when she insisted that the project was not involving health department space or personnel.[46] A few women left the study because of an inaccurate article in the newspaper that accused a nurse of a neomalthusian campaign, but there were many more waiting to take their place.[47] Thirty of the first 100 dropped out of the study, influenced by another scare story in a local newspaper, and others quit because of the side effects of nausea, vomiting, dizziness, and headache. Nevertheless, Iris Rodríquez, now the secretary of the Family Planning Association, assured Pincus that the phones never stopped ringing; there was no shortage of volunteers.[48]

Garcia said, "They came around to the idea that they were refraining from ovulation, instead of from sexual intercourse. Acceptance of that kind of thinking became very frightening to the hierarchy of the Catholic Church there. Despite admonitions by Catholic social workers, warnings from the pulpit, and outright condemnation over TV and in the Catholic press, the women just decided that the worst thing they could do was bring another baby into the world that they couldn't afford. They feared they might come to hate the child. To develop family problems was the greatest evil. For a while, when the women went to confession, if the priest noticed they hadn't been pregnant for a while he'd openly ask them, 'Are you on the pill?' On the *damn* pill was the way it was actually phrased. Then, the Catholic Social Workers Guild put on a TV program and made a lot of statements about how dangerous the pill was. About 10 percent of the volunteers dropped out. All, *all* immediately became pregnant. After that we never had a problem enlisting volunteers. They came flocking, not just the indigent population, but schoolteachers, the social workers themselves, everybody."[49]

Pincus believed the side effects were caused by the small amount of estrogen known to be a contaminant of the synthesized progestin.[50] When first produced, about 1 percent to 2 percent of norethynodrel consisted of an estrogenic compound. When this was recognized and removed, it was obvious that norethynodrel by itself was associated with a higher rate of unexpected bleeding. Pincus deliberately reintroduced the estrogen component, resulting in the combined estrogen-progestin pills that are still used today. The first trademarked combination was called "Enovid" and consisted

of 9.85 mg norethynodrel and 0.150 mg of the synthetic estrogen, mestranol. Pincus took Searle's director of biological research, Victor Drill, to Puerto Rico in the fall of 1956 to review the study. Drill was sufficiently impressed that he guaranteed sufficient pills for at least one more year of study.

SOME WOMEN had difficulties with the instructions.[51] One woman took the pills only when her husband was not traveling, another made her husband take the pills. Some thought if they took them all at once it would be that much more effective.[52] Many wanted to share with their friends. Those who quit the study had various reasons: a few husbands objected, a few responded to warnings from priests or physicians, a few moved away, and about twenty-five were frightened by the instructions at the beginning regarding the side effects, mainly nausea, vomiting, and dizziness.

The women in the study received thorough evaluations consisting of periodic cervical Pap smears, blood samples, clotting times, liver function tests, and measurement of thyroid function. This laboratory work was supported by Searle, but also by grants from the Andre and Bella Meyer Foundation, the Ford Foundation, and the American Cancer Society.[53] The logistical organization of the study was not an easy thing to accomplish.

Anne Merrill, chief assistant and technician for Pincus, flew to Puerto Rico regularly once a year in November or December. The list of supplies for the visits covered two pages, including pipettes, test tubes, batteries, lancets, chemical solutions, needles, and syringes.[54] Held up by customs when they opened the box of syringes, she had to call Foundation officials for help. Merrill learned to take a screwdriver and a list of the contents of her boxes with her after her first trip with the box of syringes. The screwdriver was to make it easy for the customs inspections on the return trip.[55]

Merrill said, "I would see these young women with many, many children, although I wouldn't know they were young women until I'd looked at their records. Some of them looked like what I would think of as a great-grandmotherly type, you know? All wizened up and gaunt to the point where you wanted to do something for them. I'd think it was due to old age, but then I'd look at the records and the women whould be thirty-four, you know, with ten children."[56]

Merrill remembered that you had to take everything you would need with you.[57] The lack of freezers and ice was a problem. She arranged to have dry ice shipped from Miami. "Carrying the dry ice in a denim bag with all

the smoke coming up, it was like voodoo."[58] On one occasion, working in Haiti where a clinical trial began in 1957, and desperate to preserve their specimens, Merrill asked to be taken to the U.S. Embassy. "I got to the Embassy and here was this gorgeous Marine standing in the door. He looked so perfect and clean, and so I said I need a freezer immediately. He took me right out to the kitchen and their freezer. He opened up the freezer and it was full of Sara Lee foods. I loved Sara Lee!"[59] Haiti was scary. Edward Wallach, a former Foundation fellow now at Johns Hopkins, recalled, "It was sort of a war-like place. Black guys with sunglasses, uniforms at the airport with submachine guns. They looked at your passport; they looked at you; they didn't smile."[60]

Garcia later remembered that "During the course of this program in Puerto Rico, the renowned biostatistician and pioneer in reproductive endocrinology, Dr. Christopher Tietze, visited the center as a tourist. He asked to see the format of the study and the record-keeping, since this was his area of expertise. He commented that he had never seen such careful documentation of patients' past history, medical problems, medication histories including tablet(s) missed, etc."[61]

After graduating from Radcliffe, Pincus's daughter, Laura, spent a year in Puerto Rico, working in the administrative office of the clinical trial. David Halberstam reported that

"Upon her return to Boston she was sent to brief Kate McCormick, who lived in a grand mansion in Back Bay, a foreboding house that seemed to have neither lights nor life to it. Laura Pincus was, in her own words, rather naïve about sex and she got a little flustered talking to this old woman about the experiments then taking place. But Kate McCormick did not become unsettled: she talked openly and frankly. The sex drive in humans was so strong, she kept insisting, that it was critical that it be separated from reproductive functions. She followed that with a brief discussion of the pleasures of sex and then added rather casually that sex between women might be more meaningful. This was spoken dispassionately, not suggestively. Nonetheless, young Ms. Pincus was stunned. Here she was in this nineteenth-century setting hearing words that seemed to come from the twenty-first century. Then, knowing that her visitor had to take the subway back to college, Mrs. McCormick summoned her butler, who brought her a silver tray with coins. She reached down and picked out two dimes and handed them to her visitor. Later, after she left, Laura Pincus looked down at the coins and noticed they were minted in 1929."[62]

A SECOND CLINICAL TRIAL was initiated in April 1957 in Humacao, Puerto Rico, but not under the direction of the Pincus-Rock group.

The reports of early success in *Science*[63,64] were sent by Clarence Gamble to Ryder Memorial Hospital, a missionary hospital in Humacao, a small town about forty miles from San Juan. Adaline Pendleton Satterthwaite, a Quaker clinician, performed most of the deliveries and gynecologic procedures in this small hospital, and also operated by herself a family planning clinic in the town. She was pleased to direct a pill project, with a social worker, Noemí Rodríguez, paid for by Clarence Gamble. By 1959, there were two projects in Humacao, with many of the patients coming from Dr. Satterthwaite's clinic. In 1963, Satterthwaite became a research associate in the department of obstetrics and gynecology at the University of Puerto Rico and continued to study the effects of the pill.[65] In 1971, she joined the Population Council and helped set up family planning clinics throughout the world.

Clarence J. Gamble is ranked with Margaret Sanger and Robert Latou Dickenson as the early leaders of the birth control movement in the U.S. Gamble, grandson of James Gamble, the co-founder of Procter & Gamble, received his first million dollars in January 1914 at the age of twenty-one. He graduated from Princeton in 1914 and Harvard Medical School in 1920. Gamble funded one of America's few birth-control clinics in 1929 with a $5,000 grant to Elizabeth Campbell, his mother's gynecologist in Cincinnati. Gamble worked to open birth-control clinics, funding only the opening of clinics, not continuing support (something he was not rich enough to do). His laboratory at the University of Pennsylvania published many research papers, investigating various methods of birth control.

Throughout the 1930s, Gamble worked with multiple birth-control organizations, holding executive positions in most. He came to the rescue of the family planning clinics in Puerto Rico, when in 1936 the Roosevelt administration, under pressure from the Catholic Church, cancelled federal support. In 1938, Gamble moved to Harvard; he continued to support the establishment of family-planning clinics in many states, and organized clinical trials demonstrating the efficacy of various methods.

By the 1950s, Gamble's activities had spread to Japan and India. He got into political trouble with leaders of the International Planned Parenthood Federation, notably with his insistence that lay people could be trained to fit diaphragms. The conflict reached its peak at the 1955 Tokyo International Planned Parenthood meeting where, despite his contribution of $3,000, Gamble was refused admittance to many of the sessions and his fieldworkers were belittled. But the Japanese, at a celebratory dinner for Margaret Sanger on the last night of the conference, presented Gamble with the Margaret Sanger Trophy, an eighteen-inch cup proclaiming his essential role in bringing an organized family planning effort to Japan.

Gamble traveled throughout Asia from 1954 to 1957, promoting birth control. To promote his work, he founded the Pathfinder Fund in 1957, which distributed birth-control supplies, mailed literature and its newsletter all over the world, and paid the salaries of workers in many countries. Gamble deliberately chose women in midlife to be his field workers, carrying the family-planning message to sixty foreign countries. In 1991, the Pathfinder Fund was renamed Pathfinder International.

Although Gamble supported the pill trial in Puerto Rico, he regarded a daily dosing method as impractical and too expensive. He enthusiastically adopted the intrauterine device (IUD), and the Pathfinder Fund became a major distributor of the device. By the time Gamble died in 1966, after struggling for two years with leukemia, the Pathfinder Fund was delivering IUDs to 504 clinicians in seventy-four countries.

EDRIS RICE-WRAY was pressured by government officials of Puerto Rico to resign from the health department only nine months into the study.[66] The secretary of health opposed her participation in the oral contraceptive trial, and in December 1956, Rice-Wray moved to Mexico, assumed a position with the World Health Organization, and initially directed a private family-planning center that carried out contraceptive trials. Her center, the Associación Pro-Salud Maternal in Mexico City, became the first family-planning clinic in Mexico. Upon leaving Puerto Rico, she summarized for Pincus the experience of 221 patients without a single pregnancy that could not be explained by incorrect use of the method.[67,68] Rice-Wray reported a 17 percent rate of side effects (breast tenderness, nausea, vomiting, and dizziness) and concluded that there was no question regarding efficacy but that the side-effect rate seemed high. Rice-Wray organized a fourth field trial in Port-au-Prince, Haiti, that began in December 1957, under the direction of Felix Laraque. In 1962, Rice-Wray reported her results with the norethindrone-containing oral contraceptive (Ortho-Novum) administered to 364 women in her Mexico City clinic.[69]

Pincus and Garcia, accompanied by their wives, visited Puerto Rico twice a year. It was usually a hectic visit, reviewing charts and arrangements and interviewing patients. Pincus and Garcia would take young physicians and their wives in the training programs at the Worcester Foundation to Puerto Rico and Haiti to perform the required examinations in the study protocols. Goody and Lizzie usually stayed at the Hotel LaRada, the Dorado Beach Hotel, or in a suite at the Condado Beach Hotel overlooking the Atlantic Ocean at the Condado Lagoon. A few hours were set aside for beach and cocktail parties.[70] Edward Wallach remembered an occasion when Goody was pouring wine for everyone and he "took his wine glass, pulled a flower from the hotel vase in the room, and put it in his ear and danced around. He was very happy, and happy that people were with him."[71] The visits to Puerto Rico *were* an exceptionally happy time for Goody and Lizzie Pincus. They even went so far as to pay a down payment of $250 for a piece of land.[72] The price was $8,000, and the purchase was never consummated.

By 1959, Pincus could summarize the data in 830 women available from Rio Piedras, the two studies in Humacao in Puerto Rico, and the trial in Port-au-Prince, Haiti, all using the trademarked product Enovid.[73,74] There were no pregnancies in the women who faithfully followed the pill regimen. The overall side-effect rate was 10.9 percent in Rio Piedras, 6.3 percent in the first Humacao study, 18.3 percent in the second Humacao project, and 7.3 percent in Haiti. The side effects were observed mostly in the first month or two of treatment, after which the rate declined.

Gregory Pincus —1959

Motivated by the side-effect rates and the concerns expressed by Rice-Wray, Pincus organized a remarkable study with Manuel E. Paniagua, Rice-Wray's replacement as director of the Family Planning Association. The number of participants was not large, but it was a placebo-controlled study in women using a conventional contraceptive method.[75,76] The side-effect rate in fifteen women administered the placebo was 17.1 percent, and in thirteen women receiving Enovid, 23.3 percent. This was not a statistically significant difference, although the size of the study was too small to provide a confident conclusion.

Pincus and Paniagua asked the question whether the side effects in the early months reflected the instructions given to the women. Omitting the baseline instructions regarding side effects in fifteen women resulted in a lowering of the rate from 17 percent to 6.3 percent.[77] The study also revealed that antacid pills (in effect, a placebo) provided to treat side effects eliminated the complaints in thirty-two of thirty-nine women.[29] This reassured Pincus, as did the observation that most side effects dissipated after a few months of treatment.

Success seemed assured. Pincus concluded, "Thus a method of oral contraception has been devised."[78] He went on to say, "Fertility and sterility are two sides of the same coin. As long as scientific inquiry into their control is freely possible, so long will we advance with new means and better insight."[79]

SATTERTHWAITE SUMMARIZED the three-year Humacao results at a conference in New York City in January 1961.[80] Efficacy was confirmed, but the side-effect rate was high, 65 percent, and 24 percent of the participants withdrew from the study because of side effects. As the study progressed, the side-effect rate decreased with the elimination of leading questions and the use of lower doses.[81] The researchers were relieved, although the patients were unhappy, that the dropouts rapidly became pregnant after discontinuing the pill, and there was a normal ratio of boys to girls.

Pincus, who was also at the New York meeting, held a press conference and surprisingly announced that according to the data from Puerto Rico the pill suppressed cancer of the cervix.[82] Satterthwaite saw this as a "publicity stunt ... to tap sources of income that wouldn't give to research on a contraceptive."[83] Pincus certainly was very much aware of what was happening in the world of endocrinology and cancer, having served as chairman of the endocrinology panel of the Cancer Chemotherapy National Service Center of the National Institutes of Health from 1956 to 1960. Allan Guttmacher, head of obstetrics and gynecology at Mt. Sinai Hospital, who a year later would become president of Planned Parenthood, was sufficiently upset that he walked out of the press conference. This was not one of Pincus's finer moments. Perhaps he was responding prematurely to statistics based on inadequate numbers of patients, or maybe Satterthwaite was right. This is the only instance in Pincus's scientific career when his interpretation and statements went beyond the data. He would later recognize that the Caribbean trials were not large enough to provide reliable data on cancer.

Pincus subsequently obtained a grant in 1961 from the American Cancer Society to study cancer of the cervix. Satterthwaite, by now devoting all of her time to contraceptive studies until she left Puerto Rico in 1966, agreed to direct the project. Pincus and Garcia published the data four years later, documenting a slightly lower incidence of abnormal cellular changes in the cervix in users of oral contraceptives, but admitted that the difference was not statistically significant.[84] A year later, in 1966, Pincus stated in a report to the National Academy of Sciences that use of the oral contraceptive *might* protect against breast cancer, cervical cancer, and atherosclerosis—an optimistic opinion that stimulated cautionary responses pointing out that the possibility of long-term effects was unknown and that on-going surveillance would be necessary.[85] Today it is recognized that epidemiologic studies indicate that the risk of cervical cancer is slightly increased in current users of oral contraceptives.[86] However, it is known that cervical cancer is caused by the human papilloma virus (HPV), and the apparent increased risk associated with oral contraceptives very likely is due to confounding factors such as more exposure to HPV in oral contraceptive users, greater use of barrier methods that protect against sexually transmitted infections among nonusers of oral contraceptives, and more Pap smears among users. No definitive evidence has emerged that oral contraceptives increase the risk of breast cancer; long-term follow-up studies have found no effect on breast cancer or cardiovascular mortality rates.[87,88] Often overlooked is the fact that use of oral contraception profoundly reduces the risk of ovarian cancer and cancer of the endometrium, the lining of the uterus.

IN JUNE 1957, Enovid was approved in the U.S. as a prescription drug for menstrual disorders. The pills were now available for American studies. One of the largest trials was that carried out by David Tyler's brother, Edward T. Tyler, in Los Angeles. Other sites included the Virginia General Hospital in Norfolk under the direction of William C. Andrews and Mason C. Andrews; the Fitzsimons Army Hospital in Denver and the Walson Army Hospital at Ford Dix, New Jersey, supervised by John A. Morris, Jr., and the West Virginia University School of Medicine by Charles S. Mahan.[89]

Edward Tyler, at one time a professional gag writer for Groucho Marx, ran his own Tyler Clinic in Los Angeles, was the medical director of family-planning clinics in Los Angeles, and had an academic appointment at the UCLA medical school. Tyler's early American studies with oral contraception were not encouraging, a high number of drop outs and side effects, but he persevered, and by 1961, he reported

his experience with 570 women with a low pregnancy rate of 1.1 percent per year.[90]

Obviously excited by results thus far, Pincus made public statements in 1957 that were widely reported in newspapers. Alan Guttmacher, chairman of the medical committee of the Planned Parenthood Federation of America, wrote to John Rock, evidently thinking an indirect approach would be more productive, and complained about "the uncritical releases Pincus has made to the lay press regarding the pill … such premature and uncritical statements may backfire badly on you, Pincus, and the whole movement. … From our armchairs here in New York it seems that the situation would be made safer by more cautious claims on Gregory's part."[91] Pincus was in Europe and Rock wrote to him in Amsterdam, admonishing him for premature statements he had presented in Stockholm, and warning him in a telegram: [92,93]

MILD STORM BREWING YOUR SPEECH SUGGEST BUTTONING UP.

The Searle officials were also cautious. Al Raymond at Searle, by now a good friend of Goody's, wrote in October 1957, "Yesterday I discussed with Mr. Searle, the question of publication of the Puerto Rican results. He appears to agree that publication would be desirable, but he would like to avoid our being associated, even by implication."[94]

But by December 1958, Pincus decided the data were sufficient. The studies were supported mainly by Katharine McCormick, with only small amounts of funding from G.D. Searle & Co. and the Planned Parenthood Federation of America. With her prodding and philanthropy, McCormick got the project off the ground and sustained it until Searle began to see the potential, and now at age eighty-one she would live to see her dream become a reality.

An article in *Fortune* magazine, however, tempered the enthusiasm, raising good questions regarding long-term side effects and reporting a consensus among scientists that at least five years of testing on at least 500 women would be necessary.[95] The article was noteworthy for its descriptions of Pincus and Rock, Pincus being the "rumpled, restless man whose deep-set eyes, bushy brows, and graying mustache make him look something like a middle-aged Einstein," and Rock was "tall, white-haired, and immaculately groomed; sixty-eight-year-old John Rock has more the air of a family physician than a scientist."

The distinguished John Rock, now sixty-nine years old, presented the results in September 1959 to the annual meeting of the American Association of Obstetricians and Gynecologists.[96] His presentation focused on the use of the new progestational drugs to treat gynecologic conditions such as painful menstrual periods (dysmenorrhea), excessive menstrual bleeding, and irregular menstrual bleeding. Tucked at the end, was a short section on conception control. In the following discussion, Edmund W. Overstreet from San Francisco pointed out that "the authors mention—calmly and almost in passing—what may prove to be the most important and dramatic use of these gestagens, their use as contraceptive agents. ... It seems to me that we as gynecologists and as a gynecologic society with a prime stake in the consequences of human reproduction, should give heed to the significance of those figures [the Puerto Rico pregnancy rates] in relation to the world's urgent population problem!" In his response, Rock, still wary of stirring a Catholic response, confined his comments to the treatment of gynecologic conditions, and carefully avoided mentioning contraception.

Pincus, however, was not so cautious. Goody never sent birth control pills before their approval to anyone he didn't know, carefully responding to requests with an explanation that his work was experimental. But that didn't keep him from supplying his young relatives, who expressed their gratitude in warm letters.[97] His niece Leila said, "Can't tell you what peace of mind this drug has brought both of us. At first it was hard to believe that a tiny orange pill could really do the job alone and I continued to use that damn diaphragm; then I said the hell with it and left it squarely up to you. And when we realized that these pills <u>really</u> work … well, you might say it was one of the most relieved moments of our married life!"[98]

Pincus published the following conclusions in 1959 in prominent journals:[99,100]

- The oral contraceptive was highly effective.
- The treatment did not cause any significant abnormalities in the menstrual cycle.
- The female reproductive tract (vagina, cervix, uterus, tubes, and ovaries) was not adversely affected.
- No major undesirable side effects had been identified.
- Sexuality in treated women was unaffected.
- Fertility after discontinuation was normal.
- A lower dosage would be possible.
- Most women found the method acceptable.

Pincus and Rock agreed: it was time to seek approval from the Food and Drug Administration, the FDA.

CHANG was uneasy that the work would just make money for the pharmaceutical industry, but Garcia said "Pincus pointed out that this was for the good of society and a necessary evil."[101] Chang recognized Pincus's role. He substituted for Pincus at a National Academy of Sciences symposium held at Duke University in 1966. Concluding his remarks, Chang said, "Without his wide knowledge in endocrinology, his organizational ability, and his good relations with the pharmaceutical industry as well as the medical profession, and above all, without his daring enterprise, all this would be on the library shelves, and the present contraceptive pills would certainly not have been on the market in such a short time."[102]

Garcia remembered Pincus as a great scientific leader. "His temperament displayed a remarkable equanimity, with profound underlying sense of social responsibility. He also was endowed with a fabulous sense of humor. In a serene manner, with the powers of his personality and the logic of his discussions, which was governed by his unyielding adherence to scientific principles, he was able to achieve unanimity of purpose with his colleagues. Through these traits he was able to nurture and coordinate the talents of many to a compulsive degree of productivity."[103]

John Rock was the essential clinician, ably assisted by Celso-Ramón Garcia. Rock, the staunch Roman Catholic, provided an unassailable public face to the effort, while Garcia provided patient care and entered clinical data with a dedicated effort that he maintained on his own time and at his own expense after the short-term objectives of the study protocols were met.

And what would these men have done without Katharine McCormick? Her drive was relentless. Katharine wrote to Goody in 1959, "These 'two decades' and 'sometime in the future' people really need to be told off. They are unwilling to face present facts, or do not know enough to understand them and have not taken the trouble to inform themselves from those who do."[104] Katharine even went so far as to hire a statistician to make sure the statistical analyses were correct when the data were presented. When Pincus was to receive the Albert D. Lasker Award from Planned Parenthood in 1960, he asked Katharine to attend the dinner as his honored guest. He said, "Mrs. Pincus and I would be very much gratified if you could find it possible to attend on this occasion, since your courageous faith has been the most responsible factor in the development of the work which is being recognized by this award."[105,106] She did attend, and this was a rare instance where she received public recognition and acknowledgment.

Albert D. Lasker Award — 1960

The complexity of Pincus's effort cannot be exaggerated. The project required the coordination of scientists and laboratory workers at the Worcester Foundation, chemists and executives at Searle, academicians, clinicians, and social workers. Pincus was a "scientific executive," and a classic multitasker.[107]

Pincus was able to conceptualize an oral contraceptive pill, and convince Searle to be involved in his project when no other drug company would consider marketing a contraceptive. The personnel and site involved in the first successful clinical trials were personally selected by Pincus, and the organizational skills of Pincus kept the components of a far-flung team operating with efficiency. Finally and importantly, he spread the word in his national and international travels, battling skepticism.

This team was pivotal in bringing oral contraceptives to the marketplace, but their efforts were made possible by those who came before them. A chemist, Russell Marker, solved the initial supply problem, and the chemical laboratories of Carl Djerassi and Frank Colton, provided the orally active progestational drugs. Each of these steps drew upon observations of preceding scientists, an essential ingredient in scientific progress. The oral contraceptive is a perfect example of what Joseph Goldzierher wrote in 1974, "… discoveries are more likely to arise from a coincidence of information, technological advances, intellectual and societal timeliness, and financial support."[108]

CHAPTER TWELVE:
JUNE 23, 1960: THE FDA APPROVES THE PILL

THE ORAL CONTRACEPTIVE was officially approved on June 23,1960, by the U. S. Food and Drug Administration (FDA). Conditional approval on May 11, 1960, was marked by a full day of celebration at the Worcester Foundation with Pincus, Rock, and McCormick sharing a bottle of champagne (paid for, of course, by Katharine).[1] The approval of an oral contraceptive was not a straightforward process. The idea of oral contraception was controversial. Would the public accept it? Would organized religion block its use? There were appropriate medical concerns. The pill represented the first long-term administration of a drug to healthy individuals. Had the clinical studies been large enough and long enough in duration? The decision was complicated by social, theological, psychological, and medical differences of opinion.

At first, G. D. Searle & Company supported the search for an effective oral contraceptive very reluctantly and with minimal funds. But by the late 1950s, Searle was beginning to see the impressive financial prospects of oral contraception. Searle management was faced with a decision: was the business opportunity sufficient to test the acceptance of an oral contraceptive by the public? The commercial prospects had to be balanced against the politics of contraception.

At Searle, the pill had two champions, John "Jack" Searle and Irwin C. Winter. Garcia said, "Most people are not aware of it, but the fact is that Jack Searle was genuinely interested in the population problem. He was very active in the population control movement and donated enormous amounts of money to it before he began making any money from the oral contraceptive."[2] Winter, a physician who was first medical director then vice-president of the company, was exposed to the problems of population growth listening to stories told by two of his sisters who were medical missionaries in India. To test public opinion, G. D. Searle & Company planted stories in 1959 about a possible birth control pill in the *Saturday Evening Post* and *Reader's Digest*.[3] To their surprise and relief, there was absolutely no reaction.

Enovid had been approved in 1957 for the regulation of menses, and by late 1959, about 500,000 women were using it allegedly for the treatment of menstrual disorders. Searle executives reasoned that the notion of a birth control pill was already spreading. Garcia and Rock were becoming enthusiastic.

> Garcia recalled, "All of the indications that we had were that there were either no side effects or none of any consequence. They were all overexaggerated because of the general opposition to the idea of birth control. Attitudes change, but at that particular time, contraception was a dirty word in the households of most people in this country. It was something that you mentioned *sotto voce*. It's hard to put yourself back in the context of those times because

> most of us forget the unpleasant things about life. That's fortunate for the human being, but unfortunate for the historian. There is still, and was then, far less concern about women's incredible burden. It's not easy to go through nine months of pregnancy. Any sort of physiological deficit may mean her life. It's one hell of an imposition to put on anybody. But no one showed the same concern for poor pregnant women that they showed over the 'hazards' the pill would subject them to."[4]

Searle management decided they were ready and submitted a request on October 29, 1959, to the Food and Drug Administration for approval of Enovid as an oral contraceptive. The data from all of the animal and human studies produced a stack of reports three-feet high.[5] The Food and Drug Administration was still hesitant, despite its earlier approval of Enovid in 1957 for the treatment of menstrual disorders. By 1960, over 2,000 women in the contraceptive clinical trials had used Enovid (1,200 women had used the 10 mg dose and 995 women the 5 mg dose) for a period ranging from a few months to almost four years.[6] There were forty-five pregnancies (1.6%), all occurring in women who failed to take their pills properly.

> Searle's Irwin Winter recalled, "The FDA was using as a part-time reviewer a

practicing thirty-five-year-old obstetrician-gynecologist, Dr. Pasquale DeFelice from Georgetown Medical Center. He was a relatively young man and obviously a Catholic. He went over the material submitted and later we got a very long letter, not very coherently expressed, stating why the FDA couldn't approve Enovid as an oral contraceptive."

DeFelice explained, "When a new drug application came in for the birth control pills, it was—needless to say—revolutionary for that indication! It was a whole new bag of beans. Everything else up to that time was a drug to treat a diseased condition. Here, suddenly, was a pill to be used to treat a healthy person and for long-term use. We really went overboard. Even though the pill had been through more elaborate testing than any drug in the FDA's history, there was a lot of opposition. Everyone was afraid of the pill. No other pill ever was put through anything like the tests for 'the pill.' Penicillin went through the FDA process very easily even though five hundred people a year still die from penicillin reactions. With the pill, however, the FDA had to come out of the licensing absolutely clean! We got all the studies, every page of them, from the projects in Puerto Rico and Haiti. Some of the women had been using the pill for as

long as five years and there just were no significant side effects. But we were in no hurry to put the FDA stamp of approval on it."

Searle asked for a hearing and brought John Rock along. On a cold day late in December 1959, in a temporary wooden building, "we had to stand in a barren little entryway for more than an hour and a half until DeFelice showed up. I felt at the time that we were left waiting to discourage us. There wasn't even a chair to sit down on. There is no question, the long, cold wait was hard on Rock. Though he was in great shape and an imposing figure, he was seventy years old at the time. Once we were inside, however, Rock carried out the whole thing. It was quite an impassioned discussion."

Rock, towering above DeFelice, kept referring to him as "young man." Rock responded to cancer allegations by saying, "I don't know how much training you've had in female cancer, young man, but I've had considerable!" DeFelice next contended that there hadn't been enough use of the pill up to that point, so it couldn't be considered proven. Rock rallied back, "If your garage is on fire, you do not wait to see if your bucket has a hole in it before trying to throw water on the blaze." He was, of course, referring to the population dilemma. Then, Winter recalled, DeFelice brought up moral and religious objections—saying the Catholic Church would never approve of it. I can still see Rock standing there, his face composed, his eyes riveted on DeFelice and then in a voice that would congeal your soul, he said, "Young man, don't you sell my Church short!"

Years later, DeFelice, now head of obstetrics-gynecology at Morris Cafritz Memorial Hospital in Washington, D.C. gave his version of the confrontation. "You have to remember, there I was, a thirty-five-year-old qualified but not yet board-certified OB-GYN man. Standing before me was John Rock, the light of the obstetrical world! ... I felt the Church was really not right about birth control and I never could understand why the popes didn't back down on it. Rock was a gentleman about the whole thing. He called me on the phone several times. ... I think abut Rock every now and then. He was a professional figure of great standing. Anything he said had to be listened to. I've only met about three doctors in my entire life who I would trust with anything. Rock was one of them. He still is."[7]

DeFelice wrote Pincus in February 1960, as he did to seventy-five academic gynecologists, asking a series of questions, including whether oral contraception would cause an early menopause or raise a risk of cancer with long-term use, and he expressed concern about future fertility and newborns.[8] Pincus addressed each question in a lengthy reply, drawing on the accumulated data from the West Indies.

DeFelice notified Searle in a letter dated April 22, 1960, that Enovid was conditionally approved pending final labeling. The approval was made public on May 11, 1960, and unconditional approval was granted on June 23, 1960.[9] Enovid's annual sales started at $20 million and rose to $40 million in 1962. By 1974, 10 million American women and 50 million women throughout the world were using the birth control pill as the sales of oral contraception paralleled individual and social changes in sexual behavior. When Enovid first came on the market, it cost $11 per month. A year later, the cost was reduced to $7.50, then to $3.50 in 1962.

Neither the Worcester Foundation nor a single investigator ever received royalties from the sale of oral contraceptives.[10] Hudson Hoagland told *The New York Times* in 1966, "They haven't made a nickel from the pill."[11] Pincus added, "I make a good salary, but I have no Cadillacs or yachts and no desire for wealth. If I became the personal beneficiary of any scientific discovery, my effectiveness as a scientist would be diminished."[12]

PINCUS DID MEET with other companies who had progestins. Parke, Davis and Co. contributed $5,000 to the Worcester Foundation but declared it would not enter the field of contraception.[13] The Upjohn Company toyed with the idea, but decided not to pursue it. The Ortho Pharmaceutical Corporation decided to wait and see what Searle's experience would be. In his book, The Control of Fertility, Pincus thanked G.D. Searle & Co. "who had the courage to assist my pioneer efforts when practically all other pharmaceutical companies had 'cold feet.'"[14]

What happened to Syntex? The company simply was not ready. With no marketing capability of its own, it was providing large wholesale quantities of compounds to other companies. Parke, Davis did acquire an exclusive license to market the Syntex product norethindrone, approved with the trade name of Norlutin for the treatment of menstrual disorders in 1957, but they were reluctant to enter the contraceptive market. Finally Syntex licensed norethindrone to be used as an oral contraceptive to the Ortho division of Johnson & Johnson. Parke-Davis refused to share its data from monkey studies, and Ortho was forced to repeat studies required for its FDA

application. Ortho's product, Ortho-Novum, was approved in 1962 and became commercially available in 1963. Parke-Davis and Syntex entered the marketplace in 1964 with Norlestrin from Parke-Davis and Norinyl from Syntex. Wyeth launched its line of oral contraceptives in 1966, featuring norgestrel, the first progestin that was totally synthesized.

The *concept* of oral contraception was never patented; only the specific progestational drugs were protected by the companies that created them. By 1970, an amazing array of oral contraceptives was available from American and European pharmaceutical companies. By the late 1960s, after seeing its profits rise dramatically, Searle had lost its lead in the oral contraceptive market, and despite making significant profits from the Enovid line of products, by the mid 1970s the company was no longer a major player. Searle was acquired by Monsanto in 1985, which then merged with Upjohn to form Pharmacia in 2000. When Pfizer acquired Pharmacia in 2003, the Searle name was retired.

THE APPROVAL in May 1960 limited the period of continuous use to two years. Two years later, anecdotal reports of venous thrombosis (clotting of blood in the veins)[15] prompted the review of accumulated cases in several geographical areas. No cases were encountered in Puerto Rico and Haiti. This review could not link the use of Enovid to venous thromboembolism, blood clots that break free and travel to the other parts of the body, notably the lungs, heart, or brain, with fatal results. The FDA established a committee of experts chaired by Irving Wright in January 1963 to evaluate all available data. The Wright Report issued in September 1963 concluded that no overall increase in thromboembolic death could be established associated with the use of Enovid, although an increase in women over age thirty-five appeared to be significant.[16] The Wright Committee cautioned that the conclusions were estimates because insufficient reliable data were available. The FDA then extended the period of use from two years to four years, with a caution for women over age thirty-five.

Blood clots are rare events and it required the study of very large numbers of pill users to accurately assess this potential side effect. It wasn't until the late 1960s that venous thrombosis was established as an actual side effect of oral contraceptives, and in the 1970s it became apparent that this side effect was related to the dose of estrogen.

Over the years, there was a steady reduction in the doses of the two hormonal components in oral contraceptives. It was immediately apparent in the first years of the Puerto Rico studies

that lower doses could still prevent pregnancy. Doses were progressively halved with no loss of efficacy.[17] Enovid-E with a dosage of 2.5 mg norethynodrel was marketed in 1964 at a cost of $2.25 per month. After 1960, the dose of the progestin decreased ten-fold, and the dose of the estrogen five-fold. Although the estrogen component has remained ethinyl estradiol, the progestin component is now any one of many progestational drugs.

Low-dose oral contraceptives have about a two-fold increase in the risk of venous thrombosis, but most of the cases occur in women at greater risk for this problem, due to conditions such as obesity or inherited clotting disorders.[18,19] It is important to point out that while elevated, this risk is six times lower than that associated with pregnancy. Arterial thrombosis, heart attacks and strokes, do not occur at a greater rate in oral contraceptive users who are under the age of thirty-five or in older women who have normal blood pressures and do not smoke.

Epidemiologic studies have documented major health benefits associated with oral contraceptives. These include the obvious such as less need for induced abortions or sterilizations, but also less endometrial and ovarian cancer, fewer ectopic pregnancies, less inflammation of the fallopian tubes, and more regular menses with less pain, less flow, and less anemia. Very probable benefits include less endometriosis, less benign breast disease, less rheumatoid arthritis, and fewer ovarian cysts. Besides contraception, oral contraceptives are used to effectively treat abnormal uterine bleeding, uterine cramps, acne, and excessive body and facial hair growth. Oral contraceptives are also now used for several months continuously or taken every day without a break, to minimize or eliminate menstrual bleeding.

TODAY, nearly 12 million American women and about 120 million women worldwide use oral contraceptives.[20] In most developed countries in the world, oral contraceptives are the most popular method of contraception. The contraceptive pill and injectable methods are the most effective reversible methods currently used by American women.[21] In the year 2002, 82 percent of American women had used the pill at some time in their lives.[22] Contraception is effectively practiced, including the use of oral contraceptives, even in countries that are predominantly Roman Catholic, but with a high standard of living, for example Italy and Spain. The most noteworthy consequence of the development and use of oral contraceptives is the avoidance of significant morbidity and mortality associated with unintended pregnancies, as well as the psychosocial consequences.

CHAPTER THIRTEEN:
THE WORLD REACTS TO THE PILL

CONTROVERSY SURROUNDED ORAL CONTRACEPTIVES, beginning about the time of the death of Gregory Pincus in 1967, reaching a peak in the 1970s and lasting a decade. Feminists and women's health advocates alleged that the pill was marketed with inadequate testing on uninformed women. Physicians voiced appropriate concerns over side effects that could emerge when the drugs were given to healthy women for an extended duration of time. As side effects were documented in on-going epidemiologic studies, they were headlined in the media, often without a balance of risks and benefits. And finally, many religious leaders had outspoken negative opinions regarding the impact of oral contraceptives on sexuality and marriage. The Catholic Church was visibly threatened by the use of oral contraception.

The birth control pill and John Rock, more than any other individual, forced the Catholic Church to reexamine its position on contraception; indeed on sexuality. The Catholic Church recognized that the birth control pill separated sexual intercourse from the possibility of pregnancy, that sexual intercourse could solely be a pleasure-seeking choice. At the time of the FDA approval of Enovid, Rock began arguing that the use of the birth control pill was a "morally permissible variant of the rhythm method."[1] He believed his position would meet the approval of the Catholic Church because in 1951 Pope Pius XII had approved the rhythm method of contraception. This was a thesis he promoted throughout the country and world in lectures before clinicians, in magazine articles, and in interviews in newspapers, on the radio, and on television; after the oral contraceptive was approved, Rock became its public defender. He argued that hormonal contraception was simply the same method used by a woman's body during pregnancy. He editorialized in the *Journal of the American Medical Association* that the pill was an evolutionary product of man's intellect, a method to maximize the opportunity to produce healthy, constructive children without violating man's sexual nature or his marriage.[2]

Rock found it hard to believe that all the women using the birth control pill were Protestants. Of course his arguments and the publicity he received drew an angry response from the Catholic establishment. He survived several attempts by Catholic colleagues and religious conservatives to have him excommunicated. It is likely that Rock received significant protection from Cardinal Richard Cushing who admired Rock.[3]

After Rock's wife died from cancer of the colon in 1961, he decided to record his thoughts in a book. If the Catholic Church deemed sexual intercourse to be moral during the days when a woman was not fertile, why should sex be immoral when the pill mimics pregnancy? *The Time Has Come: A Catholic Doctor's Proposals to End the Battle Over Birth Control* was published in spring 1963 and dedicated to Anna Thorndike Rock.[4] It sold briskly, even in its French, German, and Dutch translations. In the preface, Rock said, "It is the voice, as I hear it, of the conscience that has thus been formed within me that I am impelled to follow. I fervently pray that in doing so, I injure nobody; that I give no scandal; and that if, inadvertently, I do either, I shall be forgiven."[5] Later in his life, Rock acknowledged that although the content of the book consisted of his thoughts, they were verbally conveyed to two men who did the actual writing, Frederick Jaffe and Winfield Best, both associated with the Planned Parenthood Federation.[6] The three men shared the royalties equally.

Rock called for a change in public policy. "Finally, I have tried to demonstrate that a proper public policy, by freeing our nation's medical research establishment for a concerted effort in fertility control, offers the only practical road to the solution of both doctrinal differences between Catholics and non-Catholics on family planning methods, and the world's population explosion."[7] The reviews in newspapers and magazines were extensive. Rock became a familiar face, with his pictures and pictures of his family with nineteen grandchildren appearing in the major magazines. NBC's David Brinkley hosted an hour-long documentary of Rock. Drawing on his pipe during television interviews, the audience saw a personable, indeed avuncular, clinician who became animated only when he gestured with his pipe to emphasize a point.

John Rock maintained his frantic pace making presentations and giving interviews all over the world and publishing a seminal essay entitled, "Sex, Science, and Survival," derived from his lecture, the seventh Oliver Bird Lecture, delivered at the School of Hygiene and Tropical Medicine in London on December 8, 1963.[8] Rock confessed to believing in an almighty force called God, recognized evolutionary progress that developed in man spirituality, reason, and free will, and assigned the role of science to man's striving to know nature and, most of all, himself. Religious theories, he argued, fill the space when scientific knowledge is incomplete and often are mistakenly attributed to a celestial origin. It was the successful application of science against disease that brought humanity to a state where we are "so perilously numerous," with "confounding speed." He pointed out that the world's population was outracing its own ability for the production of food, clothes, and houses.

Without a decrease in birth rates, Rock predicted not only a decline in standards of living, but a dangerous increase in stressful living, a disorganized consequence of crowding populations. The key for Rock, of course, was the control of birth rates. He said, "There has been enough talk. It is time for action." He called for a reexamination of sacred texts. The Christian call to fill the earth was accomplished; it was time to move on. Rock believed that reproduction should not be a matter of numbers, but the production of fully capable, educated children.

Rock was a proponent of monogamy, and he viewed sexuality as a vital component of a loving relationship. He liked to say that he had a yardstick by which he measured the morality of any manifestation of sexuality, monogamy, and the monogamous unit included not only a married couple but their children. Because the marital relationship was devoted to producing healthy, proficient, and happy children, sex was more than an act of procreation. Indeed, he argued that prolonged sex-free periods within a marriage would be unnatural, and thus, sinful. At the same time, he supported short-term restraint as a method of contraception, the rhythm method. But, he pointed out that science had not yet provided the knowledge to time ovulation accurately and make this method effective.

Rock referred to his own work documenting that coitus produced a conception about 25 percent of the time.[9] He said, "Nature seems not to have recognized fertilization as an indispensable end of coitus." If a couple believed that having another child would weaken the family, then they would be "obliged to do their best to prevent conception." Rock concluded, "Like the best-informed ecologists, demographers and agriculturists, I can see no other way to avoid the impending hunger and stress which will turn our humanitarianism back to bestiality. Only by the good use of sex, can Man escape stress and insure the survival of his kind, so that healthy, educated descendants may grow in the wisdom that will surely enable them to know, to love, and to serve God."

Suddenly, major Catholic figures were holding meetings with demographers, medical investigators, political scientists, and of course, theologians. Finally, Pope John XXIII established a special commission, the Papal Commission for the Study of Population, the Family, and Birth, composed of six non-theologians, to reevaluate the Catholic position on contraception. After Pope John XXIII died in 1963, Pope Paul VI kept expanding the committee, eventually to seventy-two members. The membership was supposed to be a secret. *Newsweek* covered the story with a picture of John Rock on its cover, but Rock was excluded from participation. The size of the commission was progressively enlarged, and the names of the members were eventually leaked, an impressive array of lay people and experts in theology, medicine, psychology, and demography.[10]

The commission appeared in 1965 to favor a change in the Church's position on birth control. In 1966, the Pope restructured the committee, creating an executive group of cardinals and bishops. The world held its breath when the commission submitted its secret report in the summer of 1966. Goody Pincus was afraid the news would be bad.[11] There were rumors of a change, but the Pope postponed a decision. In April 1967, somehow the reports of the commission were obtained and published, indicating that a majority of the commission *did* favor a change in the Church's teaching.[12-14]

But John Rock was to be disappointed. The Pope finally released his encyclical entitled *Humanae Vitae* on July 25, 1968,[15] the same year that Hollywood produced a birth control pill comedy starring Deborah Kerr and David Niven, *Prudence and the Pill*. Although blasted by the critics, the movie in which vitamins or aspirin were secretly substituted for the pill symbolized the popular acceptance of the pill, rapidly making it a cultural icon. The Pope's encyclical recognized the growth of the world population and the economic problems of individual families. It also recognized a new understanding of the dignity of women, asserting that the most remarkable new development is "man's" progress and attempt to control nature, including every aspect of his own life. The Pope nicely stated the new issues, questioning whether it is not acceptable to have a less prolific and more rationally planned family.

Ultimately, however, the encyclical reinforced the Church's belief that its teachings are based on a natural law that arises in divine revelation, and that the Church is totally competent to interpret natural and moral law, as directed by Christ. Pope Paul VI stated the following principles of Catholicism:[16]

- Married love is not the effect of chance or blind evolution of natural forces. It is an institution of God.

- Married love is ordained toward procreation and education of children, and it requires responsible parenthood, which includes a decision not to have additional children. *But men and women are "not free to act as they choose in the service of transmitting life …"* Actions must correspond to the will of God, interpreted of course by the church.

- "… each and every marital act must of necessity retain its intrinsic relationship to the procreation of human life."

- Man on his own cannot break the link between union and procreation in the marriage act.

- A conjugal act of mutual love which impairs the capacity to transmit life frustrates God's design and contradicts

his will. Men and women are not "the master of the sources of life but rather the minister of the design established by the Creator." God is the source of sexual faculties for the generation of life.

- Abortion and sterilization are to be absolutely excluded as a means of regulating the number of children. Similarly excluded is any action intended to prevent procreation. Sexual intercourse which is deliberately contraceptive is intrinsically wrong.

- Sexual intercourse during those times that are infertile does not offend the moral principles of the Church. This is lawful because a married couple "rightly uses a faculty provided them by nature."

- Artificial birth control opens the way for marital infidelity and a "general lowering of moral standards." "It is an evil thing to make it easy for them (the young) to break the law."

- The Church is unwilling to accept that "the responsibility of procreating life should be left to the arbitrary decision of men, …"

- The Church "urges man not to betray his personal responsibilities by putting all his faith in technical expedients."

- Doctors and nurses should "endeavor to fulfill the demands of their Christian vocation before any merely human interest."

As far as the Catholic Church was concerned, there would be no change; all chemical and barrier methods of contraception are forbidden. Faced with this reaffirmation of tradition, many lay Catholics and Catholic clergy protested. And many Catholics continued to use oral contraceptives. By the 1990s, Catholic utilization of oral contraception and condoms was higher in the U.S. than that of protestants.[17]

R. B. Kaiser, a *Time* correspondent in Rome in the 1960s, chronicled the debates in the Second Vatican Ecumenical Council that modernized the Catholic Church, and he broke the story in 1964 that the Church was debating birth control. In 1985, Kaiser published a book, *The Politics of Sex and Religion,* that documented a play-by-play history of the deliberations of the Papal Commission, the political reasons for the Pope's rejection of the Commission's recommendations, and the aftermath, together with an Appendix that contained the fifty-seven names of the Commission members and the actual final report of the Commission.[18] It is a fascinating history that is more secular than religious. Today, the poor and uneducated people in the world are the ones that suffer the most from the Church's position.

Immediately after the release of the Pope's encyclical, Rock said, "I was disappointed, deeply saddened and embarrassed that the avowed leader of Christianity and mankind in its evolutionary progress had failed to demonstrate the insight and foresight which might have been expected." When asked, to comment on the Pope's position that every act of marriage must be dedicated to the transmission of life, Rock responded, "It's too bad that whoever arranged sexual physiology in women didn't have that in mind."[19]

In 1972, at the age of eighty-two, John Rock retreated to his farmhouse on nine acres in Temple, New Hampshire.[20] In 1972 and 1973, the last state laws prohibiting the distribution of contraceptives, including the Massachusetts law, were overthrown. Smoking his pipe, Rock, still with clear blue eyes and a full head of white hair, spent his days reading, bird watching, and swimming nude each morning until it got too cold in a pond he made by damming a stream. Garcia and Mastroianni visited at least once a year. Although a crucifix still hung above his desk, he rarely went to mass, although in the last year of his life, a local priest visited and brought him communion. Up to his death, he could not understand the Pope's decision. Rock died on December 4, 1984, at the age of ninety-four.

IN 1961, C. Lee Buxton, chairman of obstetrics and gynecology at Yale Medical School, and Estelle Griswold, the sixty-one-year-old executive director of Connecticut Planned

Parenthood, opened four Planned Parenthood clinics in New Haven, a defiant move that tested the current Connecticut law. Buxton and Griswold were arrested at the Orange Street clinic, in a prearranged scenario they scripted at the invitation of the district attorney. They were found guilty and fined $100, but imprisonment was deferred because the obvious goal was a decision by the United States Supreme Court. Buxton was forever rankled by the trivial amount of the fine. On June 7, 1965, the Supreme Court voted 7 to 2 to overturn the Connecticut law on the basis of a constitutional right of privacy.

When Margaret Sanger heard the news from the Supreme Court, she was in poor health, bed-ridden and dependent on pain killers and sleeping pills. She had friends prop her up in bed, and she celebrated by drinking champagne through a straw. About a year later, Sanger died on September 6, 1966, at the age of eighty-seven.

THE PLANNNED PARENTHOOD FEDERA-TION OF AMERICA is dedicated to resolving the problems of unregulated fertility and population growth and to the delivery of contraceptive services. The leaders of Planned Parenthood were slow to appreciate the impact of oral contraceptives. It took eighteen months of education and deliberations before the pill was accepted by Planned Parenthood's Medical Committee and available for distribution.[21] The number of women serviced by Planned Parenthood's clinics, largely low-income women, tripled between 1960 and 1965, straining resources and requiring new programs of education and service.

Aware that low-income women rarely had private physicians, Planned Parenthood campaigned for a national program of family planning services. Despite competing political and economic forces, progress in providing birth control services became reality, aided by America's first Catholic president, John F. Kennedy. Kennedy announced in 1963 his support for federal efforts to improve population control, the first president to do so. Both Katharine McCormick and John Rock were despondent beyond the norm by Kennedy's assassination. But the process had started and family planning programs multiplied rapidly. However, after 1968, these programs had to overcome a wave of negative publicity generated around oral contraceptives.

WITHIN A DECADE after the initial approval of Enovid, a storm of criticism swirled around oral contraceptives and added to the distress of John Rock's last years. Good objective appraisals of the events and reactions can be found in *Sexual Chemistry* by Lara V. Marks and *On the Pill* by Elizabeth Siegel Watkins.[22,23] A scholarly analysis of the FDA approval of oral contraception was published in 2002, concluding that the decision was appropriate because the data and conclusions were consistent with the standards of the time.[24] The oral contraceptive pill was just one part of a complicated, dynamic time period in social history, including feminist activism, the civil rights movement, and a greater openness about sexuality, the so-called sexual revolution. All of these forces interacted with each other, and scrutiny of oral contraception occasionally provided a platform for publicity from enthusiastic supporters of these social changes.

At the time an oral contraceptive was approved, the FDA was interested in only two questions: did the product work and was there any indication of lack of safety in the studies that had been performed? More extensive safety requirements emerged later in response to the thalidomide debacle. Thalidomide was a drug developed in Germany, sold worldwide, and recommended for pregnant women with morning sickness. From 1956 to 1962, thousands of children were born with severe malformations: eye and ear defects, gastrointestinal abnormalities, and especially phocomelia, the defective development of arms and legs. Although never approved in the U.S., the drug was available as an investigational drug pending approval. When

the birth defects were recognized and the lack of testing prior to use became public knowledge, the way in which the FDA approved new drugs was changed in 1962, including the number of subjects required for testing and the requirement for signed consent forms.

As Carl Djerassi wrote in 2001, "The Pill has now been around long enough that defensive or proprietary comments no longer have much effect on its use. The Pill has become part of our social fabric."[25] Although the storm has dissipated, the story of Pincus, Rock, Garcia, and McCormick requires a consideration of their critics as well.

THE FEMINIST MOVEMENT of the 1960s and 1970s followed the lead of Margaret Sanger and championed female contraception. Yet angry women saw in the oral contraceptive a male conspiracy, given the roles played by the men who at that time dominated the professional ranks of science and medicine. The important contributions of the women involved, mainly McCormick, Sanger, Rice-Wray, Rodríques, and Sattterthwaite, were ignored, as was the enthusiastic cooperation of the participants in the studies, without which nothing would have been accomplished.

Sanger and McCormick were motivated by their

desire to empower women to be able to make their own choices, a message that resonated with scores of women. It is easy to criticize retrospectively the individuals involved in their own times and their own struggles, as many feminists did. A Roman Catholic physician in England, Anne Biezanek, told her own story in a heart-tugging and thought-provoking book published in 1964, *All Things New*.[26] The story is worth a visit because it was targeted by feminists, who belittled Biezanek's honoring of those who had brought the oral contraceptive to reality.

After having seven children and experiencing eleven pregnancies before her first child was thirteen years old, Biezanek opened a family planning clinic in her own home and was rebuked by the Catholic Church. The ensuing publicity led to an outpouring of letters from men and women of all faiths all over the world, some simply addressed to Dr. Biezanek, The Clinic, England. Her story began with her conversion at age eighteen from her Quaker upbringing to Catholicism and her marriage at age twenty-one while in medical school in Scotland to Jan Biezanek, a Polish army officer left stranded in England after World War II.

By 1955, Biezanek was training as a psychiatrist in a mental hospital and had four children. Her husband, an educated lawyer prior to the war, could not obtain a license in Scotland and went to work as a ship's steward on transatlantic merchant crossings. His return from long absences inevitably led to another pregnancy. Struggling to make ends meet and to continue her medical training, Biezanek was frustrated when she sought the counsel of priests and was advised that contraception was immoral. She was told that she had to trust God and Providence and not refuse her husband. After a fifth child and a second miscarriage, and confronted with physical abuse when her husband's demands were rebuffed, Biezanek collapsed mentally and physically; she had to give up her job and move in with her parents. Working with therapists during a five-week stay as an inpatient at a mental hospital, she began to question the conflicts between her marriage and her religion, to despair at the lack of support from her church. When she returned home, she had her seventh child, and with the backing of the chaplain at the hospital where she had worked and money from two Catholic women friends, she obtained a mortgage on a house in Liverpool.

Biezanek now resolved to turn her back on her profession and devote herself to her family. Awake most nights with her children, her husband away, tied down by chores and children, handicapped by insufficient income, sex became something to be suppressed. The thought of another pregnancy drove Biezanek to use the birth control pill in 1962. Her husband accepted this as long as she didn't talk of it. Biezanek was bothered enough by this decision that she decided not to attend communion, but her children insisted. The parish priest near her home refused to accept her confession. She began to take communion secretly, without confessing her use of an oral contraceptive. Working again as a doctor and seeing the frustrations of other Catholic wives, Biezanek arranged to take a course in family planning and decided to open a family planning clinic in her own Liverpool home in 1963. She kept her local priest and bishop fully informed and received no objections. After an interview with Biezanek, the local newspaper printed her story, leading to television publicity. Now her parish priest refused her communion, and her letters to her bishop only earned his disapproval and demand for a public apology for her erroneous ways. Biezanek informed the highest ranking Catholic in England, the archbishop of Westminster in London, that she would appear for communion on May 31, 1964, and she provided a personal description complete with the clothes she would wear. She also informed the press. In front of an overflowing crowd, the archbishop, without fuss, gave her communion. The Church later claimed she had not been recognized. After the episode in London, Biezanek went to mass every Sunday but never received communion again. For every story that came to public attention, there were countless others in the silent background; thousands of

Catholic women made the choice to use oral contraception.

THE CONTROVERSY over the oral contraceptive reflected the clash of two opposing philosophies. One, as repeatedly expressed by Pincus and Rock, said that decisions should be based on the science, and the available data indicated that the pill was effective and safe. The other as expressed by many notable clinicians and scientists, focused on a concern over total safety, and that all questions regarding adverse effects of any drug treatment of healthy, normal women should be established by appropriate long-term studies before widespread use. The fundamental problem was the absence of data from large numbers of women who had been using oral contraceptives long enough to allow for the development of relatively rare but serious side effects, in short, insufficient long-term data. The proponents focused on the safety record thus far; the opponents held to a position of reasonable doubt.

Because the available studies had by 1965 failed to detect serious problems, the first camp was willing, and indeed eager, to allow oral contraceptives on the market for general use, potentially putting women at some possible risk in order to prove safety, thus the need for involvement of the medical profession. The second camp viewed the marketing of oral contraceptives as a large experiment, an experiment that was regarded as inappropriate and potentially dangerous. Pincus and his colleagues argued that the oral contraceptive had not been proven dangerous; others argued that appropriate safety had not been proven.

The two points of view were illustrated in the debate over oral contraception that took place in India beginning in 1959.[27] Pincus, acting out of his own strong beliefs as well as on the behalf of G. D. Searle & Company, devoted considerable energy into an effort to introduce oral contraception in India. This effort was sparked by the meeting of the International Planned Parenthood Federation in New Delhi in February 1959. Pincus became frustrated, convinced that Indian officials were not reasoning scientifically, whereas the Indian government refused to accept the available data, reserving the right to demand the demonstration of conclusive safety in its own population.

The conflict between the views of the opposing camps was exemplified in the U.S. by debates within the federal government at the Food and Drug Administration (FDA) and the National

Lizzie and Goody in Asia — 1959

Institutes of Health (NIH), and the public airing of the arguments at the Nelson Hearings in 1970. This was not an emotionless, objective debate. Pincus and the other experts arguing from the available science were largely individuals who had been involved in the studies of oral contraception. On the other side, passionate advocates pointed to the subjective experiences of individuals, experiences that were poignant but at the same time lacking in statistical significance. Prominent academicians and clinicians, for example, Alan Guttmacher, president of the Planned Parenthood Federation, voiced concerns regarding safety and urged a cautious approach. The scientists dismissed the individual experiences, questioning their reliability and reality. On the other hand, the scientists were accused of having a vested interest in the marketing of oral contraceptives, not financially, but professionally.

Roy Hertz and John Bailar, scientists at the National Cancer Institute, wrote a review in 1964 entitled, "An Appraisal of Some Unresolved Problems Involved in the Use of Estrogen-Progestogen Combinations for Contraception."[28] Before submitting the manuscript for publication, the authors solicited criticism from Pincus, Rock, Garcia, Joseph Goldzieher, Edward Tyler, and Robert Greenblatt. The review highlighted three major issues: cancer of the breast, endometrium, and cervix; blood clotting; and possible damage to ova with a risk of abnormalities in subsequent pregnancies. The manuscript ended by emphasizing the potential for risk and calling for more controlled studies. Pincus wrote a long letter to Hertz representing his reaction and that of Garcia's.[29] They regarded the Hertz and Bailar manuscript as biased and packed with "misstatements and misinterpretations." Goody's response was both scientific and emotional. At one point he said, "Your lack of scientific verification really appalls me." Goody told Hertz that he planned to prepare a manuscript addressing each point with the expectation that it would be submitted simultaneously with the Hertz-Bailar review. Goody concluded, "I have such a great respect for your scientific conscience that I hope to see a much better job than the one which is now on my desk."[30]

John Rock was more gracious, but he, too, argued that some of the conclusions were "unwarranted." Hertz responded to Rock, and it is clear that he was well-motivated. He said, "every patient is entitled to know whether she is accepting established therapy or volunteering for an investigative study. … These views are not to be taken as reflecting an indifference to the urgency of the population problem. On the contrary, it is because of a keen appreciation of this urgency, that insistence on scientifically sound progress is mandatory lest some of our presumed solutions discredit further efforts in this vital area."[31]

Joseph Goldzieher's comments filled an eleven-page letter.[32] Fortunately, Hertz and Goldzieher were good friends, because Goldzieher pulled no punches. "First of all, I do not really think that this is a scientific paper at all; it is a well disguised, well written polemic, presented with all the standard trappings, and thoroughly documented. … This tract of yours is deceptively simple, but it is studded with hidden premises and false assumptions, and engineered with cleverness worthy of a Jesuit. In fact, if you persevere, you may become the Aquinas of the Hormones—Cause—Cancer sect." Finally, Goldzieher pointed out that if Hertz's possibilities were true, they must be balanced against the morbidity and mortality associated with the criminal abortions performed in the U. S. per year. "What you do, in effect, is to sanction half a million crimes, including 500 murders a year in an effort to prevent the possibility of a couple of dozen breast cancers." And how about the rest of the world? "Which do you prefer—to prevent a couple of cases of carcinoma or to prevent thousands of deaths from starvation, hundreds of thousands of cases of malnutrition, squalor, and epidemic disease which everywhere in the world accompany over-population?"

It is not difficult to see both sides of the conflict and to support both points of view. The history of oral contraception tells us that Pincus, the scientists, and the pharmaceutical industry won the argument, allowing oral contraceptives to remain on the market. Roy Hertz wrote to Pincus and Garcia, "Because of cogent criticism offered by you and by other colleagues, I have decided not to publish the manuscript you so kindly reviewed for me."[33]

THE PROTESTS of the feminists and concerns regarding long-term safety raised by clinicians stimulated Senator Gaylord Nelson to hold hearings on the oral contraceptive. Nelson especially reacted to the book by Barbara Seaman, *The Doctor's Case Against the Pill*,[34] and relied upon Seaman for advice in choosing witnesses for the hearings.[35] Nelson convened the hearings under the auspices of the committee he chaired, the Subcommittee on Monopoly of the Select Committee on Small Business, but with that awkward title, the event rapidly came to be known as the Nelson Hearings. The hearings from January to March 1970 politicized the safety questions, and the event was highlighted by the media that emphasized any negative testimony. Feminists seized the opportunity to disrupt the hearings, gaining media exposure to publicize their concerns, express their anger, and to bring about change.

The proceedings produced the FDA requirement to include what is now called the package insert.

In response to an adverse reaction from the medical profession, the initial version was a mere hint of today's detailed description of the drug, its actions, and its side effects, but it was an important first step in improving communication between patients and doctors. The publicity associated with the hearings led to a temporary decline in the use of oral contraceptives, but the method rapidly regained acceptance and popularity with the introduction of newer lower-dose products and the knowledge gained from multiple epidemiologic studies.

Inaccuracy and falsehoods are for novels; reality and truth should prevail in a biography. Pincus, Rock, Garcia, and the clinicians in the later American trials were not uncaring; they *were* concerned about the safety of oral contraceptives. Their laboratory and clinical monitoring of the women and the children born in the studies is testimony to their concern, and it should be recognized that logistics, technical limitations, and socioeconomic considerations made it difficult to collect these data. The quality of the monitoring was as good as it could be for the locale and that point in time. The methods used were those that were established and acceptable in the 1950s. Garcia deserves special recognition for his repeated trips to Puerto Rico after the trials had concluded, to assess the treated women for emerging untoward consequences.

The most important side effect, the only one that carries with it an acute threat of death, is blood clotting, venous and arterial thrombosis. In the late 1950s, the data from Puerto Rico gave no indication that this would be a clinical consequence of significance. When anecdotal reports appeared in the early 1960s, reviews of available data by clinicians and epidemiologists could find no convincing link between the events and oral contraceptives. And the FDA was cautious, limiting its approval first to a two-year duration and then to four years.

Thrombosis is a relatively rare event. It was known that the risk of thrombosis is increased during pregnancy, but it wasn't until substantial numbers of women were using oral contraceptives that epidemiologists could document the reality of this estrogen-related effect. When Pincus summarized all that was known in 1966, published one year before he died, he concluded that "none of the alleged pathological adverse reactions (such as thromboembolism) to the drugs have been established as more than coincidental."[36] The progress of the historical recognition and appreciation for the side effect of thrombosis was totally appropriate for the scientific knowledge and epidemiologic data available at the time.

Cardiovascular events occur only in current users of oral contraceptives and are secondary to acute estrogen-related effects on blood clotting (thrombosis). Most, if not all, of these clinical events occur in individuals at higher risk for various reasons, such as the increased risk associated with smoking, hypertension, obesity, and inherited predispositions for clotting. Clotting in the veins and arteries is related to the estrogen dose. In the first years of oral contraception, the high doses of estrogen were associated with a six-fold increase in the risk of venous thrombosis, which still did not make this a common event. The lower-dose products used today have about a two-fold increase in this risk, an increase that is seen in the first year or two of use and concentrated in women with risk factors such as obesity and inherited clotting problems. Arterial thrombosis produces heart attacks and strokes, a side effect that is also influenced by the dose of estrogen and the presence of other risk factors. Healthy, nonsmoking women do not have an increased risk of arterial thrombosis with modern oral contraceptives, but the risk is increased in women over age thirty-five who smoke or who have elevated blood pressures.

Recent studies have documented that past users of oral contraceptives do not have a later increase in cardiovascular disease or a risk of dying from cancer.[37,38] The two longest-active oral contraception studies are in England, the Royal College of General Practitioners' study with 28,762 users of oral contraceptives and the Oxford Family Planning Association study with 17,032 women using either oral contraceptives or a diaphragm or an intrauterine device, and both cohorts of women have been followed since 1968. Neither study has documented an increase or a decrease in the risk of breast cancer, and both studies find a slight but not significant increase in cervical cancer and major reductions in endometrial and ovarian cancers.[39,40]

The high doses of the first oral contraceptives were questioned retrospectively, and indeed the doses were high. The selection of the initial doses, however, was a reasonable process by extrapolating from the effects observed in animals. The overriding concern was to prevent pregnancy; a high failure rate in the initial trials carried with it the risks of a pregnancy that left only two choices: either another unwanted child or an illegal abortion. The pharmaceutical industry had a powerful motivation to produce lower-dose oral contraceptives: the lower the dose, the less expense in the production and the greater appeal of cheaper products across all socioeconomic levels worldwide. The lowering of doses proceeded cautiously and appropriately to avoid unacceptable pregnancy rates due to pill failure.

RELIGIOUS LEADERS ACCUSED oral contraception as promoting sexual promiscuity. Many regarded the Pill as a link to the sexual revolution. But changes in sexual mores are a sociocultural phenomenon, and in retrospect, these changes were already underway when the oral contraceptive was approved for marketing. Unwanted pregnancy and legal abortion, or illegal abortion with its risk of death, are the consequences of the lack of contraceptive choices. An argument can be made that the emergence of the Pill increased the number of contraceptive choices available and made a major contribution to limiting the number of unwanted pregnancies and induced abortions that accompanied the social changes in sexuality.

An often unappreciated beneficial consequence of oral contraception was the involvement of the health care profession in family planning. Oral contraceptives required prescriptions and the participation of clinicians, and this required on-going medical education about contraception, an important advance in the clinical care of women. Prescribing oral contraceptives also increased the number of women receiving preventive health care services such as physical examinations and Pap smear screening.

JOHN ROCK'S BIOGRAPHY by Loretta McLaughlin[41] received a feminist review in *The New York Times* on March 6, 1983, which concluded that the book came close to being a cover-up.[42] The tenor of the review can be appreciated in one sentence: "If this book fails to convince the Pope that contraception is an act of piety and the pill a kind of communion wafer in the sacrament of marriage, it may still succeed as a brief for promoting John Rock to sainthood." The people who knew John Rock were quick to point out that the unassuming, mannerly Rock *was* saintly.[43,44] Castigating the lack of criticism in the book and casting the use of impoverished Caribbean women as guinea pigs, the inflammatory rhetoric of the review gives no credence to historical context and implies conspiracy in the failure to autopsy three of the test subjects who died. The three deaths are also mentioned with a similar innuendo in the 2003 film by the Public Broadcasting Service, entitled *The Pill*.[45] When did the women die, during or after treatment? What were the causes of death? Was a medical autopsy even possible in the locale of the deaths? Did the families consent to autopsies? These are just some of the questions that require answers before implying nefarious behavior on the part of the trial supervisors. It is appropriate to ask why the investigators didn't answer these questions, but it is not justified to assume an improper motivation. Writing about the past, it is easy to ignore the historical context of scientific capabilities and regulating agency requirements of the time.

By no means, were Pincus, Rock, and Garcia negligent or reckless.

CONTRACEPTION that is effective for a country and for the world's population is all about choice. The more methods there are, the better individuals and couples can choose what is most effective for their needs. The criticisms and controversies over oral contraceptives have receded into history. Oral contraceptives by virtue of lower doses and good medical screening for medical conditions, especially high blood pressure and smoking, have been demonstrated to be very safe and associated with many benefits. Women and clinicians, and women are becoming a majority in the medical profession, voted with their choices as contraception was separated from moral restrictions. Oral contraceptives today are either the first or second preferred method of contraception in most countries in the world. This worldwide popularity surely would have brought great satisfaction to Pincus, Rock, Garcia, and McCormick.

CHAPTER FOURTEEN:

FAME AND ILLNESS

THE BIRTH CONTROL PILL brought Pincus fame and travel. There is no doubt that he was very much aware of the accomplishment and its implications; he knew the social value of contraception. Nearly all scientists live in their own little worlds, experts in confined areas, and they rarely venture beyond their boundaries. Pincus knew no boundaries. He was unique in having skills in multiple levels, knowledge that crossed disciplines in science, and an appreciation of social problems and what it took to bring about change. "Pincus became a truly international figure in science. He played a major role in encouraging scientific developments outside the United States through his opinions expressed to important agencies of our government, and by stimulating the organization abroad of many international meetings."[1] Joseph Goldzieher remembered that "He was a great presenter, very verbal and lucid. He came across very clearly."[2]

Seymour Lieberman said, "He knew what he was doing and he wanted to do it, and he was glad to do it. He was an activist and always was looking to see how to do things and advance them. I once heard him give a lecture at the Rockefeller University where there were 600 physicians present, and he was teaching them how to use the pill. That's the kind of chutzpah that he had. He had a lot of chutzpah."[3]

Ego is a driving force in most, if not all, scientists. The nature of the system of "publish or perish" fosters a seeking of the attention provided by reports in scientific journals, presentations at prestigious meetings, and elections to office in academic organizations. The scientist finds his or her reward in the creation and experimental confirmation of hypotheses. But this achievement remains incomplete without the peer review and recognition derived from the public structure of publications and presentations. Indeed, the public process is an essential part of the system required to establish the accuracy and reproducibility of a scientist's achievements. In varying degrees, scientists respond to this process with ego satisfaction or frustration.

Gregory Pincus enjoyed his successful scientific career, a life that pushed him to the forefront of his colleagues, a position affirmed by his leadership of the Laurentian Hormone Conference, his chairmanship of various international and national committees, and, for example, his presidency of The Endocrine Society at a time before any work had started on oral contraception. Pincus fulfilled his scientific functions, from one-to-one interactions with junior fellows and scientists to prominent national and international roles, with a consummate grace that seemed to come naturally. There was nothing edgewise about Goody. He was straightforward, direct, and honest. "He was very sympathetic and understanding;" John McCracken said, "I don't know of anyone who disliked him. "He wasn't called 'Goody' for nothing. He was a good guy."[4]

A SPECIAL FUND WAS ESTABLISHED at the Worcester Foundation for the contributions of Katharine McCormick that were designated to support the travels of Pincus to promote the worldwide introduction and use of oral contraception. After the famed presentation at the fifth annual conference of the International Planned Parenthood Federation in Tokyo in October 1955, as described in the Prologue, Goody and Lizzie visited Hong Kong, Bangkok, Bombay, Delhi, Karachi, Beirut, Jerusalem, Athens, Rome, Madrid, Paris, London— returning home from their around-the-world trip after seventy-one days.[5] The travel airfare totaled $1,900 for Goody and $1,818 for Lizzie. In 1956, Goody embarked on a speaking tour of Europe and Asia, and in 1957, a tour of South America. Slowly but surely, Goody and Lizzie filled their house with artwork, artifacts, furniture, vases, bowls, dishes, and cups—gathered on shopping trips during their travels. Their purchases were insured and shipped to Northborough, most coming from Asia. In 1955, their trip to Asia accumulated $700 worth of goods.[6] They even sent fancy paper waste baskets home to their daughter Laura.

Many prominent individuals believed that this promotion of oral contraception was premature. To a significant degree, this reluctance was influenced by the prevalent fear of the power and influence of the Catholic Church. These travels were marked by multiple symposia and

Goody and Lizzie Passport Photos — 1960

conferences, important opportunities to develop contacts for Searle and to stimulate clinicians and government officials. The timing of this effort in the 1950s was remarkable. It wasn't until 1959 that Pincus felt confident enough to publish convincing arguments regarding the efficacy and safety of oral contraception, yet before that, he was traveling to foreign countries filling his time with promotional activities.

In the late 1950s, Pincus and Searle reached out to the United Nations, the World Health Organization, and specifically the World Health Assembly, the annual decision-making body for the World Health Organization. The intention was to spark and support oral contraceptive development throughout the world. In 1961,

Pincus participated in a meeting of experts organized to provide the National Institutes of Health with a review of contraceptive research and a proposal for targeting funding. State Department officials visited with Pincus in the early 1960s, seeking his recommendations regarding foreign funding aimed at contraception. In 1965, Pincus testified at Senate hearings on foreign aid for population control.

Newspapers throughout the U.S. reported on the presentations made by Pincus during his travels. Beginning with his first reports on oral contraception in 1956 and 1957 and ending when the birth control pill was approved for marketing, Pincus received hundreds of letters covering a wide range of subjects: men and women wanting pills, information on side effects, birth control pills for pet dogs and pet cats, suggestions of new ideas for food supplements, cures for cancer, and especially, to volunteer for his studies. It was a rare event when a religious, anti-contraception letter came in the mail. Pincus answered every letter, often with a referral to a local clinician, but always pointing out the restricted and experimental nature of the studies. These letters must have reinforced his dedication to the cause of oral contraception and his belief in the importance of his message.

Dear Doctor-

I am about 30 years old, have 6 children, oldest little over 7, youngest a few days.

My health don't seem to make it possible for me to go on this way.

We have tried to be careful and tried this & that, but I get pregnant anyway.

When I read this article I couldn't help but cry, for I thought there is my ray of hope.

As of yet can these anti-pregnancy pills be purchased? Where— How can I get them? Please help me.[7]

Dear Dr. Pincus,

… I do hope you can understand the urgency of my request, as I do not wish to practice self-denial, although I am capable of doing so, I sincerely feel it is a waste, and only to be adhered to in extreme cases. Unfortunately mine is an extreme case.[8]

Sir:

… I am already a mother of 8 children and would like to get information about the birth control pill and where they can be bought if they are being sold. I am leaving for California around the middle part of June so if it is possible to get an answer right away, I would appreciate it very much. I have no need for the pill until June because my husband is already in L.A.[9]

In 1961, Pincus organized, with Searle support, a seminar on oral contraception at the World Health Assembly meeting in New Delhi, following which he and Lizzie toured India and Australia, a trip funded with $9,900 from Katharine McCormick.[10,][11] The couple's travels were temporarily halted in the middle of 1961 as Lizzie recovered slowly after having her gall bladder removed.[12]

In March 1962, Pincus reported to Katharine McCormick that interest in oral contraception was sky rocketing.[13] In a two-month period, he listed lectures at Brandeis University, the University of Southern California, the American Cancer Society, Harvard Medical School, the Koch Memorial Lecture in Pittsburgh, the American College of Physicians, Planned Parenthood of St. Paul, and Reed College in Portland, Oregon, followed by lectures in England, Stockholm, visits to four cities in India, and attendance at the International Congress on Hormonal Steroids in Milan, Italy. Pincus recognized that his full schedule might

*Gregory Pincus–*Playboy, *May 1, 1961*

reflect "over-complaisance on my part." In February 1963, Goody and Lizzie attended the seventh annual conference of the International Planned Parenthood Federation in Singapore and combined the trip with another visit to Japan.[14,15] Goody did not want or seek privacy. His trips were full of meetings, cocktail parties, and dinners.

Goody Pincus even appeared in *Playboy*. A year after the oral contraceptive was approved for marketing, *Playboy* hailed the pill as "potent pellets" that promised a "connubial boon, ... mankind seems to have found history's biggest insurance bargain—and its best hope yet for world-wide, month-long peace of mind."[16]

In the early 1960s, the English Granada TV Network showed a thirty-minute program featuring the birth control pill.[17] A production crew had traveled from London to Shrewsbury in 1961 to film an interview with Goody. He sat behind his desk and provided practiced answers to previously prepared questions. Katharine McCormick was not impressed with the stodgy and stilted show. "I saw the TV Birth Control broadcast last night and thought it was a bore except when you were speaking, and I was very glad for what little you did say. It is so tiresome when they begin that old theological Catholic discussion. I am sorry that you had to go through the bother of rehearsing for that broadcast.[18]

Goody and Lizzie Passport Photos — 1963

Goody's schedule in 1964 was typically busy, including attendance at the Mexican Endocrine Society meeting, an appearance on national television discussing cancer, chairing a scientific group discussing the mechanism of action of sex hormones at the World Health Organization in Geneva, and a lecture at a Princeton University conference entitled "Conference on Biological Targets and Bullets."[19] Goody and Lizzie attended a symposium on hormonal contraception in Australia in October 1964 that featured his lengthy presentations on the physiological effects and the long-term effects of oral contraceptives. He was hailed in the Australian newspapers. Goody said to the symposium participants, "When we first started to do research with ovulation inhibitors as contraceptives, the mention of the word contraceptive in certain quarters was pretty dangerous, and now I think it isn't dangerous at all. And I think one of the reasons is that we've accumulated an enormous amount of basic knowledge about the utility and the usefulness and the need of the sex hormones and effectors and regulators of many processes going on in the body."[20]

Goody and Lizzie frequently visited the Ciba Foundation in London, an organization that provided facilities and the organization of conferences dedicated to the meeting and cooperation of scientists from all over the world. From 1949 to 1978, it was directed by Sir Gordon Wolstenholme who became a close friend of the Pincus family. The 100th symposium of the Ciba

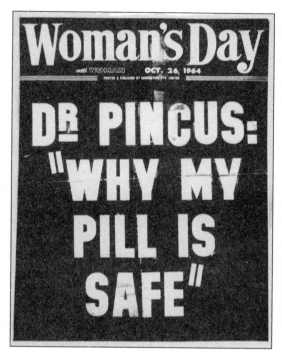

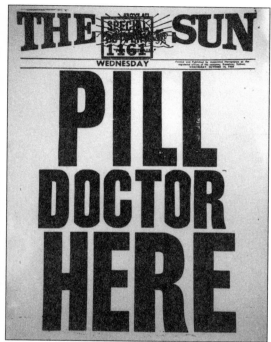

Australian newspapers — 1964

Goody and Lizzie in Australia — 1964

Foundation took place only months before Pincus died, and the published proceedings entitled "Health of Mankind" were dedicated to one of the participants, Gregory Pincus.

In an interview with *New York Times* writer Lawrence Lader in 1966, Pincus reported receiving divergent reactions on his travels.[21] In Milan, Italy, where in May 1966 Goody was the overall chairman for the Second International Congress on Hormonal Steroids, he was greeted by headlines in a Catholic newspaper asking, "Why should we welcome Dr. Pincus to Italy?" But he emphasized that far more typical was the woman who said, "You have changed my life. The pill has ended fear and uncertainty."

Katharine McCormick eagerly and enthusiastically supported Goody's travels. She wanted the message of oral contraception broadcast worldwide. She knew there was a universal need for this effective, new contraceptive method. It is impossible to measure the impact of Goody's ambassadorial efforts, but it is not far fetched to attribute some of the rapid acceptance and spread of oral contraception throughout the world to Pincus and McCormick. Goody's travels had a purpose beyond enjoyment and self-aggrandizement. He was sincerely dedicated to informing the world about oral contraception.

In the Preface to his book published in 1965, *The Control of Fertility*, Pincus said: "how a few precious facts obscurely come to in the laboratory may resonate into the lives of men everywhere, bring order to disorder, hope to the hopeless, life to the dying. That this is the magic and mystery of our time is sometimes grasped and often missed, but to expound it is inevitable."

We have conferred and lectured in many countries of the world, seen at first hand the research needs and possibilities in almost every European, Asiatic, Central, and South American country. We have faced the hard fact of overpopulation in country after country, learned of the bleak demographic future, assessed the prospects for the practice of efficient fertility control. This has been a saddening and a heartening experience; saddening because of the sight of continuing poverty and misery, heartening because of the dedicated colleagues and workers seeking to overcome the handicap of excess fertility and to promote healthy reproductive function. Among these we have made many friends, found devoted students.

It is the operation of the scientific process in the area of fertility control that this book attempts to portray. That process is neither the acme of efficiency nor the "Final Solver of All Problems." As is evident to all who read, it works by fits and starts, it leads to errors that must be painfully reviewed and critically rejected; it often dwells lengthily on minutiae, overstresses conditional findings, and for long periods fails to illumine factual obscurities. Nonetheless it gets ahead, haltingly perhaps, but inevitably. The mystery and wonder of conception becomes describable in terms of gametes and their movements, in terms of fertilization reactions and the operation of replication mechanisms, in terms of oviduct chemistry and hormonal regulation. In each of these is also mystery and wonder, for there is still more to discover than we now know. But in the blazing or flickering light of what we do know, a priori judgments and willful prejudices fade. And our considered and tested knowledge offers a firm basis for what we can and should do."[22]

IT IS EASY TO THINK that the oral contraceptive was Goody's all-encompassing focus during the last ten years of his life. But this was far from the case. He had a serious problem; he could never say no. Pincus was constantly reviewing research proposals forwarded from private foundations, the National Institutes of Health, and the National Science Foundation. He filled every request for letters of recommendations for promotions, clinical and scientific appointments, medical and graduate school applicants, and job candidates who

ranged from high school students to professors. He answered every letter asking for scientific materials or professional advice. And he rarely refused an invitation to speak and never refused a request to chair a meeting, both nationally and internationally. He was so busy that many of his letters began with the phrase, "When I returned to my office, I found your letter." Goody's secretary, Pauline Pertell, became quite good at providing adequate replies in his absence.

The studies in the Caribbean did not end with FDA approval of oral contraception. Goody and Lizzie continued to visit Puerto Rico and Haiti for a week once or twice a year, flying first class.[23] This was a time when first-class airfare from New York to San Juan was only $65, and a hotel suite only $30 daily. In 1963, six projects were on-going, located in Haiti and three sites in Puerto Rico: Rio Piedras, Caguas, and Ponce. The studies included the follow-up of long-term users, metabolic effects on the liver and thyroid glands, the impact on lactation, and even the transmission of the contraceptive steroids in breast milk.[24] Newer low-dose products were being tested, and oral administration of the pill was being compared with vaginal administration. A low-dose product was being given daily without interruption to totally prevent menstruation, a method that wasn't marketed until forty-four years later. In 1964, Hector Rocamora came to the Worcester Foundation to assume supervision of the oral contraceptive studies and Bernardo Santamarina took over in Puerto Rico. The year that Pincus died, he was involved in a study of the children born to his steroid-treated mothers in collaboration with Priscilla White at the Joslin Clinic in Boston.[25] It is striking that the Pincus group thought of these many topics so early in the history of oral contraception. These issues would not be studied on a larger scale in different countries throughout the world until more than twenty and thirty years later.

Pincus was honest and fastidious in his finances. He kept track of every expense, no matter how small, including the cost of entertaining colleagues, and submitted them for reimbursement, either to the Worcester Foundation or to sponsoring pharmaceutical companies and organizations.[26-28] In his interactions with industry, he was always on the lookout for ways to benefit the Foundation. For example, Pincus was working with the Julius Schmid Company studying the efficacy and toxicity in animals of new anti-progestins, anti-estrogens, and anti-androgens. He assigned his potential 5 percent royalty to the Worcester Foundation.[29] His focus was always on his science.

Goody was an honorable man whose life was enriched not by money, but by his science and his personal relationships. He did not take relationships lightly; he came to know the family members of his friends, and invited them into his home. In the hundreds of letters he wrote to associates and friends, he always gave his warm regards by personal names to the wives (a female scientist was a rare occurrence in those days).

Pincus did accept some opportunities to become affluent, but not one amounted to significant wealth. As a paid consultant to Searle, Goody was eligible to participate in the employee's stock option plan. Small numbers of Searle shares, ten to twenty at a time, were obtained and assigned to his children.[30] Goody paid for his stock purchases with Searle payroll deductions of about $72 per month.[31] In addition, he was able to supplement his life and health insurance with group programs at Searle. In 1951, he was receiving $600 per month as a consultant and he purchased a $7,000 life insurance policy for $2.10 per month.[32]

The progesterone used by Pincus, Chang, and Rock in their very first studies was obtained from a Syntex subsidiary, Chemical Specialties in New York City. Irvin V. Sollins was involved with the New York company, but in the early 1950s, he created a new enterprise, Root Chemicals, Inc. This became a family-run business producing steroid products from the Mexican yam and a research operation in Puerto Rico seeking new methods of synthesis and production. In 1954, the Puerto Rico branch of the company provided 40,000 progesterone tablets for the initial clinical study in San Juan, at a cost of $3,000.[33] Sollins and Goody became friends and in the first years of the company's existence, Goody invested small amounts ($2,500) in Root in anticipation of future profits.[34] The company never became a major player, and never made a meaningful contribution to Goody's finances. Eventually Root Chemicals was obtained by G. D. Searle by an exchange of stock holdings, and a small number of Searle shares were acquired by Lizzie who held the Root shares.[35]

Goody never slowed down. In 1967, the last year of his life, Goody's name appeared on fifteen publications, with subjects such as the metabolism and secretion of aldosterone, anabolic steroid effects in elderly patients, the effect of irradiation on cortisol production, and of course, the long-term effects of oral contraception.[36]

Pincus belonged to twenty-six national and international scientific societies.[37] These were not memberships for window dressing. He participated in the meetings and often chaired committees. Over the years, he was responsible for organizing and leading multiple scientific meetings.

Final Days

Goody Pincus didn't anticipate his death. In the last months of his life, he was accepting invitations to meetings and conferences scheduled after his death for the last half of 1967 and all of 1968. In the six months before he died, Goody lectured at Cornell University and at the Harvard Medical Society. He attended the Ciba Foundation Symposium in London, and afterwards visited Paris and Morocco. And he went to Russia.

John McCracken recalled that "A year before he died, he looked gaunt. Lizzie and his friends tried to persuade him not to go to Russia, but he had a sense of obligation and went. You could vaguely tell that he wasn't well, but you really didn't know."[38] The trip to Russia, only three months before he died, was a testimony to Goody's sense of obligation. Under the joint sponsorship of the National Academy of Sciences and the Russian Academy of Sciences, he was scheduled to visit

Some Noteworthy Committees

1949–1951	Mental Health Research Study Section, U.S. Public Health Service
1951–1957	Endocrinology Study Section, NIH, Chairman 1955–1957
1956–1960	Chairman, Endocrinology Panel, Cancer Chemotherapy National Service Center, NIH
1955–1967	Research Study Committee, National Association for Mental Health
1959–1967	Committee on Research, International Planned Parenthood Federation
1960	Chairman, Program Committee, First International Congress of Endocrinology
1961–1967	Medical Council, Planned Parenthood Federation of America

Honors and Awards

1939	Fellow, American Academy of Arts and Sciences
1951–1952	President, The Endocrine Society
1957	Oliver Bird Prize
1960	Albert D. Lasker Award in Planned Parenthood
1962	Sixth Annual Julius A. Koch Award
1964	Modern Medicine Award for Distinguished Achievement
1964	City of Hope National Medical Center Award
1965	Member, National Academy of Sciences
1966	Cameron Prize in Practical Therapeutics, University of Edinburgh
1966	Barren Foundation Medal
1967	Cyril Foster Lecturer, Oxford University
1968	American Medical Association Scientific Achievement Award

with many Russian scientists; he was unwilling to disappoint the Russians, and he was expected to provide a written report on Russian science. Goody kept a journal of this trip that produced seventeen single-spaced pages when his secretary typed it on his return.[39] There is no hint in this journal that he was even a little tired, let alone sick, as he and Lizzie maintained a busy, hectic pace throughout the four-week trip from Moscow to Leningrad to Peterhof to Sukhum to Tbilisi and back to Moscow.

Goody and Lizzie arose early each day, did some touring, visiting museums, and checking out art galleries, during which Goody, who had some knowledge of the Russian language from his childhood, was impressed that "Liz's Russian does a good job mostly." Occasionally Goody

was able to converse in French and to understand some German. Most days, a chauffeured limousine carted Goody, usually accompanied by Lizzie, to research institutes and hospitals, where he visited patient-care facilities, gave lectures, and talked science. Goody exchanged books with department heads, handing out copies of his book, *The Control of Fertility,* and spent a lot of time listening to summaries of Russian medicine and science, which he duly recorded in his journal.

Goody and Lizzie usually returned to the hotel for a late afternoon siesta, awakening for late suppers in the European tradition. For evening dinners at hotels, Goody made sure he found a bottle of Scotch. Goody's gregarious nature often enticed another group of tourists to join them.

Goody and Lizzie were taken on excursions to museums and to rural areas with lunches lengthened by extensive toasts. In Peterhof, they enjoyed seeing *Swan Lake*, "superbly done." But in Sukhumi, they were not impressed by their small hotel room and the bathroom down the hall with a broken toilet, "Pretty poor stuff for eminent invitee!" On a ride to the countryside, lunch at a Georgian roadside eating house was marked by "mush tasteless, meat tough, wine dago red acid." It was time to go home.

IN PINCUS'S LAST MONTHS, the staff of the Worcester Foundation became aware of his condition but not its cause. His jaundice could not be hidden, stimulating speculation whether it was alcohol or cancer.[40] His incurable illness, agnogenic myeloid metaplasia with myelofibrosis, originated in a mutation in bone marrow stem cells, the cells that differentiate to form platelets, and red and white blood cells. It is a cancer of bone marrow cells. Over time, the bone marrow is replaced with scar tissue (myelofibrosis). Other tissues that can produce red and white blood cells try to compensate for the ensuing deficiency, leading to enlargements of the liver and spleen. It is a rare disorder and no known specific cause can be identified. Agnogenic myeloid metaplasia with myelofibrosis occurs at any age, even in newborn infants, but usually it

occurs in individuals older than fifty years, with most diagnoses made from age sixty to sixty-five. Only 20 percent of individuals live as long as ten years after diagnosis.

An increased risk has been associated with exposure to industrial solvents such as benzene and toluene, but this would require daily exposure over a lengthy duration.[41,42] It has often been written that Pincus's illness was a consequence of overexposure to toxic chemicals in the laboratory. This is extremely unlikely. For many, if not nearly most years of his life, Pincus ventured into the laboratory for only a few minutes at a time to talk with the younger scientists doing the work. Although myeloid metaplasia has been linked with exposure to industrial solvents, no suggestion has emerged indicating that the scientists exposed to laboratory chemicals have had an increase in blood disorders.

Myeloid metaplasia usually causes no symptoms until the pain of an enlarged spleen leads to its diagnosis. It is also often detected when a routine blood count is performed. An examination of the blood reveals anemia and an increase in white-blood cells in about one-fourth of patients and low white–blood-cell counts in one-third. The diagnosis is established by obtaining a sample of bone marrow. The early symptoms largely reflect the resulting anemia: fatigue, weakness, difficulty breathing. Rapid progression can cause severe bleeding in the skin or gastrointestinal tract, the coughing up of blood, seizures, and an inability to breathe. But the course is usually slower, and this appeared to be the case with Pincus, and the findings are usually limited to the enlarged liver and spleen plus skin hemorrhages.

Today, stem cell transplantation offers a potential cure, but in general no treatment can overcome this condition. Blood transfusions are provided periodically to overcome the anemia and the low platelet counts; however, transfusions are only supportive in that no treatment produces a cure.

FOR MOST OF HIS LIFE, Goody Pincus was in good health except for occasional bouts of

Gregory Pincus — 1964

abdominal discomfort. In August 1955 when he was fifty-two years old and six months after he made in Tokyo his first public presentation on a potential oral contraceptive, Pincus endured a total examination of his gastrointestinal tract by x-rays.[43] A small duodenal ulcer was discovered and appropriate dietary adjustments were recommended. A return of this complaint prompted another x-ray examination seven years later in June 1963. The small ulcer was still there, but a disturbing new finding was noted, an enlarged spleen.[44]

An admission to Massachusetts General Hospital was arranged after Pincus first attended the 1963 Laurentian Hormone Conference. In September 1963, his complaints were fatigue and night sweats. His physical examination revealed a pale appearance and an enlarged spleen, liver, and prostate gland.[45] Blood studies documented his anemia, and a microscopic examination of his blood smear suggested a diagnosis of myeloid metaplasia. The question was whether to perform a splenectomy, an operation that would be harmful if the diagnosis of myeloid metaplasia was correct because the blood being formed in the enlarged spleen was essential for his life. A bone marrow biopsy from his iliac crest confirmed the diagnosis and revealed the replacement of marrow cells with fibrosis.

Goody's doctors monitored him with periodic

blood tests that were often submitted under a pseudonym.[46] He remained anemic, and a year later his spleen was larger. Nevertheless, he was relatively stable, and no treatment was recommended.

In May 1965, Pincus, now sixty-two years old, was again admitted to Massachusetts General Hospital, with a severe anemia that required transfusion with five pints of blood (approximately half of a normal man's full blood volume).[47] A repeat x-ray examination of his gastrointestinal tract found the ulcer to be gone, although he had diverticulitis of his colon. Three months later, Pincus required another two pints of red blood cells. A sophisticated study with radioactive tracers documented active erythropoiesis (blood formation) in the spleen and sacrum. A month later, treatment was begun with weekly intramuscular injections of testosterone (a boost to blood formation) and Myleran.

Until Myleran was first used in 1953, the standard palliative therapy for myeloid leukemias was irradiation of the splenic area to control splenic enlargement. Myleran is busulfan, a cytotoxic drug that suppresses the bone marrow. The drug is related to the toxic nitrogen mustards, sharing a mechanism, the alkylation of DNA in bone marrow cells. Although not curative, it is still considered an appropriate therapy for chronic myelogeous leukemias, better than irradiation, to

Gregory Pincus — 1965

relieve symptoms and increase survival time by improving the blood counts and reducing splenic and hepatic size. Excessive dosage and complete shut down of blood production are avoided by monitoring blood counts.

Goody Pincus didn't want people, even his family, to know that he was sick. His sister Sophie remembered seeing Goody at a party and saying, "Goody, you're getting fat!"[48] She had to be told by the hostess of the party that Goody was sick and had an enlarged spleen. In a letter written on March 28, 1966, Goody said, "Oscar Hechter tells me that you have been informed that I am a seriously ill man. This is entirely untrue, and I wish you would do your utmost to scotch this rumor. At the moment I am healthier than I have

been in many years. As nearly as I can make out, a minor setback which occurred about a year ago has been the source of the unfounded rumor."[49]

But at that same time early in 1966, Anne Merrill was in her laboratory on a Saturday morning. Gregory Pincus dropped by and embarrassingly asked if Merrill would take his blood sample and perform a blood-cell count. He requested that she not mention it to anyone, explaining that he had recently had a blood transfusion and wanted to know if he needed another. Merrill recalled, "I never saw such funny blood in my life. In fact a little later, when I took a count just before he went into the hospital his last time, I remember calling them to say, 'You better take a good look at this, because I can't find *any* white cells at all."[50] "We knew he was going for transfusions, but we didn't know why. I don't think we ever asked. I just felt we were assistants and it wasn't our place to be asking. I think we all knew he wasn't well."[51]

Gregory Pincus in Paris — November, 1966

IN PICTURES TAKEN during his last year, Pincus, for the first time in his life, had the round, protruding abdomen typically seen in older men who gain weight. It is likely that Pincus passed it off as such to many he encountered during that year. But he had not gained weight.

To compensate for his steadily failing bone marrow, blood-forming tissue in his spleen and liver progressively increased in size, pushing outward when his intra-abdominal space was fully occupied. Luigi Mastroianni remembered that when Goody visited Philadelphia in the last year of his life, "you could see his spleen from across the room."[52]

In April 1967, Goody's physician observed that "It is difficult to catch him between numerous lectures and conferences. For the most part I am quite impressed how well he has lived with his myeloid metaplasia during the past few years."[53] Goody always did set a hectic pace, but his ability to do so in the last months of his life may have been aided by the large doses of testosterone he was receiving. Pincus weighed 160 pounds (his usual weight ranged from 156 to 160), complained of fatigue and moderate diarrhea every few weeks, and some night sweating. Because of abdominal discomfort secondary to his enlarged spleen and liver, he was eating frequent small meals. His treatment consisted of daily Myleran pills and testosterone injections every two weeks. The possibility of a small dose of irradiation to the spleen was raised. Three months later, Pincus required another transfusion, with three pints of blood.[54] The question was whether this worsening of his anemia was due to the destruction of blood cells by the spleen or by excessive doses of Myleran. The plan was to repeat radioactive isotope studies of his spleen and to further consider the use of irradiation.

Perhaps Pincus's buoyant optimism was beginning to fade because in early July 1967 he started to liquidate some of his investments. He sold two hundred shares of his Searle stock and one hundred shares of stock in the Parke Davis company; in addition, he transferred shares of Searle to his brother-in-law, Myron Notkin, a physician who lived in Montreal.[55] Nevertheless, he wrote to Katharine McCormick on July 18, 1967, reviewing his latest research data and seeking to arrange a visit with Katharine in the fall.[56]

The increasing hematopoietic function of his spleen and liver was vital for his life, but eventually the size of the organs and the crowding of his abdomen began to cause unbearable discomfort and pain. The pain caused Pincus to be admitted to Peter Bent Brigham Hospital in Boston on July 24, 1967.[57] His spleen, normally high under the left side of the rib cage, was now enormous, easily palpated by his physician as far down as the pelvic bones, like a tumor overfilling the abdomen. Goody, his family, and his physician faced a crucial decision. Celso-Ramón Garcia was probably involved in the decision-making as well, because as Luigi Mastroianni put it, "Every time they tried something new, Celso was right there by

his side, even when he was dying. ... Lizzie would call him at the drop of a hat."[58] Surgery was out of the question; Pincus depended on his blood-producing spleen for adequate levels of red blood cells to keep him oxygenated, platelets to prevent spontaneous hemorrhaging, and white blood cells to fight infection. Irradiation of the spleen with an appropriate dose of x-rays offered the possibility of shrinkage without a total loss of hematopoiesis. The problem was that fixing the dose had to be an educated estimate, but guesswork all the same. It was decided to administer 100 rads to his abdomen. There was an obvious salutary response. Despite a sore throat and fall of his white count to 800 (normal is up to 10,000), Goody was discharged and was back in his office dictating letters the first week of August.

Pincus was hospitalized again on August 11, 1967 with a red ulcerated throat and swollen, tender salivary glands. He was anemic and had only a few white blood cells in his circulation. In addition, his platelet count was low, putting him at risk for spontaneous hemorrhaging. On his sixth hospital day, Pincus became febrile and went into shock. His blood cultures were positive for E. coli that at first seemed to respond to treatment with three antibiotics. But his white count fell to fifty, which is essentially zero. Every body function deteriorated rapidly, and Pincus, only sixty-four years old, died at 7:40

PM on August 22nd. Three days later, Pincus was buried in the Mountain View Cemetery in Shrewsbury. The words on his gravestone, "A Great And Kindly Man," are a final tribute from his wife and children.

Because of the failure to form sufficient white cells and platelets, the causes of death were overwhelming infection and hemorrhage. Gregory Pincus's diagnosis was confirmed at autopsy. He had a blood infection and hemorrhage in the lungs, spinal canal, and gastrointestinal tract, plus kidney damage.[59,60] His esophagus and lungs, which were filled with pneumonia, were heavily infected with yeast. The large bowel had a perforation of a diverticulum, probably secondary to a fungal infection that caused a partial obstruction of his intestine, intensified by his huge spleen (2080 grams, normal being 150 grams) and liver (3620 grams, normal is about 1500 grams). The bone marrow was totally replaced by fibrotic tissue. The spleen had a complete loss of white cell precursors. His enlarged prostate consisted of benign growth. The downhill course began with the splenic irradiation, because as the pathologist wrote, the spleen was "the sole remaining site of effective hematopoiesis and proved highly sensitive to the radiation."[61]

Goody and Lizzie were not religious.[62,63] Like Hudson Hoagland, Goody was a pure scientist. Nevertheless, a memorial service was conducted at the Temple Emanuel in Worcester by Rabbi Joseph Klein on Friday morning, August 25, 1967. Celso-Ramón Garcia began his remarks at the service by saying, "It is difficult to believe that Gregory Pincus has left us. To me he was invincible. He was the strongest man I have known. … only those who have worked closely with him could know his flashes of imaginative insight in attacking tough scientific problems and his patient pursuit of truth, his meticulous self-criticism and his prodigious output of brilliant research in fields as diverse as basic endocrinology, cancer, cardiovascular problems, aging and especially, the physiology of reproduction."[64] Hudson Hoagland spoke and pointed out that "Though his discoveries offered him opportunities for great financial gain, he left no fortune. Instead he bequeaths to all mankind a heritage of great and useful discoveries."[65]

AFTER PINCUS DIED, "His death seemed to tear the heart out of the Foundation."[66] Pauline Pertell, Goody's secretary in his last years, "was like a dragon that guarded him."[67] When she heard of Goody's death, Pertell collapsed and had to be hospitalized.[68] "Many of the scientists had been drawn to the Foundation by Pincus's charisma, and his death left them bewildered and exposed."[69] Pincus was both mentor and fund raiser for the young scientists. The young scientists never had to apply for grants or worried about funding; Goody "arranged for the money to come."[70] Gabrial Bialy said, "One thing I never had to worry about funding as long as Goody was alive. Where he found the money to pay my salary and laboratory expenses, I do not know and I never asked him. Now this involved good and bad. It's good that you didn't have to worry; it's bad because you never learn about grantsmanship."[71] The young scientists were abruptly on their own. As Joseph Goldzieher said, "The Foundation was an institution that was put together by powerful personalities. And it lived and died with them."[72]

After the death of Pincus, Hudson and then Mahlon Hoagland repeatedly tried, without success, to persuade the pharmaceutical companies that benefited from oral contraception to provide an endowed position or some meaningful token of gratitude to the Worcester Foundation.[73] Six months before his death, Goody had formulated an agreement with Daniel C. Searle, executive vice president of Searle, that Searle would provide a lifetime monthly payment of $600 when he retired at age sixty-seven in 1970.[74] This was not an impressive amount, less than that paid to junior research fellows at that time. After his death or if he died before 1970,

Searle agreed to pay Lizzie $300 per month, and this they did. Lizzie also collected $18,000 from the Searle group life insurance program.[75] The Board of Trustees of the Worcester Foundation granted Lizzie a gift of $5,000 plus $1,000 per month for a year.[76]

Goody's total income the year that he died was $55,790; the portion from G.D. Searle was $12,206, his Worcester Foundation salary was $29,583, and he earned $14,001 business income that included consultant fees, dividends, and royalties.[77] Pincus recorded in 1966 a $25,601 sale of stock in Searle, acquired since 1963. Beginning in the early 1950s, Goody received a royalty payment from Searle for the development of Vallestril, a synthetic estrogen; the payment amounted to about $600 per year.[78] He also collected an annual royalty of about $600 from Vineland Poultry.[790] Dividend income totaled $3,975 from stocks in eighteen companies, including the pharmaceutical companies G. D. Searle, Parke Davis, and Merck. By today's standards, Pincus's investments in companies that stood to profit from the sales of oral contraceptives, even though they were not large investments, would be open to criticism that he had a vested interest in the success of his studies. This can only be judged by the accuracy and honesty of his publications and presentations. Pincus allowed the data to speak for him; there never has been an indication of anything less

than open truthfulness. Even the one time in 1961 when Pincus prematurely suggested that oral contraceptives reduced cervical cancer, he was reflecting the experience in his clinical trials. Later, he acknowledged that the number of women in his studies was not large enough to provide definitive answers regarding any cancers.

In 1974, Searle presented Harvard with $400,000 to support a fellowship or faculty position.[80] The presentation was marked by the unveiling of a portrait of Goody at a luncheon attended by Lizzie and son John. The Gregory Pincus Memorial Endowment in the Harvard School of Public Health grew substantially over the years and is currently used, but unfortunately with no publicly visible recognition of Pincus, to support faculty salaries and research. The Pincus family did not like the portrait; Harvard gave it to Lizzie and today the portrait cannot be found.

There is one building in the world that bears only Goody's name. The French National Institute for Health and Medical Research (INSERM) was created in 1964 as a public institution dedicated to the study of human health and diseases. Several hundred research laboratories are located in university hospitals, cancer treatment centers, and research campuses such as the Pasteur Institute. The prominent French scientist, Etienne-Emile Baulieu, honored his friend and colleague, by

designating the main building housing INSERM as the Gregory Pincus Building.

Lizzie moved to be with her family in Montreal. But after suffering several strokes, John Pincus arranged for her to be in an assisted living center in Georgetown. Finally Lizzie had to be in a nursing home, and the family sent her to be near her son and grandchildren who had moved to California. Lizzie died in Santa Monica in 1988, almost eighty-nine years old. She was buried next to Goody in the Mountain View Cemetery in Shrewsbury, with a humble grave stone that lies flat with the ground and says, "They Always Stood Together."

ANNE MERRILL said it best, "He was kind, generous, tolerant, understanding, driving, dedicated. I pity the people that haven't known him, I really do."[81]

EPILOGUE

GOODY PINCUS has been called the "Father of the Pill" by many, even by Carl Djerassi, who proclaimed himself the "Mother of the Pill" when he presented the Gregory Pincus Memorial Lecture at the last Laurentian Hormone Conference in 1994.[1] Djerassi took the opportunity to complain that Pincus never gave sufficient credit or recognition to the chemists responsible for the orally active progestational drugs. M-C. Chang's wife, Isabelle, had "Father of the Pill" engraved on Chang's gravestone. And where does that leave John Rock and Celso-Ramón Garcia? For that matter, where does that leave Katharine McCormick who gave more than her money to the project?

After two years of writing and rewriting, Pincus published his second book, *The Control of Fertility*, in 1965. The book was dedicated to Mrs. Stanley McCormick "because of her steadfast faith in scientific inquiry and her unswerving encouragement of human dignity."[2] It was more than a summary of the work on oral contraceptives. With 1,459 references, Pincus pointed out in his Preface that he had examined more than twice that number, the book summarized the contemporary knowledge of male and female reproductive physiology before concluding with an emphasis on contraception. As noted, Djerassi criticized Pincus for not citing the chemists who made orally active progestins possible. It would certainly have been easy for Pincus to add a sentence or two about this history. However, Pincus was a physiologist. His book is about physiology, and it is understandable that he left chemistry to the chemists.

In 1968, Celso Ramón Garcia wrote, "Goody was a creative, productive biologist. He had equanimity, a fabulous sense of humor and a profound sense of responsibility. In a serene manner, the logic of his presentations demonstrated the correctness of his decisions. These were strengthened by the influence of his personality and above all by his unyielding faith in scientific principles."[3] Thirty-six years later, Garcia opined, "I am often amused by those who claim to be the father of the pill, the godfather of the pill, or the grandfather of the pill. Most of these accounts are by Johnny-come-latelies or those who allege that they have researched the history of the pill and publish monographs on the subject but allow poetic license to run wild."[4]

What did Pincus think? In an article published one year before he died, Pincus said, "Although there was a well-established background for its launching, the initiation of the present-day practice of oral contraception may fairly be marked by the publication in 1953 of a report by Chang and me on the ovulation-inhibiting potency of progesterone and some of its derivatives as administered by several routes (subcutaneous, intravaginal, oral)."[5] But Pincus's early death deprived us of his further thoughts in invited historical articles or in his personal memoir.

Although Goody would at human moments have enjoyed the acknowledgment and title of "Father of the Pill," I believe that the purity of his scientific soul would have found it unacceptable. Scientific

and clinical accomplishments build upon the work of others. To be sure, at critical junctures, an individual can make a penetrating insight or provide the required drive and perseverance—and thus, discoveries and accomplishments will occur earlier than they might have. But the pressure of accumulating knowledge will eventually have its way. The birth control pill did not suddenly appear; it was the result of scientific development, one achievement leading to another. Joseph Goldzieher thought that Goody would dislike being called the Father of the Pill because "He was the right man in the right place at the right time."[6]

In his last days, Goody's illness galvanized talk at the Worcester Foundation about the Nobel Prize; would Pincus receive the award before he died? He was nominated once, in 1963 and again in 1965 by his friend Hermann Joseph Muller, a noted geneticist.[7] Muller, like Goody, had graduated from Morris High School, although much earlier, in 1907. Muller received the Nobel Prize in Physiology or Medicine in 1946 for his work describing the damaging effects of x-rays on genes. There is no way to know how Muller's nomination of Pincus was received in Sweden, or whether there were other nominations. Conversations about the Nobel Prize inevitably brought up the early controversial work on parthenogenesis, and there was speculation that the difficulty in reproducing Goody's work was working against him.[8]

Titles and prizes are created by the world outside of science. Egos are assuaged and satisfaction comes with public recognition. There was no shortage of public recognition during Goody's last years, but it would be a disservice to Pincus for him to be known only as the "Father of the Pill." His accomplishments were greater than that single achievement. There are 429 citations on his list of scientific publications. Pincus developed new methods of measuring hormones and made original contributions to understanding the physiology of mammalian ova, the effect of hormones on early development, and the metabolism of hormones.

His early work on parthenogenesis earned Pincus notoriety, but his book, *The Eggs of Mammals,* published in 1936, was acclaimed by scientists in the field as a seminal contribution. Although it summarized the scientific literature on the subject, every chapter was buttressed with Pincus's own studies and results.

From his days at Harvard until his death, Pincus mentored a huge number of young scientists, many of whom went on to distinguished careers of scientific contributions and leadership. In addition, he secured financial support for dozens enabling them to concentrate on their work without worrying about funding. The educational programs at the Worcester Foundation that Hoagland and Pincus created gave a substantial boost to many who pursued academic careers in the U.S. and in many foreign countries. For twenty-three years, Pincus was the organizer, director, and shepherd for the Laurentian Hormone Conference. He deserves accolades for that endeavor alone. The Laurentian Hormone Conference gave young scientists a public platform, and it provided for important networking that led to new ideas and significant collaborations.

Pincus was known throughout the world. He was the scientific statesman for the field of endocrinology, especially in steroid hormones and reproductive physiology. He freely shared his thinking, his accomplishments, and his ideas. And all of this was achieved with warmth and grace. He made friends wherever he went.

Gregory Pincus, in the story of his life, can continue to teach contemporary young scientists. Today, it has become fashionable to speak of "translational research," the translation of scientific knowledge into daily living, the application of research findings into clinical practice.[9] This is an old philosophy with a new title. Gregory Pincus was a translational scientist. His work was part of the foundation for in vitro fertilization, and bringing oral contraception to the world as a cooperative effort between bench scientists and clinicians can be easily viewed as the epitome of translational research. Burton Caldwell remembered his fellowship days when Goody told him: "A method itself is never of any value unless you have a specific application, and so in your writing you have to make it more concrete by being very careful about delineating what you really want to do with the method, because the method is never the end."[10]

Pincus learned from his uncles, Charles and Jacob Lipman, and from the supervisor of his doctorate work, William J. Crozier, that the goal of science is to benefit human life. These mentors only reinforced a basic philosophy that Pincus was already expressing in his personal dairy written in his last year of high school. The most fundamental discovery in basic research ultimately makes its way to an impact on public health, indeed this is translational research. From the bench to the bedside is the motto of translational research, and in Goody's case, it was from the bench to everyone's beds.

In 1968, exactly one year after the death of Pincus, I arrived in Shrewsbury as a fellow in the Steroid Training Program at the Worcester Foundation. I came to interact with many of Pincus's friends and colleagues, and, through them, I realized what I had just missed knowing: Goody Pincus was truly a good man.

APPENDIX:
THE ENDOCRINOLOGY OF
FEMALE REPRODUCTION

To appreciate fully the importance of the studies of Gregory Pincus with rabbit eggs and to understand the methods used by Pincus to produce an oral contraceptive, a brief review of the way a woman's hormones are involved in human reproduction is useful to provide the appropriate background. This summary covers nearly a century of science, and it starts with hormones.

Hormones are substances that are produced in special tissues, released into the bloodstream and travel to distant, responsive cells where each hormone sends a specific message. Hormone production in the endocrine glands, such as the ovaries, testicles, and adrenal glands, is regulated by protein hormones originating in the brain, specifically the hypothalamus and the pituitary gland. The different organs in this system, therefore, use hormones to talk with each other—from the brain to the ovaries with protein hormones, the gonadotropins, and from the ovaries to the brain with the sex hormones, estrogen and progesterone.

The sex hormones produced by the ovary belong to a chemical group called steroids. The generic name of steroids is derived from the Greek *stereos*, meaning solid. Although steroids are members of the alcohol family, they differ from other alcohols in that they can be crystallized into a solid form, hence the name steroids. All steroid hormones are of basically similar structure with relatively minor chemical differences that result in striking variations in how they affect the body.

The sex steroids are divided into three main groups according to the number of carbon atoms they possess. The 21-carbon series includes the corticoids, the main products of the adrenal gland, and progesterone, the main hormone secreted by the ovary after ovulation. The 19-carbon series includes all the androgens (male hormones), whereas the estrogens are 18-carbon steroids. The normal human ovary produces all three classes of sex steroids: estrogens, progestins, and androgens. The major products of the ovary are estrogen (the most potent and the most important being estradiol) and progesterone, with a small amount of the male hormones, androstenedione and testosterone. The ovary does not have the enzymes required to make glucocorticoids and mineralocorticoids (the hormones made in the adrenal glands that regulate metabolism).

CHOLESTEROL
(27 CARBONS)

PREGNANE DERIVATIVES
(21 CARBONS)   PROGESTINS
                                                CORTICOIDS

ANDROSTANE DERIVATIVES
(19 CARBONS)   ANDROGENS

ESTRANE DERIVATIVES
(18 CARBONS)   ESTROGENS

PROGESTERONE   TESTOSTERONE   ESTRADIOL

Just before and during menses, when ovarian hormone secretion reaches a low point, escape from the inhibitory feedback of estrogen, progesterone, and a regulating protein secreted in the ovary, inhibin, results in increased follicle-stimulating hormone (FSH) secretion by the anterior pituitary gland in the brain. As the name implies FSH is the required hormone for the growth of an ovarian follicle, the structure in the ovary that contains the egg, surrounded by the cells that produce hormones. With continued growth of the follicle, factors produced within the follicle maintain follicular sensitivity to FSH, allowing conversion from a microenvironment dominated by androgens to one dominated by estrogen, a change necessary for a complete and successful follicular lifespan.

Estrogen is released into the bloodstream in increasing amounts, causing the lining of the uterus to grow in thickness. Continuing and combined action of FSH and another follicular protein, activin, leads to the appearance of luteinizing hormone (LH) receptors on the granulosa cells (the cells in the follicle that surround the egg). This is a prerequisite for ovulation and the formation of the corpus luteum (discussed below). The pituitary hormones, FSH and LH, are called gonadotropins because of their ability to stimulate both the male and female sex organs, the gonads.

Ovulation is triggered by a rapid rise in circulating levels of estradiol, the main estrogen produced by the ovarian follicle. A positive response to this rise in estrogen at the level of the anterior pituitary (and perhaps at the hypothalamus as well) results in the midcycle surge of LH necessary for final maturation of the follicle, expulsion of the egg (ovulation), and subsequent formation of the corpus luteum.

After ovulation, the egg and its surrounding cells are in the fallopian tube within two or three minutes. The fertilizable life of the human egg is unknown, but most estimates

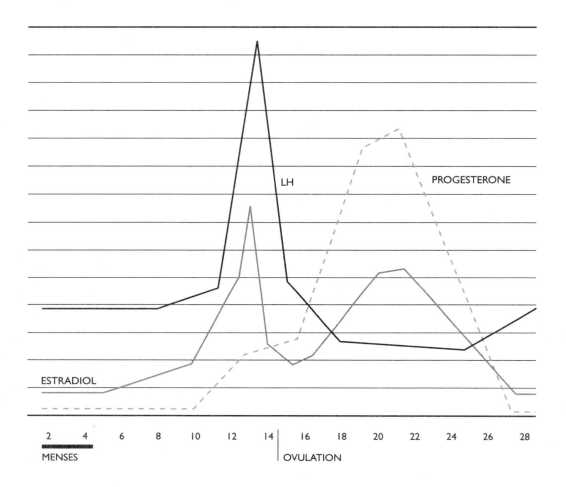

LH

PROGESTERONE

ESTRADIOL

| 2 | 4 | 6 | 8 | 10 | 12 | 14 | 16 | 18 | 20 | 22 | 24 | 26 | 28 |

MENSES

OVULATION

range between twelve and twenty-four hours. The great majority of pregnancies occur when intercourse takes place within the three-day interval just before ovulation. Gregory Pincus's colleague, Min-Chueh Chang, working at the Worcester Foundation for Experimental Biology (Chapter 6), discovered in 1951 that rabbit and rat spermatozoa must spend some hours in the female tract before acquiring the capacity to penetrate ova.[1] Chang called this transformation of sperm, *capacitation*, denoting the cellular changes that ejaculated sperm must undergo in order to fertilize.

Ejaculated sperm reach the fallopian tube within minutes and remain there for hours, even days. Of an average of 200 to 300 million sperm deposited in the vagina, at most only a few hundred, and often less, achieve proximity to the egg. But it only takes one capacitated sperm to achieve fertilization.

After fertilization, the egg begins dividing into multiple cells while remaining in the tube for about eighty hours. This time is necessary to allow the lining of the uterus to prepare for implantation. The fertilized product reaches the uterus about four days after ovulation. The cells continue to multiply, reaching the stage of a blastocyst, a thirty-two- to 256-cell early embryo before implantation. Implantation begins two to four days after the fertilized egg has entered the uterine cavity.

The corpus luteum is literally a yellow body, formed from the cells remaining in the follicle after expulsion of the egg. It continues to produce the major female sex hormones, especially progesterone. It is characterized by an accumulation of a yellow pigment called lutein, which lends its name to the process of luteinization and the corpus luteum. A rise in progesterone follows ovulation along with a second rise in estradiol, producing the fourteen-day luteal phase characterized by low FSH and LH levels. Prior to ovulation the granulosa layer, the cells that surround the egg, is characterized by conversion of androgens to estrogens, an FSH-mediated

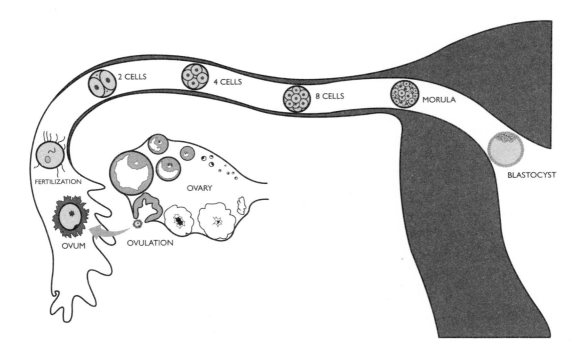

activity. After ovulation the granulosa layer secretes progesterone and estrogens directly into the bloodstream, an LH-mediated activity. These sex hormones, principally progesterone, are responsible for preparing the lining of the uterus for implantation.

After ovulation, the marked increase in progesterone levels, in the presence of estrogen, exerts a profound inhibition of gonadotropin secretion, preventing new follicular growth until it is certain a pregnancy has not occurred. This increase in progesterone after ovulation produces a small but measurable rise in body temperature, and one of the tests for ovulation is the detection of this temperature change in a daily record of morning temperatures.

In the absence of pregnancy, the demise of the corpus luteum two weeks after ovulation, results in a fall in hormone levels, allowing the lining of the uterus (the endometrium) to slough and FSH to increase again, thus initiating a new monthly cycle. Recognition of low FSH and LH levels during the life of the corpus luteum and during pregnancy was the first hint that the sex steroids could suppress the secretion of the pituitary gonadotropins and prevent ovarian follicular growth and ovulation. High levels of a progestational drug, therefore, inhibit ovulation by suppressing the brain's secretion of gonadotropins. This is

the mechanism exploited by Pincus, Chang, and Rock in their studies dedicated to oral contraception.

If pregnancy occurs, the corpus luteum fails to undergo regression and continues to function, secreting the hormone required to maintain pregnancy, progesterone. Progesterone is produced by the corpus luteum until about ten weeks of gestation. Indeed, until approximately the seventh week, the pregnancy is dependent on the presence of the corpus luteum. After a transition period of shared function between the seventh week and tenth week, the placenta emerges as the major source of progesterone synthesis, and maternal circulating levels of progesterone progressively increase throughout pregnancy.

Progesterone prepares and maintains the endometrium to allow implantation. The human corpus luteum makes significant amounts of estradiol, but it is progesterone and not estrogen that is required for successful implantation. A successful pregnancy requires that the corpus luteum be rescued from demise after a two-week lifespan. This rescue is orchestrated by a protein hormone made by the blastocyst and the placenta, human chorionic gonadotropin (HCG). Because implantation normally occurs about five or six days after ovulation, human chorionic gonadotropin must appear by the tenth day after ovulation to rescue the corpus luteum. The blastocyst must successfully implant and secrete HCG within a narrow window of time.

The menstrual cycle is regulated by substances functioning as classic hormones (FSH, LH, estradiol, progesterone, and inhibin) transmitting messages between the ovary and the hypothalamic-pituitary axis and local factors (inhibin, and activin, among others), which coordinate sequential activities within the follicle destined to ovulate. The inhibitory feedback on the pituitary gland by the secretory products of the corpus (estradiol, progesterone, and inhibin) is lost at the time of corpus luteum regression prior to menses and results in the critical initial rise in FSH, which initiates new follicular growth and the beginning of a new cycle.

This is a very logical mechanism. The remarkable degree of coordination between the ovary and the brain (the hypothalamus and pituitary gland) and the exquisite timing involved are achieved by the hormones produced in only one ovarian follicle, the very one destined to ovulate. In this way the ovarian follicle is in charge of its own destiny.

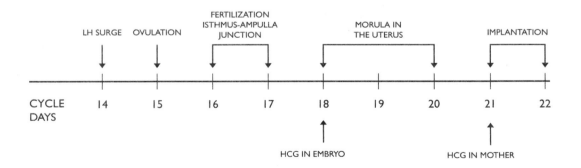

CHAPTER REFERENCES

PROLOGUE

1. **Box 18,** Program, Fifth International Conference on Planned Parenthood, *Papers of Gregory Pincus, Manuscript Division, Library of Congress, Washington, D.C.,* October 28, 1955.

2. **Bernard LP,** Personal interview, May 23, 2007.

3. **Sandrof I,** Worcester's Dr. Pincus Famed for Probing Secrets of Life Begins Program of Atomic Research, *The Worcester Sunday Telegram,* March 4, 1951.

4. **Vaughn P,** *The Pill on Trial,* Coward-Mc-Cann, Inc., New York, 1970, p. 32.

5. Ibid., p. 33.

6. Ibid., pp. 33-34.

7. **McLaughlin L,** *The Pill, John Rock, and the Church: The Biography of a Revolution,* Little, Brown and Company, Boston, 1982, pp. 121-122.

8. **Vaughn P,** *The Pill on Trial,* Coward-Mc-Cann, Inc., New York, 1970, pp. 33-34.

9. **Ramírez de Arellano AB, Seipp C,** *Colonialism, Catholicism, and Contraception,* The University of North Carolina Press, Chapel Hill, 1983, p. 111.

10. **Parkes AS,** Gregory Pincus, as I knew him—an appreciation, *Persp Biol Med* Spring:422-426, 1968.

11. **Segal S,** Personal interview; December 27, 2007.

12. **Parkes AS,** Gregory Pincus, as I knew him—an appreciation, *Persp Biol Med* Spring:422-426, 1968.

13. **Vaughn P,** *The Pill on Trial,* Coward-Mc-Cann, Inc., New York, 1970, p. 36.

14. Ibid., p. 6.

CHAPTER ONE

1. **Drucker S,** Our Teacher, In: Sabsovich K, ed. *Adventures in Idealism: A Personal Record of the Life of Professor Sabsovich,* 1975 Reprint Edition of the original 1922 edition, Arno Press, New York, 1922, p. 183.

2. **Gitelman Z,** *A Century of Ambivalence: The Jews of Russia and the Soviet Union, 1881 to the Present,* second, expanded edition, Indiana University Press, Bloomington, 2001, p. 28.

3. Ibid.

4. **Klier JD,** The Pogrom Paradigm in Russian History, In: Klier JD, Lambroza S, eds. *Pogroms: Anti-Jewish Violence in Modern Russian History,* Cambridge University Press, Cambridge, 1992, p. 34.

5. Ibid., pp. 3-38.

6. **Aronson M,** The Anti-Jewish Pogroms in Russia in 1881, In: Klier JD, Lambroza S, eds. *Pogroms: Anti-Jewish Violence in Modern Russian History,* Cambridge University Press, Cambridge, 1992, pp. 44-61.

7. **Pincus E,** Russian American Episodes, Year unknown, pp. 1-17.

8. **Gitelman Z,** *A Century of Ambivalence: The Jews of Russia and the Soviet Union, 1881 to the Present,* second, expanded edition, Indiana University Press, Bloomington, 2001, p. 10.

9. Ibid., p. 12.

10. **Robinson GT,** *Rural Russia Under the Old Regime,* Longmans, Green and Company, New York, 1932.

11. **Maynard J,** *The Russian Peasant and Other Studies,* Collier Books, New York, 1941, Collier Books Edition, 1962.

12. **Troyat H,** *Daily Life in Russia under the Last Tsar,* Stanford University Press, Stanford, California, 1979, original French edition, 1959.

13. **Lincoln WB,** *In War's Dark Shadow: The Russians Before the Great War,* The Dial Press, New York, 1983, pp. 35-67.

14. **Bonnell VE,** ed, *The Russian Worker: Life and Labor under the Tsarist Regime,* University of California Press, Berkeley, 1983.

15. **Gitelman Z,** *A Century of Ambivalence: The Jews of Russia and the Soviet Union, 1881 to the Present,* second, expanded edition, Indiana University Press, Bloomington, 2001, p. 49.

RUSSIAN HISTORY

1. **Gooding J,** *Rulers and Subjects: Government and People in Russia 1801–1991,* Arnold, London, 1996, p. 1.

CHAPTER TWO

1. **Sabsovich K,** *Adventures in Idealism: A Personal Record of the Life of Professor Sabsovich,* Reprint edition of the 1922 original by Arno Press, New York, 1975, pp. 2-3.

2. Ibid., p. 7.

3. Ibid., p. 10.

4. **Rogger H,** Conclusion and Overview, In: Klier JD LS, ed. *Pogroms: Anti-Jewish Violence in Modern Russian History,* Cambridge University Press, Cambridge, 1992, p. 328.

5. **Sabsovich K,** *Adventures in Idealism: A Personal Record of the Life of Professor Sabsovich,* Reprint edition of the 1922 original by Arno Press, New York, 1975, p. 15.

6. Ibid.

7. Ibid., p. 20.

8. Ibid., p. 24.

9. **Pincus A,** Memories about Gregory Pincus, Family Memoir, *Papers of Gregory Pincus.* Washington, D.C., Library of Congress. 1989, Box 5, pp. 1-30.

10. Ibid.

11. Ibid.

12. Ibid.

13. Ibid.

14. **Pincus E,** Russian American Episodes, Year unknown, pp. 1-17.

15. Ibid.

16. Ibid.

17. **Pincus S,** Personal Recorded Interview with Sophie Pincus Dutton by Honor White, January 8 and 14, 1980.

18. **Waksman SA,** *Jacob G. Lipman: Agricultural Scientist and Humanitarian,* Rugers University Press, New Brunswick, New Jersey, 1966, p. 10.

19. **Pincus E,** Russian American Episodes, Year unknown, pp. 1-17.

20. Ibid.

21. **Pincus S,** Personal Recorded Interview with Sophie Pincus Dutton by Honor White, January 8 and 14, 1980.

22. **Reed HS,** Obituary, Charles B. Lipman, *Science* 100:464-465, 1944.

23. Ibid.

24. **Pincus A,** Memories about Gregory Pincus, Family Memoir, *Papers of Gregory Pincus.* Washington, D.C., Library of Congress, 1989, Box 5, pp. 1-30.

25. **Herlihy P,** The ethnic composition of the city of Odessa in the nineteenth century, *Ukrainian Research Institute, Harvard University,* 1:53-78, 1977, p. 121.

26. **Zipperstein SJ,** *The Jews of Odessa: A Cultural History, 1794–1881,* Stanford University Press, Stanford, California, 1986, p. 121.

27. Ibid. p. 21.

28. **Pincus JW,** The Jewish Farmers' Best Friend, In: Sabsovich K, ed. *Adventures in Idealism: A Personal Record of the Life of Professor Sabsovich,* 1975 Reprint Edition of the 1922 edition, Arno Press, New York, 1922, pp.194-203.

29. **Joseph S,** *History of the Baron de Hirsch Fund,* Augustus M. Kelley, Publishers, Fairfield, New Jersey, 1978, p. 58.

30. **Pincus JW,** The Jewish Farmers' Best Friend, In: Sabsovich K, ed. *Adventures in Idealism: A Personal Record of the Life of Professor Sabsovich,* 1975 Reprint Edition of the 1922 edition, Arno Press, New York, 1922, pp. 194-203.

CHAPTER THREE

1. **Sabsovich K,** *Adventures in Idealism: A Personal Record of the Life of Professor Sabsovich,* Reprint edition of the 1922 original by Arno Press, New York, 1975, pp. 38-39.

2. Ibid., p. 46.

3. Ibid., p. 52.

4. **Singer I, Straus OS,** Hirsch, Baron Maurice de (Moritz Hirsch, Freiherr auf Gereuth): *http://www.jewishencyclopedia. com/view/jsp?artid=771&letter=H,* July 19, 2007.

5. **de Hirsch B,** My Views on Philanthropy, *North Am Rev* 416, 1891.

6. **Jewish Encyclopedia,** Clara de Hirsch, *http://www.jewishencyclopedia.com/view. jsp?artid=758?letter=H,* August 8, 2007.

7. **Singer I, Straus OS,** Hirsch, Baron Maurice de (Moritz Hirsch, Freiherr auf Gereuth): *http://www.jewishencyclopedia.com/view/ jsp?artid=771&letter=H,* July 19, 2007.

8. **Joseph S,** *History of the Baron de Hirsch Fund,* Augustus M. Kelley, Publishers, Fairfield, New Jersey, 1978, p. 41.

9. **Teltsch K,** Fund guides jobless Soviet immigrants, *The New York Times,* May 26, 1991.

10. **Davidson G,** (The Jewish Agricultural Society), The Jewish Agricultural Society, Inc. Report of the Managing Director for the Period 1900–1949, Report No. 1950.

11. **The AJHS Manuscript Catalog,** Jewish Agricultural Society, *http://data.jewishgen. org.wconnect/wc.dll?jg~ajhs_pb~r!!389,* July, 2007.

12. **Sabsovich K,** *Adventures in Idealism: A Personal Record of the Life of Professor Sabsovich,* Reprint edition of the 1922 original by Arno Press, New York, 1975, p. 53.

13. Ibid., p. 54.

14. **Eisenberg E,** *Jewish Agricultural Colonies in New Jersey, 1882-1920,* Syracuse University Press, Syracuse, New York, 1995.

15. **Brandes J,** *Immigrants to Freedom: Jewish Communities in Rural New Jersey since 1882,* University of Pennsylvania Press for the Jewish Publication Society of America, Philadelphia, 1971, p. 77.

16. **Sabsovich K,** *Adventures in Idealism: A Personal Record of the Life of Professor Sabsovich,* Reprint edition of the 1922 original by Arno Press, New York, 1975, p. 57.

17. **Joseph S,** *History of the Baron de Hirsch Fund,* Augustus M. Kelley, Publishers, Fairfield, New Jersey, 1978, p. 50.

18. **Brandes J,** *Immigrants to Freedom. Jewish Communities in Rural New Jersey since 1882,* University of Pennsylvania Press for the Jewish Publication Society of America, Philadelphia, 1971, p. 115.

19. **Ludins DG,** Memories of Woodbine: 1891–1894, *Jewish Frontier* June:7-15, 1960.

20. Ibid.

21. **Sabsovich K,** *Adventures in Idealism: A Personal Record of the Life of Professor Sabsovich,* Reprint edition of the 1922 original by Arno Press, New York, 1975, p. 61.

22. **Joseph S,** *History of the Baron de Hirsch Fund,* Augustus M. Kelley, Publishers, Fairfield, New Jersey, 1978, p. 51.

23. **Sabsovich K,** *Adventures in Idealism: A Personal Record of the Life of Professor Sabsovich,* Reprint edition of the 1922 original by Arno Press, New York, 1975, p. 81.

24. **Pincus E,** Russian American Episodes, Year unknown, pp. 1-17.

25. **Sabsovich K,** *Adventures in Idealism: A Personal Record of the Life of Professor Sabsovich,* Reprint edition of the 1922 original by Arno Press, New York, 1975, p. 79.

26. **Joseph S,** *History of the Baron de Hirsch Fund,* Augustus M. Kelley, Publishers, Fairfield, New Jersey, 1978, p. 53.

27. **Ludins DG,** Memories of Woodbine: 1891–1894, *Jewish Frontier* June:7-15, 1960.

28. **Sabsovich K,** *Adventures in Idealism: A Personal Record of the Life of Professor Sabsovich,* Reprint edition of the 1922 original by Arno Press, New York, 1975, p. 95.

29. Ibid., p. 96.

30. **Ludins DG,** Memories of Woodbine: 1891–1894, *Jewish Frontier* June:7-15, 1960.

31. **Joseph S,** *History of the Baron de Hirsch Fund,* Augustus M. Kelley, Publishers, Fairfield, New Jersey, 1978, p. 55.

32. **Brandes J,** *Immigrants to Freedom: Jewish Communities in Rural New Jersey since 1882,* University of Pennsylvania Press for the Jewish Publication Society of America, Philadelphia, 1971, p. 123.

33. **Herscher UD,** *Jewish Agricultural Utopias in America, 1880–1910,* Wayne State University Press, Detroit, 1981, pp. 93-98.

34. **Sabsovich K,** *Adventures in Idealism: A Personal Record of the Life of Professor Sabsovich,* Reprint edition of the 1922 original by Arno Press, New York, 1975, p. 114.

35. **Joseph S,** *History of the Baron de Hirsch Fund,* Augustus M. Kelley, Publishers, Fairfield, New Jersey, 1978, p. 58.

36. **Lipman JG,** The Baron de Hirsch Agricultural School, In: Sabsovich K, ed. *Adventures in Idealism: A Personal Record of the Life of Professor Sabsovich,* 1975 Reprint Edition of 1922 edition, Arno Press, New York, 1922, pp. 188-193.

37. **Pincus JW,** The Jewish Farmers' Best Friend, In: Sabsovich K, ed. *Adventures in Idealism: A Personal Record of the Life of Professor Sabsovich,* 1975 Reprint Edition of the 1922 edition, Arno Press, New York, 1922, p. 197.

38. **Sabsovich K,** *Adventures in Idealism: A Personal Record of the Life of Professor Sabsovich,* Reprint edition of the 1922 original by Arno Press, New York, 1975, pp. 73-75.

39. **Brandes J,** *Immigrants to Freedom. Jewish Communities in Rural New Jersey since 1882,* University of Pennsylvania Press for the Jewish Publication Society of America, Philadelphia, 1971, pp. 135-140.

40. Ibid., p. 136.

41. Ibid., pp. 277-278.

42. **Davidson G,** *Our Jewish Farmers and the Story of the Jewish Agricultural Society,* L.B. Fischer, New York, 1943, p. 260.

43. **Joseph S,** *History of the Baron de Hirsch Fund,* Augustus M. Kelley, Publishers, Fairfield, New Jersey, 1978, p. 87.

44. **Pincus JW,** The Jewish Farmers' Best Friend, In: Sabsovich K, ed. *Adventures in Idealism: A Personal Record of the Life of Professor Sabsovich,* 1975 Reprint Edition of the 1922 edition, Arno Press, New York, 1922, p. 195

45. Ibid., p. 201.

46. **Brandes J,** *Immigrants to Freedom. Jewish Communities in Rural New Jersey since 1882,* University of Pennsylvania Press for the Jewish Publication Society of America, Philadelphia, 1971, p. 130.

47. Ibid., p. 349.

48. **Joseph S,** *History of the Baron de Hirsch Fund,* Augustus M. Kelley, Publishers, Fairfield, New Jersey, 1978, p. 103.

49. **Brandes J,** *Immigrants to Freedom. Jewish Communities in Rural New Jersey since 1882,* University of Pennsylvania Press for the Jewish Publication Society of America, Philadelphia, 1971, p. 258.

50. **Sabsovich K,** *Adventures in Idealism: A Personal Record of the Life of Professor Sabsovich,* Reprint edition of the 1922 original by Arno Press, New York, 1975, p. 60.

51. **Waksman SA,** *Jacob G. Lipman: Agricultural Scientist and Humanitarian,* Rugers University Press, New Brunswick, NJ, 1966, p. 27.

52. Ibid., p. 62.

53. Ibid., p. 60.

54. Ibid., p. 55.

55. Ibid., p. 86.

56. Ibid., p. 69.

57. Ibid. p. 58.

58. Ibid., P. 59.

59. Ibid., p. 70.

60. Ibid.

61. Ibid., p. 71.

62. Ibid., p. 101.

63. Ibid., p. 74.

64. Ibid., p. 765.

65. Ibid., p. 85.

66. Ibid., P. 84.

67. Ibid., p. 87.

68. **Lipman JG,** The conservation of our land resources, *Science* 83:65-69, 1936.

69. **Waksman SA,** *Jacob G. Lipman: Agricultural Scientist and Humanitarian,* Rugers University Press, New Brunswick, NJ, 1966, p. 97.

70. **McCall AG,** Obituary, Jacob Goodale Lipman, *Science* 89:378-379, 1939.

71. **Pincus G,** Jacob Goodale Lipman (1874–1939), *Proc Am Acad Arts Sci* 74:142-143, 1940.

72. **Pincus E,** Russian American Episodes, Year unknown, pp. 1-17.

73. Ibid.

74. **Brandes J,** *Immigrants to Freedom: Jewish Communities in Rural New Jersey since 1882,* University of Pennsylvania Press for the Jewish Publication Society of America, Philadelphia, 1971, p. 255.

75. **Eisenberg E,** *Jewish Agricultural Colonies in New Jersey, 1882–1920,* Syracuse University Press, Syracuse, New York, 1995, pp. 126-127.

76. **Ludins DG,** Memories of Woodbine: 1891–1894, *Jewish Frontier* June,:7-15, 1960.

77. **Pincus E,** Russian American Episodes, Year unknown, pp. 1-17.

78. Ibid.

79. Ibid.

80. Ibid.

81. Ibid.

82. Ibid.

83. **Brandes J,** *Immigrants to Freedom: Jewish Communities in Rural New Jersey since 1882,* University of Pennsylvania Press for the Jewish Publication Society of America, Philadelphia, 1971, p. 153.

84. **Pincus E,** Russian American Episodes, Year unknown, pp. 1-17.

85. Ibid.

86. **Sabsovich K,** *Adventures in Idealism: A Personal Record of the Life of Professor Sabsovich,* Reprint edition of the 1922 original by Arno Press, New York, 1975, p. 121.

87. **Pincus E,** Russian American Episodes, Year unknown, pp. 1-17.

88. Ibid.

89. **Pincus A,** Memories about Gregory Pincus, Family Memoir, *Papers of Gregory Pincus.* Washington, D.C., Library of Congress, 1989, Box 5, pp. 1-30.

90. Ibid.

91. Ibid.

92. Ibid.

93. Ibid.

94. Ibid.

95. Ibid.

96. **Davidson G,** *Our Jewish Farmers and the Story of the Jewish Agricultural Society,* L.B. Fischer, New York, 1943, p. 38.

97. **Joseph S,** *History of the Baron de Hirsch Fund,* Augustus M. Kelley, Publishers, Fairfield, New Jersey, 1978, p. 145.

98. **Brandes J,** *Immigrants to Freedom. Jewish Communities in Rural New Jersey since 1882,* University of Pennsylvania Press for the Jewish Publication Society of America, Philadelphia, 1971, pp. 96-97.

99. **Box 1,** Personal diary, *Papers of Gregory Pincus, Manuscript Division, Library of Congress, Washington, D.C.,* 1920.

100. **Sabsovich K,** *Adventures in Idealism: A Personal Record of the Life of Professor Sabsovich,* Reprint edition of the 1922 original by Arno Press, New York, 1975, p. 17.

101. **Pincus E,** Russian American Episodes, Year unknown, pp. 1-17.

CHAPTER FOUR

1. **Garcia C-R,** Dedication, *Int J Fertil* 13:267-269, 1968.

2. **Pincus A,** Memories about Gregory Pincus, Family Memoir, *Papers of Gregory Pincus.* Washington, D.C., Library of Congress, 1989, Box 5, pp. 1-30.

3. **Bernard LP,** Personal interview, May 23, 2007, August 11, 2008.

4. **Pincus A,** Memories about Gregory Pincus, Family Memoir, *Papers of Gregory Pincus.* Washington, D.C., Library of Congress, 1989, Box 5, pp. 1-30.

5. Ibid.

6. **Foss J,** Personal interview, May 21, 2007.

7. **Pincus A,** Memories about Gregory Pincus, Family Memoir, *Papers of Gregory Pincus.* Washington, D.C., Library of Congress, 1989, Box 5, pp. 1-30.

8. Ibid.

9. **Box 209,** Letter, Sophie to Pincus, *Papers of Gregory Pincus, Manuscript Division, Library of Congress, Washington, D.C.,* Unknown date.

10. **Pincus S,** Personal Recorded Interview with Sophie Pincus Dutton by Honor White, January 8 and 14, 1980.

11. **Pincus A,** Memories about Gregory Pincus, Family Memoir, *Papers of Gregory Pincus.* Washington, D.C., Library of Congress, 1989, Box 5, pp. 1-30.

12. Ibid.

13. Ibid.

14. **Pincus S,** Personal Recorded Interview with Sophie Pincus Dutton by Honor White, January 8 and 14, 1980.

15. **Pincus A,** Memories about Gregory Pincus, Family Memoir, *Papers of Gregory Pincus.* Washington, D.C., Library of Congress, 1989, Box 5, pp. 1-30.

16. **Pincus S,** Personal Recorded Interview with Sophie Pincus Dutton by Honor White, January 8 and 14, 1980.

17 **Pincus A,** Memories about Gregory Pincus, Family Memoir, *Papers of Gregory Pincus.* Washington, D.C.: Library of Congress; 1989: Box 5, pp. 1-30.

18. **Bernard LP,** Personal interview, May 23, 2007, August 11, 2008.

19. **Box 4,** Letter, Papa to Goody, *Papers of Gregory Pincus, Manuscript Division, Library of Congress, Washington, D.C.,* August 19, 1948.

20. **Box 204,** Letter, McElvain to Pincus, *Papers of Gregory Pincus, Manuscript Division, Library of Congress, Washington, D.C.,* October 30, 1950.

21. **Box 209,** Letter, Gregory to Maurice, *Papers of Gregory Pincus, Manuscript Division, Library of Congress, Washington, D.C.,* December 5, 1950.

22. **Box 212,** Death Certificate, Joseph Pincus, *Papers of Gregory Pincus, Manuscript Division, Library of Congress, Washington, D.C.,* 1951.

23. **Pincus A,** Memories about Gregory Pincus, Family Memoir, *Papers of Gregory Pincus.* Washington, D.C., Library of Congress, 1989, Box 5, pp. 1-30.

24. Ibid.

25. **Vaughn P,** *The Pill on Trial,* Coward-McCann, Inc., New York, 1970, p. 22.

26. **Pincus A,** Memories about Gregory Pincus, Family Memoir, *Papers of Gregory Pincus.* Washington, D.C., Library of Congress, 1989, Box 5, pp. 1-30.

27. Ibid.

28. **Hermalyn G,** *Morris High School and the Creation of the New York City Public High School System,* The Bronx County Historical Society, The Bronx, New York, 1995.

29. **Polokow S,** Bronx: Small Schools at Morris High, *http://www.goodsmallschools. org/information.asp?schoolIID=4,* 2007.

30. **Hermalyn G,** *Morris High School and the Creation of the New York City Public High School System,* The Bronx County Historical Society, The Bronx, New York, 1995.

31. **Kase N,** Personal interview, December 19, 2007.

32. **Matzke H**, ed, *The Morris Annual, 1920,* Morris High School, courtesy of the Bronx County Historical Society Bronx, New York.

33. **Box 1,** Personal diary, *Papers of Gregory Pincus, Manuscript Division, Library of Congress, Washington, D.C.,* 1920.

34. **Pincus A,** Memories about Gregory Pincus, Family Memoir, *Papers of Gregory Pincus.* Washington, D.C.. Library of Congress, 1989, Box 5, pp. 1-30.

35. **Box 1,** Personal diary, *Papers of Gregory Pincus, Manuscript Division, Library of Congress, Washington, D.C.,* 1920.

36. **Box 85,** Letter, Harris to Pincus, *Papers of Gregory Pincus, Manuscript Division, Library of Congress, Washington, D.C.,* June 10, 1965.

37. **Marcello AA,** Popping Questions, *The Worcester Sunday Telegram,* June 29, 1952.

38. Ibid.

39. **Sandrof I,** Worcester's Dr. Pincus Famed for Probing Secrets of Life Begins Program of Atomic Research, *The Worcester Sunday Telegram,* March 4, 1951.

40. **Box 212,** Transcript, Cornell University, *Papers of Gregory Pincus, Manuscript Division, Library of Congress, Washington, D.C.*

41, **Box 1,** Personal diary, *Papers of Gregory Pincus, Manuscript Division, Library of Congress, Washington, D.C.,* 1920.

42. Ibid.

43. Ibid.

44. **Box 212,** Transcript, Cornell University, *Papers of Gregory Pincus, Manuscript Division, Library of Congress, Washington, D.C.*

45. **Pincus G,** Nocturne, *The Literary Review of Cornell,* December, 1922.

46. **Bernard LP,** Personal interview, May 23, 2007, August 11, 2008.

47. **The Editors,** Comments, *The Literary Review of Cornell,* June, 1923.

48. **Pincus G,** New York, *The Literary Review of Cornell,* December, 1923.

49. **Pincus A,** Memories about Gregory Pincus, Family Memoir, *Papers of Gregory Pincus.* Washington, D.C., Library of Congress, 1989, Box 5, pp. 1-30.

50. Ibid.

51. **Box 6,** Visa application, *Papers of Gregory Pincus, Manuscript Division, Library of Congress, Washington, D.C.*

52. **Pincus A,** Memories about Gregory Pincus, Family Memoir, *Papers of Gregory Pincus.* Washington, D.C.: Library of Congress; 1989: Box 5, pp. 1-30.

53. **Bernard LP,** Personal interview, May 23, 2007, August 11, 2008.

54. **Pincus A,** Memories about Gregory Pincus, Family Memoir, *Papers of Gregory Pincus.* Washington, D.C.: Library of Congress; 1989: Box 5, pp. 1-30.

55. Ibid.

56. **Bernard LP,** Personal interview, May 23, 2007, August 11, 2008.

57. **Pincus A,** Memories about Gregory Pincus, Family Memoir, *Papers of Gregory Pincus.* Washington, D.C.: Library of Congress; 1989: Box 5, pp. 1-30.

58. **Box 6,** Visa application, *Papers of Gregory Pincus, Manuscript Division, Library of Congress, Washington, D.C.,* 1929.

59. **Pincus A,** Memories about Gregory Pincus, Family Memoir, *Papers of Gregory Pincus.* Washington, D.C., Library of Congress, 1989, Box 5, pp. 1-30.

60. Ibid.

61. Ibid.

62. **Sandrof I,** Worcester's Dr. Pincus Famed for Probing Secrets of Life Begins Program of Atomic Research, *The Worcester Sunday Telegram,* March 4, 1951.

63. **Goldzieher J,** Personal interview, October 30, 2007.

64. **Bernard LP,** Personal interview, May 23, 2007, August 11, 2008.

65. **Pincus A,** Memories about Gregory Pincus, Family Memoir, *Papers of Gregory Pincus.* Washington, D.C., Library of Congress, 1989, Box 5, pp. 1-30.

66. Ibid.

67. **Wallach E,** Personal interview, January 23, 2008.

68. **Foss J,** Personal interview, May 21, 2007.

69. Ibid.

70. **Kase N,** Personal interview, December 19, 2007.

71. **Fridhandler L,** Personal interview, February 8, 2008.

72. **Bedford JM,** Personal interview, April 16, 2008.

73. **Bialy G,** Personal interview, August 27, 2007.

74. **Neves e Castro M,** Personal email, May 28, 2008.

75. Ibid.

76. **Goldzieher J,** Personal interview, October 30, 2007.

77. **Wallach E,** Personal interview, January 23, 2008.

78. **Bialy G,** Personal interview, August 27, 2007.

79. **Box 5,** Letter, Pincus to Fortnum & Mason, *Papers of Gregory Pincus, Manuscript Division, Library of Congress, Washington, D.C.,* February 6, 1956.

80. **Box 209,** Letter, Lizzie to Goody, *Papers of Gregory Pincus, Manuscript Division, Library of Congress, Washington, D.C.,* 1967.

CHAPTER FIVE

1. **Reed J,** *The Birth Control Movement and American Society: From Private Vice to Public Virtue,* Princeton University Press, Princeton, New Jersey, 1978, p. 317.

2. **Vaughn P,** *The Pill on Trial,* Coward-Mc-Cann, Inc., New York, 1970, p. 22.

3. **Foss J,** Personal interview, May 21, 2007.

4. **Pincus A,** Memories about Gregory Pincus, Family Memoir, *Papers of Gregory Pincus.* Washington, D.C., Library of Congress, 1989, Box 5, pp. 1-30.

5. Ibid.

6. Ibid.

7. Ibid.

8. Ibid.

9. **Box 212,** U.S. Civil Service Application, *Papers of Gregory Pincus, Manuscript Division, Library of Congress, Washington, D.C.*, 1940.

10. **Pincus GG,** Observations on the living eggs of the rabbit, *Proc Roy Soc* 197B:132-167, 1930.

11. **Pincus A,** Memories about Gregory Pincus, Family Memoir, *Papers of Gregory Pincus.* Washington, D.C., Library of Congress, 1989, Box 5, pp. 1-30.

12. **Pincus G,** *The Eggs of Mammals,* The Macmillan Company, New York, 1936.

13. **Chang MC,** Mammalian sperm, eggs, and control of fertility, *Persp Biol Med* Spring:376-383, 1968.

14. **Hoagland H,** *The Road to Yesterday,* privately printed, Worcester, Massachusetts, 1974, p. 66.

15. Ibid.

16. Ibid., p. 62.

17. **Pincus A,** Memories about Gregory Pincus, Family Memoir, *Papers of Gregory Pincus.* Washington, D.C., Library of Congress, 1989, Box 5, pp. 1-30.

18. **Rabbits Born In Glass**, *The New York Times,* May 13, 1934.

19. **Bottles Are Mothers**, *The New York Times,* April 21, 1935.

20. **Laurence WL,** Life is generated in a scientist's tube, *The New York Times,* March 27, 1936.

21. **Editorial**, *The New York Times,* , March 28, 1936.

22. **His Experiment Gives Vision of Manless World,** *Ames Daily Tribune and Times,* March 31, 1936.

23. **Pincus A,** Memories about Gregory Pincus, Family Memoir, *Papers of Gregory Pincus.* Washington, D.C., Library of Congress, 1989, Box 5, pp. 1-30.

24. **Ratcliff JD,** No father to guide them, *Colliers,* March 20, 1937, pp. 19, 73.

25. **Pincus A,** Memories about Gregory Pincus, Family Memoir, *Papers of Gregory Pincus.* Washington, D.C., Library of Congress, 1989, Box 5, pp. 1-30.

26. **Pincus G,** The breeding of some rabbits produced by recipients of artifically activated ova, *Proc Nat Acad Sci* 25:557-559, 1939.

27. **Vaughn P,** *The Pill on Trial,* Coward-McCann, Inc., New York, 1970, p. 37.

28. **Laurence WL,** First Step Shown in Human Creation, *The New York Times,* April 28, 1939.

29. **Pincus Says Test Tube Babies 'Out',** *The Kingsport Times, Kingsport, Tennessee,* May 16, 1939.

30. **Doctor Embarrassed by Report He Is Trying to Make Test Tube Baby,** *The Evening News, Sault Ste. Marie, Michigan,* May 17, 1939.

31. **Mammal Created Without a Father,** *The New York Times,* November 2, 1939.

32. **Editorial,** Rabbits Without Fathers, *The New York Times,* November 3, 1939.

33. **Laurence WL,** Test Tube Babies Come Step Nearer, *The New York Times,* April 30, 1941.

34. **Werthessen NT, Johnson RC,** Pincogenesis—parthenogenesis in rabbits by Gregory Pincus, *Persp Biol Med* 18:81-93, 1974.

35. Ibid.

36. **Pincus G,** *Proc Roy Soc* 107:132-167, 1930.

37. **Pincus G, Enzmann EV,** Can mammalian eggs undergo normal development in vitro?, *Proc Nat Acad Sci* 20:121-122, 1934.

38. **Pincus G, Enzmann EV,** The comparative behavior of mammalian eggs in vivo and in vitro. I. The activation of ovarian eggs, *J Exp Med* 62:665-675, 1935.

39. **Pincus G, Enzmann EV,** The comparative behavior of mammalian eggs in vivo and in vitro. II. The activation of tubal eggs of the rabbit, *J Exp Zoology* 73:195-208, 1936.

40. **Pincus G, Werthessen N,** The comparative behavior of mammalian eggs in vivo and in vitro. III. Factors controlling the growth of the rabbit blastocyst, *J Exp Zoology* 78:1-18, 1938.

41. **Pincus G,** The comparative behavior of mammalian eggs in vivo and in vitro. IV. The development of fertilized and artificially activated rabbit eggs, *J Exp Zoology* 82:85-129, 1939.

42. **Pincus G, Werthessen NT,** The maintenance of embryo life in ovariectomized rabbits, *Am J Physiol* 124:484-490, 1938.

43. **Werthessen NT, Johnson RC,** Pincogenesis—parthogenesis in rabbits by Gregory Pincus, *Persp Biol Med* 18:81-93, 1974.

44. **Pincus G, Werthessen N,** The comparative behavior of mammalian eggs in vivo and in vitro. III. Factors controlling the growth of the rabbit blastocyst, *J Exp Zoology* 78:1-18, 1938.

45. **Pincus G,** The breeding of some rabbits produced by recipients of artifically activated ova, *Proc Nat Acad Sci* 25:557-559, 1939.

46. **Pincus G,** The comparative behavior of mammalian eggs in vivo and in vitro. IV. The development of fertilized and artificially activated rabbit eggs, *J Exp Zoology* 82:85-129, 1939.

47. **Pincus G, Shapiro H,** Further studies on the parthenogenetic activation of rabbit eggs, *Proc Nat Acad Sci* 26:163-165, 1940.

48. **Beatty RA,** *Parthenogenesis and Polyploidy in Mammalian Development,* Cambridge University Press, Cambridge, 1957.

49. **Kono T, Obata Y, Wu Q, Niwa K, Ono Y, Yamamoto Y, Park ES, Seo J-S, Ogawa H,** Birth of parthenogenetic mice that can develop to adulthood, *Nature* 428:860-864, 2004.

50. **Kono T,** Genomic imprinting is a barrier to parthenogenesis in mammals, *Cytogenet Genome Res* 113:31-35, 2006.

51. **Kono T,** Personal email, July 8, 2008.

52. **Yanagimachi R,** Personal email, July 9 & 10, 2008.

53. **Werthessen NT, Johnson RC,** Pincogenesis—parthogenesis in rabbits by Gregory Pincus, *Persp Biol Med* 18:81-93, 1974.

54. **Pincus A,** Memories about Gregory Pincus, Family Memoir, *Papers of Gregory Pincus.* Washington, D.C., Library of Congress, 1989, Box 5, pp. 1-30.

55. **Lieberman S,** Personal interview, October 17, 2007.

56. **Pincus A,** Memories about Gregory Pincus, Family Memoir, *Papers of Gregory Pincus.* Washington, D.C., Library of Congress, 1989, Box 5, pp. 1-30.

CHAPTER SIX

1. **Hoagland H,** *The Road to Yesterday,* privately printed, Worcester, Massachusetts, 1974, p. 17.

2. Ibid., p. 87.

3. Ibid., p. 107.

4. **Hoagland M,** *Toward the Habit of Truth: A Life in Science,* W.W. Norton & Company, New York, 1990, p. 16.

5. **Koelsch WA,** *Clark University 1887–1987. A Narrative History,* Clark University Press, Worcester, Massachusetts, 1987.

6. **Hoagland H,** *Pacemakers in Relation to Aspects of Behavior,* The MacMillan Company, New York, 1935.

7. **Hoagland H,** *The Road to Yesterday,* privately printed, Worcester, Massachusetts, 1974, p. 62.

8. Ibid., p. 64.

9. Ibid., P. 66.

10. **Goldzieher J,** Personal interview, October 30, 2007.

11. **Box 4,** Letter, Hoagland to Pincus, *Papers of Gregory Pincus, Manuscript Division, Library of Congress, Washington, D.C.,* May 24, 1938.

12. **Box 4,** Letter, Hoagland to Pincus, *Papers of Gregory Pincus, Manuscript Division, Library of Congress, Washington, D.C.,* April 25, 1938.

13. **Box 4,** Letter, Castle to Pincus, *Papers of Gregory Pincus, Manuscript Division, Library of Congress, Washington, D.C.,* April 26, 1938.

14. **Box 4,** Letter, Hoagland to Fremont-Smith, *Papers of Gregory Pincus, Manuscript Division, Library of Congress, Washington, D.C.,* May 24, 1938.

15. **Hoagland H,** *The Road to Yesterday,* privately printed, Worcester, Massachusetts, 1974, p. 67.

16. **Pincus A,** Memories about Gregory Pincus, Family Memoir, *Papers of Gregory Pincus.* Washington, D.C., Library of Congress, 1989, Box 5, pp. 1-30.

17. Ibid.

18. Ibid.

19. Ibid.

20. **Mother Was a Thoroughbred,** *Time,* April 4, 1949.

21. **Coleman L,** *Tom Slick: True Life Encounters in Cryptozoology,* Craven Street Books, Fresno, California, 2002.

22. **Cooke CN,** *Tom Slick: Mystery Hunter,* Paraview, Inc., Bracey, Virginia, 2005.

23. **Goldzieher J,** Personal interview, October 30, 2007.

24. **Jordan RG,** Research Foundation Opened in Ceremony at Essar Ranch Near City, *San Antonio Express,* April 6, 1947.

25. **Pincus G,** Studies on the role of the adrenal cortex in the stress of human subjects, *Rec Prog Hor Res* 1:123-145, 1947.

26. **Hoagland H,** *The Road to Yesterday,* privately printed, Worcester, Massachusetts, 1974, p. 73.

27. Ibid. p. 74.

28. Ibid., p. 78.

29. **Pincus A,** Memories about Gregory Pincus, Family Memoir, *Papers of Gregory Pincus.* Washington, D.C., Library of Congress, 1989, Box 5, pp. 1-30.

30. **Hoskins RG, Pincus G,** Sex-hormone relationships in schizophrenic men, *Psychosom Med* 11:102-109, 1949.

31. **Hoagland H, Pincus G,** The nature of the adrenal stress response failure in schizophrenic man, *J Nerve Ment Dis* 111:434-439, 1950.

32. **Hoagland H,** *The Road to Yesterday,* privately printed, Worcester, Massachusetts, 1974, p. 95.

33. Ibid., p. 80.

34. **Hoagland M,** *Toward the Habit of Truth: A Life in Science,* W.W. Norton & Company, New York, 1990, p. 7.

35. **Pederson T,** The battle that launched the Worcester Foundation for Experimental Biology, *Lecture presented at the Worcester Club,* April 7, 2008, Personal communication.

36. **McCracken J,** Personal interview, May 21, 2007.

37. **Hoagland H,** *The Road to Yesterday,* privately printed, Worcester, Massachusetts, 1974, p. 83.

38. Ibid., p. 84.

39. **Pederson T,** The battle that launched the Worcester Foundation for Experimental Biology, *Lecture presented at the Worcester Club* Personal communication, April 7, 2008, Personal communication.

40. **Hoagland H,** *The Road to Yesterday,* privately printed, Worcester, Massachusetts, 1974, p. 87.

41. **Pincus G,** The Worcester Foundation for Experimental Biology, *AIBS Bulletin* 6:8-9, 1956.

42. **Halberstam D,** *The Fifties,* Fawcett Columbine, New York, 1993, p. 290.

43. **Reed J,** *The Birth Control Movement and American Society: From Private Vice to Public Virtue,* Princeton University Press, Princeton, N. J., 1978, p. 330.

44. **Hoagland M,** *Toward the Habit of Truth: A Life in Science,* W.W. Norton & Company, New York, 1990, p. 8.

45. **Wilson RE,** Science Marches On, *The Worcester Sunday Telegram*, April 19, 1964.

46. **McCracken J,** Personal interview, May 21, 2007.

47. **Shaw J,** Personal interview, April 16, 2008.

48. **McCracken J,** Personal interview, May 21, 2007.

49. **Lieberman S,** Personal interview, October 17, 2007.

50. **Box 44,** Letter, Pincus to McCormick, *Papers of Gregory Pincus, Manuscript Division, Library of Congress, Washington, D.C.,* August 30, 1960.

51. **Box 74,** Letter, Pincus to McCormick, *Papers of Gregory Pincus, Manuscript Division, Library of Congress, Washington, D.C.,* 1964.

52. **Neves e Castro M,** Personal email, May 28, 2008.

53. **Box 212,** U.S. Civil Service application, *Papers of Gregory Pincus, Manuscript Division, Library of Congress, Washington, D.C.,* 1940.

54. **Reed J,** *The Birth Control Movement and American Society: From Private Vice to Public Virtue,* Princeton University Press, Princeton, N. J., 1978.

55. **Hoagland H,** *The Road to Yesterday,* privately printed, Worcester, Massachusetts, 1974, p. 96.

56. Ibid., 87.

57. **Merrill A,** Personal interview, May 23, 2007.

58. **Bernard LP,** Personal interview, May 23, 2007, August 11, 2008.

59. **Foss J,** Personal interview, May 21, 2007.

60. Ibid.

61. Ibid.

62. **Halberstam D,** *The Fifties,* Fawcett Columbine, New York, 1993, p. 292.

63. **Caldwell B,** Personal interview, December 5, 2007.

64. **McCracken J,** Personal interview, May 21, 2007.

65. Ibid.

66. **Kase N,** Personal interview, December 19, 2007.

67. **Neves e Castro M,** Personal email, May 28, 2008

68. **Caldwell B,** Personal interview, December 5, 2007.

69. **Merrill A,** Personal interview, May 23, 2007.

70. **Bialy G,** Personal interview, August 27, 2007.

71. **Peron F,** Personal email, April 13, 2007.

72. **McCracken J,** Personal interview, May 21, 2007.

73. Ibid.

74. **Bialy G,** Personal interview, August 27, 2007.

75. **Brooks J,** Personal interview, June 30, 2008.

76. **Fridhandler L,** Personal interview, February 8, 2008.

77. **Wallach E,** Personal interview, January 23, 2008.

78. **Caldwell B,** Personal interview, December 5, 2007.

79. **Lader L,** Three Men Who Made a Revolution, *The New York Times Magazine*, April 10, 1966.

80. **Bernard LP,** Personal interview, May 23, 2007, August 11, 2008.

81. Ibid.

82. **White AB,** Gregory Goodwin Pincus (1903–1967), *Endocrinology* 82:651-654, 1968.

83. **Bernard LP,** Personal interview, May 23, 2007, August 11, 2008.

84. **Box 209,** Letter, John Pincus to White, *Papers of Gregory Pincus, Manuscript Division, Library of Congress, Washington, D.C.*, October 20, 1967.

85. **Box 91,** Letter, Putney School to Pincus, *Papers of Gregory Pincus, Manuscript Division, Library of Congress, Washington, D.C.*, 1963.

86. **Merrill A,** Personal interview, May 23, 2007.

87. **Peron F,** Personal email, April 13, 2007.

88. **Box 211,** *Papers of Gregory Pincus, Manuscript Division, Library of Congress, Washington, D.C.*

89. **Box 203,** Financial papers, *Papers of Gregory Pincus, Manuscript Division, Library of Congress, Washington, D.C.*

90. **Bernard LP,** Personal interview, May 23, 2007, August 11, 2008.

91. **Peron F,** Personal email, April 13, 2007.

92. **McCracken J,** Personal interview, May 21, 2007.

93. **Garcia C-R,** Gregory Goodwin Pincus (1903–1967), *J Clin Endocrin Metab* 28:1245-1248, 1968.

94. **Box 212,** Pincus wine cellar, *Papers of Gregory Pincus, Manuscript Division, Library of Congress, Washington, D.C.*, September, 1967.

95. **Greep RO,** Min Chueh Chang, 1908–1991, *Biograph Memoirs* 68:3-19, 1995.

96. **Chang MC,** Recollections of 40 years at the Worcester Foundation for Experimental Biology, *The Physiologist* 28:400-401, 1985.

97. Ibid.

98. **Fridhandler L,** Personal interview, February 8, 2008.

99. **McCracken J,** Personal interview, May 21, 2007.

100. **Bialy G,** Personal interview, August 27, 2007.

101. **Box 8,** Letter, Pincus to Slick, *Papers of Gregory Pincus, Manuscript Division, Library of Congress, Washington, D.C.*, August 18, 1950.

102. **Chang MC,** Recollections of 40 years at the Worcester Foundation for Experimental Biology, *The Physiologist* 28:400-401, 1985.

103. Ibid.

104. **Chang MC,** Mammalian sperm, eggs, and control of fertility, *Persp Biol Med* Spring:376-383, 1968.

105. **Chang MC,** Recollections of 40 years at the Worcester Foundation for Experimental Biology, *The Physiologist* 28:400-401, 1985.

106. Ibid.

107. Ibid.

108. **Greep RO,** Min Chueh Chang, 1908–1991, *Biograph Memoirs* 68:3-19, 1995.

109. **Chang MC,** Recollections of 40 years at the Worcester Foundation for Experimental Biology, *The Physiologist* 28:400-401, 1985.

110. **Halberstam D,** *The Fifties,* Fawcett Columbine, New York, 1993, p. 293.

111. **Chang I,** Personal interview, May 22, 2007.

112. **Greep RO,** Min Chueh Chang, 1908–1991, *Biograph Memoirs* 68:3-19, 1995.

113. Ibid.

114. **Bernard LP,** Personal interview, May 23, 2007, August 11, 2008.

115. **Chang I,** Personal interview, May 22, 2007.

116. Ibid.

117. Ibid.

118. **McCann J,** Personal interview, May 22, 2007.

119. **Greep RO,** Min Chueh Chang, 1908–1991, *Biograph Memoirs* 68:3-19, 1995.

120. **McCann J,** Personal interview, May 22, 2007.

121. **Chang I,** Personal interview, May 22, 2007.

122. **Bedford JM,** Personal interview, April 16, 2008.

123. **Pincus G,** *The Control of Fertility,* Academic Press, New York, 1965, p. xi.

124. **Chang MC,** Recollections of 40 years at the Worcester Foundation for Experimental Biology, *The Physiologist* 28:400-401, 1985.

125. Ibid.

126. **Chang I,** Personal interview, May 22, 2007.

127. **Pincus A,** Memories about Gregory Pincus, Family Memoir, *Papers of Gregory Pincus.* Washington, D.C., Library of Congress, 1989: Box 5, pp. 1-30.

128. **Hoagland H,** *The Road to Yesterday,* privately printed, Worcester, Massachusetts, 1974, p. 101.

129. **Hoagland M,** *Toward the Habit of Truth: A Life in Science,* W.W. Norton & Company, New York, 1990, p. 136.

130. Ibid.

131. **Hoagland H,** *The Road to Yesterday,* privately printed, Worcester, Massachusetts, 1974, p. 19.

131. **Hoagland H,** Some reflections on science and regligion, In: Shapley H, ed. *Science Ponders Religion,* Appleton-Century-Crofts, Inc., New York, 1960, p. 25.

CHAPTER SEVEN

1. **Ingle DJ,** *Gregory Goodwin Pincus, 1903–1967,* Vol. XLII, Columbia University Press, New York, 1971.

2. **Lieberman S,** Personal interview, October 17, 2007.

3. **Bates RW,** The first 25 years of the Laurentian Hormone Conference, *Rec Prog Hor Res* 24:vii-xi, 1968.

4. **Parkes AS,** Gregory Pincus, as I knew him—an appreciation, *Persp Biol Med* Spring:422-426, 1968.

5. **Bates RW,** The first 25 years of the Laurentian Hormone Conference, *Rec Prog Hor Res* 24:vii-xi, 1968.

6. **Ingle DJ,** *Gregory Goodwin Pincus, 1903–1967,* Vol. XLII, Columbia University Press, New York, 1971, p. 234.

7. **Lieberman S,** Personal interview, October 17, 2007.

8. Ibid.

9. Ibid.

10. **Jensen EV,** Remembrance: Gregory Pincus—catalyst for early receptor studies, *Endocrinology* 131:1581-1582, 1992.

11. **Jensen EV, Jacobson HI, Flesher JW, Saha N, Gupta GN, Smith S, Colucci V, Shiplacoff D, Neumann HG, DeSombre ER, Jungblut PW,** Estrogen Receptors in Target Tissues, In: Pincus GN, T, Tait JF, eds. *Steroid Dynamics: Proceeedings of the Symposium on the Dynamics of Steroid Hormones held in Tokyo, May, 1965,* Academic Press, New York, 1966, pp. 133-158.

12. **Ingle DJ,** *Gregory Goodwin Pincus, 1903–1967,* Vol. XLII, Columbia University Press, New York, 1971, pp. 233-234.

13. **Goldzieher J,** Personal interview, October 30, 2007.

14. **Pincus G,** Preface, *Rec Prog Hor Res* 6:i, 1951.

15. **McCracken J,** Personal interview, May 21, 2007.

16. Ibid.

17. **White AB,** Gregory Goodwin Pincus (1903–1967), *Endocrinology* 82:651-654, 1968.

18. **Baulieu EE,** Personal interview, November 17, 2007.

19. **Lieberman S,** Personal interview, October 17, 2007.

20. **Foss J,** Personal interview, May 21, 2007.

21. **Lieberman S,** Personal interview, October 17, 2007.

22. Ibid.

23. **Segal S,** Personal interview, December 7, 2007.

24. **McCracken J,** Personal interview, May 21, 2007.

25. **Segal S,** Personal interview, December 7, 2007.

26. **Parkes AS,** Gregory Pincus, as I knew him—an appreciation, *Persp Biol Med* Spring:422-426, 1968.

27. Ibid.

28. **Pincus G,** Preface, *Rec Prog Hor Res* 1:i, 1947.

29. **McCracken J,** Personal interview, May 21, 2007.

30. **Garcia C-R,** Gregory Goodwin Pincus (1903–1967), *J Clin Endocrin Metab* 28:1245-1248, 1968.

31. **Ingle DJ,** *Gregory Goodwin Pincus, 1903–1967,* Vol. XLII, Columbia University Press, New York, 1971, p. 238.

32. **Pincus A,** Memories about Gregory Pincus, Family Memoir, *Papers of Gregory Pincus.* Washington, D.C., Library of Congress, 1989, Box 5, pp. 1-30.

33. **Bates RW,** Gregory Goodwin Pincus, *Rec Prog Hor Res* 24:v-vi, 1968.

34. **Schwartz NB,** A model for the regulation of ovulation in the rat, (Gregory Pincus Memorial Lecture), *Rec Prog Hor Res* 25:1-55, 1969.

35. **Djerassi C,** *This Man's Pill: Reflections on the 50th Birthday of the Pill,* Oxford University Press, Oxford, 2001, pp. 59-60.

CHAPTER EIGHT

1. **Maisel AQ,** *The Hormone Quest,* Random House, New York, 1965.

2. **Medvei VC,** *The History of Clinical Endocrinology,* The Parthenon Publishing Group, New York, 1993.

3. **O'Dowd MG, Philipp EE,** *The History of Obstetrics and Gynaecology,* The Parthenon Publishing Group, New York, 1994.

4. **Sneader W,** The discovery of oestrogenic hormones, *J Br Menopause Soc* December:129-133, 2000.

5. **Speert H,** *Obstetric & Gynecologic Milestones Illustrated,* The Parthenon Publishing Group, New York, 1996.

6. **Fosbery WHS,** Severe climacteric flushings successfully treated by ovarian extract, *Br Med J* i:1039, 1897.

7. **Parkes AS,** The rise of reproductive endocrinology, 1926–1940, *J Endocrinol* 34:20-32, 1966.

8. Ibid.

9. **Maisel AQ,** *The Hormone Quest,* Random House, New York, 1965, p. 44.

10. **Simmer HH,** On the history of hormonal contraception. I. Ludwig Haberlandt (1885–1932) and his concept of "hormonal sterilization", *Contraception* 1:3-20, 1970.

11. **Simmer HH,** On the history of hormonal contraception. II. Otfried Otto Fellner (1873–19??) and estrogens as antifertility hormones, *Contraception* 3:1-21, 1971.

12. **Maisel AQ,** *The Hormone Quest,* Random House, New York, 1965.

13. **Lehman F PA, Bolivar GA, Quintero RR,** Russell E. Marker. Pioneer of the Mexican steroid industry, *J Chem Education* 50:195-199, 1973.

14. **Asbell B,** *The Pill: A Biography of the Drug that Changed the World,* Random House, New York, 1995.

15. **Halberstam D,** *The Fifties,* Fawcett Columbine, New York, 1993.

16. **Perone N,** The progestins, In: Goldzieher JW, ed. *Pharmacology of the Contraceptive Steroids,* Raven Press, Ltd., New York, 1994, pp. 5-20.

17. **Marker RE,** The early production of steroid hormones, *CHOC News, The Center for History of Medicine, University of Pennsylvania* 4:3-6, 1987.

18. **Russell E. Marker, interview by Jeffrey L. Sturchio at Pennsylvania State University,** *Chemical Heritage Foundation, Philadelphia,* Oral History Transcript No. 0068, April 17, 1987.

19. **Maisel AQ,** *The Hormone Quest,* Random House, New York, 1965, p. 47.

16. **Applezweig N,** The big steroid treasure hunt, *Chemical Week* January 31:38-52, 1959.

21. **Applezweig N,** *Steroid Drugs,* McGraw-Hill Book Company, Inc., New York, 1962.

22. **Lehman F PA,** Early history of steroid chemistry in Mexico: the story of three remarkable men, *Steroids* 57:403-408, 1992.

23. **Marker RE,** The early production of steroid hormones, *CHOC News, The Center for History of Medicine, University of Pennsylvania* 4:3-6, 1987.

24. **Aztecs,** *http://www.mexicolore.co.uk/index.php?one=azt&two=sto&id=149,* March 17, 2008.

25. **Maisel AQ,** *The Hormone Quest,* Random House, New York, 1965, p. 55.

26. **Djerassi C,** Problems of Manufacture and Distribution. The manufacture of steroidal contraceptives: technical versus political aspects, *Proc Roy Soc* 195:175-186, 1976.

27. **Lehman F PA,** Early history of steroid chemistry in Mexico: the story of three remarkable men, *Steroids* 57:403-408, 1992.

28. Ibid.

29. **Rosenkranz G,** The early days of Syntex, *Chemical Heritage* 23:2,10,12, 2004.

30. **Rosenkranz G,** From Ruzicka's terpenes in Zurich to Mexican steroids via Cuba, *Steroids* 57:409-418, 1992.

31. Ibid.

32. **Djerassi C,** *The Pill, Pygmy Chimps, and Degas' Horse,* Basic Books, New York, 1992.

33. **Djerassi C,** Steroid research at Syntex: "the Pill" and cortisone, *Steroids* 57:631-641, 1992.

34. **Maisel AQ,** *The Hormone Quest,* Random House, New York, 1965, pp. 68-70.

35. **Hench PS, Kendall EC, Slocumb CH, Polley HF,** The effect of a hormone of the adrenal cortex (17-hydroxy-11-dehydrocorticosterone (compound E) and of pituitary adrenocorticotropic hormone on rheumatoid arthritis, *Proc Staff Meetings Mayo Cl* 24:181-197, 1949.

36. **Rosenkranz G, Pataki J, Djerassi C,** Synthesis of cortisone, *J Am Chem Soc* 76:4055, 1951.

37. **Djerassi C,** A steroid autobiography, *Steroids* 43:351-361, 1984.

38, **Maisel AQ,** *The Hormone Quest,* Random House, New York, 1965, p. 70.

39. **Peterson DH,** Autobiography, *Steroids* 45:1-17, 1985.

40. **Colton FB,** Steroids and "the Pill": early steroid research at Searle, *Steroids* 57:624-630, 1992.

41. **Hechter O,** Homage to Gregory Pincus, *Persp Biol Med* Spring:358-370, 1968.

42. Ibid.

43. Ibid.

44. **Hechter O, Jacobsen RP, Jeanloz R, Levy H, Marshall CW, Pincus G, Schenker V,** The bio-oxygenation of steroids at C-11, *Arch Biochem* 15:457-460, 1950.

45. **Hechter O, Jacobsen RP, Jeanloz R, Levy H, Pincus G, Schenker V,** Pathways of corticosteroid synthesis, *J Clin Endocrin Metab* 10:827-828, 1950.

46, **Hechter O,** Homage to Gregory Pincus, *Persp Biol Med* Spring:358-370, 1968.

47. **Box 105,** Searle letter to Pincus, *Papers of Gregory Pincus, Manuscript Division, Library of Congress, Washington, D.C.,* July 18, 1946.

48. **Hechter O,** Homage to Gregory Pincus, *Persp Biol Med* Spring:358-370, 1968.

49. Ibid.

50. **Box 105,** Letter, Pincus to Raymond, *Papers of Gregory Pincus, Manuscript Division, Library of Congress, Washington, D.C.,* November 30, 1951.

51. **Hechter O,** Homage to Gregory Pincus, *Persp Biol Med* Spring:358-370, 1968.

52. Ibid.

53. **Box 105,** Assignment, *Papers of Gregory Pincus, Manuscript Division, Library of Congress, Washington, D.C.,* 1946.

54. **Box 105,** Searle meetings, *Papers of Gregory Pincus, Manuscript Division, Library of Congress, Washington, D.C.*

55. **Maisel AQ,** *The Hormone Quest,* Random House, New York, 1965, pp. 73-75.

56. **Sarett LH,** Partial synthesis of pregnene-4-triol-17(ß),20(ß),21-dione-3,11 and pregnene-4-diol-17(ß),21-trione-3,11,20 monoacetate, *J Biol Chem* 162:601-631, 1946.

57. **Maisel AQ,** *The Hormone Quest,* Random House, New York, 1965, p. 76.

58. **Peterson DH,** Autobiography, *Steroids* 45:1-17, 1985.

59. Ibid.

60. Ibid.

61. **Rosenkranz G,** From Ruzicka's terpenes in Zurich to Mexican steroids via Cuba, *Steroids* 57:409-418, 1992.

62. **Ehrenstein M,** Investigations on steroids. VIII. Lower homologs of hormones of the pregnane series: 10-nor-11-desoxycorticosterone acetate and 10-norprogesterone, *J Org Chem* 9:435-456, 1944.

63. **Djerassi C,** Steroid research at Syntex: "the Pill" and cortisone, *Steroids* 57:631-641, 1992.

64. **Djerassi C,** *This Man's Pill. Reflections on the 50th Birthday of the Pill,* Oxford University Press, Oxford, 2001, p. 47.

65. **Djerassi C,** Steroid research at Syntex: "the Pill" and cortisone, *Steroids* 57:631-641, 1992.

66. **Djerassi C, Miramontes L, Rosenkranz G, Sondheimer F,** Synthesis of 19-nor-17α-ethynyltestosterone and 19-nor-17α-methyltestosterone, *J Am Chem Soc* 76:4092-4094, 1954.

67. **Tullner WW, Herz R,** High progestational activity of 19-norprogesterone, *Endocrinology* 52:359-361, 1953.

68. **Herz R, Waite JH, Thomas LB,** Progestational effectiveness of 19-nor-ethinyl-testosterone by oral route in women, *Proc Soc Exp Biol* 91:418-420, 1956.

69. **Tullner WW, Hertz R,** Progestational activity of 19-norprogesterone and 19-norethisterone in the Rhesus monkey, *Proc Soc Exp Biol* 94:298-300, 1957.

70. **Tyler ET,** Comparative evaluation of various types of administration of progesterone, *J Clin Endocrin Metab* 15:881, 1955.

71. **Colton FB,** Steroids and "the Pill": early steroid research at Searle, *Steroids* 57:624-630, 1992.

72. Ibid.

73. **Djerassi C,** Steroid research at Syntex: "the Pill" and cortisone, *Steroids* 57:631-641, 1992.

74. **Rosenkranz G,** The early days of Syntex, *Chemical Heritage* 23:2,10,12, 2004.

75. **Zaffaroni A,** Life after Syntex, *Chemical Heritage* 23:2,10,12, 2004.

76. **Rosenkranz G,** The early days of Syntex, *Chemical Heritage* 23:2,10,12, 2004.

77. Ibid.

CHAPTER NINE

1. **Vaughn P,** *The Pill on Trial,* Coward-McCann, Inc., New York, 1970, pp. 23-24.

2. **Asbell B,** *The Pill: A Biography of the Drug that Changed the World,* Random House, New York, 1995, pp. 8-9.

3. **Halberstam D,** *The Fifties,* Fawcett Columbine, New York, 1993, p. 283.

4. **Chesler E,** *Woman of Valor: Margaret Sanger and the Birth Control Movement in America,* Simon & Schuster, New York, 1992.

5. **Tone A**, ed, *Controlling Reproduction: An American History,* Scholarly Resources Inc. Wilmington, Delaware, 1997, pp. 156-157.

6. **Gray M,** *Margaret Sanger: A Biography of the Champion of Birth Control,* Richard Marek Publishers, New York, 1979.

7. **Chesler E,** *Woman of Valor: Margaret Sanger and the Birth Control Movement in America,* Simon & Schuster, New York, 1992, pp. 118-122.

8. **PBS Video AMER 6509,** The Pill: American Experience, 2003.

9. **Borell M,** Biologists and the promotion of birth control research, 1918–1938, *J Hist Biology* 20:51-87, 1987.

10. **Jaffe FS,** Knowledge, perception, and change: notes on a fragment of social history, *Mt. Sinae J Med* 42:286-299, 1975.

11. **Mudd EH,** Dr. Abraham Stone, *Marriage and Family Living* May:174-175, 1960.

12. **Maisel AQ,** *The Hormone Quest,* Random House, New York, 1965, p. 113.

13. Ibid.

14. Ibid.

15. **Kurzrok R,** The prospects for hormonal sterilization, *J Contraception* 2:27-29, 1937.

16. **Maisel AQ,** *The Hormone Quest,* Random House, New York, 1965, p. 114.

17. **Reed J,** *The Birth Control Movement and American Society: From Private Vice to Public Virtue,* Princeton University Press, Princeton, N. J., 1978, p. 340.

18. **Box 12,** Planned Parenthood budget, *Papers of Gregory Pincus, Manuscript Division, Library of Congress, Washington, D.C.*, March 16, 1951.

19. **Fields A,** *Katharine Dexter McCormick: Pioneer for Women's Rights,* Praeger Publishers, Westport, Connecticut, 2003, p. 261.

20. **Fields A,** *Katharine Dexter McCormick: Pioneer for Women's Rights,* Praeger Publishers, Westport, Connecticut, 2003.

21. Ibid., p. 300.

22. **Reed J,** *The Birth Control Movement and American Society: From Private Vice to Public Virtue,* Princeton University Press, Princeton, N. J., 1978, p. 335.

23. **Fields A,** *Katharine Dexter McCormick: Pioneer for Women's Rights,* Praeger Publishers, Westport, Connecticut, 2003, pp. 38-45.

24. Ibid., p. 157.

25. Ibid. p. 156.

26. **Fields A,** *Katharine Dexter McCormick: Pioneer for Women's Rights,* Praeger Publishers, Westport, Connecticut, 2003.

27. Ibid., p. ix.

28. Ibid., p. 252.

29. **Reed J,** *The Birth Control Movement and American Society: From Private Vice to Public Virtue,* Princeton University Press, Princeton, N. J., 1978, p. 337.

30. **Fields A,** *Katharine Dexter McCormick: Pioneer for Women's Rights,* Praeger Publishers, Westport, Connecticut, 2003, pp. 181-182.

31. Ibid., p. 284.

32. **Reed J,** *The Birth Control Movement and American Society: From Private Vice to Public Virtue,* Princeton University Press, Princeton, N. J., 1978, p. 338.

33. Ibid., p. 339.

34. **Chang MC,** Mammalian sperm, eggs, and control of fertility, *Persp Biol Med* Spring:376-383, 1968.

35. **Reed J,** *The Birth Control Movement and American Society: From Private Vice to Public Virtue,* Princeton University Press, Princeton, N. J., 1978, p. 339.

36. **Vaughn P,** *The Pill on Trial,* Coward-Mc-Cann, Inc., New York, 1970, p.25.

37. **Reed J,** *The Birth Control Movement and American Society: From Private Vice to Public Virtue,* Princeton University Press, Princeton, N. J., 1978, p. 341.

38. Ibid, p. 342.

39. **Box 14,** Letters, Henshaw to Pincus, Pincus to Henshaw, *Papers of Gregory Pincus, Manuscript Division, Library of Congress, Washington, D.C.,* 1953.

40. **Reed J,** *The Birth Control Movement and American Society: From Private Vice to Public Virtue,* Princeton University Press, Princeton, N. J., 1978, p. 342.

41. Ibid.

42. **Fields A,** *Katharine Dexter McCormick: Pioneer for Women's Rights,* Praeger Publishers, Westport, Connecticut, 2003, p. 265.

43. **Garcia C-R,** Development of the pill, *Ann N Y Acad Sci* 1038:223-226, 2004.

44. **Box 16,** Letter, McCormick to Hoagland, *Worcester Foundation for Biomedical Research (WFBR) Papers, (formerly) Worcester Foundation for Experimental Biology (WFEB), The Lamar Soutter Library, University of Massachusetts Medical School, Worcester, Massachusetts,* August 13, 1954.

45. **Reed J,** *The Birth Control Movement and American Society: From Private Vice to Public Virtue,* Princeton University Press, Princeton, N. J., 1978, p. 343.

46. **Vaughn P,** *The Pill on Trial,* Coward-Mc-Cann, Inc., New York, 1970, p.25.

47. Ibid.

48. **McCormick KD,** Letter to Margaret Sanger: Margaret Sanger Papers, Sophia Smith Collection, Smith College; July 19, 1954.

49. **Merrill A,** Personal interview, May 23, 2007.

50. Ibid.

51. **Asbell B,** *The Pill: A Biography of the Drug that Changed the World,* Random House, New York, 1995, pp. 347-348.

52. **Box 1,** *Candide* Interview, *Papers of Gregory Pincus, Manuscript Division, Library of Congress, Washington, D.C.,* 1966.

53. **Fields A,** *Katharine Dexter McCormick: Pioneer for Women's Rights,* Praeger Publishers, Westport, Connecticut, 2003, p. 298.

54. Ibid. p. 304.

55. Ibid, p. xii.

56. Ibid., p. 159.

57. **Hoagland H,** Lamar Soutter Lecture, University of Massachusetts Medical Center, *Worcester Foundation for Biomedical Research (WFBR) Papers, (formerly) Worcester Foundation for Experimental Biology (WFEB), The Lamar Soutter Library, University of Massachusetts Medical School, Worcester, Massachusetts,* September 10, 1975.

58. **Simmer HH,** On the history of hormonal contraception. I. Ludwig Haberlandt (1885–1932) and his concept of "hormonal sterilization", *Contraception* 1:3-20, 1970.

59. **Pincus G, Werthessen N,** The continued injection of oestrin into young rats, *Am J Physiol* 103:631-636, 1933.

60. **Makepeace AW, Weinstein GL, Friedman MH,** *Am J Physiol* 119:512, 1927.

61. **Pincus G, Chang MC,** The effects of progesterone and related compounds on ovulation and early development in the rabbit, *Acta Physiol. Latinoamericana* 3:177-183, 1953.

62. **Chang MC,** Mammalian sperm, eggs, and control of fertility, *Persp Biol Med* Spring:376-383, 1968.

63. Ibid.

64. **Slechta RF, Chang MC, Pincus G,** Effects of progesterone and related compounds on mating and pregnancy in the rat, *Fertil Steril* 5:282-293, 1954.

65. **Box 4,** Letter, Pincus to Raymond, *Papers of Gregory Pincus, Manuscript Division, Library of Congress, Washington, D.C.,* 1951.

66. **Pincus G,** Control of conception by hormonal steroids, *Science* 153:493-500, 1966.

67. **Hoagland H,** *The Road to Yesterday,* privately printed, Worcester, Massachusetts, 1974, p. 91.

68. **Maisel AQ,** *The Hormone Quest,* Random House, New York, 1965, p. 122.

69. **Tullner WW, Herz R,** High progestational activity of 19-norprogesterone, *Endocrinology* 52:359-361, 1953.

70. **Herz R, Waite JH, Thomas LB,** Progestational effectiveness of 19-nor-ethinyl-testosterone by oral route in women, *Proc Soc Exp Biol* 91:418-420, 1956.

71. **Tullner WW, Hertz R,** Progestational activity of 19-norprogesterone and 19-norethisterone in the Rhesus monkey, *Proc Soc Exp Biol* 94:298-300, 1957.

72. **Pincus G,** The hormonal control of ovulation and early development, *Postgrad Med* 24:654-660, 1958.

73. **Hunt DM,** *Evolution of the Pill,* privately printed, Northborough, Massachusetts, 2002.

74. **Box 107,** Searle correspondence, *Papers of Gregory Pincus, Manuscript Division, Library of Congress, Washington, D.C.*

75. **Pincus G,** Some effects of progesterone and related compounds upon the reproduction and early development in mammals, *Acta Endocrinol* Suppl 28:18-36, 1956.

76. Ibid.

77. **Pincus G, Chang MC, Hafez ESE, Zarrow MX, Merrill A,** Effects of certain 19-nor steroids on reproductive processes in animals, *Science* 124:890-891, 1956.

78. **Rock J, Pincus G, Garcia C-R,** Effects of certain 19-nor steroids on the normal human menstrual cycle, *Science* 124:891-893, 1956.

79. **Fields A,** *Katharine Dexter McCormick: Pioneer for Women's Rights,* Praeger Publishers, Westport, Connecticut, 2003, p. 281.

80. **Pincus G, Chang MC, Zarrow MX, Hafez ESE, Merrill A,** Studies of the biological activity of certain 19-nor steroids in female animals, *Endocrinology* 59:695-707, 1956.

81. **Rock J, Pincus G, Garcia C-R,** Effects of certain 19-nor steroids on the normal human menstrual cycle, *Science* 124:891-893, 1956.

82. **Rock J, Garcia C-R, Pincus G,** Synthetic progestins in the normal human menstrual cycle, *Rec Prog Hor Res* 13:323-329, 1957.

83. **Garcia C-R, Pincus G, Rock J,** Effects of three 19-nor steroids on human ovulation and menstruation, *Am J Obstet Gynecol* 75:82-97, 1958.

84. **McLaughlin L,** *The Pill, John Rock, and the Church: The Biography of a Revolution,* Little, Brown and Company, Boston, 1982, p. 117.

85. **Pincus G, Rock J, Chang MC, Garcia C-R,** Effects of certain 19-nor steroids on reproductive processes and fertility, *Fed Proc* 18:1051-1056, 1959.

86, **Rock J, Garcia C-R, Pincus G,** Synthetic progestins in the normal human menstrual cycle, *Rec Prog Hor Res* 13:323-329, 1957.

87. **McLaughlin L,** *The Pill, John Rock, and the Church: The Biography of a Revolution,* Little, Brown and Company, Boston, 1982, pp. 122-123.

88. **Rock J, Garcia C-R, Pincus G,** Synthetic progestins in the normal human menstrual cycle, *Rec Prog Hor Res* 13:341, 1957.

89. Ibid., p. 340.

90. Ibid., p. 344.

91. **McLaughlin L,** *The Pill, John Rock, and the Church: The Biography of a Revolution,* Little, Brown and Company, Boston, 1982, p. 45.

92. **Reed J,** *The Birth Control Movement and American Society: From Private Vice to Public Virtue,* Princeton University Press, Princeton, N. J., 1978, p. 344.

93. **Pincus G,** *The Control of Fertility,* Academic Press, New York, 1965, pp. 6-8.

CHAPTER TEN

1. **Halberstam D,** *The Fifties,* Fawcett Columbine, New York, 1993, p. 601.

2. **McLaughlin L,** *The Pill, John Rock, and the Church: The Biography of a Revolution,* Little, Brown and Company, Boston, 1982.

3. Ibid., p. 18.

4. Ibid., p. 27.

5. **Rock J, Loth D,** *Voluntary Parenthood,* Random House, New York, 1949.

6. Ibid., p. 3.

7. **Halberstam D,** *The Fifties,* Fawcett Columbine, New York, 1993, p. 601.

8. **McLaughlin L,** *The Pill, John Rock, and the Church: The Biography of a Revolution,* Little, Brown and Company, Boston, 1982, p. 125.

9. **Speroff L, Darney PD,** *A Clinical Guide for Contraception,* Fourth Edition, Lippincott Williams & Wilkins, Philadelphia, 2005, pp. 11-13.

10. **McLaughlin L,** *The Pill, John Rock, and the Church: The Biography of a Revolution,* Little, Brown and Company, Boston, 1982, p. 60.

11. Ibid., p. 66.

12. **Hertig AT, Rock J, Adams EC, Menkin MF,** Thirty-four fertilized human ova, good, bad and indifferent, recovered from 210 women of known fertility; a study of biologic wastage in early human pregnancy, *Pediatrics* 23:202-211, 1959.

13. **McLaughlin L,** *The Pill, John Rock, and the Church: The Biography of a Revolution,* Little, Brown and Company, Boston, 1982, p. 70.

14. **Rock J, Menkin MF,** In vitro fertilization and cleavage of human ovarian eggs, *Science* 100:105-107, 1944.

15. **Rock J,** *The Time Has Come: A Catholic Doctor's Proposal to End the Battle over Birth Control,* Alfred A. Knopf, New York, 1963, p. 163.

16. **Vaughn P,** *The Pill on Trial,* Coward-McCann, Inc., New York, 1970, p. 30.

17. **Reed J,** *The Birth Control Movement and American Society: From Private Vice to Public Virtue,* Princeton University Press, Princeton, N. J., 1978, p. 355.

18. **Pincus G,** The hormonal control of ovulation and early development, *Postgrad Med* 24:654-660, 1958.

19. Ibid.

20. **Reed J,** *The Birth Control Movement and American Society: From Private Vice to Public Virtue,* Princeton University Press, Princeton, N. J., 1978, p. 352.

21. Ibid.

22. **Halberstam D,** *The Fifties,* Fawcett Columbine, New York, 1993, p. 602.

23. **McLaughlin L,** *The Pill, John Rock, and the Church: The Biography of a Revolution,* Little, Brown and Company, Boston, 1982, p. 194.

24. Ibid., p. 200.

CHAPTER ELEVEN

1. **Rock J,** *The Time Has Come: A Catholic Doctor's Proposal to End the Battle over Birth Control,* Alfred A. Knopf, New York, 1963, p. 159.

2. **Ramírez de Arellano AB, Seipp C,** *Colonialism, Catholicism, and Contraception,* The University of North Carolina Press, Chapel Hill, 1983, p. 108.

3. **Box 21,** Letters, McCormick to Pincus, *Papers of Gregory Pincus, Manuscript Division, Library of Congress, Washington, D.C.,* 1956.

4. **Box 21,** Letter, McCormick to Pincus, *Papers of Gregory Pincus, Manuscript Division, Library of Congress, Washington, D.C.,* June 14, 1956.

5. **Ramírez de Arellano AB, Seipp C,** *Colonialism, Catholicism, and Contraception,* The University of North Carolina Press, Chapel Hill, 1983, p. 109.

6. **Box 18,** Letter, Tyler to Pincus, *Papers of Gregory Pincus, Manuscript Division, Library of Congress, Washington, D.C.,* July 8, 1955.

7. **Ramírez de Arellano AB, Seipp C,** *Colonialism, Catholicism, and Contraception,* The University of North Carolina Press, Chapel Hill, 1983, p. 110.

8. **Box 22,** Letter, Díaz Carazo to Pincus, *Papers of Gregory Pincus, Manuscript Division, Library of Congress, Washington, D.C.,* January 31, 1956.

9. **Box 22,** Letter, Hinman to Pincus, *Papers of Gregory Pincus, Manuscript Division, Library of Congress, Washington, D.C.,* October 25, 1956.

10. **McLaughlin L,** *The Pill, John Rock, and the Church: The Biography of a Revolution,* Little, Brown and Company, Boston, 1982, p. 120.

11. **Fields A,** *Katharine Dexter McCormick: Pioneer for Women's Rights,* Praeger Publishers, Westport, Connecticut, 2003, p. 274.

12. **Chang I,** Personal interview, May 22, 2007.

13. **Box 21,** Letter, Crawford to McCormick, *Papers of Gregory Pincus, Manuscript Division, Library of Congress, Washington, D.C.,* 1955.

14. **Fields A,** *Katharine Dexter McCormick: Pioneer for Women's Rights,* Praeger Publishers, Westport, Connecticut, 2003, p. 275.

15. **Birth Control Pill Reported by Expert**, *Pasadena Independent*, October 19, 1955.

16. **Box 21,** Letters, Pincus to Ishidawa, *Papers of Gregory Pincus, Manuscript Division, Library of Congress, Washington, D.C.,* 1955.

17. **Box 21,** Letter, Stone to McCormick, *Papers of Gregory Pincus, Manuscript Division, Library of Congress, Washington, D.C.,* March 30, 1956.

18. **Box 109,** Long term administration of vilane to human subjects, *Papers of Gregory Pincus, Manuscript Division, Library of Congress, Washington, D.C.,* April 18, 1957.

19. **Box 112,** Activities at Worcester State Hospital, *Papers of Gregory Pincus, Manuscript Division, Library of Congress, Washington, D.C.,*

20. **Box 29,** Letter, Rock to Winter, *Papers of Gregory Pincus, Manuscript Division, Library of Congress, Washington, D.C.,* August 10, 1957.

21. **Box 21,** Letter, Pincus to McCormick, *Papers of Gregory Pincus, Manuscript Division, Library of Congress, Washington, D.C.,* March 14, 1956.

22. **Box 21,** Letter, Crawford to McCormick, *Papers of Gregory Pincus, Manuscript Division, Library of Congress, Washington, D.C.,* 1955.

23. **Box 39,** Letter, Pincus to McCormick, *Papers of Gregory Pincus, Manuscript Division, Library of Congress, Washington, D.C.,* May 6, 1959.

24. **Box 29,** Letter, Crawford to Grahn, *Papers of Gregory Pincus, Manuscript Division, Library of Congress, Washington, D.C.,* February 26, 1957.

25. **Box 27,** Letter, Crawford to McCormick, *Papers of Gregory Pincus, Manuscript Division, Library of Congress, Washington, D.C.,* June 21, 1957.

26. **Box 33,** Budget, *Papers of Gregory Pincus, Manuscript Division, Library of Congress, Washington, D.C.,* 1959.

27. **Box 74,** Letter, Crawford to McCormick, *Papers of Gregory Pincus, Manuscript Division, Library of Congress, Washington, D.C.,* September 28, 1964.

28. Ibid.

29. **Box 74,** Letter, Pincus to McCormick, *Papers of Gregory Pincus, Manuscript Division, Library of Congress, Washington, D.C.,* May 15, 1964.

30. **Reed J,** *The Birth Control Movement and American Society: From Private Vice to Public Virtue,* Princeton University Press, Princeton, N. J., 1978, p. 356.

31. Ibid.

32. **Fields A,** *Katharine Dexter McCormick: Pioneer for Women's Rights,* Praeger Publishers, Westport, Connecticut, 2003, p. 281.

33. **Box 27,** Letter, Crawford to McCormick, *Papers of Gregory Pincus, Manuscript Division, Library of Congress, Washington, D.C.,* June 21, 1957.

34. **Ramírez de Arellano AB, Seipp C,** *Colonialism, Catholicism, and Contraception,* The University of North Carolina Press, Chapel Hill, 1983, p. 113.

35. **Vaughn P,** *The Pill on Trial,* Coward-McCann, Inc., New York, 1970, p. 42.

36. **Strauss III JF, Mastroianni Jr L,** In memoriam: Celso-Ramon Garcia, M.D. (1922–2004), reproductive medicine visionary, *J Exp Clin Assist Reprod* 2:2-7, 2005.

37. **Garcia C-R,** Gregory Goodwin Pincus (1903–1967), *J Clin Endocrin Metab* 28:1245-1248, 1968.

38. **Strauss III JF, Mastroianni Jr L,** In memoriam: Celso-Ramon Garcia, M.D. (1922–2004), reproductive medicine visionary, *J Exp Clin Assist Reprod* 2:2-7, 2005.

39. **Vaughn P,** *The Pill on Trial,* Coward-McCann, Inc., New York, 1970, p. 125.

40. **Strauss III JF, Mastroianni Jr L,** In memoriam: Celso-Ramon Garcia, M.D. (1922–2004), reproductive medicine visionary, *J Exp Clin Assist Reprod* 2:2-7, 2005.

41. **Fields A,** *Katharine Dexter McCormick: Pioneer for Women's Rights,* Praeger Publishers, Westport, Connecticut, 2003, p. 277.

42. **Strauss III JF, Mastroianni Jr L,** In memoriam: Celso-Ramon Garcia, M.D. (1922–2004), reproductive medicine visionary, *J Exp Clin Assist Reprod* 2:2-7, 2005.

43. **Box 22,** Letter, Pincus to Rice-Wray, *Papers of Gregory Pincus, Manuscript Division, Library of Congress, Washington, D.C.*, July 6, 1956.

44. **Ramírez de Arellano AB, Seipp C,** *Colonialism, Catholicism, and Contraception,* The University of North Carolina Press, Chapel Hill, 1983, p. 113.

45. **Pincus G, Rock J, Garcia C-R, Rice-Wray E, Paniagua M, Rodriguez I,** Fertility control with oral medication, *Am J Obstet Gynecol* 75:1333-1346, 1958.

46. **Box 137,** Study Project of SC-4642, *Papers of Gregory Pincus, Manuscript Division, Library of Congress, Washington, D.C.,* January, 1957.

47. **Box 22,** *El Imparcial* article, *Papers of Gregory Pincus, Manuscript Division, Library of Congress, Washington, D.C.,* April 21, 1956.

48. **Box 22,** Letter, Rodríguez to Pincus, *Papers of Gregory Pincus, Manuscript Division, Library of Congress, Washington, D.C.,* May 8, 1956.

49. **McLaughlin L,** *The Pill, John Rock, and the Church: The Biography of a Revolution,* Little, Brown and Company, Boston, 1982, p. 130.

50. **Pincus G, Rock J, Garcia C-R, Rice-Wray E, Paniagua M, Rodriguez I,** Fertility control with oral medication, *Am J Obstet Gynecol* 75:1333-1346, 1958.

51. **Reed J,** *The Birth Control Movement and American Society: From Private Vice to Public Virtue,* Princeton University Press, Princeton, N. J., 1978, p. 132.

52. **Merrill A,** Personal interview, May 23, 2007.

53. **Hoagland H,** *The Road to Yesterday,* privately printed, Worcester, Massachusetts, 1974, p. 93.

54. **Box 16,** Supplies to be taken to Haiti, *Worcester Foundation for Biomedical Research (WFBR) Papers, (formerly) Worcester Foundation for Experimental Biology (WFEB), The Lamar Soutter Library, University of Massachusetts Medical School, Worcester, Massachusetts,* November, 1961.

55. **Merrill A,** Personal interview, May 23, 2007

56. **Vaughn P,** *The Pill on Trial,* Coward-McCann, Inc., New York, 1970, p. 46.

57. **Merrill A,** Personal interview, May 23, 2007

58. Ibid.

59. Ibid.

60. **Wallach E,** Personal interview, January 23, 2008.

61. **Garcia C-R,** Development of the pill, *Ann N Y Acad Sci* 1038:223-226, 2004.

62. **Halberstam D,** *The Fifties,* Fawcett Columbine, New York, 1993, p. 640.

63. **Pincus G, Chang MC, Hafez ESE, Zarrow MX, Merrill A,** Effects of certain 19-nor steroids on reproductive processes in animals, *Science* 124:890-891, 1956.

64. **Rock J, Pincus G, Garcia C-R,** Effects of certain 19-nor steroids on the normal human menstrual cycle, *Science* 124:891-893, 1956.

65. **Reed J,** *The Birth Control Movement and American Society: From Private Vice to Public Virtue,* Princeton University Press, Princeton, N. J., 1978, pp. 362-364.

66. **Box 22,** Letter, Rice-Wray to Pincus, *Papers of Gregory Pincus, Manuscript Division, Library of Congress, Washington, D.C.,* December 20, 1956.

67. **Box 137,** Study project of SC-4642, *Papers of Gregory Pincus, Manuscript Division, Library of Congress, Washington, D.C.,* January, 1957.

68. **Pincus G, Rock J, Garcia C-R, Rice-Wray E, Paniagua M, Rodriguez I,** Fertility control with oral medication, *Am J Obstet Gynecol* 75:1333-1346, 1958.

69. **Rice-Wray E, Schulz-Contreeras M, Guerrero I, Aranda-Rosell A,** Long-term administration of norethindrone in fertility control, *JAMA* 180:355-358, 1962.

70. **Wallach E,** Personal interview, January 23, 2008.

71. Ibid.

72. **Box 5,** Receipt, *Papers of Gregory Pincus, Manuscript Division, Library of Congress, Washington, D.C.,* December 17, 1962.

73. **Pincus G, Garcia C-R, Rock J, Paniagua M, Pendleton A, Laraque F, Nicolas R, Borno R, Pean V,** Effectiveness of an oral contraceptive; effects of a progestin-estrogen combination upon fertility, menstrual phenomena, and health, *Science* 130:81-83, 1959.

74. **Pincus G, Rock J, Chang MC, Garcia C-R,** Effects of certain 19-nor steroids on reproductive processes and fertility, *Fed Proc* 18:1051-1056, 1959.

75. **Pincus G,** The hormonal control of ovulation and early development, *Postgrad Med* 24:654-660, 1958.

76. **Pincus G, Garcia C-R, Rock J, Paniagua M, Pendleton A, Laraque F, Nicolas R, Borno R, Pean V,** Effectiveness of an oral contraceptive; effects of a progestin-estrogen combination upon fertility, menstrual phenomena, and health, *Science* 130:81-83, 1959.

77. Ibid.

78. **Pincus G,** The hormonal control of ovulation and early development, *Postgrad Med* 24:654-660, 1958.

79. Ibid.

80. **Ramírez de Arellano AB, Seipp C,** *Colonialism, Catholicism, and Contraception,* The University of North Carolina Press, Chapel Hill, 1983, pp. 119-120.

81. **Satterthwaite AP, Gamble CJ,** Conception control with norethynodrel. Progress report of a four-year field study at Humacao, Puerto Rico, *J Am Women's Assoc* 17:797-802, 1962.

82. **Ramírez de Arellano AB, Seipp C,** *Colonialism, Catholicism, and Contraception,* The University of North Carolina Press, Chapel Hill, 1983, p. 120.

83. Ibid, p. 137.

84. **Pincus G, Garcia C-R,** Studies on vaginal, cervical and uterine histology, *Metabolism* 14:344-347, 1965.

85. **Carrey F,** Denies Oral Pills Cause of Cancer, *The Lowell Sun,* April 25, 1966.

86. **International Collaboration of Epidemiological Studies of Cervical Cancer,** Cervical cancer and hormonal contraceptives: collaborative reanalysis of individual data for 16573 women with cervical cancer and 35509 women without cervical cancer from 24 epidemiological studies, *Lancet* 370:1609-1621, 2007.

87. **Wingo PA, Austin H, Marchbanks PA, Whiteman MK, Hsia J, Mandel MG, Peterson HB, Ory HW,** Oral contraceptives and the risk of death from breast cancer, *Obstet Gynecol* 110:793-800, 2007.

88. **Graff-Iversen S, Hammar N, Thelle DS, Tonstad S,** Use of oral contraceptives and mortality during 14 years' follow-up of Norwegian women, *Scand J Public Health* 34:11-16, 2006.

89. **Vaughn P,** *The Pill on Trial,* Coward-Mc-Cann, Inc., New York, 1970, p. 52.

90. **Tyler ET, Olson HJ, Wolf L, Finkelstein S, Thayer J, Kaplan N, Levin M, Weintraub J,** An oral contraceptive. A 4-year study of norethindrone, *Obstet Gynecol* 18:363-367, 1961.

91. **Box 29,** Letter, Rock to Pincus, *Papers of Gregory Pincus, Manuscript Division, Library of Congress, Washington, D.C.,* June 26, 1957.

92. Ibid.

93. **Box 29,** Telegram, *Papers of Gregory Pincus, Manuscript Division, Library of Congress, Washington, D.C.,* June 25, 1957.

94. **Box 109,** Letter, Raymond to Pincus, *Papers of Gregory Pincus, Manuscript Division, Library of Congress, Washington, D.C.,* October 4, 1957.

95. **Sheehan R,** The Birth-Control "Pill", *Fortune* April:154-155, 220-222, 1958.

96. **Rock J, Garcia C-R, Pincus G,** Use of some progestational 19-nor steroids in gynecology, *Am J Obstet Gynecol* 79:758-767, 1960.

97. **Box 5,** Letter, Pincus to Stockwell, *Papers of Gregory Pincus, Manuscript Division, Library of Congress, Washington, D.C.,* June 3, 1959.

98. **Box 209,** Letter, Leila to Pincus, *Papers of Gregory Pincus, Manuscript Division, Library of Congress, Washington, D.C.,* June 5, 1958.

99. **Pincus G, Garcia C-R, Rock J, Paniagua M, Pendleton A, Laraque F, Nicolas R, Borno R, Pean V,** Effectiveness of an oral contraceptive; effects of a progestin-estrogen combination upon fertility, menstrual phenomena, and health, *Science* 130:81-83, 1959.

100. **Pincus G, Rock J, Chang MC, Garcia C-R,** Effects of certain 19-nor steroids on reproductive processes and fertility, *Fed Proc* 18:1051-1056, 1959.

101. **Vaughn P,** *The Pill on Trial,* Coward-Mc-Cann, Inc., New York, 1970, p. 42.

102. **Chang MC,** Mammalian sperm, eggs, and control of fertility, *Persp Biol Med* Spring:376-383, 1968.

103. **Garcia C-R,** Dedication, *Int J Fertil* 13:267-269, 1968.

104. **Box 39,** Letter, McCormick to Pincus, *Papers of Gregory Pincus, Manuscript Division, Library of Congress, Washington, D.C.,* May 21, 1959.

105. **Fields A,** *Katharine Dexter McCormick: Pioneer for Women's Rights,* Praeger Publishers, Westport, Connecticut, 2003, p. 299.

106. **Box 44,** Letter, Pincus to McCormick, *Papers of Gregory Pincus, Manuscript Division, Library of Congress, Washington, D.C.,* August 30, 1960.

107. **Reed J,** *The Birth Control Movement and American Society. From Private Vice to Public Virtue,* Princeton University Press, Princeton, N. J., 1978, p. 349.

108. **Goldzieher JW,** How the oral contraceptives came to be developed, *JAMA* 230:421-425, 1974.

CHAPTER TWELVE

1. **Fields A,** *Katharine Dexter McCormick: Pioneer for Women's Rights,* Praeger Publishers, Westport, Connecticut, 2003, p. 291.

2. **McLaughlin L,** *The Pill, John Rock, and the Church: The Biography of a Revolution,* Little, Brown and Company, Boston, 1982, p. 135.

3. Ibid., p. 138.

4. Ibid., p. 140.

5. **Reed J,** *The Birth Control Movement and American Society: From Private Vice to Public Virtue,* Princeton University Press, Princeton, N. J., 1978, p. 142.

6. **Junod SW, Marks L,** Women's trials: the approval of the first oral contraceptive pill in the United States and Great Britain, *J Hist Med Allied Sci* 57:117-160, 2002.

7. **McLaughlin L,** *The Pill, John Rock, and the Church: The Biography of a Revolution,* Little, Brown and Company, Boston, 1982, pp. 141-143.

8. **Box 42,** Letters, DeFelice to Pincus; Pincus to DeFelice, *Papers of Gregory Pincus, Manuscript Division, Library of Congress, Washington, D.C.,* February 12, 1960.

9. **Junod SW, Marks L,** Women's trials: the approval of the first oral contraceptive pill in the United States and Great Britain, *J Hist Med Allied Sci* 57:117-160, 2002.

10. **Hoagland H,** *The Road to Yesterday,* privately printed, Worcester, Massachusetts, 1974, p. 92.

11. **Lader L,** Three Men Who Made a Revolution, *The New York Times Magazine*, April 10, 1966.

12. Ibid.

13. **Reed J,** *The Birth Control Movement and American Society: From Private Vice to Public Virtue,* Princeton University Press, Princeton, N. J., 1978, p. 362.

14. **Pincus G,** *The Control of Fertility,* Academic Press, New York, 1965, p. xii.

15. **Jordan WM,** Pulmonary embolism, *Lancet* ii:1140-1141, 1961.

16. **Amador E, Zimmerman TS, Wacker WE,** FDA report on Enovid. Ad hoc advisory committee for the evaluation of a possible etiologic relation with thromboembolic conditions, *JAMA* 185:776, 1963.

17. **Pincus G, Garcia C-R, Rock J, Paniagua M, Pendleton A, Laraque F, Nicolas R, Borno R, Pean V,** Effectiveness of an oral contraceptive; effects of a progestin-estrogen combination upon fertility, menstrual phenomena, and health, *Science* 130:81-83, 1959.

18. **Dinger JC, Heinemann LA, Kühl-Habich D,** The safety of a drospirenone-containing oral contraceptive: final results from the European Active Surveillance Study on oral contraceptives based on 142,475 women-years of observation, *Contraception* 75:344-354, 2007.

19. **Pomp ER, le Cessie S, Rosendaal FR, Doggen CJ,** Risk of venous thrombosis: obesity and its joint effect with oral contraceptive use and prothrombotic mutations, *Br J Haematol* 139:289-296, 2007.

20. **Trussell J, Wynn LL,** Reducing unintended pregnancy in the United States, *Contraception* 77:1-5, 2008.

21. **Kost K, Singh S, Vaughan B, Trussell J, Bankole A,** Estimates of contraceptive failure from the 2002 National Survey of Family Growth, *Contraception* 77:10-21, 2008.

22. **Mosher WD, Martinez GM, Chandra A, Abma JC, Wilson SJ,** Use of contraception and use of family planning services in the United States: 1982–2002., *Advance data from vital and health statistics; no. 350* National Center for Health Statistics, Hyattsville, Maryland, 2004.

CHAPTER THIRTEEN

1. **McLaughlin L,** *The Pill, John Rock, and the Church: The Biography of a Revolution,* Little, Brown and Company, Boston, 1982, p. 155.

2. **Rock J,** Population growth, *JAMA* 177:58-60, 1961.

3. **McLaughlin L,** *The Pill, John Rock, and the Church: The Biography of a Revolution,* Little, Brown and Company, Boston, 1982, pp. 157-158.

4. **Rock J,** *The Time Has Come: A Catholic Doctor's Proposal to End the Battle over Birth Control,* Alfred A. Knopf, New York, 1963.

5. Ibid., p. xiv.

6. **Marsh M, Ronner W,** *The Fertility Doctor. John Rock and the Reproductive Revolution,* The Johns Hopkins University Press, Baltimore, 2008, p 237.

7. **Rock J,** *The Time Has Come: A Catholic Doctor's Proposal to End the Battle over Birth Control,* Alfred A. Knopf, New York, 1963, p. 201.

8. **Rock J,** Sex, science and survival, *J Reprod Fertil* 8:397-409, 1964.

9. **Hertig AT, Rock J, Adams EC, Menkin MF,** Thirty-four fertilized human ova, good, bad and indifferent, recovered from 210 women of known fertility; a study of biologic wastage in early human pregnancy, *Pediatrics* 23:202-211, 1959.

10. **McLaughlin L,** *The Pill, John Rock, and the Church: The Biography of a Revolution,* Little, Brown and Company, Boston, 1982, p. 176.

11. **Neves e Castro M,** Personal email, May 28, 2008.

12. **Kneeland DE,** Majority report seeks papal shift on contraception, *The New York Times,* p. 1, April 17, 1967.

13. **McLaughlin L,** *The Pill, John Rock, and the Church: The Biography of a Revolution,* Little, Brown and Company, Boston, 1982, p. 186.

14. **Asbell B,** *The Pill: A Biography of the Drug that Changed the World,* Random House, New York, 1995, pp. 283-285.

15. **Pope Paul VI,** Humanae Vitae: Encyclical of Pope Paul VI on the Regulation of Birth, July 25, 1968.

16. Ibid.

17. **Goldscheider C, Mosher WD,** Patterns of contraceptive use in the United States: the importance of regligious factors, *Studies Fam Plann* 22:102-115, 1991.

18. **Kaiser RB,** *The Politics of Sex and Religion: A Case History in the Development of Doctrine, 1962–1984,* Leaven Press, Kansas City, 1985.

19. **Dr. Rock Regrets Pope's Stand,** *Boston Globe,* August 4, 1968.

20. **McLaughlin L,** *The Pill, John Rock, and the Church: The Biography of a Revolution,* Little, Brown and Company, Boston, 1982, pp. 226-233.

21. **Jaffe FS,** Knowledge, perception, and change: notes on a fragment of social history, *Mt. Sinae J Med* 42:286-299, 1975.

22. **Marks LV,** *Sexual Chemistry: A History of the Contraceptive Pill,* Yale University Press, New Haven, 2001.

23. **Watkins ES,** *On the Pill: A Social History of Oral Contraceptives 1950–1970,* The Johns Hopkins University Press, Baltimore, 1998.

24. **Junod SW, Marks L,** Women's trials: the approval of the first oral contraceptive pill in the United States and Great Britain, *J Hist Med Allied Sci* 57:117-160, 2002.

25. **Djerassi C,** *This Man's Pill: Reflections ont he 50th Birthday of the Pill,* Oxford University Press, Oxford, 2001, p. 69.

26. **Biezanek AC,** *All Things New: A Declaration of Faith,* Harper & Row, Publishers, New York, 1964.

27. **Courey RM,** Participants in the Development, Marketing and Safety Evaluation of the Oral Contraceptive, 1950–1965: Mythic Dimensions of a Scientific Solution, *Dissertation for the Degree of Doctor of Philosophy in History,* Graduate Division, University of California at Berkeley, 1994.

28. **Box 72,** Hertz Manuscript and Correspondence, *Papers of Gregory Pincus, Manuscript Division, Library of Congress, Washington, D.C.,* 1964.

29. Ibid.

30. Ibid.

31. Ibid.

32. Ibid.

33. Ibid.

34. **Seaman B,** *The Doctor's Case Against the Pill,* Dobleday & Company, Inc., Garden City, New York, 1980 (First Edition: 1969).

35. **Watkins ES,** *On the Pill: A Social History of Oral Contraceptives 1950–1970,* The Johns Hopkins University Press, Baltimore, 1998, pp. 103-108.

36. **Pincus G,** Control of conception by hormonal steroids, *Science* 153:493-500, 1966.

37. **Stampfer MJ, Willett WC, Colditz GA, Speizer FE, Hennekens CH,** Past use of oral contraceptives and cardiovascular disease: a meta-analysis in the context of the Nurses' Health Study, *Am J Obstet Gynecol* 163:285-291, 1990.

38. **Wingo PA, Austin H, Marchbanks PA, Whiteman MK, Hsia J, Mandel MG, Peterson HB, Ory HW,** Oral contraceptives and the risk of death from breast cancer, *Obstet Gynecol* 110:793-800, 2007.

39. **Hannaford PC, Selvaraj S, Elliot AM, Angus V, Iversen L, Lee AJ,** Cancer risk among users of oral contraceptives: cohort data from the Royal College of General Practitioner's oral contraception study, *Brit Med J* 335:651, 2007.

40. **Vessey M, Painter R,** Oral contraceptive use and cancer. Findings in a large cohort study, 1968–2004, *Br J Cancer* 95:385-389, 2006.

41. **McLaughlin L,** *The Pill, John Rock, and the Church: The Biography of a Revolution,* Little, Brown and Company, Boston, 1982.

42. **Ehrenreich B,** Bitter Pill, *The New York Times,* March 6, 1983.

43. **Kase N,** Personal interview, December 19, 2007.

44. **Bedford JM,** Personal interview, April 16, 2008.

44. **PBS Video AMER 6509,** The Pill: American Experience, 2003.

CHAPTER FOURTEEN

1. **White AB,** Gregory Goodwin Pincus (1903–1967), *Endocrinology* 82:651-654, 1968.

2. **Goldzieher J,** Personal interview, October 30, 2007.

3. **Lieberman S,** Personal interview, October 17, 2007.

4. **McCracken J,** Personal interview, May 21, 2007.

5. **Box 18,** Around the world itinerary, *Papers of Gregory Pincus, Manuscript Division, Library of Congress, Washington, D.C.,* 1955.

6. **Box 18,** Letter, Lundgren to Feingold, *Papers of Gregory Pincus, Manuscript Division, Library of Congress, Washington, D.C.,* January 26, 1956.

7. **Box 25,** Letter, Chancellor to Pincus, *Papers of Gregory Pincus, Manuscript Division, Library of Congress, Washington, D.C.,* October 31, 1957.

8. **Box 25,** Letter, Anderson to Pincus, *Papers of Gregory Pincus, Manuscript Division, Library of Congress, Washington, D.C.,* June 28, 1957.

9. **Box 43,** Letter, Caraway to Pincus, *Papers of Gregory Pincus, Manuscript Division, Library of Congress, Washington, D.C.,* May 4, 1960.

10. **Box 44,** Letter, Pincus to McCormick, *Papers of Gregory Pincus, Manuscript Division, Library of Congress, Washington, D.C.,* November 19, 1960.

11. **Box 44,** Letter, Pincus to McCormick, *Papers of Gregory Pincus, Manuscript Division, Library of Congress, Washington, D.C.,* December 6, 1960.

12. **Box 203,** Lizzie's gall bladder, *Papers of Gregory Pincus, Manuscript Division, Library of Congress, Washington, D.C.,* 1961.

13. **Box 53,** Letter, Pincus to McCormick, *Papers of Gregory Pincus, Manuscript Division, Library of Congress, Washington, D.C.,* March 20, 1962.

14. **Box 65,** Seventh International Conference on Planned Parenthood, *Papers of Gregory Pincus, Manuscript Division, Library of Congress, Washington, D.C.,* February 1963.

15. **Box 64,** Itinerary in Japan, *Papers of Gregory Pincus, Manuscript Division, Library of Congress, Washington, D.C.,* February 1963.

16. **Box 51,** *Playboy, Papers of Gregory Pincus, Manuscript Division, Library of Congress, Washington, D.C.,* May 1, 1961.

17. **Granada TV Network,** The Pill, 1961.

18. **Box 74,** Letter, McCormick to Pincus, *Papers of Gregory Pincus, Manuscript Division, Library of Congress, Washington, D.C.,* November 16, 1964.

19. **Box 74,** Travels, *Papers of Gregory Pincus, Manuscript Division, Library of Congress, Washington, D.C.,* 1964.

20. **Box 69,** Australian Symposium Presentations, *Papers of Gregory Pincus, Manuscript Division, Library of Congress, Washington, D.C.,* October, 1964.

21. **Lader L,** Three Men Who Made a Revolution, *The New York Times Magazine,* April 10, 1966.

22. **Pincus G,** *The Control of Fertility,* Academic Press, New York, 1965, pp. viii-ix.

23. **Box 54,** Sullivan Travel Service, *Papers of Gregory Pincus, Manuscript Division, Library of Congress, Washington, D.C.,* September 28, 1962.

24. **Box 54,** Letter, Pincus to Winter, *Papers of Gregory Pincus, Manuscript Division, Library of Congress, Washington, D.C.,* November 8, 1962.

25. **Box 104,** Letters to Priscilla White, 1966-1967, *Papers of Gregory Pincus, Manuscript Division, Library of Congress, Washington, D.C.,*

26. **Box 76,** Expense report, *Papers of Gregory Pincus, Manuscript Division, Library of Congress, Washington, D.C.,* 1963.

27. **Box 76,** Expense report, *Papers of Gregory Pincus, Manuscript Division, Library of Congress, Washington, D.C.,* 1964.

28. **Box 100,** Expense report, *Papers of Gregory Pincus, Manuscript Division, Library of Congress, Washington, D.C.,* 1965.

29. **Box 66,** *Papers of Gregory Pincus, Manuscript Division, Library of Congress, Washington, D.C.,*

30. **Box 105,** Letter, Searle to Pincus, *Papers of Gregory Pincus, Manuscript Division, Library of Congress, Washington, D.C.,* November 3, 1950.

31. **Box 107,** Letter, Searle to Pincus, *Papers of Gregory Pincus, Manuscript Division, Library of Congress, Washington, D.C.,* June 28, 1954.

32. **Box 105,** Letter, Searle to Pincus, *Papers of Gregory Pincus, Manuscript Division, Library of Congress, Washington, D.C.,* December 26, 1951.

33. **Box 16,** Letter, Crawford to McCormick, *Worcester Foundation for Biomedical Research (WFBR) Papers, (formerly) Worcester Foundation for Experimental Biology (WFEB), The Lamar Soutter Library, University of Massachusetts Medical School, Worcester, Massachusett.,* December 29, 1954.

34. **Box 5,** Letter, Sollins to Pincus, *Papers of Gregory Pincus, Manuscript Division, Library of Congress, Washington, D.C.,* May 3, 1955.

35. **Box 5,** Letter, Sollins to Elizabeth Pincus, *Papers of Gregory Pincus, Manuscript Division, Library of Congress, Washington, D.C.,* March 13, 1958.

36. **Box 1,** Curriculum Vitae, *Papers of Gregory Pincus, Manuscript Division, Library of Congress, Washington, D.C.*

37. Ibid.

38. **McCracken J,** Personal interview, May 21, 2007.

39. **Pincus G,** A Journal: Trip to Russia, *Worcester Foundation for Biomedical Research (WFBR) Papers, (formerly) Worcester Foundation for Experimental Biology (WFEB), The Lamar Soutter Library, University of Massachusetts Medical School, Worcester, Massachusetts.* May, 1967.

40. **Caldwell B,** Personal interview, December 5, 2007.

41. **Tefferi A,** The forgotten myeloproliferative disorder: myeloid metaplasia, *The Oncologist* 8:225-231, 2003.

42. **Lal A,** Agnogenic myeloid metaplasia with myelofibrosis, *http://www.emedicine.com/MED/topic78.htm,* 2004.

43. **Box 5,** Letter, Solomon to Klaiber, *Papers of Gregory Pincus, Manuscript Division, Library of Congress, Washington, D.C.,* June 13, 1963.

44. Ibid.

45. Ibid.

46. **Box 209,** Letter, Jacobson to Pincus, *Papers of Gregory Pincus, Manuscript Division, Library of Congress, Washington, D.C.,* June 22, 1964.

47. **Box 6,** Letter, Gardner to Jacobson, *Papers of Gregory Pincus, Manuscript Division, Library of Congress, Washington, D.C.,* October 18, 1965.

48. **Pincus S,** Personal Recorded Interview with Sophie Pincus Dutton by Honor White, January 8 and 14, 1980.

49. **Ingle DJ,** *Gregory Goodwin Pincus, 1903–1967,* Vol. XLII, Columbia University Press, New York, 1971, p. 238.

50. **Asbell B,** *The Pill: A Biography of the Drug that Changed the World,* Random House, New York, 1995, p. 317.

51. **Merrill A,** Personal interview, May 23, 2007.

52. **Mastroianni L,** Personal interview, August 28, 2007.

53. **Box 6,** Letter,Gardner to Jacobson, *Papers of Gregory Pincus, Manuscript Division, Library of Congress, Washington, D.C.,* April 25, 1967.

54. **Box 6,** Letter, Gardner to Cooley, *Papers of Gregory Pincus, Manuscript Division, Library of Congress, Washington, D.C.,* July 21, 1967.

55. **Box 6,** Letter, Pincus to French, *Papers of Gregory Pincus, Manuscript Division, Library of Congress, Washington, D.C.,* July 6, 1967.

56. **Box 103,** Letter, Pincus to McCormick, *Papers of Gregory Pincus, Manuscript Division, Library of Congress, Washington, D.C.,* July 18, 1967.

57. **Box 209,** Autopsy No. A67-235, Peter Bent Brigham Hospital Department of Pathology, *Papers of Gregory Pincus, Manuscript Division, Library of Congress, Washington, D.C.,* June 24, 1968.

58. **Mastroianni L,** Personal interview, August 28, 2007

59. **Certificate of Death of Gregory Pincus,** *The Commonwealth of Massachusetts, Department of Public Health, Registry of Vital Records and Statistics,* 1967.

60. **Box 209,** Autopsy No. A67-235, Peter Bent Brigham Hospital Department of Pathology, *Papers of Gregory Pincus, Manuscript Division, Library of Congress, Washington, D.C.,* June 24, 1968.

61. Ibid.

62. **Foss J,** Personal interview, May 21, 2007.

63. **Bernard LP,** Personal interview, May 23, 2007; August 11, 2008.

64. **Obituary,** Fellow Scientists Laud Researcher Dr. Pincus, *The Worcester Daily Telegram,* August 26, 1967.

65. Ibid.

66. **Hoagland M,** *Toward the Habit of Truth: A Life in Science,* W.W. Norton & Company, New York, 1990, p. 18.

67. **Bernard LP,** Personal interview, May 23, 2007; August 11, 2008.

68. **Foss J,** Personal interview, May 21, 2007.

69. **Hoagland M,** *Toward the Habit of Truth: A Life in Science,* W.W. Norton & Company, New York, 1990, p. 18.

70. **Fridhandler L,** Personal interview, February 8, 2008.

71. **Bialy G,** Personal interview, August 27, 2007.

72. **Goldzieher J,** Personal interview, October 30, 2007.

73. **Hoagland M,** *Toward the Habit of Truth: A Life in Science,* W.W. Norton & Company, New York, 1990, p. 17.

74. **Box 211,** Letter, Searle to Pincus, *Papers of Gregory Pincus, Manuscript Division, Library of Congress, Washington, D.C.,* March 1, 1966.

75. **Box 212,** Letter, Solomonson to John Pincus, *Papers of Gregory Pincus, Manuscript Division, Library of Congress, Washington, D.C.,* September 22, 1967.

76. **Box 15,** Minutes of an executive committee meeting of the Worcester Foundation for Experimental Biology, Inc., *Worcester Foundation for Biomedical Research (WFBR) Pa-*

pers, (formerly) Worcester Foundation for Experimental Biology (WFEB), The Lamar Soutter Library, University of Massachusetts Medical School, Worcester, Massachusetts, September 6, 1967.

77. **Box 212,** Income tax return, *Papers of Gregory Pincus, Manuscript Division, Library of Congress, Washington, D.C.,* 1966.

78. **Box 203,** Financial papers, *Papers of Gregory Pincus, Manuscript Division, Library of Congress, Washington, D.C.*

79. Ibid.

80. **The 'Pill' Ushered In Golden Age of Womenhood,** *Boston Herald-American,* November 1, 1974.

81. **Vaughn P,** *The Pill on Trial,* Coward-McCann, Inc., New York, 1970, p. 37.

EPIILOGUE

1. **Djerassi C,** The Mother of the Pill, *Rec Prog Hor Res* 50:1-17, 1995.

2. **Pincus G,** *The Control of Fertility,* Academic Press, New York, 1965.

3. **Garcia C-R,** Gregory Goodwin Pincus (1903–1967), *J Clin Endocrin Metab* 28:1245-1248, 1968.

4. **Garcia C-R,** Development of the pill, *Ann N Y Acad Sci* 1038:223-226, 2004.

5. **Pincus G,** Control of conception by hormonal steroids, *Science* 153:493-500, 1966.

6. **Goldzieher J,** Personal interview, October 30, 2007.

7. **Box 86,** Letters, Muller to Pincus, Pincus to Muller, *Papers of Gregory Pincus, Manuscript Division, Library of Congress, Washington, D.C.,* 1965.

8. **Caldwell B,** Personal interview, December 5, 2007.

9. **Plebani M, Marincola FM,** Research translation: a new frontier for clinical laboratories, *Clin Chem Lab Med* 44:1301-1312, 2006.

10. **Caldwell B,** Personal interview, December 5, 2007.

APPENDIX

1. **Chang M-C,** Fertilizing capacity of spermatozoa deposited into the fallopian tubes, *Nature* 168:697-698, 1951.

ILLUSTRATION ACKNOWLEDGMENTS

Photographs are used with the acknowledgments listed below. Photographs not acknowledged are by the author. Maps, diagrams, and chapter icons are by Aimee Genter and Josef Garibaldi.

COVER AND TITLE PAGE

Box 45, Papers of Gregory Pincus, Manuscript Division, Library of Congress, Washington, D.C.

PROLOGUE

Gregory Pincus — 1955

Library of Congress, Washington D.C.

CHAPTER TWO

Zena, Victor, William, Joseph, Alex, Sophie, Alexander Pincus

Courtesy of Michael Pincus

CHAPTER THREE

Baron Maurice de Hirsch

Print and Picture Collection, The Free Library of Philadelphia, Pennsylvania

H. L. Sabsovich

Sabsovich K, Adventures in Idealism. A Personal Record of the Life of Professor Sabsovich, Reprint edition of the 1922 original by Arno Press, New York, 1975.

Sabsovich House

The Sam Azeez Museum of Woodbine Heritage, Woodbine, New Jersey

Woodbine Houses

The Sam Azeez Museum of Woodbine Heritage, Woodbine, New Jersey

Woodbine, New Jersey

The Sam Azeez Museum of Woodbine Heritage, Woodbine, New Jersey

Woodbine Houses

The Sam Azeez Museum of Woodbine Heritage, Woodbine, New Jersey

Woodbine Railroad Station

The Sam Azeez Museum of Woodbine Heritage, Woodbine, New Jersey

Baron de Hirsch Agricultural School

The Sam Azeez Museum of Woodbine Heritage, Woodbine, New Jersey

A Woodbine Factory

The Sam Azeez Museum of Woodbine Heritage, Woodbine, New Jersey

Jacob Lipman, Rutgers student

Waksman SA, Jacob G. Lipman: Agricultural Scientist and Humanitarian, Rutgers University Press, New Brunswick, New Jersey, 1966.

Jacob Lipman, Dean of Agriculture	The Sam Azeez Museum of Woodbine Heritage, Woodbine, New Jersey
Woodbine School	The Sam Azeez Museum of Woodbine Heritage, Woodbine, New Jersey
Joseph Pincus	Courtesy of Michael Pincus
Elizabeth and Joseph — 1902	Courtesy of Michael Pincus
Pincus and Lipman Families	Waksman SA, Jacob G. Lipman: Agricultural Scientist and Humanitarian, Rutgers University Press, New Brunswick, New Jersey, 1966.

CHAPTER FOUR

Lizzie and Joseph	Courtesy of Michael Pincus
Alex, Sophie, Lee, Maurice, Bun, Goody	Courtesy of Michael Pincus
Lizzie with Alex, Lee, Goody, Maurice, Bun, Sophie	Courtesy of Michael Pincus
Joseph with donated seeds	Courtesy of Michael Pincus
Morris High School	The Bronx County Historical Society, The Bronx, New York.
Goody at Morris High School	Courtesy of Michael Pincus
Goody and Evelyn	Courtesy of Michael Pincus

Goody, Goldie, Evelyn, Leon   Courtesy of Michael Pincus

Gregory Pincus — 1924   Cornellian Yearbook, Cornell University Library, Ithaca, New York

Portrait of Lizzie   Courtesy of Laura Pincus Bernard

Lizzie — about 1930   Courtesy of Laura Pincus Bernard

Lizzie — 1937   Box 204, Papers of Gregory Pincus, Manuscript Division, Library of Congress, Washington, D.C.

Lizze — about 1945   Courtesy of Laura Pincus Bernard

Lizzie and Goody — 1951   Box 212, Papers of Gregory Pincus, Manuscript Division, Library of Congress, Washington, D.C.

Lizzie and Goody — 1950s   Courtesy of Laura Pincus Bernard

CHAPTER FIVE

Gregory Pincus, Assistant Professor   The Worcester Foundation for Biomedical Research, University of Massachusetts Medical School Archives, The Lamar Soutter Library, University of Massachusetts Medical School, Worcester, Massachusetts

Goody — 1929   Box 204, Papers of Gregory Pincus, Manuscript Division, Library of Congress, Washington, D.C.

Pincus Family — 1937   Box 204, Papers of Gregory Pincus, Manuscript Division, Library of Congress, Washington, D.C.

CHAPTER SIX

Hudson Hoagland — 1940	The Worcester Foundation for Biomedical Research, University of Massachusetts Medical School Archives, The Lamar Soutter Library, University of Massachusetts Medical School, Worcester, Massachusetts
Pincus — 1940	Courtesy of Geoffry Dutton
Hudson Hoagland and Gregory Pincus	The Worcester Foundation for Biomedical Research, University of Massachusetts Medical School Archives, The Lamar Soutter Library, University of Massachusetts Medical School, Worcester, Massachusetts
Laura, Lizzie, Goody — 1947	Box 204, Papers of Gregory Pincus, Manuscript Division, Library of Congress, Washington, D.C.
The Hovey Estate — 1939	The Worcester Foundation for Biomedical Research, University of Massachusetts Medical School Archives, The Lamar Soutter Library, University of Massachusetts Medical School, Worcester, Massachusetts
The Worcester Foundation for Experimental Biology — 1949	The Worcester Foundation for Biomedical Research, University of Massachusetts Medical School Archives, The Lamar Soutter Library, University of Massachusetts Medical School, Worcester, Massachusetts

Pincus's Office and Laboratory	The Worcester Foundation for Biomedical Research, University of Massachusetts Medical School Archives, The Lamar Soutter Library, University of Massachusetts Medical School, Worcester, Massachusetts
The Worcester Foundation for Experimental Biology — 1976	The Worcester Foundation for Biomedical Research, University of Massachusetts Medical School Archives, The Lamar Soutter Library, University of Massachusetts Medical School, Worcester, Massachusetts
Gregory Pincus — 1958	Box 212, Papers of Gregory Pincus, Manuscript Division, Library of Congress, Washington, D.C.
Pincus House, Northborough	Northborough Historical Society, Northborough, Masachusetts
Lizzie — around 1960	Courtesy of Geoffrey Dutton
Hoagland and Pincus — 1960s	The Worcester Foundation for Biomedical Research, University of Massachusetts Medical School Archives, The Lamar Soutter Library, University of Massachusetts Medical School, Worcester, Massachusetts
M-C. Chang — 1933	Courtesy of Isabelle Chang
M-C. Chang — 1941	Courtesy of Isabelle Chang
M-C. Chang — 1946	Courtesy of Isabelle Chang

M-C. Chang — 1969	Courtesy of Isabelle Chang
M-C. Chang — 1970	Courtesy of Isabelle Chang
Gregory Pincus, Sir John Hammond, M-C. Chang, unknown date	Courtesy of Isabelle Chang
Hudson and Anna Hoagland	The Worcester Foundation for Biomedical Research, University of Massachusetts Medical School Archives, The Lamar Soutter Library, University of Massachusetts Medical School, Worcester, Massachusetts

CHAPTER SEVEN

Gregory Pincus — 1950	Library of Congress, Washington, D.C.

CHAPTER EIGHT

Russell Marker and Dean Frank Whitmore	Penn State University Archives, The Pennsylvania State University Libraries
Russell Marker	Penn State University Archives, The Pennsylvania State University Libraries
Russell Marker and Cabeza de negra	Roche Palo Alto LLC, Palo Alto, California
Photo staged for *Life* magazine —Rozenkranz with test tube of cortisone pointing to the Mexican yam; Djerassi in suit on the right.	Roche Palo Alto LLC, Palo Alto, California
Carl Djerassi	Roche Palo Alto LLC, Palo Alto, California

Djerassi pointing to norethindrone, Zaffaroni on left, Rozenkranz on right

Roche Palo Alto LLC, Palo Alto, California

CHAPTER NINE

Gregory Pincus — 1950s

The Worcester Foundation for Biomedical Research, University of Massachusetts Medical School Archives, The Lamar Soutter Library, University of Massachusetts Medical School, Worcester, Massachusetts

Katharine Dexter in MIT Lab

MIT Libraries, Massachusetts Institute of Technology, Cambridge, Massachusetts

Katharine McCormick — about 1910

MIT Libraries, Massachusetts Institute of Technology, Cambridge, Massachusetts

Katharine McCormick — about 1915

MIT Libraries, Massachusetts Institute of Technology, Cambridge, Massachusetts

Katharine McCormick, at Dedication of Stanley McCormick Hal

MIT Libraries, Massachusetts Institute of Technology, Cambridge, Massachusetts

CHAPTER TEN

John Rock

Library of Congress, Washington, D.C.

John Rock

Harvard Medical Library in the Francis A. Countway Library of Medicine, Cambridge, Massachusetts

CHAPTER ELEVEN

Goody and Lizzie — 1955	Box 204, Papers of Gregory Pincus, Manuscript Division, Library of Congress, Washington, D.C.
Gregory Pincus — 1955	The Worcester Foundation for Biomedical Research, University of Massachusetts Medical School Archives, The Lamar Soutter Library, University of Massachusetts Medical School, Worcester, Massachusetts
Garcia, Pincus, Rock	The Worcester Foundation for Biomedical Research, University of Massachusetts Medical School Archives, The Lamar Soutter Library, University of Massachusetts Medical School, Worcester, Massachusetts
Celso Ramón Garcia	Strauss III JF, Mastroianni Jr L, In memoriam: Celso-Ramon Garcia, M.D, (1922–2004), reproductive medicine visionary, J Exp Clin Assist Reprod 2:2-7, 2005.
Gregory Pincus — 1959	Box 204, Papers of Gregory Pincus, Manuscript Division, Library of Congress, Washington, D.C.
Albert T. Lasker Award	Box 45, Papers of Gregory Pincus, Manuscript Division, Library of Congress, Washington, D.C.

CHAPTER THIRTEEN

Goody and Lizzie in Asia	Box 212, Papers of Gregory Pincus, Manuscript Division, Library of Congress, Washington, D.C.

CHAPTER FOURTEEN

Passport Pictures — 1960	Box 204, Papers of Gregory Pincus, Manuscript Division, Library of Congress, Washington, D.C.
Gregory Pincus — Playboy, 1961	Box 51, Papers of Gregory Pincus, Manuscript Division, Library of Congress, Washington, D.C.
Passport Pictures — 1963	Box 64, Papers of Gregory Pincus, Manuscript Division, Library of Congress, Washington, D.C.
Australian newspapers — 1964	Box 69, Papers of Gregory Pincus, Manuscript Division, Library of Congress, Washington, D.C.
Goody and Lizzie, Australia – 1964	Box 69, Papers of Gregory Pincus, Manuscript Division, Library of Congress, Washington, D.C.
Gregory Pincus — 1964	Box 212, Papers of Gregory Pincus, Manuscript Division, Library of Congress, Washington, D.C.
Gregory Pincus — 1965	Box 204, Papers of Gregory Pincus, Manuscript Division, Library of Congress, Washington, D.C.
Gregory Pincus in Paris — 1966	Box 95, Papers of Gregory Pincus, Manuscript Division, Library of Congress, Washington, D.C.

BIBLIOGRAPHY

COLLECTIONS

Russell E. Marker, interview by Jeffrey L. Sturchio at Pennsylvania State University, *Chemical Heritage Foundation, Philadelphia,* Oral History Transcript No. 0068, April 17, 1987.

Papers of Gregory Pincus, Manuscript Division, Library of Congress, Washington, D.C.

Worcester Foundation for Biomedical Research (WFBR) Papers, (formerly) Worcester Foundation for Experimental Biology (WFEB), The Lamar Soutter Library, University of Massachusetts Medical School, Worcester, Massachusetts.

BOOKS

Early accounts of the history of the birth control pill had the advantage of personal interviews with key figures. This includes the books written by Asbell, Maisel, McLauglin, Reed, and Vaughn.

Applezweig N, *Steroid Drugs,* McGraw-Hill Book Company, Inc., New York, 1962.

Asbell B, *The Pill: A Biography of the Drug that Changed the World,* Random House, New York, 1995.

Bascomb N, *Red Mutiny: Eleven Fateful Days on the Battleship Potemkin,* Houghton Mifflin Company, Boston, 2007.

Beatty RA, *Parthenogenesis and Polyploidy in Mammalian Development,* Cambridge University Press, Cambridge, 1957.

Bernheimer CS, *The Russian Jew in the United States,* The John C. Winston Co., Philadelphia, 1905.

Biezanek AC, *All Things New: A Declaration of Faith,* Harper & Row, Publishers, New York, 1964.

Bonnell VE, ed, *The Russian Worker: Life and Labor under the Tsarist Regime,* University of California Press Berkeley, 1983.

Brandes J, *Immigrants to Freedom: Jewish Communities in Rural New Jersey since 1882,* University of Pennsylvania Press for the Jewish Publication Society of America, Philadelphia, 1971.

Briggs L, *Reproducing Empire. Race, Sex, Science, and U.S. Imperialism in Puerto Rico,* University of California Press, Berkeley, 2002.

Chesler E, *Woman of Valor: Margaret Sanger and the Birth Control Movement in America,* Simon & Schuster, New York, 1992.

Coleman L, *Tom Slick: True Life Encounters in Cryptozoology,* Craven Street Books, Fresno, California, 2002.

Cooke CN, *Tom Slick: Mystery Hunter,* Paraview, Inc., Bracey, Virginia, 2005.

Critchlow DT, editor, *The Politics of Abortion and Birth Control in Historical Perspective,* The Pennsylvania State University Press, University Park, Pennsylvania, 1996.

Davies N, *God's Playground. A History of Poland,* Vol. II, 1795 to the Present, Columbia University Press, New York, 2005.

Davidson G, *Our Jewish Farmers and the Story of the Jewish Agricultural Society,* L.B. Fischer, New York, 1943.

Dioxon-Mueller R, *Population Policy & Women's Rights: Transforming Reproductive Choice,* Praeger, Westport, Connecticut, 1993.

Djerassi C, *The Politics of Contraception,* W.W. Norton & Company, New York, 1979.

Djerassi C, *The Pill, Pygmy Chimps, and Degas' Horse,* Basic Books, New York, 1992.

Djerassi C, *This Man's Pill: Reflections on the 50th Birthday of the Pill,* Oxford University Press, Oxford, 2001.

Dubnow SM, *History of the Jews in Russia and Poland: From the Earliest Times until the Present Day,* Vol. III, From the accession of Nicholas II, until the present day with bibliography and index, Friedlaender I, Translator; The Jewish Publication Society of America, 1920, Kessinger Publishing's Legacy Reprints, Philadelphia, 2007.

Eisenberg E, *Jewish Agricultural Colonies in New Jersey, 1882–1920,* Syracuse University Press, Syracuse, New York, 1995.

Fields A, *Katharine Dexter McCormick: Pioneer for Women's Rights,* Praeger Publishers, Westport, Connecticut, 2003.

Gitelman Z, *A Century of Ambivalence: The Jews of Russia and the Soviet Union, 1881 to the Present,* Vol. second, expanded edition, Indiana University Press, Bloomington, 2001.

Gooding J, *Rulers and Subjects: Government and People in Russia 1801–1991,* Arnold, London, 1996.

Gordon L, *The Moral Property of Women: A History of Birth Control Politics in America,* University of Illinois Press, Urbana, 2007.

Gray M, *Margaret Sanger: A Biography of the Champion of Birth Control,* Richard Marek Publishers, New York, 1979.

Halberstam D, *The Fifties,* Fawcett Columbine, New York, 1993.

Hartman CG, editor, *Mechanisms Concerned with Contraception: Proceedings of a Symposium Prepared under the Auspices of the Population Council and the Planned Parenthood Federation of America,* The Macmillan Company New York, 1963.

Hermalyn G, *Morris High School and the Creation of the New York City Public High School System,* The Bronx County Historical Society, The Bronx, New York, 1995.

Herscher UD, Chyet SF, (translators), *On Jews, America and Immigration: A Socialist Perspective by Boris M. Frumkin, 1907,* American Jewish Archives, Cincinnati, 1980.

Herscher UD, *Jewish Agricultural Utopias in America, 1880–1910,* Wayne State University Press, Detroit, 1981.

Hoagland H, *Pacemakers in Relation to Aspects of Behavior,* The MacMillan Company, New York, 1935.

Hoagland H, *The Road to Yesterday,* privately printed, Worcester, Massachusetts, 1974.

Hoagland M, *Toward the Habit of Truth: A Life in Science,* W.W. Norton & Company, New York, 1990.

Hunt DM, *Evolution of the Pill,* privately printed, Northborough, Massachusetts, 2002.

Joseph S, *History of the Baron de Hirsch Fund,* Augustus M. Kelley, Publishers, Fairfield, New Jersey, 1978.

Klier JD, Lambroza S, editors, *Pogroms: Anti-Jewish Violence in Modern Russian History,* Cambridge University Press, Cambridge, 1992.

Kaiser RB, *The Politics of Sex and Religion: A Case History in the Development of Doctrine, 1962–1984,* Leaven Press, Kansas City, 1985.

Koelsch WA, *Clark University 1887–1987: A Narrative History,* Clark University Press, Worcester, Massachusetts, 1987.

Lincoln WB, *In War's Dark Shadow: The Russians Before the Great War,* The Dial Press, New York, 1983.

Lipman JG, *Bacteria in Relation to Country Life,* The Macmillan Company, New York, 1908.

Maisel AQ, *The Hormone Quest,* Random House, New York, 1965.

Marks LV, *Sexual Chemistry: A History of the Contraceptive Pill,* Yale University Press, New Haven, 2001.

Marsh M, Ronner W, *The Fertility Doctor. John Rock and the Reproductive Revolution,* The Johns Hopkins University Press, Baltimore, 2008.

Maynard J, *The Russian Peasant and Other Studies,* Collier Books, New York, 1941, Collier Books Edition 1962.

McLaughlin L, *The Pill, John Rock, and the Church: The Biography of a Revolution,* Little, Brown and Company, Boston, 1982.

Medvei VC, *The History of Clinical Endocrinology,* The Parthenon Publishing Group, New York, 1993.

Nathans B, *Beyond the Pale: The Jewish Encounter with Late Imperial Russia,* University of California Press, Berkeley, 2002.

O'Dowd MG, Philipp EE, *The History of Obstetrics and Gynaecology,* The Parthenon Publishing Group, New York, 1994.

Oudshoorn N, *Beyond the Natural Body: An Archeology of Sex Hormones,* Routledge, London, 1994.

Pincus G, *The Eggs of Mammals,* The Macmillan Company, New York, 1936.

Pincus G, Vollmer EP, editor, *Biological Activities of Steroids in Relation to Cancer,* Academic Press, New York, 1960.

Pincus G, *The Control of Fertility,* Academic Press, New York, 1965.

Pincus G, Nakao T, Tait JF, editors, *Steroid Dynamics: Proceedings of the Symposium on the Dynamics of Steroid Hormones held in Tokyo, May, 1965,* Academic Press New York, 1966.

Ramírez de Arellano AB, Seipp C, *Colonialism, Catholicism, and Contraception,* The University of North Carolina Press, Chapel Hill, 1983.

Robinson GT, *Rural Russia Under the Old Regime,* Longmans, Green and Company, New York, 1932.

Reed J, *The Birth Control Movement and American Society: From Private Vice to Public Virtue,* Princeton University Press, Princeton, N. J., 1978.

Reed M, *Margaret Sanger. Her Life in Her Words,* Barricade Books Inc., Fort Lee, New Jersey, 2003.

Rock J, Loth D, *Voluntary Parenthood,* Random House, New York, 1949.

Rock J, *The Time Has Come: A Catholic Doctor's Proposal to End the Battle over Birth Control,* Alfred A. Knopf, New York, 1963.

Sabsovich K, *Adventures in Idealism: A Personal Record of the Life of Professor Sabsovich,* Reprint edition of the 1922 original by Arno Press, New York, 1975.

Seaman B, Seaman G, *Women and the Crisis in Sex Hormones,* Bantam Books, New York, 1977.

Seaman B, *The Doctor's Case Against the Pill,* Doubleday & Company, Inc., Garden City, New York, 1980 (First Edition: 1969).

Segal SJ, *Under the Banyan Tree: A Population Scientist's Odyssey,* Oxford University Press, Oxford, 2993.

Speert H, *Obstetric & Gynecologic Milestones Illustrated,* The Parthenon Publishing Group, New York, 1996.

Speroff L, Darney PD, *A Clinical Guide for Contraception,* Fourth Edition, Lippincott Williams & Wilkins, Philadelphia, 2005.

Tait AS, Tait JF, *A Quartet of Unlikely Discoveries: The Double Helix, the Pill, a Pinch of Salt, then Saturation,* Athena Press, London, 2004.

Tone A, editor, *Controlling Reproduction: An American History,* Scholarly Resources Inc. Wilmington, Delaware, 1997.

Tone A, *Devices and Desires: A History of Contraceptives in America,* Hill and Wang, New York, 2001.

Troyat H, *Daily Life in Russia under the Last Tsar,* Stanford University Press, Stanford, California, 1979, original French edition 1959.

Vaughn P, *The Pill on Trial,* Coward-McCann, Inc., New York, 1970.

Waksman SA, *Jacob G. Lipman: Agricultural Scientist and Humanitarian,* Rugers University Press, New Brunswick, NJ, 1966.

Watkins ES, *On the Pill: A Social History of Oral Contraceptives 1950–1970,* The Johns Hopkins University Press, Baltimore, 1998.

Zipperstein SJ, *The Jews of Odessa: A Cultural History, 1794–1881,* Stanford University Press, Stanford, California, 1986.

BOOK CHAPTERS

Aronson M, The Anti-Jewish Pogroms in Russia in 1881, In: Klier JD, Lambroza S, eds. *Pogroms. Anti-Jewish Violence in Modern Russian History,* Cambridge University Press, Cambridge, 1992, 44-61.

Drucker S, Our Teacher, In: Sabsovich K, editor. *Adventures in Idealism: A Personal Record of the Life of Professor Sabsovich,* 1975 Reprint Edition of the original 1922 edition, Arno Press, New York, 1922, 183-187.

Hoagland H, Some reflections on science and religion, In: Shapley H, editor. *Science Ponders Religion,* Appleton-Century-Crofts, Inc., New York, 1960, pp. 17-31.

Jensen EV, Jacobson HI, Flesher JW, Saha N, Gupta GN, Smith S, Colucci V, Shiplacoff D, Neumann HG, DeSombre ER, Jungblut PW, Estrogen Receptors in Target Tissues, In: Pincus GN, T, Tait JF, editors. *Steroid Dynamics: Proceedings of the Symposium on the Dynamics of Steroid Hormones held in Tokyo, May, 1965,* Academic Press, New York, 1966, 133-158.

Lipman JG, The Baron de Hirsch Agricultural School, In: Sabsovich K, editor. *Adventures in Idealism: A Personal Record of the Life of Professor Sabsovich,* 1975 Reprint Edition of 1922 edition, Arno Press, New York, 1922, 188-193.

Pincus JW, The Jewish Farmers' Best Friend, In: Sabsovich K, editor. *Adventures in Idealism: A Personal Record of the Life of Professor Sabsovich,* 1975 Reprint Edition of the 1922 edition, Arno Press, New York, 1922, 194-203.

Klier JD, The Pogrom Paradigm in Russian History, In: Klier JD, Lambroza S, editors. *Pogroms: Anti-Jewish Violence in Modern Russian History,* Cambridge University Press, Cambridge, 1992, 3-38.

Perone N, The progestins, In: Goldzieher JW, editor. *Pharmacology of the Contraceptive Steroids,* Raven Press, Ltd., New York, 1994, pp. 5-20.

Rogger H, Conclusion and Overview, In: Klier JD LS, editor. *Pogroms. Anti-Jewish Violence in Modern Russian History,* Cambridge University Press, Cambridge, 1992, 314-372.

JOURNAL ARTICLES

Amador E, Zimmerman TS, Wacker WE, FDA report on Enovid. Ad hoc advisory committee for the evaluation of a possible etiologic relation with thromboembolic conditions, *JAMA* 185:776, 1963.

Applezweig N, The big steroid treasure hunt, *Chemical Week* January 31:38-52, 1959.

Bates RW, Gregory Goodwin Pincus, *Rec Prog Hor Res* 24:v-vi, 1968.

Bates RW, The first 25 years of the Laurentian Hormone Conference, *Rec Prog Hor Res* 24:vii-xi, 1968.

Borell M, Biologists and the promotion of birth control research, 1918–1938, *J Hist Biology* 20:51-87, 1987.

Chang M-C, Fertilizing capacity of spermatozoa deposited into the fallopian tubes, *Nature* 168:697-698.

Chang M-C, Mammalian sperm, eggs, and control of fertility, *Persp Biol Med* Spring:376-383, 1968.

Chang M-C, Development of the oral contraceptives, *Am J Obstet Gynecol* 132:217-219, 1978.

Chang M-C, Recollections of 40 years at the Worcester Foundation for Experimental Biology, *The Physiologist* 28:400-401, 1985.

Clarke AE, Controversy and the development of reproductive sciences, *Social Problems* 37:18-37, 1990.

Colton FB, Steroids and "the Pill": early steroid research at Searle, *Steroids* 57:624-630, 1992.

de Hirsch B, My views on philanthropy, *North Am Rev* 416, 1891.

Davis KS, The story of the pill, *American Heritage* 29:80-91, 1978.

Dinger JC, Heinemann LA, Kühl-Habich D, The safety of a drospirenone-containing oral contraceptive: final results from the European Active Surveillance Study on oral contraceptives based on 142,475 women-years of observation, *Contraception* 75:344-354, 2007.

Djerassi C, Problems of Manufacture and Distribution. The manufacture of steroidal contraceptives: technical versus political aspects, *Proc Roy Soc* 195:175-186, 1976.

Djerassi C, A steroid autobiography, *Steroids* 43:351-361, 1984.

Djerassi C, Steroid research at Syntex: "the Pill" and cortisone, *Steroids* 57:631-641, 1992.

Djerassi C, The Mother of the Pill, *Rec Prog Hor Res* 50:1-17, 1995.

Djerassi C, Miramontes L, Rosenkranz G, Sondheimer F, Synthesis of 19-nor-17α-ethynyltestosterone and 19-nor-17α-methyltestosterone, *J Am Chem Soc* 76:4092-4094, 1954.

Drill VA, History of the first oral contraceptive, *J Toxicol Environ Health* 3:133-138, 1977.

Ehrenstein M, Investigations on steroids. VIII. Lower homologs of hormones of the pregnane series: 10-nor-11-desoxycorticosterone acetate and 10-norprogesterone, *J Org Chem* 9:435-456, 1944.

Fosbery WHS, Severe climacteric flushings successfully treated by ovarian extract, *Br Med J* i:1039, 1897.

Garcia C-R, Pincus G, Rock J, Effects of three 19-nor steroids on human ovulation and menstruation, *Am J Obstet Gynecol* 75:82-97, 1958.

Garcia C-R, Dedication, *Int J Fertil* 13:267-269, 1968.

Garcia C-R, Gregory Goodwin Pincus (1903–1967), *J Clin Endocrin Metab* 28:1245-1248, 1968.

García C-R, Development of the pill, *Ann N Y Acad Sci* 1038:223-226, 2004.

Goldscheider C, Mosher WD, Patterns of contraceptive use in the United States: the importance of religious factors, *Studies Fam Plann* 22:102-115, 1991.

Goldzieher JW, How the oral contraceptives came to be developed, *JAMA* 230:421-425, 1974.

Graff-Iversen S, Hammar N, Thelle DS, Tonstad S, Use of oral contraceptives and mortality during 14 years' follow-up of Norwegian women, *Scand J Public Health* 34:11-16, 2006.

Greep RO, Min Chueh Chang, 1908–1991, *Biograph Memoirs* 68:3-19, 1995.

Hannaford PC, Selvaraj S, Elliot AM, Angus V, Iversen L, Lee AJ, Cancer risk among users of oral contraceptives: cohort data from the Royal College of General Practitioner's oral contraception study, *Brit Med J* 335:651, 2007.

Hechter O, Jacobsen RP, Jeanloz R, Levy H, Marshall CW, Pincus G, Schenker V, The bio-oxygenation of steroids at C-11, *Arch Biochem* 15:457-460, 1950.

Hechter O, Jacobsen RP, Jeanloz R, Levy H, Pincus G, Schenker V, Pathways of corticosteroid synthesis, *J Clin Endocrin Metab* 10:827-828, 1950.

Hechter O, Homage to Gregory Pincus, *Persp Biol Med* Spring:358-370, 1968.

Hench PS, Kendall EC, Slocumb CH, Polley HF, The effect of a hormone of the adrenal cortex (17-hydroxy-11-dehydrocorticosterone (compound E) and of pituitary adrenocorticotropic hormone on rheumatoid arthritis, *Proc Staff Meetings Mayo Cl* 24:181-197, 1949.

Herlihy P, The ethnic composition of the city of Odessa in the nineteenth century, *Ukrainian Research Institute, Harvard University,* 1:53-78, 1977.

Hertig AT, Rock J, Adams EC, Menkin MF, Thirty-four fertilized human ova, good, bad and indifferent, recovered from 210 women of known fertility; a study of biologic wastage in early human pregnancy, *Pediatrics* 23:202-211, 1959.

Herz R, Tullner WW, Raffelt E, Progestational activity of orally administered 17α-ethinyl-19-nortestosterone, *Endocrinology* 54:228-230, 1954.

Herz R, Waite JH, Thomas LB, Progestational effectiveness of 19-nor-ethinyl-testosterone by oral route in women, *Proc Soc Exp Biol* 91:418-420, 1956.

Hoagland H, Pincus G, The nature of the adrenal stress response failure in schizophrenic man, *J Nerve Ment Dis* 111:434-439, 1950.

Hoskins RG, Pincus G, Sex-hormone relationships in schizophrenic men, *Psychosom Med* 11:102-109, 1949.

Ingle DJ, Gregory Goodwin Pincus, 1903–1967, *Biographical Memoirs,* Columbia University Press, Vol. XLII, 1971.

International Collaboration of Epidemiological Studies of Cervical Cancer, Cervical cancer and hormonal contraceptives: collaborative reanalysis of individual data for 16573 women with cervical cancer and 35509 women without cervical cancer from 24 epidemiological studies, *Lancet* 370:1609-1621, 2007.

Jaffe FS, Knowledge, perception, and change: notes on a fragment of social history, *Mt. Sinae J Med* 42:286-299, 1975.

Jensen EV, Remembrance: Gregory Pincus—catalyst for early receptor studies, *Endocrinology* 131:1581-1582, 1992.

Johnson RC, Feminism, philanthropy and science in the development of the oral contraceptive pill, *Pharmacy in History* 19:63-78, 1977.

Jordan WM, Pulmonary embolism, *Lancet* ii:1140-1141, 1961.

Junod SW, Marks L, Women's trials: the approval of the first oral contraceptive pill in the United States and Great Britain, *J Hist Med Allied Sci* 57:117-160, 2002.

Kabat GC, Miller AB, Rohan TE, Oral contraceptive use, hormone replacement therapy, reproductive history and risk of colorectal cancer in women, *Int J Cancer* 122:643-646, 2008.

Kono T, Obata Y, Wu Q, Niwa K, Ono Y, Yamamoto Y, Park ES, Seo J-S, Ogawa H, Birth of parthenogenetic mice that can develop to adulthood, *Nature* 428:860-864, 2004.

Kono T, Genomic imprinting is a barrier to parthenogenesis in mammals, *Cytogenet Genome Res* 113:31-35, 2006.

Kost K, Singh S, Vaughan B, Trussell J, Bankole A, Estimates of contraceptive failure from the 2002 National Survey of Family Growth, *Contraception* 77:10-21, 2008

Kurzrok R, The prospects for hormonal sterilization, *J Contraception* 2:27-29, 1937.

Lehman F PA, Bolivar GA, Quintero RR, Russell E. Marker. Pioneer of the Mexican steroid industry, *J Chem Education* 50:195-199, 1973.

Lehman F PA, Early history of steroid chemistry in Mexico: the story of three remarkable men, *Steroids* 57:403-408, 1992.

Lipman JG, The conservation of our land resources, *Science* 83:65-69, 1936.

Ludins DG, Memories of Woodbine: 1891–1894, *Jewish Frontier* June,:7-15, 1960.

Makepeace AW, Weinstein GL, Friedman MH, *Am J Physiol* 119:512, 1927.

Marker RE, The early production of steroid hormones, *CHOC News, The Center for History of Medicine, University of Pennsylvania* 4:3-6, 1987.

McCall AG, Obituary, Jacob Goodale Lipman, *Science* 89:378-379, 1939.**Mintz M,** The pill. Press and public at the experts' mercy, *Columbia Journalism Rev* Winter:4-10, 1968.

Mosher WD, Martinez GM, Chandra A, Abma JC, Wilson SJ, Use of contraception and use of family planning services in the United States: 1982–2002., *Advance Data from Vital and Health Statistics; no. 350* National Center for Health.Statistics, Hyattsville, Maryland, 2004.

Mudd EH, Dr. Abraham Stone, *Marriage and*

Family Living May:174-175, 1960.

Parkes AS, The rise of reproductive endocrinology, 1926–1940, *J Endocrinol* 34:20-32, 1966.

Parkes AS, Gregory Pincus, as I knew him—an appreciation, *Persp Biol Med* Spring:422-426, 1968.

Peterson DH, Autobiography, *Steroids* 45:1-17, 1985.

Pincus GG, Observations of the living eggs of the rabbit, *Proc Roy Soc* 197B:132-167, 1930.

Pincus G, Baum OS, On the interaction of oestrin and the ovary-stimulating principles of extracts of the urine of pregnancy, *Am J Physiol* 102:241-248, 1932.

Pincus G, Werthessen N, The continued injection of oestrin into young rats, *Am J Physiol* 103:631-636, 1933.

Pincus GG, The parthenogenetic activation of rabbit eggs, *Anat Record* 67(Suppl No. 1):7, 1934.

Pincus G, Enzmann EV, Can mammalian eggs undergo normal development in vitro?, *Proc Nat Acad Sci* 20:121-122, 1934.

Pincus G, Enzmann EV, The comparative behavior of mammalian eggs in vivo and in vitro. I. The activation of ovarian eggs, *J Exp Med* 62:665-675, 1935.

Pincus G, Enzmann EV, The comparative behavior of mammalian eggs in vivo and in vitro. II. The activation of tubal eggs of the rabbit, *J Exp Zoology* 73:195-208, 1936.

Pincus G, Werthessen N, The comparative behavior of mammalian eggs in vivo and in vitro. III. Factors controlling the growth of the rabbit blastocyst, *J Exp Zoology* 78:1-18, 1938.

Pincus G, Werthessen NT, The maintenance of embryo life in ovariectomized rabbits, *Am J Physiol* 124:484-490, 1938.

Pincus G, The comparative behavior of mammalian eggs in vivo and in vitro. IV. The development of fertilized and artificially activated rabbit eggs, *J Exp Zoology* 82:85-129, 1939.

Pincus G, The breeding of some rabbits produced by recipients of artifically activated ova, *Proc Nat Acad Sci* 25:557-559, 1939.

Pincus G, Jacob Goodale Lipman (1874–1939), *Proc Am Acad Arts Sci* 74:142-143, 1940.

Pincus G, Shapiro H, Further studies on the parthenogenetic activation of rabbit eggs, *Proc Nat Acad Sci* 26:163-165, 1940.

Pincus G, Preface, *Rec Prog Hor Res* 1:i, 1947.

Pincus G, Studies on the role of the adrenal cortex in the stress of human subjects, *Rec Prog Hor Res* 1:123-145, 1947.

Pincus G, Preface, *Rec Prog Hor Res* 6:i, 1951.

Pincus G, Chang MC, The effects of progesterone and related compounds on ovulation and early development in the rabbit, *Acta Physiol. Latinoamericana* 3:177-183, 1953.

Pincus G, Some effects of progesterone and related compounds upon the reproduction and early development in mammals, *Acta Endocrinol* Suppl 28:18-36, 1956.

Pincus G, The Worcester Foundation for Experimental Biology, *AIBS Bulletin* 6:8-9, 1956.

Pincus G, Control of conception by hormonal

steroids, *Science* 153:493-500, 1966.

Pincus G, Chang M-C, Zarrow MX, Hafez ESE, Merrill A, Studies of the biological activity of certain 19-nor steroids in female animals, *Endocrinology* 59:695-707, 1956.

Pincus G, Chang M-C, Hafez ESE, Zarrow MX, Merrill A, Effects of certain 19-nor steroids on reproductive processes in animals, *Science* 124:890-891, 1956.

Pincus G, The hormonal control of ovulation and early development, *Postgrad Med* 24:654-660, 1958.

Pincus G, Rock J, Garcia C-R, Rice-Wray E, Paniagua M, Rodriguez I, Fertility control with oral medication, *Am J Obstet Gynecol* 75:1333-1346, 1958.

Pincus G, Garcia C-R, Rock J, Paniagua M, Pendleton A, Laraque F, Nicolas R, Borno R, Pean V, Effectiveness of an oral contraceptive; effects of a progestin-estrogen combination upon fertility, menstrual phenomena, and health, *Science* 130:81-83, 1959.

Pincus G, Rock J, Chang M-C, Garcia C-R, Effects of certain 19-nor steroids on reproductive processes and fertility, *Fed Proc* 18:1051-1056, 1959.

Pincus G, Garcia C-R, Studies on vaginal, cervical and uterine histology, *Metabolism* 14:344-347, 1965.

Pincus G, Control of conception by hormonal steroids, *Science* 153:493-500, 1966.

Plebani M, Marincola FM, Research translation: a new frontier for clinical laboratories, *Clin Chem Lab Med* 44:1301-1312, 2006.

Pomp ER, le Cessie S, Rosendaal FR, Doggen CJ, Risk of venous thrombosis: obesity and its joint effect with oral contraceptive use and prothrombotic mutations, *Br J Haematol* 139:289-296, 2007.

Reed HS, Obituary, Charles B. Lipman, *Science* 100:464-465, 1944.

Rice-Wray E, Schulz-Contreeras M, Guerrero I, Aranda-Rosell A, Long-term administration of norethindrone in fertility control, *JAMA* 180:355-358, 1962.

Rock J, Menkin MF, In vitro fertilization and cleavage of human ovarian eggs, *Science* 100:105-107, 1944.

Rock J, Pincus G, Garcia C-R, Effects of certain 19-nor steroids on the normal human menstrual cycle, *Science* 124:891-893, 1956.

Rock J, Garcia C-R, Pincus G, Synthetic progestins in the normal human menstrual cycle, *Rec Prog Hor Res* 13:323-329, 1957.

Rock J, Garcia C-R, Pincus G, Use of some progestational 19-nor steroids in gynecology, *Am J Obstet Gynecol* 79:758-767, 1960.

Rock J, Population growth, *JAMA* 177:58-60, 1961.

Rock J, Sex, science and survival, *J Reprod Fertil* 8:397-409, 1964.

Rosenkranz G, From Ruzicka's terpenes in Zurich to Mexican steroids via Cuba, *Steroids* 57:409-418, 1992.

Rosenkranz G, The early days of Syntex, *Chemical Heritage* 23:2,10,12, 2004.

Rosenkranz G, Pataki J, Djerassi C, Synthesis of cortisone, *J Am Chem Soc* 76:4055, 1951.

Sarett LH, Partial synthesis of pregnene-4-triol-17(ß),20(ß),21-dione-3,11 and pregnene-4-diol-17(ß),21-trione-3,11,20 monoacetate, *J Biol Chem* 162:601-631, 1946.

Satterthwaite AP, Gamble CJ, Conception control with norethynodrel. Progress report of a four-year field study at Humacao, Puerto Rico, *J Am Women's Assoc* 17:797-802, 1962.

Schwartz NB, A model for the regulation of ovulation in the rat. (Gregory Pincus Memorial Lecture), *Rec Prog Hor Res* 25:1-55, 1969.

Schwartz NB, Perspective: reproductive endocrinology and human health in the 20th century—a personal retrospective, *Endocrinology* 142:2163-2166, 2001.

Shpall L, Jewish agricultural colonies in the United States, *Agricultural History* XXIV:120-146, 1950.

Simmer HH, On the history of hormonal contraception. I. Ludwig Haberlandt (1885–1932) and his concept of "hormonal sterilization", *Contraception* 1:3-2, 1970.

Simmer HH, On the history of hormonal contraception. II. Otfried Otto Fellner (1873–19??) and estrogens as antifertility hormones, *Contraception* 3:1-21, 1971.

Slechta RF, Chang M-C, Pincus G, Effects of progesterone and related compounds on mating and pregnancy in the rat, *Fertil Steril* 5:282-293, 1954.

Smith TL, New approaches to the history of immigration in twentieth-century America, *Am Hist Rev* LXXI:1265-1279, 1966.

Sneader W, The discovery of oestrogenic hormones, *J Br Menopause Soc* December:129-133, 2000.

Spar DL, Huntsberger B, The business of birth control, *Harvard Health Policy Rev* 6:6-18, 2005.

Stampfer MJ, Willett WC, Colditz GA, Speizer FE, Hennekens CH, Past use of oral contraceptives and cardiovascular disease: a meta-analysis in the context of the Nurses' Health Study, *Am J Obstet Gynecol* 163:285-291, 1990.

Strauss III JF, Mastroianni Jr L, *In memoriam:* Celso-Ramon Garcia, M.D. (1922–2004), reproductive medicine visionary, *J Exp Clin Assist Reprod* 2:2-7, 2005.

Szajkowski Z, The Alliance Israélite Universelle in the United States, 1860–1949, *Am Jewish Hist Soc* XXXIX:389-443, 1950.

Tefferi A, The forgotten myeloproliferative disorder: myeloid metaplasia, *The Oncologist* 8:225-231, 2003.

Trussell J, Wynn LL, Reducing unintended pregnancy in the United States, *Contraception* 77:1-5, 2008.

Tullner WW, Herz R, High progestational activity of 19-norprogesterone, *Endocrinology* 52:359-361, 1953.

Tullner WW, Hertz R, Progestational activity of 19-norprogesterone and 19-norethisterone in the Rhesus monkey, *Proc Soc Exp Biol* 94:298-300, 1957.

Tyler ET, Comparative evaluation of various types of administration of progesterone, *J Clin Endocrin Metab* 15:881, 1955.

Tyler ET, Olson HJ, Wolf L, Finkelstein S, Thayer J, Kaplan N, Levin M, Weintraub J, An oral contraceptive. A 4-year study of norethindrone, *Obstet Gynecol* 18:363-367, 1961.

Vessey M, Painter R, Oral contraceptive use and cancer. Findings in a large cohort study, 1968–2004, *Br J Cancer* 95:385-389, 2006.

Werthessen NT, Johnson RC, Pincogenesis—parthogenesis in rabbits by Gregory Pincus, *Persp Biol Med* 18:81-93, 1974.

White AB, Gregory Goodwin Pincus (1903–1967), *Endocrinology* 82:651-654, 1968.

Wingo PA, Austin H, Marchbanks PA, Whiteman MK, Hsia J, Mandel MG, Peterson HB, Ory HW, Oral contraceptives and the risk of death from breast cancer, *Obstet Gynecol* 110:793-800, 2007.

Zaffaroni A, Life after Syntex, *Chemical Heritage* 23:2,10,12, 2004.

MAGAZINE ARTICLES

Gladwell M, John Rock's Error. What the co-inventor of the Pill didn't know: menstruation can endanger women's health, *The New Yorker* pp. 52-63, March 13, 2000.

Lader L, Three Men Who Made a Revolution, *New York Times Magazine*, April 10, 1966.

Pincus G, Nocturne, *The Literary Review of Cornell*, December, 1922.

Pincus G, New York, *The Literary Review of Cornell,* December, 1923.

Ratcliff JD, No father to guide them, *Colliers,* pp. 19, 73, March 20, 1937.

Pincogenesis, *Time,* November 13, 1939.

Mother Was a Thoroughbred, *Time,* April 4, 1949.

Sheehan R, The Birth-Control "Pill", *Fortune,* April:154-155, 220-222, 1958.

NEWSPAPER ARTICLES

Rabbits Born In Glass, *The New York Times,* May 13, 1934.

Bottles Are Mothers, *The New York Times,* April 21, 1935.

Editorial, *New York Times,* , March 28, 1936.

Laurence WL, Life is generated in a scientist's tube, *The New York Times,* March 27, 1936.

His Experiment Gives Vision of Manless World, *Ames Daily Tribune and Times,* March 31, 1936.

Laurence WL, First Step Shown in Human Creation, *The New York Times,* April 28, 1939.

Pincus Says Test Tube Babies 'Out', *The Kingsport Times, Kingsport, Tennessee,* May 16, 1939.

Doctor Embarrassed by Report He Is Trying to Make Test Tube Baby, *The Evening News, Sault Ste. Marie, Michigan,* , May 17, 1939.

Mammal Created Without a Father, *The New York Times,* November 2, 1939.

Rabbits Without Fathers, *The New York Times,* November 3, 1939.

Laurence WL, Test Tube Babies Come Step Nearer, *The New York Times,* April 30, 1941.

Jordan RG, Research Foundation Opened in Ceremony at Essar Ranch Near City, *San Antonio Express,* April 6, 1947.

O'Neill JJ, Texan Operates Unique University to Develop Ideas Useful to Society, *Winnipeg Free Press,* July 25, 1949.

Sandrof I, Worcester's Dr. Pincus Famed for Probing Secrets of Life Begins Program of Atomic Research, *The Worcester Sunday Telegram,* March 4, 1951.

Marcello AA, Popping Questions, *The Worcester Sunday Telegram,* June 29, 1952.

Birth Control Pill Reported by Expert, *Pasadena Independent,* October 19, 1955.

Pincus G, Paradoxical Hormone is Basis of Birth Control Pill, *The Washington Post,* August 2, 1959.

Wilson RE, Science Marches On, *The Worcester Sunday Telegram,* April 19, 1964.

Carrey F, Denies Oral Pills Cause of Cancer, *The Lowell Sun,* April 25, 1966.

Obituary, Fellow Scientists Laud Researcher Dr. Pincus, *The Worcester Daily Telegram,* August 26, 1967.

Kneeland DE, Majority report seeks papal shift on contraception, *The New York Times*: p. 1, April 17, 1967.

Dr. Rock Regrets Pope's Stand, *Boston Globe*, August 4, 1968.

Wojtyla K, The Truth of the Encyclical "Humanae Vitae", *L'Osservatore Romano*, January 16, 1969.

Michelson DP, Study of Thirty Deaths Shows 'The Pill' Had No Connection, *Burlington (N.C.) Times-News*, March 27, 1970.

The 'Pill' Ushered In Golden Age of Womenhood, *Boston Herald-American*, November 1, 1974.

Vaughan P, The Pill Turns Twenty, *The New York Times Magazine*, June 13, 1976.

Ehrenreich B, Bitter Pill, *The New York Times*, March 6, 1983.

INTERNET

Aztecs, *http://www.mexicolore.co.uk/index.php?one=azt&two=sto&id=149*, March 17, 2008.

Jewish Encyclopedia, Clara de Hirsch, *http://www.jewishencyclopedia.com/ viewjsp?artid=758?letter=H*, August 8, 2007.

Lal A, Agnogenic myeloid metaplasia with myelofibrosis, *http://www.emedicine.com/MED/topic78.htm*, 2004.

Polokow S, Bronx: Small Schools at Morris High, *http://www.goodsmallschools.org/information. asp?schoolIID=4*, 2007.

Reinsdorf W, Reflections on Humanae Vitae, *http://www.catholic.net/RCC/Periodicals/ Faith/0708-96/article6.html*, June 2007.

Singer I, Straus OS, Hirsch, Baron Maurice de (Moritz Hirsch, Freiherr auf Gereuth): *http://www. jewishencyclopedia.com/view/jsp?artid=771&letter=H*, July 19, 2007.

The AJHS Manuscript Catalog, Jewish Agricultural Society, *http://data.jewishgen.org.wconnect/ wc.dll?jg~ajhs_pb~r!!389*, July, 2007.

UNPUBLISHED MANUSCRIPTS

Pincus, Alex, Memories about Gregory Pincus, Family Memoir, Courtesy of *Papers of Gregory Pincus*. Box 5. Washington, DC: Library of Congress; 1989: pp. 1-30.

Pincus, Eizabeth, Russian American Episodes, Courtesy of Laura Pincus Bernard; Year unknown, pp.1-17.

Yanagimachi R, Dr. M.C. Chang, the founder of modern fertilization study, and my work, *Worcester Foundation for Biomedical Research (WFBR) Papers, (formerly) Worcester Foundation for Experimental Biology (WFEB)*, The Lamar Soutter Library, University of Massachusetts Medical School, Worcester, Massachusetts

DISSERTATIONS

Courey RM, Participants in the Development, Marketing and Safety Evaluation of the Oral Contraceptive, 1950–1965: Mythic Dimensions of a Scientific Solution, Dissertation for the Degree of Doctor of Philosophy in History Graduate Division, University of California at Berkeley, 1994.

MISCELLANEOUS

Certificate of Death of Gregory Pincus, *The Commonwealth of Massachusetts, Department of Public Health, Registry of Vital Records and Statistics,* 1967.

Davidson G, (The Jewish Agricultural Society), The Jewish Agricultural Society, Inc., Report of the Managing Director for the Period 1900–1949, Report No. 1950.

Granada TV Network, The Pill, 1961.

Hoagland H, Lamar Soutter Lecture, University of Massachusetts Medical Center, *Worcester Foundation for Biomedical Research (WFBR) Papers, (formerly) Worcester Foundation for Experimental Biology (WFEB),* The Lamar Soutter Library, University of Massachusetts Medical School, Worcester, Massachusetts, September 10, 1975.

Pincus G, A Journal. Trip to Russia, May 1967, *Worcester Foundation for Biomedical Research (WFBR) Papers, (formerly) Worcester Foundation for Experimental Biology (WFEB),* The Lamar Soutter Library, University of Massachusetts Medical School, Worcester, Massachusetts.

Pope Paul VI, Humanae Vitae. Encyclical of Pope Paul VI on the Regulation of Birth, July 25, 1968.

Matzke H, ed, *The Morris Annual, 1920,* Morris High School, courtesy of the Bronx County Historical Society Bronx, New York.

Pederson T, The battle that launched the Worcester Foundation for Experimental Biology, Lecture presented at the Worcester Club, April 7, 2008, Personal communication August 11, 2008.

The Pill. An American Experience, PBS Video AMER6509, 2003.

Dutton, S, Audio recording of an interview with Sophie Pincus Dutton by Honor White, January 8 and 14, 1980, (courtesy of Geoffrey Dutton).

PERSONAL INTERVIEWS OR COMMUNICATIONS

Etienne-Emile Baulieu	November 17, 2007
J. Michael Bedford	April 16, 2008
Laura Pincus Bernard	May 23, 2007; August 11, 2008
Gabrial Bialy	August 27, 2007
Jerry Brooks	June 30, 2008
Sumner Burstein	May 22, 2007
Burton Caldwell	December 5, 2007
Sara Caspi	May 22, 2007
Isabelle Chang	May 22, 2007
Geoffry Dutton	August 11, 2008
Jacqueline (Jackie) Foss	May 21, 2007
Louis Fridhandler	February 8, 2008
Joseph Goldzieher	October 30, 2007
Michael Harper	April 15, 2008
Nathan Kase	December 19, 2007
Alexia Lalli	September 14, 2008
Seymour Lieberman	October 17, 2007
Luigi Mastroianni	August 28, 2007
Judy McCann	May 22, 2007
John McCracken	May 21, 2007; August 12, 2008
Anne Merrill	May 23, 2007
Manuel Neves e Castro	May 28, 2008
Fernand Peron	April 13, 2007
Michael Pincus	August 4, 2008
Sheldon Segal	December 7, 2007
Jane Shaw	April 16, 2008
Edward Wallach	January 23, 2008
Koji Yoshinaga	August 27, 2007

INDEX

In the Index, Gregory Pincus is referred to as Goody

A

adrenal cortex responses to pilot performances, 104

adrenal gland function in schizophrenic patients, 105, 174

agnogenic myeloid metaplasia with myelofibrosis, 263

All Things New (Biezanek), 241

Allen, Edgar, 141

Allen, Willard Myron, 142

Alliance Israélite Universelle, 23

American Birth Control League, 167

Am-olam, 10–11

Amtorg Trading Corporation, 58

anti-Semitism, 1, 85, 101

Applezweig, Norman, 148

arterial thrombosis, 230, 247

Atwood, Wallace W., 99

B

Bailar, John, 244

Baker, Newton D., Jr., 173

Baron de Hirsch Agricultural School, 33
  closure of, 36
  Pincus, Joseph, teaching at, 48

Baron de Hirsch Fund
  establishment of, 24
  farming controversy and, 32
  lawsuit against, 32

Baron de Hirsch Trade School, 25

Bemis, William H., 173, 206

Bialy, Gabrial, 121, 270

Biezanek, Anne, 241

Birkhahn Family, 12

birth control. *See also* oral contraceptives; Sanger, Margaret
  first clinic for, 167
  mortality and morbidity, effect on, 196
  organizations for, 167
  population growth and, 194–196
  rhythm method, 193

Birth Control Federation of America, 167

blood clots (venous thrombosis), 229, 230

Botanica-Mex, 150

Brown-Sequard, Charles Edouard, 141

Bush, Ian, 109, 111

Buxton, C. Lee, 238

C

cabeza de negro, 147

Caldwell, Burton, 114, 115, 116

Cambridge University, 93

cancer

    birth control pills and, 219, 220, 263

    Goody's, 263, 265

capacitation of sperm, 123, 282

Castle, William E., 81

Catholic Church

    contraception and, 233

    excommunication attempts against Rock, 234

    Humanae Vitae, 236

    Papal Commission for the Study of Population, the Family, and Birth, 236

    Pope Paul VI on, 237

cervical cancer, birth control pills and, 219

Chang, Isabelle (Chin), 125

Chang, Min-Chueh, 119, xvi

    death of, 126

    degrees of, 120

    marriage of, 125

    philosophy of, 124

    second family of, 125

    Worcester Foundation for Experimental Biology and, 120

Château de Prangins, 171

Chemical Specialties, 149, 203

Chin, Isabelle. *See* Chang, Isabelle (Chin)

Clark University, 98

    in 1943, 106

    physiological laboratory, funding for, 103

    Visiting Professor of Experimental Biology, 101

clinical studies. *See also* Puerto Rico studies

    in Caribbean, 259

    in Haiti, 217

placebo-controlled study, 218

Colliers, 87

Colton, Frank, 161

Comstock laws, 167

Conant, James Bryant, 86

Conference of the International Planned Parenthood Federation, fifth annual, 199, 203, xv

Connecticut law, 239

contraception. *See* birth control; oral contraceptives

Cordoba, Mexico, 147

Cornell University, 67

Corner, George W., 142

corpus luteum, 283

cortisol, 155

cortisone

    cortisol, conversion to, 155

    race for, 152

criticism of work, 92

Crozier, William E., 82, 85

D

de Hirsch, Clara, 23

de Hirsch, Maurice, 22. *See also entries beginning with Baron*

    Baron de Hirsch Fund, establishment of, 24

    Jewish Colonization Association, establishment of, 24

    wife of, 23

DeFelice Pasquale, 227, 228

definitions

    capacitation of sperm, 282

    corpus luteum, 283

    endocrine, 141

    gonadotropins, 281

    hormones, 279

    steroids, 279

diary during high school, 64

Dioscorea barbasco, 150
Dioscorea mexicana, 145
   location of, 147
   Moreno, Alberto and, 147
Djerassi, Carl, 139, 154, 275
   Stanford job, 156
   Syntex invitation and, 155
   Wayne State University job offer, 155
The Doctor's Case Against the Pill (Seaman), 245
Doisy, Edward, 141

E

Eggs of Mammals (Pincus), 84
emergency contraception, 179
emigration of Jewish people, 4
endocrine, 141
endocrinology of female reproduction. *See*
   female reproduction, endocrinology of
endometrium cancer, 220
Enovid, 185
   annual sales and cost of, 228
   approval of, 220, 228
   use of, 226
Enzmann, E.V., 85
estrin, 142
estrogen, 213, 280
Ethyl Gasoline Corporation, 144
excommunication attempts against Rock, 234

F

"Father of the Pill," 276. *See also* Pincus,
   Gregory Goodwin "Goody"
Fellner, Otfried Otto, 143
Fellowship in Reproductive Physiology
   program, 111
female reproduction, endocrinology of
   activin, 281
     blastocyst, 283
     capacitation of sperm and, 282
     corpus luteum, 283

fertilizable life of the human egg, 281
FSH (follicle-stimulating hormone), 280
gonadotropins, 281
hint that sex steroids could suppress
   ovulation, 284
hormones, 279
human chorionic gonadotropin, 284
implantation, 283
inhibin, 280
luteinizing hormone, 281
ovaries, 279
ovulation, 281
pregnancy and progesterone, 284
steroids, 279
feminist movement, 240
Fernald, Mason, 127
follicle-stimulating hormone (FSH), 281
Food and Drug Administration
   birth control pills, approval of, 225
   Enovid, approval of, 220
   package insert and, 245
   request for birth control pills submitted to, 226
Foss, Jackie, 114
FSH (follicle-stimulating hormone), 281
funding for research
   Foundation, membership dues for, 107
   G.D. Searle Company, 102, 113, 156
   Hudson Hoagland Society, 129
   Ittleson, Henry and, 101
   McCormick, Katharine and, 106, 111, 169,
     174, 177
   Parke-Davis research grants, 144
   physiological laboratory of Clark University
     and, 103
   reproductive projects budget, 206
   Slick, Tom and, 122

G

Gamble, Clarence, 215

Garcia, Celso-Ramón, 119, 137, 186, 208, 268, 275
    education of, 209
    memorial service, remarks at, 270
G.D. Searle Company
    FDA approval request by, 226
    founding of, 156
    funding for research by, 102, 113, 156
    Goody, relationship with, 156, 158
    reluctance of initial support by, 225
Girard, A., 142
Goldzieher, Joseph, 103, 135, 162, 245, 270, 276
gonadotropins, 281
"Goody." See Pincus, Gregory Goodwin "Goody"
Granada TV Network, 255
Graubard, Mark, 102
Greep, Roy, 125
Gregory Pincus Medal, 129
Gregory Pincus Memorial Lecture, 138
Griswold, Estelle, 238
Gut, Marcel, 121
Guttmacher, Allan, 219, 220, 244

H
Haberlandt, Ludwig, 143
Haiti, clinical trial in 1957, 217
Hall, G. Stanley, 99
Harvard education
    Goody, 81
    Hoagland, Hudson, 98
Harvard employment
    Goody, 85, 89
    Hoagland, Hudson and, 100
Harvard's Neuroendocrine Research Foundation, 106
HCG (human chorionic gonadotropin), 284
Hechter, Oscar, 156

Hench, Philip S., 155
Henshaw, Paul, 177
Hertig, Arthur, 196, 197
Hertz, Roy, 244
Hoagland, Hudson, 97
    Columbia University and, 100
    death of, 129
    education, committment to, 111
    education of, 98
    Eighth Air Force and, 104
    employment of, 98
    funding for Goody and, 101
    Goody, meeting with, 100
    Harvard and, 100
    memorial service, remarks at, 270
    schizophrenia research and, 174
Hoagland, Mahlon, 98, 128, 129
hormones. See also Marker, Russell E.
    defined, 279
    follicle-stimulating hormone, 281
    supply problems for research, 142
Hoskins, Roy, 106, 174
Hovey, Harry P., 109
Howes, Raymond F., 69
Hudson Hoagland Society, 129
human chorionic gonadotropin (HCG), 284
Humanae Vitae, 236

I
in vitro fertilization, 86, 197
India, 243
Infecundin, 143
Ingle, Dwight, 132, 135
International Planned Parenthood, fifth annual conference, 199, 203, xv
Isaacson, Joseph, 16
Ittleson, Henry, 101

J

Jensen, Elwood, 135
Jewish Agricultural Society, 25
Jewish Colonization Association, 24
The Jewish Farmer (magazine), 51
Jewish people
    anti-Semitism and, 1, 85, 101
    emigration of, 4
    as farmers, 37
    Pale of Settlement, 2
    in Russian Empire, 1
Josephson, Dena, 64
Julian, Percy, 131

K
Kamm, Oliver, 147
Kendall, Edward C., 155
Kennedy, John F., 239
Kurzok, Raphael, 168

L
Laboratorios Hormona, 148
Laurence, William L., 86
Laurentian Hormone Conference
    attendance at, 132
    beginning of, 132
    Committee of Arrangements, 132
    Goody cocktail party for, 136
    Gregory Pincus Memorial Lecture, 138
    presentation by Rock of first human studies,
        187
Lehman, Frederick A., 148
LH (luteinizing hormone), 281
Lieberman, Seymour, 111, 131, 134, 136, 251
Lifschitz, Leon, 66, 82
Lipman, Alexis "Alex," 52
Lipman, Charles, 17
Lipman, Daniel, 42
Lipman, Edward, 42
Lipman, Elizabeth. *See* Pincus, Elizabeth

"Lizzie" (Lipman)
Lipman, Ethel, 18
Lipman, Evelyn, 64
Lipman, Ida, 38
Lipman, Isaac, 17
Lipman, Jacob, 17, 38–44
    children of, 42
    death of, 43
    education of, 40
    employment of, 40
    marriage of, 42
    obituary of, 44
Lipman, Leonard, 42
Lipman, Michael Gregory, 12, 44
    death of, 38
    move to U.S., 15
    sending for family, 15
    Woodbine Jewish Farmers Colony and, 27
Lipman, Raymond, 16
Lipman, William (Willie), 16
    powerhouse of, 28
Lipman Family, 12
The Literary Review of Cornell, 69–72
Loth, David, 193
luteinizing hormone (LH), 281

M
Malthus, Thomas Robert, 194
Malthusian Hypothesis, 194–195
Margaret Sanger Center, 168
Margaret Sanger Research Bureau, 167
Marker, Russell E.
    artwork, collecting of, 152
    birth of, 144
    death of, 152
    education of, 143, 144
    employment of, 144
    isolation of diosgenin by, 147
    Marker degradation, development of, 144

Mexico, trips to, 145
  Order of the Aztec Eagle award, 152
  at Pennsylvania State University, 144
  search for *Dioscorea* by, 147
  Syntex and, 149, 150
  synthesizing of progesterone by, 148
  Tláloc (rain god) statue and, 150
  work in Applezweig's lab, 148
Marker degradation, 144
Massachusetts General Hospital, Goody's
    admission to, 265
Massachusetts Institute of Technology, 98, 171
  Stanley McCormick Hall, 179
Mastroianni, Luigi, Jr., 186, 210, 267
  as chairman of department, 211
Mayer, Hannah, 167
M-C. Chang Building, 185
"McCarthyism," 59
McCormick, Katharine, 169–180, xvi
  birth control movement, beginning of
      involvement in, 175
  birth of, 170
  contract with Worcester Foundation, 178
  death of, 180
  education of, 171
  funding for research by, 106, 111, 169, 175,
      176, 177
  funding for travel to promote use of pills,
      252, 258
  husband's mental illness and, 172
  inheritance of, 173, 174
  legal battles with husband's family and,
      172–173, 174
  marriage of, 172
  relationship with husband, 171, 172
  Sanger and, 169
  Stanley McCormick Hall and, 179
  support, uniqueness of, 206
  will, provisions of, 180

McCormick, Stanley, 171
  death of, 174
  marriage of, 172
  schizophrenia and, 172
McCracken, John, 107, 111, 114, 115, 119, 121,
    135, 137, 252, 261
McLaughlin, Loretta, 249
Menkin, Miriam, 196
Merrill, Anne, 115, 178, 214, 266, 273
Miramontes, Luis, 161
Moreno, Alberto, 147
"morning after" pill, 178
Morris High School, 62
Mountain View Cemetary (Shrewsbury), 269
Muller, Hermann Joseph, 276
Murray, H.C., 159
Myleran, 265

N
National Research Council fellowship, 83
natural family planning, 193
Nelson, Gaylord, 245
Nelson, Warren, 177
Nelson Hearings, 245
Neuroendocrine Research Foundation, 106, 175
Neves e Castro, Manuel, 112
New Jersey Agricultural Experiment Station,
    40, 41
The New York Times, 86
Nilevar, 185
Nobel Prize, 276
norethandrolone, 184
norethindrone, 159, 184
  infringement claims, 161
  synthesizing of, 161
norethynodrel, 159, 184, 207
  infringement claims, 161
  patent for on August 31, 1953, 161
Norlutin, 185

Northborough house, 117

O

oral contraceptives. *See also* female
    reproduction, endocrinology of; Puerto
    Rico studies
  approval by FDA of, 225
  cancer risk and, 219–220
  cardiovascular events and, 246
  Catholic Church and, 233
  combination pill, mechanism for, 181
  emergency contraception, 179
  Enovid and, 185, 220, 226, 228
  feminist movement and, 240
  first collaboration of Goody and Rock and, 197
  first human studies, 186
  first oral contraception studies in
      Massachusetts, 180
  Goody's initial involvement in, 176
  health benefits associated with, 230
  in India, 243
  letters from others about, 253–254
  "morning after" pill, 178
  number of people using, 231
  package insert for, 245
  press conference and cervical cancer, 219
  publication of Goody's conclusions about,
      222
  publicity for, 255
  questions to be answered in clinical trials, 201
  reduction in doses of, 230
  risks of, 246–247
  royalties and, 228
  sexual promiscuity and, 247
  side effects, estrogen and, 213
  summary of first studies, 217
  testing of compounds for, 184
  thrombosis and, 229–230, 246
  travels of Goody to support use of, 252, 258,
      261
  two opposing philosophies and, 242
  Worcester State Hospital clinical trials, 205
Order of the Aztec Eagle, 152
Orizaba, Mexico, 147
Ortho Pharmaceutical Corporation, 229
ovarian cancer, 220
ovarian hormones, 142
ovaries, as estrogen producers, 280
ovulation, 281
Oxford Family Planning Association study, 247

P

package insert, 245
Pale of Settlement, 2
Paniagua, Manuel E., 218
Papal Commission for the Study of Population,
    the Family, and Birth, 236
Parke-Davis and Co., 229
  chemists, 147
  infringement claims over norethindrone and
      norethynodrel, 161
  research grants, 144
Parkes, Alan S., 132, 137, xvii
parthenogenesis, 92, 94
parthenogenic full-term rabbits, 94
patents
  infringement claims over norethindrone and
      norethynodrel, 161
  norethindrone, synthesizing of, 161
  norethynodrel, 161
  perfusion method, 158
Pathfinder Fund, 216
Pathfinder International, 216
Pederson, Thoru, 129
Pennsylvania State University, 144
  Russell and Mildred Marker Professorship of
      Natural Product Chemistry, 152
Pererson, Durey H., 158

perfusion method, 156
    patent for, 158
Péron, Fernand, 115
Pertell, Pauline, 270
Peter Bent Brigham Hospital, Goody's
        admission to, 268
pilot fatigue, 103
    adrenal cortex responses and, 104
"Pincogenesis," 85, 90, 94
Pincus, Alex John, 82
Pincus, Alexander, 20
    marriage of, 18
Pincus, Alexis, 56
Pincus, Bernard "Bun," 54
Pincus, Elizabeth "Lizzie" (Lipman), 44–47
    at age 15, 47
    birth of, 14, 73
    as boarder at Pincus house, 74
    character of, 53
    children of, 50, 52
    early employment of, 45
    employment of, 30
    marriage of, 50
    move to New York City, 50
    Sabsovich, work for, 47
Pincus, Elizabeth "Lizzie" (wife of Goody)
    death of, 273
    dinners at her house, 78
    marriage of, 72, 74
    personality of, 77
    as smoker, 114
    teaching certificate, obtaining of, 73
Pincus, Gregory Goodwin "Goody"
    accomplishments of, 89, 277
    agnogenic myeloid metaplasia with
        myelofibrosis and, 263
    as assistant professor of biology, 85
    autopsy of, 269
    birth of, 50

children of, 82
collaboration with Rock, 197
college majors of, 67
complexity of his projects, 223
confidence of, xvii
as consultant for G.D. Searle, 156, 158
at Cornell, 67
death of, 268
degrees of, 81
diary of, 64
education, commitment to, 111
"Father of the Pill," 275–276
final illness and death of, 261–270
financial situation of, 260, 271
grades during college, 68
Harvard education and, 81
Hoagland, meeting with, 100
as honor student, 63
letters from others, 253–254
Lifschitz, Leon, and, 66
Lipman's obituary and, 44
Literary Review of Cornell and, 69–72
marriage of, 72, 74
"McCarthyism" and, 59
memorial service for, 270
at Morris High School, 62
mother of, 53
move to 30 Main Street, 117
move to New York City, 50
National Research Council fellowship of, 83
Nobel Prize, nomination for, 276
poetry of, 66
at P.S. 40, 60
Puerto Rico and, 202
scientific philosophy, foundation of, 85
scientific societies, membership in, 261
Scrabble and, 117
siblings of, 54
as smoker, 114

stock purchases by, 260
swimming and, 116
teenage romances of, 64
as a teenager, 57
termination of Harvard appointment, 85, 89
timeline, xix
as translational scientist, 277
travels to support use of pills, 252, 258, 261
Pincus, Joseph, 18, 48–52
children of, 50, 52
death of, 60
employment at Amtorg Trading Corporation, 58
employment at exporting company, 58
employment at Woodbine Agricultural School, 48
graduation of, 48
as magazine editor, 51
marriage of, 50
move to New York City, 50
New York residences of, 51, 52
Sabsovich's influence on, 37
schooling of, 19
as secretary of County Agricultural Society, 37
Pincus, Laura Jane, 82
Pincus, Leopold Lincoln "Lee," 55
Pincus, Maurice, 56
Pincus, Sophie, 20, 56
birth of, 52
Pincus, William, 19
Pincus Family, 18
Pincus laboratory work, 89, 92
Planned Parenthood Federation
beginning of, 167
mission of, 239
New Haven offices, 239
New York office, 176
Planned Parenthood, International, fifth annual

conference, xv
Playboy, 255
Plummer, Anna (Hoagland), 98
Podolsky, Zena, 18
pogrom, 3
Pope Paul VI, 237
Population Council, 177
population growth, 194–196
pregnancy and progesterone, 284
progesterone, 142, 148
ovulating-inhibiting properties of, 168
pregnancy and, 284
purpose of, 284
promiscuity, 247
P.S. 40, 60
publicity, 86, 212, 255
publish or perish, 251
Puerto Rico studies, 202, 203
1954 clinical trial, 203
1956 clinical trial, 208
1957 clinical trial, 215
efficacy of, 217
negative publicity about studies, 212
problems during studies, 203
Rio Piedras, recruitment of women in, 208

R
Raymond, Albert L., 156, 182, 220
Recent Progress in Hormone Research, 137
rhythm method, 193
Rice-Wray, Edris, 208, 217
Richardson, George S., 187
Rio Piedras, Puerto Rico, 208
Rocamora, Hector, 259
Rock, John, 178, 191–200, xvi
biography of, 249
birth of, 191
book by, 234
collaboration with Goody, 186, 197

death of, 238
education of, 191–192
employment at Harvard, 192
eviction from his clinic, 200
excommunication attempts against, 234
at FDA hearing, 227
fertilized eggs, obtaining of, 196
financial situation of, 200
marriage of, 192
monogamy, belief in, 235
presentation in 1959, 221
presentation of human studies at Laurentian
     Hormone Conference, 187
Rock Reproductive Clinic, 200
Rockefeller Institute, 144
Rodríques, Iris, 212
Root Chemicals, Inc., 260
Rosenkranz, George, 153
Rosenthal, Cecilia, 42
Royal College of General Practitioner's study,
     247
Russell and Mildred Marker Professorship of
     Natural Product Chemistry, 152
Russian Empire
   history of, 5
   Jewish population of, 1
Rutgers tomato, 40

S
Sabsovich, H.L., 9
   Am-olam and, 10
   "breakdown" of, 32
   Elizabeth working for, 47
   exhibits and, 33
   illness and death of, 36
   influence on Joseph Pincus, 37
   marriage to Katherine, 11
   move to New York City, 35
   Woodbine Jewish Farmers Colony and, 26

Sabsovich, Katherine, 11
Sanger, Margaret
   Comstock laws and, 167
   McCormick and, 169
   meeting with Goody, 165
   writings in *The Woman Rebel*, 165
Satterthwaite, Adaline Pendleton, 215
Saunders, Francis, 206
schizophrenic patients, adrenal gland function
     and, 105, 174
School in the Bronx, 60
Schwartz, Neena, 139
Science, reports in, 186
scientific societies, membership in, 261
Scrabble, 117
Seaman, Barbara, 245
Searle, John "Jack," 225
Searle Company. *See* G.D. Searle Company
Segal, Sheldon, 136, 177, xviii
Seltzer, Evelyn, 16
sexual promiscuity, 247
Shrewsbury, Massachusetts, 109
Slick, Tom, 102, 122
Sollins, Irvin V., 260
Somlo, Emeric, 148
sperm, capacitation of, 123, 282
Stanford University, 156
Stanley McCormick Hall, 179
steroids, 279
Stone, Abraham, 165, 167
stress, research on, 107
Supreme Court decision on Connecticut law, 239
swimming, 116
Syntex, 229
   Djerassi, Carl and, 155
   formation of, 149
   Marker leaves, 150
   norethindrone, synthesizing of, 161

T

thalidomide, 240
Thorndike, Anna, 192
thrombosis, 246
Tietze, Christopher, 214
The Time Has Come: A Catholic Doctor's Proposals to End the Battle Over Birth Control (Rock), 234
Time magazine, 90
Tláloc (rain god) statue, 150
Training Program in Steroid Chemistry, 112
translational research, 277
Tyler, David, 202
Tyler, Edward T., 161, 187, 220

U

Umbaugh, Ray E., 102, 122
Upjohn method, 159

V

venous thrombosis, 229, 230
Voluntary Parenthood (Loth), 193

W

Wallach, Edward, 214, 217
Wayne State University, 155
Werthessen, Nicholas, 92, 122
White, Abraham, 135
Whitmore, Frank, 144
wine collection, 118
Winter, Irwin C., 225
The Woman Rebel, 165
Woodbine Brotherhood Synagogue, 31
Woodbine factories, 30, 37
Woodbine Jewish Farmers Colony, 21, 38
Woodbine stores, 31
Worcester Foundation for Experimental Biology
    animal house, funding for, 176
    budget and, 109, 113

Fellowship in Reproductive Physiology program, 111
    founding of, 107
    G.D. Searle Company funding for, 102, 113, 156
    after Goody, 127
    Goody, job titles at, 127
    Gregory Pincus Medal, 129
    Hoagland, Mahlon and, 128, 129
    Hudson Hoagland Society and, 129
    McCormick's contract with, 178
    name, issues with, 107
    purchase of Shrewsbury building, 109
    reproductive projects budget, 206
    staff, growth of, 109
    Training Program in Steroid Chemistry, 112
Worcester State Hospital, 105, 205
World Health Organization meeting proceedings, 137
world population, 194–196
Wright, Irving, 230
Wright Report, 230

Y

yams, 152. *See also Dioscorea entries*

Z

Zaffaroni, Alejandro, 162
Zuckerman, Solly, xvii

To order additional copies of

A Good Man

Gregory Goodwin Pincus

$29.95 US / $31.86 Canada

Contact:

PUBLISHING, INC.

3880 SE 8th Ave. #110
Portland, OR 97202
P: 503.225.9900 / F: 503.225.9901
info@arnicacreative.com

Or order online at:

http://www.arnicacreative.com